OF LAW AND MAN

OF LAW AND MAN

ESSAYS IN HONOR OF HAIM H. COHN

under the Auspices of the Faculty of Law
Tel Aviv University

Edited By
SHLOMO SHOHAM

SABRA BOOKS NEW YORK AND TEL AVIV, 1971

The Editor and Publishers wish to acknowledge
the devoted and invaluable assistance of Mrs. Rivka Banitt
throughout the preparation of this volume

Composed By Keter Publishing House Ltd., Jerusalem
Printed in Israel

CONTENTS

PROCESSES OF LAW

LAWS AND CRIME

PREFACE

In a country such as Israel, which has no formal constitution, there is an almost endemic tendency towards a positivist concept of the Rule of Law. The law as promulgated by Israel's Knesset (Parliament) is equated with the Rule of Law. The other meaning of the Rule of Law, that which embodies ideas and values standing outside and above positive law, tends to be disregarded. The borderline between technical law enforcement and the principles which should govern the legislator becomes nebulous. The Rule of Law is equated with the law which the people enact through their legislative assembly—or, if one may paraphrase Gertrude Stein, a law is a law is a law.

This positivist concept, needless to say, harbors some dangers. Totalitarian democracy and authoritarian majorities are not unknown in contemporary history. The very idea of entrenched human rights—when applied to democratic societies—implies some distrust of the democratic machinery: it cannot be the sole guarantor of civil liberties and basic rights. Israel not only lacks constitutional guarantees but is, and has been since its creation, governed by one party—Labour in its various guises. In such a regime, there is an obvious temptation to abuse the powers conferred by a parliamentary majority. It is indeed a measure of the maturity of the people and the sophistication of its leaders that such an abuse hardly exists, and that the climate of legality which pervades the country could stand up to criteria applicable to peaceful democracies.

That the Israeli courts, and the Supreme Court in particular, should be credited with creating this atmosphere is a truism which need not be reiterated. From the first day, the courts have established their independence and have demonstrated their concern for the rights of the individual, spurning government disapproval, ignoring possible political repercussions. In the Israeli War of Independence, when the Egyptian army was advancing on Tel Aviv, the Supreme Court calmly heard a *habeas corpus* application lodged by an Arab who had been detained under the Emergency Regulations.

While a desperate war was being waged 30 miles south of its seat, the Supreme Court made the order *nisi* absolute and freed the Arab suspected of sabotage, because the arrest warrant issued by the Chief of Staff did not conform with the formalities laid down by law. There is a direct link between that decision and the abolition of State privilege, even when claimed on grounds of state security, enacted by the Knesset in 1968. The whole essence of the Israeli legal system lies in this belief that the Rule of Law, in its substantive meaning, can coexist with a state of emergency and preparedness. This does not imply that the Israeli record is spotless. There are many ambits of the law which require immediate reform—the exclusive religious jurisdiction in matters of personal status springs to mind as an evident example. But the objective observer who is familiar with the legal record of other countries at war will have to admit that the Israeli legal system has fared remarkably well and that Israel shares with a shrinking number of countries a regime in which the Rule of Law thrives.

Behind this achievement stand men like Haim Cohn, in honour of whose sixtieth birthday we have published this book. This is neither the time nor the place to assess the contribution of a judge who is active on the bench and whose decisions, lectures and articles continue to stimulate our legal system. Yet, even at this stage, his contribution to the climate of legality in Israel is more than impressive. As Attorney General he was responsible for establishing a respect for legality and for the rights of the individual among Government officers. In many cases he refused to defend the Government officer against whom an application was lodged in the High Court, even when such a defense could technically be made. With a single stroke of his pen, he, has, in effect, annulled some of the harsh laws which Israel inherited from the British Mandatory regime. He issued a directive to the police and prosecuting authorities not to institute proceedings against consenting adults accused of homosexuality and other "unnatural" offenses, unless there is some element of public indecency involved. From a law-enforcement point of view, the directive may be questionable. But if the Rule of Law means the equal protection under law of all minorities, including sexual minorities, the directive must be regarded as a step towards a better and more humane legal system. As a Supreme Court judge, Haim Cohn has pursued the same line. Thus, in a famous case he said:

Preface

"The freedom of religion has been assured to every Israeli in
the Declaration of Independence, and although the Declaration
is not a law upon which a cause of action can be founded, freedom
of religion is but one of the fundamental rights of the individual
guaranteed in every enlightened and democratic regime."

In that case a local authority had refused to let its hall to a reformed
Jewish congregation but the court, invoking the notion of inherent
fundamental rights, ordered it to do so.

These are merely two illustrations of the tenacity with which Haim
Cohn adheres to his principles. He has left his imprint on Israeli case law
in many decisions. By accepting as canons of interpretation both the
Universal Declaration of Human Rights and Israel's Declaration
of Independence which guarantees equality and freedom of conscience
to all Israelis, regardless of race, religion or creed, he has established
an important precedent which, from a practical point of view, may be
tantamount to a formal constitutional guarantee.

Decisions and attitudes of men like Haim Cohn have shown that
respect for the Rule of Law and the rights of men can survive even the
prolonged state of war and emergency existing in Israel.

Amnon Rubinstein
Dean of the Faculty of Law
Tel Aviv University, Israel
January 1971.

HUMAN RIGHTS

FROM THE TEN COMMANDMENTS TO
THE RIGHTS OF MAN

RENE CASSIN*

From the very day that the Universal Declaration of Human Rights was adopted by the United Nations, on December 10, 1948, the world could not help but compare it to the Ten Commandments. Happily, the relationship between the two has generally been confirmed. On the occasion of the twentieth anniversary of the adoption of the Declaration in 1968, numerous studies on its origin and its impact were published, and once again links with the Ten Commandments were evoked. It seems, however, that so far there have been more bold assertions among them than careful examinations. The jubilee of a great Israeli jurist, Haim Cohn, who has consecrated an important part of his full career to the problems of Human Rights can serve as a suitable occasion for one of the artisans of the Declaration to present his contribution to this subject.

At the outset, a preliminary clarification as to the immediate origins of the Declaration is in order. For during the preparatory phases of the work of the United Nations Commission on Human Rights then at its inception, and particularly in the collection of Declarations and constitutions carefully assembled in 1947 by the staff of the U.N. General Secretariat's Social and Economic Division, there was no mention of or reference to such monuments of the ancient religious history as the Ten Commandments. Only modern juridical instruments of a national character were alluded to, in connection with each Right of Man likely to be included in the future "International Declaration." Moreover, in one of the first articles of the first draft of the Declaration which my colleagues of the Working Group of the Commission had assigned to me to write at the beginning of June 1947, I had expressly made mention

* Nobel Peace Prize Laureate, 1968

of the Duties of man and attempted to state the principal ones in a concise —not too perfect—sentence. But at the initial study of that draft, which was to serve as the basis for discussion, the idea of reasserting the duties of man at the threshold of the Declaration, in a general and direct form, met with objections from important members of the Commission, known either for their liberal or for their religious convictions, and foremost among them, the President of the Commission, Mrs. Eleanor Roosevelt.

Thoroughly influenced as she was by the knowledge of both the American (1778) and the French (1789) Declarations of Human Rights which pass in silence over the duties, and dearly attached as she was to the principles of individual liberty which had just achieved the upper hand at such cost over the racial and totalitarian doctrines of Hitlerism and Fascism, Mrs. Roosevelt objected vehemently to the idea of setting forth anything but the rights of man. Animated by the same spirit, she successfully argued in favor of starting off each article of the new Declaration with the word "Man," endowed with the particular Right mentioned in that article.

The prevailing formula, as we know, reads: "Each person has the right . . ." or "Everyone has the right . . ." At the end of that discussion, in which the Commission's delegates from the relevant countries maintained a more reserved attitude, it was accepted that the examination of the problem of mentioning the duties of man would be taken up again, when the enumeration of the rights had been completed. And so it was. The spirit prevailing during the preparation of the Universal Declaration was completely at variance with any intention of drawing deliberate and direct inspiration from the Ten Commandments.

This fact leads to a number of important conclusions. First of all, if any relationship between the universal Declaration and more generally the place of the rights of man in the modern world on the one hand, and the Decalogue as the first formulation of man's basic duties on the other hand does exist, this relation is not a formal one. Nevertheless, its reality is evident and must be traced back to the earliest periods of ancient history, when man, standing erect, mastering fire, and enjoying the benefits of written language, became aware of his innate dignity.

The expression: "God created Man in his own Image" characterizes both that *prise de conscience* and the religious form which it adopted initially. Secularization followed. The dignity of man has been reaffirmed by philosophers, sociologists, and statesmen regardless of religious beliefs, and has been detached from religious credos or cults. What is incontestable is the permanence of the idea through the centuries and despite the most profound divergences of interpretation of the doctrine.

The first article of the Declaration—for the sake of achieving unanimity—does not contain the affirmation of the "divine origin of man," which several delegations would have wished to insert. It does proclaim, however, that "all human beings are born free and equal in dignity and in rights. They are endowed with reason and with conscience, and should act towards each other in a spirit of brotherhood." Thus, though man is mortal and civilizations come and go, from Biblical times to our days, there has been a fixed pivot for the thoughts of all generations and for men of all continents: the equal dignity inherent in the human personality.

* * *

The Decalogue, one of the most ancient documents of Israel's tradition, is essentially religious and monotheistic in its first commandments, and subsequently lays down principles of morals and justice. The first commandment states the monotheistic principle: "I am the Lord thy God . . . Thou shalt have no other Gods before me."* The Decalogue then dictates to man rules of conduct, some positive ("Remember the Sabbath day, to keep it holy . . .," "Honour thy father and thy mother . . .") and some negative ("Thou shalt not murder," "Thou shalt not steal," "Thou shalt not bear false witness," "Thou shalt not covet . . .") Although we can infer from these commandments that other human beings (ordinary men, parents, spouses, servants, property-owners, etc.) must be respected, there is no direct formulation in the Decalogue of a correlative prerogative, or of any subjective right. It is only "duty" which the legislator of Israel stresses in man's relationship to man.

Formulations of this style are by no means limited to the Decalogue— we find them further in Leviticus XIX: 18: "Thou shalt love thy neighbour as thyself . . ." and :33 "The stranger that sojourneth with you . . . thou shalt love him as thyself. . . ." Later, Isaiah expresses himself in similar manner: "Learn to do well; seek justice, relieve the oppressed, judge the fatherless, plead for the widow" (Isaiah I:17).

The monotheistic creed of the Jewish people, epitomized in the idea of one God, father of all men, and strengthened by the bitter memories of slavery in Egypt, inspired in them rather early a vivid repugnance to serfdom. To them, that institution is neither natural, nor just (Job XXXI: 15); Jeremiah considers outrageous the curtailment of the liberty of

---

* In a later development of the Decalogue, the Deutoronomist phrases this statement as a positive commandment: "Therefore thou shalt love the Lord thy God . . ." (Deut. XI:1).

the Hebrew servant (XXXIV: 13 to 16); the law of the jubilee and of the seventh year prescribes the release of every Hebrew slave. As to the heathen slave, he is to be dealt with in kindness; his manumission is to be favored. A person from abroad seeking refuge in Israel, is not to be returned to his former master, and is to enjoy the right of asylum.

The fact that all men were considered sons of the same father, implied that they were equal in the Covenant of the people with its God: "Ye are standing this day all of you before the Lord your God: your heads, your tribes, your elders, and your officers, even all the men of Israel, your little ones, your wives, and thy stranger that is in the midst of thy camp, from the hewer of thy wood unto the drawer of thy water" (Deuteronomy XXIX: 9–10). It is true that history reveals that precepts of the Torah and of the Prophets are not always observed. The latter frequently denounce the violation of those precepts. One of the last Prophets, Ezekiel, proclaims human responsibility for what has resulted from man's abuse of his own liberty. But the great potential for human action offered by the Bible and the institutions of the nation of Israel cannot be underestimated.

* * *

At approximately the same period in history, Buddhism, in India, teaches men respect for life and condemnation of violence. Chinese civilization exalts civic responsibility and altruism, and elaborates upon the duties of the citizen as well as the duties of man. On the shores of the Mediterranean, polytheism flourished. The fact that the worship of a multitude of gods does not embody the same degree of moral principle as expressed in the Bible, will surprise nobody. It was the monarchs of great empires who strove to dictate the conduct of men. In Babylonia, it was Hammourabi who authored a famous code of laws—a very demanding one at that—which aimed at justice. In Egypt, the Book of the Dead attributed an examination of conscience, based on the ideal of moral perfection, to the soul of a King of the XVIIIth dynasty, appearing before Osiris.

Nowhere more than among the Greeks, founders of both the exact and the political sciences, was the spirit of independence expressed as loftily: Sophocles' Antigone, and the words of Socrates condemned to die, have come down through history and are as timely today as in their own time. However, freedom is restricted to certain men, and Aristotle, the great genius, considers the distinction between free men and those doomed by nature to slavery to be self-evident.

In Rome, similarly, an elite of thinkers (Cicero, Epictetus, Seneca, etc . . .) formulated exalted principles. Roman jurists elaborated a code of law that was never matched. The Roman Empire, nevertheless, carried on its expansion by fierce conquests—even to the point of total destruction of any adversary who resisted and of his civilization as well. Gaul is one illustration. At the eastern end of the Mediterranean, the destruction of the State (Kingdom) of Israel and the dispersion of its population constitute an even more perfect example.

At that particular moment in history, Christianity had already come into being. During the period of its early expansion, it was intended to combat its violent and barbarian surroundings. Basing himself on the need for purity and altruism already expressed in the Bible and evident before the birth of Christ, Saint Paul draws from the teachings of Jesus and from his torture a dynamic force for the promotion of brotherly love and universal fraternity: there is to be no more distinction between Jew and Gentile, between free men and slaves. All form one large family, the human family. All men, whatever their earthly state, are equal before God. Christianity is first and foremost a religion of redemption: to gain redemption for his soul, man must strive to be worthy thereof by his acts, by fulfilling his duty to God, to his fellowmen and to himself. Far from mentioning the rights of the individual, the sole concern is to prepare on earth for a good death.

Ominous events, in the form of barbarian invasions into christianized societies, brought in their wake such unheard-of troubles that the Bishops and other heads of the Clergy were drawn into temporal activities to ensure the security, not only of individual co-religionists, but of the cities. The Church has entered the realm of the Temporal. In the IVth century, under Constantine, it even becomes the official religion. In addition, progressively, the chiefs of the barbarian invaders and their troops are converted (Clovis, *et al.*) and the emperors are taken under its protection (Charlemagne, *et al.*), and thus its authority is consolidated, step by step.

From that point on, and for several ensuing centuries, the Church functions on two planes. As a Christian institution, the Church shows its belief in the idea of the equality of all before God and carries out forceful activities in the realm of charity—acts of spontaneous, voluntary giving, leading to the purification of the one who offers his heart or his property, and preparing him for a good death. Within this conception, the one who helps the sick, the old, the infirm, the poor, or who creates a foundation for their benefit, has acquitted himself of his duty towards them, with no correlative right on them. This is opposed to the situation created in a modern system of social security, and opposed, too, to the

Jewish concept of *Tsedek*. The Church very soon takes charge of the education of the young, instils them with the precepts of religion, and prepares them for future leadership cooperating with monarchs or acting independently in this mission.

The other aspect of the Church's policy was to deal with sovereigns and temporal lords on an equal footing or rather, from a superior position, to stimulate the obedience of their subjects, to influence by suggestion or sometimes by arbitration (the truces of God, etc.) in the political sphere of war and peace. This type of action leads the Church to a serious disregard of man's fundamental aspiration to freedom. In this guise, beyond the original apostolic aim, the Inquisition shows the sad picture of an institution that censures all writings with severity, and converts by forceful baptism under the menace of death by fire, exile and persecution, and participates in crusades and conquests. Even after losing his supremacy over Chiefs of State, the Pope remains for several centuries a temporal sovereign, and does not forsake subjection of a political character.

* * *

The awakening of human aspirations to emancipation—restrained by oppression or by virtue of obedient resignation—manifests itself as early as the XIth century. Aside from the peasant revolts, it starts with the emancipation of the mercantile cities, weary of heavy feudal or episcopal tutelage, and proceeds to the nobility in opposition to royal arbitrariness. The *Magna Carta* in England dates from 1215, and the *habeas corpus* follows. Some monarchs promulgate charters, granting their subjects guarantees for their corporal freedom.

But it is the Reformation and the Renaissance which inaugurate a new era, in the XVth, and XVIth centuries. The former restores the right to read the Bible and proclaims, on the religious plane, freedom of conscience and thought, and succeeds in making these ideas triumph in a number of countries. Nearly simultaneously, the Renaissance championed the freedom of intellectual, scientific and artistic creation. Galileo is one of its symbols. In the XVIIth century man's aspiration to political freedom manifests itself in the toppling of kings and the declarations of rights in England. Both there and in France, political philosophers exert much influence. The American Declaration of Independence gives the final consecration to the ideal of the juridical autonomy of the individual in his relation to the monarch or to the State, even if it is a republic.

The French Revolution marked the crowning point in this return of man to a minimum of freedom. In the summer of 1789, the famous Declaration of the Rights of Man and Citizen proclaimed to the world universal principles asserting rights. Their explosive force spread to other countries of Europe, Latin America and even Africa and Asia. Russia of the Czars remained untouched; this temporary immunity may not have been without influence on the form and character of the Russian Revolution of 1917.

The slogan of "Liberty, Equality, Fraternity" was one of the characteristic symbols of this upheaval. But it was the official abolition of slavery— even temporarily—which characterized most distinctively the impact of the Revolution's principles. For during thousands of years that institution was fostered by economic conditions, prior to what is known as the industrial revolution. Regardless of attempts to temper it, it constituted the most flagrant negation of the personality inherent in every human being, and existed in defiance of all moral condemnations leveled at it. Never was the slave-trade from Africa to the New World as intense as during the XVIIIth century. Even now, after nearly two centuries of international agreements and even civil wars, the scourge of slavery has not yet been completely eradicated, and, unfortunately, millions of human beings—men, women and children—are literally still slaves, reduced to the condition of objects, or merchandise, or subjected to a regime very much like slavery. Nevertheless the formulation of the principle that men are free and by law are equal by their very essence, made the French Revolution one of the major turning points in human history.

The history of Human Rights in the century following the 1789 Declaration has been recorded frequently. They developed in two directions: extension to more people, and inclusion of more rights and freedoms conceived as fundamental.

To begin with the extension to more human beings: Abbé Grégoire, who played such a considerable role in the Declaration of 1789 and the emancipation of black slaves, in 1791 also succeeded in obtaining the declaration that Jews were citizens with equal rights. Inspired by the same spirit, in 1860 seven French Jewish citizens founded the "Alliance Israélite Universelle" with the aim of extending to all Jews the Rights of Man. Among other things, they were responsible for the provision in the Treaty of Berlin (in 1878) whereby the newly-recognized independent Balkan States, were to confer the nationality of the state, and legal equality with their other nationals, upon Jews in their respective countries.

As to the list of the rights and freedoms of man, we know that in France itself the *Déclaration Montagnarde* of 1793 modified in a restrictive sense the sacred character of private property, and thereby multiplied the consequences of the principle of equality. In the following century, and right up to the second world war, the movement of expansion continued. Rights of workmen, the right to education, the right to social solidarity for protection against the risks of life, the right of individuals to life itself, all these became in France subjects for legislative action or projects; on the other hand, in a growing number of cases the law began to put a stop to abuses of property and of contracts, in order to protect the poor and the weak against the more severe cases of exploitation committed in the names of contractual freedom.

In recent constitutions of Latin American states, a powerful, though limited movement in favor of social justice has become sanctioned in more and more explicit and precise terms. But in the U.S.S.R. Constitution of 1920, and later in 1937, the rights of man as an individual were dealt with in the framework of a system, and were expressed in a new form, corresponding to Marxist doctrines, opposing individual ownership of the means of production, and putting the rights of man under the protection of socialist legalism. The birth of I.L.O. in 1919 has resulted in the organized protection of the workers without hindering the principle of free competition.

As to the Catholic Church, the *Syllabus* of Pope Pius IX violently objected to the Declaration of Human Rights of 1789. But even before the beginning of the XXth century the Popes came out in favor of legal protection for workers—while remaining true to the principles of private property and the rights of the employers. In 1893, Leo XIII published his famous *Encyclical* on the rights of workers. His successors, Pius X, Benedict XV and Pius XI were mainly interested in peace and quiet; Pius XI had the courage in 1934 to be the first to publicly voice his apprehension in the face of Nazi infringements on human rights, and he warned the world in vain of the grave menace to peace which that regime constituted.

For the past thirty years, numerous studies have been published on the methods by which Hitler assumed power in Germany, consolidated it, and then began his campaigns against neighboring countries, and finally, after contracting alliances, came to attack distant and mighty States in order to achieve global domination. History's answer is categorical. It was by announcing their flagrant contempt for liberty, the equality of man and races, and of human solidarity, by frenzied anti-Semitism and violent attacks on human rights, that Hitler and his gang-leaders launched the most formidable assault ever attempted against the principles of the French Revolution.

The Fascists of Mussolini actually preceded him in this. The techniques of governing by terror were on the rise. But as soon as Hitler came to power he applied them in full. The Versailles Treaty and the Jews were his main targets from the outset. Nominated Chancellor in 1933, he set fire to the *Reichstag* in order to be able to blame his political adversaries. He had to account to the League of Nations which accused him of violating the 1922 Calonder Treaty with Poland, regarding the minorities of Upper Silesia. After a very mild request to respect the basic rights of his nationals, he ostentatiously broke away from the League in September, and reaffirmed his absolute sovereignty.

Since there was no vigorous reaction throughout the world he allowed himself to intensify his domestic policies of repression and terror. In other European countries, he took the offensive by planning and executing a series of assassinations of heads of State, and setting off a process of moral disintegration within those countries. Having progressed sufficiently with this process of dividing social classes and ethnic groups, he was in a position to allow himself, in the sphere of international politics, to interfere in other countries' affairs, under the pretext of protecting German minorities or of requiring *"Lebensraum."*

Just before the war, on the morrow of Munich, "Kristallnacht" was the sinister forerunner of what was to follow: war, and the systematic extermination of so-called "inferior" races and the *intelligentsia* of the occupied countries. Finally, it was the Jews who, after having benefited completely or partially in 19th century Europe from the Human Rights proclaimed in the Declaration of 1789, now became the actual victims and also the most notable symbols of their systematic violation. This is the horrifying history of the Holocaust visited upon six million Jews by means of segregation, hunger, deportation, forced labor, the destruction of the ghettos and the death camps.

So many crimes, not prevented between 1932 and 1944, could not have gone without later judgment, nor could their recurrence be averted without preventive measures. The severe condemnations, in the Nuremberg trials of 1946, of the major war criminals, constituted the main repressive instrument. Later prosecutions, carried out with various degrees of energy, speed, and effectiveness in the countries of the guilty had a far from sufficient moral effect. Eichmann's condemnation strikes in the midst of that greyness.

As to the Convention designed to prevent genocide and combat any occurrences of it, this was adopted by the United Nations on December 9, 1948, and ratified by at least 75 States, but has never been applied for lack of an International Court. It is hard to envisage how it could be implemented by judges functioning in a dictatorial regime or in the midst of anarchy.

The protest of the human conscience was expressed more positively in the Preamble and first articles of the United Nations Charter—which reconfirms the belief of nations in the dignity of man, and which defines safeguarding and promotion of human rights as one of the main concerns of the United Nations, along with peace. In fact, the Commission on Human Rights, created by the Charter, worked between 1947 and 1954 to develop the three basic instruments of the Charter of Human Rights, as promised to the nations.

These are the Universal Declarations, adopted by the United Nations General Assembly on December 10, 1948, and two Pacts, one relating to the civil and political rights of man, and the other to his economic, social and cultural rights. The pacts were adopted unanimously on December 16, 1966, but are not yet in force, because of an insufficient number of ratifications. The Commission also prepared a convention aiming at the elimination of racial discrimination in all forms. This was adopted in 1965 and, having received the required number of ratifications, is at present valid. The framework of this study does not allow an analysis of these instruments, nor an examination of the total accomplishments of the Commission on Human Rights.

But as we approach the end of a panoramic look at the history of Human Rights, of their eclipse and development since the Decalogue, it is worth making a comparison between the Decalogue, which is the point of departure, and the present Charter which is our temporary point of arrival.

There is no doubt that the contrast is striking. The tone of the Decalogue, of religious inspiration and absolute unity, is both imperative and concise. The style of the Universal Declaration of 1948, a purely human instrument adopted by 56 States of profoundly differing ideologies is formulated in thirty rather long and complex articles. We must, however, insist on another difference which is characteristic. The Decalogue, a religious act, contains only prescriptions and prohibitions. It imposes duties on man, positive or negative ones. The Universal Declaration, a human instrument, proclaims first and foremost man's rights, and only at the very end articulates his duties. One might say that the difference is unimportant: rights and duties are correlative. A man against whom the commission of murder or robbery is forbidden has therefore implicitly the right to his life and his property!*

* Some Talmudic sages argue that the imposition of a duty grants a right.

From the Ten Commandments to the Rights of Man

In reality, the inversion in the formulation, already striking in the American and French Declarations of the XVIIIth century, has great significance. In the Decalogue, man is considered a creature and servant of God, one who receives orders. In the XVIIth century Declarations we find the influence of a long evolution in the course of which man has gradually affirmed his liberty, his responsibility, his legal autonomy in relation to the temporal powers conducting society. Those powers are not unlimited. The State, the pre-eminent form of social organization, cannot for instance control the consciences, the thoughts, the speech of its nationals. Nor can it arbitrarily dispose of their lives or their liberty. It is they, the human beings, who form the living reality, and they have the right to participate, directly or through their representatives, in governing their society and in levying their taxes.

The evolution pointed up by the inverted formulation of the Decalogue in the XVIIIth century Declarations went so far as to bring about the omission of so much as a mention of the general duties of man, notably in the French Declaration. The most it said was that a citizen should contribute to public expenses within his means. It is a manifesto in favor of the basic freedom of man, and of the equality of rights too long despised and trampled upon, a manifesto issued after prolonged struggle. As such, it insists on representing man and even the citizen as the responsibility of society, and not only of other men. It is society which must institute an adequate system of justice which will insure that a man is not punished retroactively nor imprisoned arbitrarily, and also that he may participate without fear in peaceful assemblies, and express his thoughts without being molested.

Such exalted individualism could not reach so high a level in the middle of the XXth century. Already in the middle of the XIXth century, abuses of liberty to the disadvantage of the weak—notably in the matters of private property and of contract—had provoked protesting voices from social reformers and religious circles. Auguste Comte, the founder of positivism, expressed his opposition in this way: "There is no right but the one to do one's duty." A half-century later, Gandhi echoed him when, upon being asked about human rights, he answered: "The only rights man has are those that enable him to do his duty." In Africa, the notion of duty in man's relation to his family and tribe is of tremendous importance.

The Declaration to be drawn up came in the wake of two world wars which had crushed millions of human beings and had concentrated untold power in the hands of governments, even in the most democratic of countries.

Upon completion of the list of fundamental rights and freedoms, the writers of the Declaration were confronted by the insistence of the socialist countries that express mention be made in what is Article 27, of the duties of the individual towards the community. They were supported by the Latin American countries whose representatives had adopted an "American Declaration of the Rights and Duties of Man" in Bogota in the winter of 1948. However, they did not insist—nor did I—on attempting what would have been an arbitrary enumeration of the principal duties of man and citizen.

The text adopted by the Commission on Human Rights was rejected by the representative of the Soviet Union, before the third Commission of the General Assembly. He achieved partial success in his aim. But the defenders of the individual's rights against the totalitarianism of the State took certain precautions so that their limitation in the general interest should be solely "such as were required by the exigencies of moral climate, public order, and general welfare in a democratic society." Giving our attention to the manner in which the Declaration envisages the duties of the individual to his fellow-men, one notes that it formulates the most important mutual duty in these terms: "They must act towards each other in a spirit of fraternity."

In regard to the other duties, one can only regret the defective presentation in Article 29, para. 2, which states: "The recognition of and respect for the rights and liberties of others," as a limitation on the rights and liberties of everyone. This is patently insufficient: the abuse of the rights, and the problem of the individual's general duties are not two interchangeable notions. It should have been specifically noted that "every person is generally bound not to interfere with the satisfaction of other people's rights and liberties, and thus respect the exercise of those rights."

The Head of the Catholic Church, Pope John XXIII, was not misled. After years of silence and of profound study, and after thorough thought and reflection, he described the United Nations Declaration in his Encyclical of 1963, *Pacem in Terris*, as "one of the most important acts of the United Nations" and as "a step towards the politico-judicial organization of the world community." In the chapter on "Duties" of the Encyclical (no. 30) he was even careful to specify that "in social life, every right conferred on man by nature creates in others (individuals and collectivities) a duty, that of recognizing and respecting that right."

This approval, indeed, was not an isolated phenomenon. In fact, the Declaration speeded up the change in the general position of the Church. For a very long time it had been concerned with the condition of man on earth only insofar as it promoted the fulfillment of his duties and obtained eternal salvation for him. But, since Leo XIII, and mainly since it ceased being a temporal power, the Church has been devoting more and more attention to the lot of the living individual, and of peoples; the most recent Encyclicals, those of Paul VI, as well as those of John XXIII, show that the Catholic Church—as well as the other Christian sects, reformed and orthodox—are becoming increasingly conscious of their duty to foster respect for the freedom and rights of man.

A characteristic example of this evolution can be found in the recent visit of the Pope to Cagliari, in Sardinia. Addressing himself to the slum-dwellers, he first said: "If civilian authorities . . . do not feel it their duty to collaborate for the protection of the sacred rights of man . . . grave dangers loom on the horizons of such a nation, as history has shown." But he continued: "We have come to honor you, to demand for you the dignified place you deserve within the Church, and also in civilian society to raise your needs (and how numerous they are) to the level of rights; right to a decent home of sufficient size, to daily bread, to work, to schooling, to sanitary installations, to participation in the general welfare, for yourselves and for your children." If we set these words alongside passages in the Encyclical *Populorum Progressio*, which states that the right to private property cannot go counter to the general welfare, and alongside the action for peace and the public protest of the Holy See against the tortures inflicted in Brazil on the numerous people arrested there, one can but rejoice at the orientation currently given to one of the most widespread of world religions among those considering the Bible as their Book.

Centuries have passed. Judaism has, throughout unparalleled trials, preserved its passion for justice and its desire to contribute to the defense of the rights of men of all races and origins, along the lines of the very principle with which it was entrusted two thousand years ago. The Ten Commandments, the first Code of the essential duties of man, have suffered many an outrage in history and continue to suffer. Their moral authority remains intact.

The emblem of the Universal Declaration recalls the duty of human fraternity, inspired by that master precept "Love thy neighbor as thyself." May it partake, despite its purely human origin, of the greatness of the Decalogue and appear as its worthy extension.

HUMAN RIGHTS AT THE U.N.
ILLUSION AND REALITY

WILLIAM KOREY*

I

For the thousands who annually write to the United Nations alleging
violation of some provision of the Universal Declaration of Human
Rights by one or another state, there is a standard typed response from
the Secretariat which concludes " . . . the Commission on Human Rights
has no power to take any action in regard to any complaints concerning
human rights."

It is a testimonial to the faith which the public holds in the United
Nations—and the illusions concerning it—that aggrieved or concerned
individuals continue to turn to the world organization seeking redress
or amelioration of the human rights condition in particular countries.

During most of the fifties, the average annual number of complaints
sent to the U.N. was in the 2–6,000 range, jumping to 25,000 in 1951–52
and to 63,700 in 1957. In 1968, International Human Rights Year,
the total was 18,394. Since the founding of the United Nations, an estimated one-quarter million petitions about human rights violations
have been addressed to the United Nations. All have been gathering
dust in the storerooms of the U.N.

The statistics highlighted the irony of commemorating International
Human Rights Year in 1968 to mark the twentieth anniversary of the
adoption of the Universal Declaration of Human Rights. On the eve
of the commemoration, René Cassin, who was to be awarded the Nobel
Peace Prize for his distinguished contributions to the advancement of
human rights, commented that violations of the Declaration have not
been "sufficiently reduced either in number or seriousness." The Year,
indeed, saw perhaps the most flagrant violations of human rights in
the Universal Declaration's 20–year history—the assault on Czecho-
slovak freedom, the threat of genocide in Biafra, the destruction of

* Director, U.N. Office of B'nai Brith International Council

Greek liberties, continuing massive deprivations in Southern Africa, mounting anti-Semitism in Poland, military takeovers in various Latin American countries.

Yet, it would be an error to dismiss the significance of the Universal Declaration. Both legally-binding international conventions covering various aspects of human rights and post-war peace treaties have incorporated direct reference to the Declaration. Its provisions have been included in the constitutions of many of the new states and have even been applied, in several instances, by national courts. As a "statement of principles," the Declaration is often appealed to as the fount of moral authority. A dramatic example was the manuscript of Professor Andrei D. Sakharov, privately circulated in 1968 in the Soviet Union, which, in its bold demand for greater freedom of speech and expression, repeatedly and expressly took its point of departure from the Declaration.

An assembly of international legal experts meeting in Montreal in March, 1968 concluded that the Universal Declaration "has over the years become a part of customary international law." But, if so, it is law without implementation provisions. The U.N. Charter (of which the Declaration, according to Cassin, is "an authoritative interpretation") does obligate member states, in Articles 55 and 56, to "take joint and separate action in cooperation with the Organization" to achieve "universal respect for and observance of human rights and fundamental freedoms for all without distinction as to race, sex, language or religion." While the words clearly specify an activist, not a passive, orientation, the Charter also throws up a built-in obstacle designed to safeguard the sovereign authority of the state. Article 2(7) stipulates that "nothing contained in the present Charter shall authorize the United Nations to intervene in matters which are essentially within the domestic jurisdiction of any state . . ."

The limitation leaves undefined two key words: "essentially" and "intervene." In any given situation violations of human rights may become a matter that transcends "essentially" domestic jurisdictional concerns and may enter the realm of international concern. "Intervention" has traditionally been defined as "dictatorial interference." As clarified by the great international legal authority, Professor Hersch Lauterpacht, such interference involves physical enforcement or threat of enforcement in the event of non-compliance. Excluded from this definition are such forms of human rights implementation as fact-finding, conciliation, and adjudication—forms that are utilized by the International Labor Organization or the Council of Europe, and to a lesser extent by the Organization of American States.

Not surprisingly, many governments which have been or are fearful of any international inquiry into their own human rights practices have given the term "intervene" the broadest possible interpretation and argue that the "domestic jurisdiction" clause of the Charter precludes consideration, in any form, of their internal practices. This has not prevented the same governments from advocating or acquiescing in various forms of intervention when it involved the condition of human rights elsewhere. The fact is that when a strong enough majority prevailed on any given human rights issue, neither the General Assembly nor other U.N. organs have hesitated to utilize various forms of intervention, short of military intervention.

More recently the burgeoning Southern Africa issues have prompted U.N. "intervention." But even earlier the General Assembly has, from time to time, attempted to deal with human rights violations notwithstanding Article 2(7). In most instances, the technique used was a resolution designed to expose to public attention a particular transgression of the Universal Declaration. Thus, in 1948, an Assembly resolution highlighted the refusal of the U.S.S.R. to permit their nationals who were married to foreigners to leave and join their spouses abroad. In 1949, the Assembly called upon Bulgaria and Hungary, and later Romania, each of whom had been accused of persecuting religion, in violation of post-war treaty obligations, to observe human rights and fundamental freedoms. A resolution condemning the three Governments followed in 1950. Of the same order were resolutions adopted in 1959 and 1961 concerning Tibet which had been directly absorbed into Communist China. Appeal for the observance of human rights was emphasized. It was clear that Western predominance in the Assembly made these exhortatory actions possible just as Cold War factors provided them with the essential, although by no means only, motivation.

Fact-finding through an *ad hoc* committee made its appearance as a technique in 1957 with the appointment of a Special Committee to investigate conditions in Hungary. One year earlier the Assembly had condemned the action of the Soviet regime in using military force against the rebel Government of Hungary and thereby depriving the Hungarian people of the exercise of their "fundamental rights." The Committee's report spelled out deprivations of political rights and led the Assembly the following year to deplore repression of the "fundamental rights" of the Hungarian people.

A similar approach was tried in October 1963 but with few Cold War overtones. Broad concern with the repression of the Buddhists by the Government of South Viet Nam led the Assembly, at the invitation of

South Viet Nam, to appoint a Commission to conduct an investigation. The group, after an on-the-spot inquiry, including the receipt of petitions and the hearing of witnesses, submitted a comprehensive report to the General Assembly. But the issue had already been mooted by the overthrow of the Diem Government.

The work and significance of these *ad hoc* instruments paled before two new organs created in 1961–62 by the Assembly under the powerful influence of the Afro-Asian bloc, now greatly enlarged by the admission of new states. The "Special Committee on the Situation with regard to the Implementation of the Declaration on the Granting of Independence to Colonial Countries and Peoples" was established in 1961 with 17 members. In 1963, with the addition of 7 new members, it came to be known as the Committee of Twenty-Four. The Committe was to constitute an elaborate machinery of implementation, far more extensive than anything heretofore created by the U.N. Subsidiary organs were established to deal with petitions and requests for hearings, the preparation of questionnaires, and individual territories.

The right of self-determination was of course the basic concern of the Committee, which it pursued through the technique of fact-finding and reporting. The petition system was a central feature of its operation. During 1962–66, it received a total of 1,283 communications of which 1,208 were circulated as petitions. On-the-spot investigations and hearings supplemented this procedure. In addition to self-determination, the Committee was concerned with human rights in the territories within its purview. Thus the questionnaires it sent out inquired into "the statutory and constitutional safeguards, if any, in regard to the observance of human rights and fundamental freedoms."

The second important instrument was the Special Committee on Apartheid established in November, 1962. The Committee received communications from organizations and individuals, held hearings from petitioners, and published reports on its findings. It became the moving force for action on *apartheid* by the General Assembly.

The effective functioning of these General Assembly mechanisms made it clear, if proof was ever needed, that the "domestic jurisdiction" argument constituted no obstacle to a determined majority which had the acquiescence or support of the major powers, anxious to court the Afro-Asians. And it also demonstrated that the U.N. could throw up an elaborate machinery for implementation, to which individuals had access through petitions and hearings. Of course, these mechanisms were political creations, designed to serve political ends. But these ends coincided with human rights purposes. The crucial point was that the human rights embraced by the mechanisms were severely limited in scope. Human rights encompass a far broader gamut, as clauses of the Universal Declaration make evident.

Even the Security Council which is empowered by the Charter to apply the ultimate form of implementation—sanctions—has not lagged far behind. On December 16, 1966, in an unprecedented decision, it voted selective mandatory sanctions against the rebel regime in Rhodesia on grounds that efforts of a small minority to suppress the political rights of a majority and to extend practices of racial discrimination were abhorrent to the United Nations and constituted a growing danger to peace. Article 41 of the Charter which gives the Council authority to order any measure, short of armed force, was invoked.

In three other decisions, the Security Council has come close to recognizing the existence of an actual and immediate threat to the peace, but backed away from a final determination and decisive action. Concerning the Portuguese territories of Angola, Mozambique and Guinea, the Security Council declared that "the situation resulting from the policies of Portugal both as regards the African population of its colonies and the neighboring states seriously disturbs international peace and security." Thus far, the Council has but demanded that Portugal recognize rights of self-determination and independence. With reference to South Africa, the Council ruled in 1960 that the situation "has led to international friction and if continued might endanger international peace and security." Three years later, in August 1963, the Council stated that the situation in South Africa "is seriously disturbing international peace and security" and recommended an arms embargo, which has been complied with by a number of the major powers.

II

But aside from the South African issues, abridgements of human rights today are all but neglected at the United Nations. (The rhetoric of delegates is, of course, another matter: human rights receive the most reverential of obeisances.) Their proper locus should have been the U.N. Commission on Human Rights, the body on which Justice Haim Cohn so ably served and the only functional U.N. organ specifically referred to in the Charter itself. In inserting it in the Charter, the U.N. Founding Fathers responded to a plea that the creation of a Commission dealing with human rights "was expected and hoped for by a great many people and there would be profound disappointment if it were not accepted."

WILLIAM KOREY

The Commission was given broad terms of reference and its role as an implementing organ was underscored. But in 1947 the body adopted a historic self-denying rule which was to restrict decisively its function in the area of human rights protection. The organ declared that it "recognizes that it has no power to take any action in regard to any complaints concerning human rights." Over the years, repeated suggestions have been made that the Commission end its self-restraining commitment, but it was reaffirmed by a decisive resolution of the Economic and Social Council, the Commission's superior organ, in 1959.

The self-denying resolution places the numerous complaints addressed to the U.N. in a nether world. The procedure adopted for dealing with them is as follows: a confidential list of complaints is drawn up and distributed at a private meeting to members of the Commission early in its annual session; the identity of the authors of the complaints is not divulged except in cases where they have no objection; and comments by the Government against which the complaint is lodged are also presented to the Commission; no discussion takes place at the private meeting except upon procedural grounds; and the writer of the communication is informed by the Secretary General that his complaint will be handled in accordance with the self-denying U.N. resolution, and that the Commission has no power to take any action with regard to human rights complaints.

The current conduct of the Commission, comprising 32 governmental representatives, stands in sharp contrast with the operation of the U.N. Trusteeship Council which during 1947–59 received and examined 16,232 petitions from private sources; with the General Assembly special Committees on Colonialism and Apartheid; and, indeed, with its own Ad Hoc Working Group of Experts on South African prisoners and detainees. This last independent body was created in 1967 by the Commission to assemble, evaluate and air pertinent information from all sources, especially non-governmental ones. The purpose, as one witness put it, was "the focussing of attention on what is going on and . . . [thereby] to exercise something of a brake on the [South African] authorities." Twenty-five witnesses were heard and twenty-three written statements were received in what the Director of the Human Rights Division called "one of the first occasions that an inquiry of this type has been organized under United Nations auspices."

The principal source of information for the Commission on general human rights matters is the sanitized reporting of governments. In 1950, Cassin had proposed that State-members forward annually "for consideration by the Commission" a report on the steps "they have taken to ensure respect for and the promotion of human rights . . ." But when adopted in 1953 as a "periodic reporting system," the proposal was emptied of all content, with the Commission restricted to making comments and recommendations of "an objective and general character." The term "general" was aimed at excluding references to specific situations in specific countries.

Not unexpectedly, the voluminous governmental reports that poured into the Commission were *apologias* describing laws on the books, not how they operated. In 1964 the Commission attempted to relieve itself of this burden by requesting its subordinate organ, the Sub-Commission on Prevention of Discrimination and Protection of Minorities, to examine the reports. This 18-member body was theoretically composed of "experts" who presumably do not represent governments. The Sub-Commission was also asked to study the "objective information" submitted by non-governmental organizations.

The experience proved illuminating in revealing the deep distrust, on the part of both Communist powers and Afro-Asian countries, of non-governmental criticisms that are not specifically related to *apartheid* and racial discrimination. The Sub-Commission in January, 1967 called upon its *Rapporteur*, Judge Zeev Zeltner of Israel, to prepare a special study on "salient developments and trends" based upon the periodic reports. After scrutinizing the government submissions, the Judge found such inadequacies in reportage that he declared it impossible to point to "trends."

More important was the "restricted" document prepared by the *Rapporteur* for only Sub-Commission members. It summarized allegations made by a half-dozen prominent non-governmental organizations about civil and political rights violations in a number of countries. These included World Young Women's Christian Association, International League for the Rights of Man, Amnesty International, Friends Peace and International Relations Committee, Open Door International and the International Federation of Christian Trade Unions. Where governments had commented upon the allegations, these comments, too, were included. The document of eleven pages covered almost every geographical area. Among countries criticized were a number in West Europe as well as in East Europe; South Africa and Black Africa; Central Asia and South East Asia; Central America and South America.

The range of charges was broad, stretching from enforced servitude to deprivation of freedom of thought, conscience and religion; from violations of freedom of opinion and expression to restrictions upon the formation of trade unions.

The reaction of the Soviet member was violent. A flow of invective directed against non-governmental organizations was accompanied by a demand for the suppression of the document. African and Asian members, sensitive to criticism directed against their own Governments, joined in the criticism. When the vote was taken, an extraordinary result emerged. A majority—8 to 6—decided to suppress the document of its own specially designated *Rapporteur*.

The repercussions were decisive in determining the direction of the periodic reporting system. The Commission deprived the Sub-Commission of further study of the periodic reports.

At another session of the Sub-Commission held in October, 1967 the body displayed far more courage. Acting under instructions of the Commission to examine *for the first time* the mass of "communications" (the euphemistic term for complaints) alleging violations of human rights, the Sub-Commission was asked to report on situations which reveal a "consistent pattern" of "gross" violations of human rights. The Sub-Commission, drawing upon both published reports and information supplied by Amnesty International in particular, called attention to "consistent patterns" of "gross" violations in Haiti and Greece and recommended that the Commission "establish a Special Committee of Experts" to investigate situations of this nature. The proposal marked a crucial breakthrough in the heretofore virtually silent treatment of instances of human rights violations.

Observers keenly awaited the reaction of the Commission at its February-March 1968 session—the session taking place during International Human Rights Year. Would it pursue the matter further? Would it focus a powerful public searchlight upon situations known to be ugly and needing exposure? Not only were the observers to be disappointed; they were to be stunned by the Commission's reaction.

The Haitian Ambassador found it expedient to appear before the Commission to deny all charges and to initiate a counterattack which accused members of the Sub-Commission of attempting to divert attention from *apartheid* by attacking Haiti. He further implied that Sub-Commission members were motivated by an anti-black bias. The Greek representative on the Commission also engaged in a lengthy *apologia* at the same time as he chastised the Sub-Commission for singling out his own country as a violator of human rights. Both warned that if the Commission permitted itself to condemn governments on the basis of unofficial communications received by the U.N., then no government would be safe from condemnation. Haiti called attention to the fact that a certain power had been accused of genocide in Viet Nam and that a certain European country had been accused of denying religious freedom to Jews. The Greek representative, no doubt aware that Nigeria was a member of the Commission, observed that he had been approached by Biafran spokesmen concerning their alleged mistreatment. These warnings proved decisive.

Strikingly, not a single Western state, aside from Sweden, proposed that the evidence warranted action by the Commission. Nor were the Communist bloc members prepared to accept a formal resolution on the subject even though the U.S.S.R. representative singled out Greece for a strong verbal attack. The United States, which had already recognized the Greek military junta, had its representative table a bland resolution which after stating that the information on the two cases had not been sufficient to require Commission action, took note of the assertions of Greece and Haiti in the session and expressed hope that further information would become available next year. The resolution would have further required the Sub-Commission to continue considering *all* situations "which appear to involve consistent patterns of gross violations of human rights."

But even this mild version was unacceptable to the Communist bloc or the Afro-Asian bloc. The Nigerian delegate declared that it would be an undesirable precedent for the Commission to deal with violations on the basis of non-governmental evidence. The Tanzanian delegate went further. He submitted a resolution which would have virtually censured the Sub-Commission and would have required it to limit its reports on gross violations to Southern Africa. He threatened that if the Sub-Commission were to continue focussing attention on areas other than Southern Africa, he would request it to consider violations of human rights in Viet Nam and in the United States itself.

The U.S. was not prepared to do battle on the issue and, by agreement with Tanzania, withdrew its own, now greatly weakened, resolution. In turn Tanzania withdrew paragraphs from its resolution and accepted a proposal that the Commission, not the wayward Sub-Commission, give annual consideration to "all situations, which it has reasonable cause to believe, reveal a consistent pattern of gross violations of human rights and fundamental freedoms" as "exemplified by the policy of *apartheid*" in South Africa and "racial discrimination" in Rhodesia.

Ultimately, the jointly-prepared draft was withdrawn when the Commission agreed not to take any action at all on the Sub-Commission resolution. "We have all gone back to zero," said one member. While the matter of violations in Greece and Haiti was left suspended in mid-air, it was unclear how the Sub-Commission was expected to interpret the mandate given it the previous year beyond the mere studying of "consistent patterns" of violations in Southern Africa. To make certain that this was the intent of the majority, the Tanzanian moved a resolution—successfully—which would have ECOSOC increase the membership of the Sub-Commission from 18 to 26 by adding to it persons principally from Africa and Asia.

The drastic Commission setback to human rights progress in 1968 was dramatically highlighted by a further development relating to the *Rapporteur's* official report of the Commission session. Ambassador Arthur Goldberg had appeared before that body and, in a major address, called attention to "current and serious transgressions" against freedom of expression in the U.S.S.R. as illustrated by the secret Sinyavsky-Daniel trial and the arrest and sentencing of those who had protested the trial. The U.S.S.R. demanded that three paragraphs in the official Commission Report which carried most of Goldberg's charges be expunged. And, by a vote of 10 to 8 with 4 abstentions, this startling act of censorship was accomplished.

The Soviet Union had argued that Goldberg was interfering in its internal affairs, an act presumably proscribed by the Charter. But, as the former Supreme Court Justice commented, violations of human rights do not occur on "celestial bodies"; they take place only within states. This truth has yet to be recognized by the Commission.

If the Commission's action relative to Greece and Haiti once more had the effect of pigeon-holing complaints, few would doubt that the Afro-Asian bloc was the decisive factor (the Soviet opposition to the U.N.'s dealing with private complaints having long been established). An African diplomat later revealed at the Montreal Assembly on Human Rights that the "corridor gossip" among bloc members considered the Haiti and Greek issues to be a deliberate "diversionary" effort of the West aimed at avoiding the South African question. That the "corridor gossip" was a "damned lie"—as an informed source observed—made little difference to the African. He delivered the pointed warning that unless the West satisfies African demands on *apartheid*, "the work of human rights must suffer."

III

But the *apartheid* issue is only a part of the African concern. Supranational authorities inquiring into matters unrelated to racial discrimination or *apartheid* are regarded by many African representatives as but the "Trojan horse" of neo-colonialism. With this argument, the Africans and Asians joined the Communist bloc in severely weakening implementation provisions of the draft International Covenant on Civil and Political Rights, adopted by the Assembly in December, 1966. As one African diplomat explained: "Africans have learned from bitter experience that human rights could not be guaranteed unless the security of the state was guaranteed." The interests of the state preceded that of the individual—except, of course, in matters involving racial discrimination. Thus, the international treaty barring all forms of racial discrimination, adopted the year before the Covenant, was equipped with the strongest implementation devices of any international instrument.

With the Commission on Human Rights virtually impotent, the U.N. has relied upon the use of legally-binding human rights treaties to bring about a modicum of implementation. Sixteen of these have been adopted, ranging from genocide and slavery to discrimination on grounds of sex and race. In addition, the U.N. specialized agencies, I.L.O. and UNESCO, have adopted several human rights treaties. But these treaties are restricted in their application to only those Governments which ratify them, and the record of ratification is hardly encouraging. A statistical study shows that the total number of ratifications as of January, 1968 was 21.3 per cent of the maximum attainable number. Only three treaties—the Genocide Convention, the 1926 (League of Nations) Slavery Convention as amended in 1953, and the Supplementary Slavery Convention—have received more than half of the maximum number of ratifications. A mere seven states have ratified a majority of human rights treaties; 125 states have ratified less than one-half the number of treaties. 59 states have ratified two or less treaties. 14 states have ratified none. The International Covenants on Human Rights, a product of 18 years of labor in drafting two all-embracing human rights treaties, have received only a single ratification since their adoption in December, 1966.

Somewhat more significant than the question of ratification is the fact that only two U.N. treaties provide for independent organs of enforcement: the Convention on the Elimination of All Forms of Racial Discriminaton and the Covenant on Civil and Political Rights. The former, adopted in December, 1965 creates an 18-member organ carrying significant powers in the area of fact-finding, reporting and conciliation. An optional clause—which has yet to acquire the necessary ten declarations to become operable—would enable the organ to initiate actions based on complaints submitted by aggrieved individuals. But the implementation machinery has yet to be tested and there is considerable doubt as to whether it will amount to much. And, it should be

emphasized, the machinery is applicable only to ratifying powers—
a comparatively small number. The weaker enforcement organ contemplated by the Covenant is not likely to see the light of day for a long
period.

An Asian member of the Commission on Human Rights recently
commented that the body was like a trade union and "one shouldn't
attack other members of the union." He was responding to criticism
that the body avoided taking hold of the crucial human rights issues
of the day. In March, 1968 the Commission met at a moment when
world headlines were carrying the news that Britain, in violation of
solemn commitments, was restricting the right of her citizens of Asian
origin living in Kenya to come to England. Not a word about it was
uttered at the session. Nor had the issue of Biafra been raised either in
that organ or in any other U.N. body. Several years ago when a massive,
possibly genocidal, campaign was conducted by Army nationalists in
Indonesia against native Communists and residents of the Chinese
quarter, no voice was raised in the U.N. chambers.

The fact is, unfortunately, that the Commission has become, like
the major U.N. organs, a highly political body where the vote and interests of blocs and of the great powers are decisive. Before such organs
an individual or group whose rights have been abused can seek no
redress. While the I.L.O. and such regional bodies as the Council of
Europe and, to a lesser extent, the Organization of American States
have created permanent independent implementation instruments,
to a considerable degree insulated from overt political pressures, the
U.N., twenty years after proclaiming the Universal Declaration of
Human Rights, has established no institution to which the aggrieved
and the oppressed can appeal.

Deliberation over the question of implementation was to have been
a major concern of the U.N.-sponsored International Conference on
Human Rights held in Teheran in April-May, 1968. For three weeks,
delegates from 84 countries sat and pondered and brought forth a "Proclamation of Teheran" which, in most respects, was a rehash of numerous
resolutions adopted by the U.N. or a series of platitudinous assertions.
No serious consideration was given to the question of implementation
machinery. After months of preparation, the accumulation of massive
documentation, and the spilling of an enormous quantity of words in
preparatory debates and memoranda, Teheran—the high point of
International Human Rights Year—produced little to show for the
effort. Inevitably, public attention to the proceedings flagged and disappeared.

Politics, not human rights, was the principal order of the day. An example was the extraordinary amount of time devoted to the Middle East question even though the question was not originally on the agenda. Arab states and their friends in the Communist and Afro-Asian blocs, monopolized a substantial part of the conference's limited time to ventilate anti-Israel grievances. They succeeded in obtaining a strong resolution expressing "grave concern for the violation of human rights in Arab territories occupied as a result of the June, 1967 hostilities," and in asking the General Assembly to appoint a special committee to investigate the alleged violations. (This request the Assembly later approved.) The character of the sponsors of the resolution provided an ironic commentary upon and demonstrated the political nature of the proceedings. The three sponsors were Spain, Sudan and Saudi Arabia. As champions of human rights, whether at home or abroad, they left something to be desired.

Politics also played a shamefully decisive role in the selection of the first U.N. Human Rights Awards presented on December 9, 1968. Along with such distinguished names as Mrs. Eleanor Roosevelt, Chief Albert Luthuli and René Cassin, the U.N. gave an award to an obscure Ukrainian law professor, Petr Emelyanovich Nedbailo who, while representing his Government at the Commission on Human Rights, defended a notorious anti-Semitic book *Judaism Without Embellishment,* written by his countryman, Trofim K. Kichko.

IV

While the twentieth anniversary of the Universal Declaration of Human Rights passed into history, the international community remained in desperate need of at least minimal forms of compliance machinery. The United Nations Charter gave emphasis to the truism that peace and human rights are inter-related. President John F. Kennedy was to underscore this theme when he rhetorically asked in his historic American University address of June 10, 1963: "Is not peace, in the last analysis, a matter of human rights?"

Human rights were at the core of the U.N. Charter when it was adopted twenty-five years ago. Its Preamble and six of its Articles placed emphasis upon civil rights and civil liberties. The opening words of the Charter underscored, at least indirectly, the principle that it was the rights of individuals that were primary, not those of states. "We, the Peoples of the United Nations"—not "We, the Member-States of the United Nations"—was how the founding fathers of the U.N.

phrased it. Implicit was the right of people, of individuals, to petition for redress of grievances.

Since May, 1969 a spate of petitions has attracted wide public attention to the failure of the U.N. to deal with human rights violations. That month, 52 Soviet intellectual dissidents wrote to the U.N. spelling out a series of abridgements of civil liberties and ethnic rights by Soviet authorities and called upon the U.N. "to come to the defense of human rights that are being trampled upon in our country." In September, 46 of the original group again petitioned the U.N., calling upon Secretary General Thant to "speak out against violations of human rights in our country." The signers voiced anxiety that they had not received word as to how their initial appeal had been treated. They then went on to comment: "The silence of international . . . organizations frees the hand of those who inspire further repressions."

More recently, 18 heads of Jewish families in Soviet Georgia called upon the U.N. Commission on Human Rights "to help us leave for Israel." Their request to Soviet authorities had gone unanswered. "No one cares about our fate," the petitioners sadly observe. And in January, 1970, 25 Jews in Moscow complained to the U.N. that they were "being kept forcibly" by Soviet authorities from exercising their right to leave the U.S.S.R. to join relatives in Israel. They specifically appealed to Article 13/2 of the Universal Declaration of Human Rights which stipulates that "everyone has a right to leave any country including his own," and to the International Convention on the Elimination of All Forms of Racial Discrimination which carries reference to the same right. The Soviet Government has endorsed the Universal Declaration and has ratified the International Convention (January 22, 1969).

At least a dozen more similar appeals have come to light since the beginning of the year. Yet, these as well as the petitions of the Soviet intellectuals have not been acted upon and will not be considered by any U.N. body. Instead, the petitions have simply been filed away while the signers, who have clearly run great personal risks, have been notified by the U.N. Secretariat that the U.N. has no power to take any action in regard to any complaints concerning human rights.

In the Fall of 1969, the U.N. Secretary General officially reported that 14,214 petitions had been received during the year. Independent knowledgeable sources, not connected with the U.N. Secretariat, indicate that, on the one hand, the scale of alleged violations is indeed broad and, on the other hand, personal situations requiring redress of grievances are poignant.

Thirteen Articles of the Universal Declaration of Human Rights are alleged to have been abridged by at least three score governments in literally every corner of the globe. The largest number of complaints, by far, concerned the "right to leave" (Article 13/2). The next largest number dealt with Article 2, which requires fulfillment of the rights and freedoms in the Universal Declaration "without distinction of any kind, such as race, colour, sex, language, religion, political or other opinion, national or social origin, property, birth or other status." Third in the number of complaints were those relating to infringements of Article 3: "Everyone has the right to life, liberty and security of person."

A considerable number of grievances were also concerned with violations of Article 9 which prohibits "arbitrary arrest, detention or exile"; with Article 18 which guarantees "freedom of thought, conscience and religion"; and with Article 19 which upholds "the right to freedom of opinion and expression."

In addition there was a massive outpouring of complaints to the U.N., by no means restricted to the West, concerning the public executions that had taken place in Baghdad, Iraq. A heavy volume of complaints were also received, some from high officials in various countries, demanding an end to persecution of Jews in Iraq, Syria, and Egypt. The extraordinary number of these communications may have been among the factors that prompted Secretary General Thant formally to express concern to the Iraqi authorities about the public executions and to urge, in the Introduction to his Annual Report to the U.N. in September, 1969, that the "departure" of the Jews from Arab countries be "sanctioned and arranged" by the Arab Governments. Formal intervention by the Secretary General in human rights matters is rare.

Beyond the complaints which, because of either their significance or scale, obviously have an international concern, there are numerous simple appeals of ordinary people seeking assistance from the only global body that they believe may offer aid. A few samples suggest the extent and character of these petitions.

A West European woman complains that her sister, while travelling in Asia, had been arbitrarily arrested and deprived of travel documents by a particular Asian country.

A mother in a Central American state seeks assistance in obtaining news of the whereabouts of her son who is thought to have mysteriously disappeared.

An East European woman asks aid in being permitted to leave her country so that she might marry her lover in a West European country.

A sailor in West Europe complains that his Government deprived him of his disability pension because he had worked for foreign countries.

A Southeast Asian charges that he has been deprived of employment because he refused to adopt the Islamic faith.

An East African alleges that he was denied his nationality by his Government.

An East Asian complains that his right to work was denied.

A South Asian complains that during his absence while visiting another country he was deprived of his property by the authorities.

A blind woman in Southeast Europe asserts that she and other blind people in her country were inhumanly treated.

A Latin American asks that his immediate deportation on grounds that he has no birth certificate be halted.

A Southeast Asian living on the borderland of two states alleges that he was refused citizenship by both, thereby making it impossible for him to find work in either.

At times, the appeals have a character that might intrigue a Hollywood producer: a petition signed by 1200 political prisoners in a camp in Southeast Europe, charging that they had been held in detention without trial for two years, is smuggled to a Central European country and forwarded to U.N. headquarters; a prominent composer in the same Southeastern country spells out the details of his detention in a communication sent to a major West European newspaper, then transmitted to the U.N.; a letter from mothers and relatives of political prisoners in a Caribbean country appeals to the U.N. for its intercession.

V

The fact that twenty-five years after the Charter's adoption there exists no adequate machinery for dealing with the great mass of petitions concerning human rights violations constitutes a major imperfection in the U.N. structure. In 1969, the Commission, drawing upon suggestions advanced in the Sub-Commission by Professor John Humphrey of Canada, tried to correct this imperfection by drafting the following guidelines: all complaints would be channeled through the Secretary General to be considered by a special Working Group of the Sub-Commission on Prevention of Discrimination and Protection of Minorities. The Working Group would then consider whether certain complaints reveal a consistent pattern of gross violations of human rights.

The proposal has aroused considerable anxiety among numerous states especially those whose standards in the human rights field leave much to be desired. Strong resistance arose at the 1970 session of the

Commission held in March. The Soviet bloc, supported by Arab and Moslem states, halted further progress while emphasizing that any investigation must have the approval of the state against which charges of "consistent patterns of gross violations" have been lodged.

A compromise proposal was approved in May, 1970 by the Economic and Social Council. It would allow the Sub-Commission to create a 5–man Working Group, but observers are nonetheless uncertain about the effectiveness of any machinery emerging from the highly politicized organs of the United Nations. Many State-members are notoriously reluctant to open their internal structure to public scrutiny, shielding themselves in the meantime behind the so-called "domestic jurisdiction" clause of the Charter.

The most ardent defender of the "domestic jurisdiction" clause has been the U.S.S.R. whose delegation at the U.N. has fiercely resisted the public airing of issues which bear upon, for example, the Soviet treatment of Jews. When United States Ambassador Rita Hauser, at the 1969 session of the General Assembly, read an eloquent plea from a Soviet Jewish citizen, Mrs. Elizaveta Issakovna Kapshitser, asking that her son be permitted to emigrate to Israel, she was so repeatedly and rudely interrupted by Soviet spokesmen, that she finally quit reading the plea altogether.

The sensitivity of the Soviet authorities to public discussion of their internal human rights inadequacies and their determination to utilize considerable pressure to halt or limit embarrassing disclosures were especially highlighted in October, 1969 after the second petition from Soviet intellectual dissidents had arrived at U.N. headquarters. The outcome was to take a scandalous turn with the Secretariat lending itself to the shutting down of an established channel for the mere transmission of petitions.

The background was this: Soviet dissenters, in both May and September, had approached the U.N. Information Center in Moscow asking it to transmit their petitions to U.N. Headquarters. They obviously feared that Soviet censors would prevent their use of the mail for that purpose. (Their suspicions were no doubt legitimate. Their petitions, mailed from Moscow, never arrived in New York. Instead, copies of the original petitions, had to be brought to the U.N. by the London-based Amnesty International, a non-governmental organization holding consultative status with ECOSOC. Western correspondents in Moscow were aware of the first petition on May 22, but the U.N. did not receive a copy until June 18.)

But the Acting Director of the U.N. Information Center in Moscow,

Igor Chechetkin, refused to accept the petitions for transmission. It did not go unnoticed that the Moscow Center was one of only two Information Centers—the other being Prague—which, in violation of established U.N. rules, is staffed by nationals of the country. The other 49 U.N. Information Centers, scattered all over the globe, are staffed by non-nationals.

Nor did it go unnoticed that Information Centers had traditionally been used as a "post-office" for the transmission of petitions to the U.N. If relatively few utilized this channel, nonetheless they were especially important for petitions in countries where there are difficulties about direct contact with U.N. headquarters.

Yet, on October 3, the Secretariat, responding to Soviet objections, broke a twenty-year U.N. tradition by ordering U.N. Information Centers not to accept petitions for transmission. The U.N. argued that "from the inception of the Information Centers in many Member countries, no instructions were ever issued to them to accept and transmit complaints from individuals or groups of individuals regarding breaches of human rights . . ." The reasoning was somewhat tortured, for instructions had not been issued to the contrary and, as the Secretary General acknowledged, Directors of Information Centers had, over the years, "used their own discretion and forwarded some letters or communications from individuals or organizations which, in the judgment of the Directors, were worth consideration at headquarters."

The non-governmental community at the U.N. was stunned and made their displeasure felt. Various governmental delegates joined the chorus of criticism. Particularly eloquent was the Permanent Representative of Norway, Edvard Hambro, who was elected President of the General Assembly in the fall of 1970. He called the action of the Secretariat a "most serious matter" and emphasized that "it is urgently important to furnish an open channel of communication for people who feel that their human rights have been curtailed or violated."

But the decision was not revoked. Nor did members of the Commission on Human Rights feel compelled to challenge it. The following episode which occurred on March 26, 1970 at the Commission session suggests the indifference of many governmental delegates to the vital issue of complaint petitions generally. The Chairman of the Commission stated: "We now come to the item dealing with communications. It has been our custom in the past that if any member has observations on communications we go into closed session in order to hear those observations. Does any member of the Commission have any observations?" Thirty seconds of silence elapsed. Then the Chair commented: "There being no obervations, we have finished that agenda item and we now go on to the next item."

Ambassador Edvard Hambro of Norway emphasized the major imperfection in the U.N. human rights structure. "And certainly," he declared in an Assembly speech in November, 1969, "if world order and world organizations shall have any meaning we must realize that suffering and humiliation of human beings everywhere is ultimately the concern of all of us. The way of the future must therefore be to place an ever greater emphasis on human rights." Such "emphasis" would require the establishment of international machinery for bringing about compliance with the human rights provisions of the Charter. One proposal that has been advanced, particularly by Costa Rica, would create an Office of U.N. High Commissioner for Human Rights. That office would have access to the currently pigeon-holed "communications" and attempt, in a tactful, diplomatic manner, to deal with them. But few observers are optimistic about the Costa Rica proposal being adopted in the near future. The problem underscored by Ambassador Hambro remains.

THE STRUGGLE FOR HUMAN RIGHTS AND ITS IMPLICATIONS

Zeev Zeltner*

Among his manifold activities in a life dedicated to the service of the State of Israel, the Jewish people and the whole freedom loving world, not the least is Haim Cohn's incessant struggle for the implementation of Human Rights and the upholding of Human Dignity.

On being elected a member of the United Nations Expert Committee and later on, of the Commission on Human Rights, he brought to those bodies the brilliance of an outstanding lawyer and statesman and the culture of a sensitive human being. Haim Cohn's numerous contributions to the deliberations of these institutions are now milestones in the emergence of a modern Law of Nations.

The struggle for peace and the fight for Human Rights are inextricably interwoven. Nazism could not have triumphed in Germany without having previously destroyed the fundamental rights of the German people themselves. The lesson of World War II is that national governments provide insufficient protection for human rights. International protection has, therefore, become a condition for survival.

However, a sober review and reasonable preview of the history of human rights in the United Nations discloses in the area of human rights the failure rather than the success of this organization in all but lip-service. Future prospects are gloomy.

Two milestones may be noted on the progress towards a possible doomsday. The *Universal Declaration of Human Rights,* accepted in 1948, constitutes *merely a program.* Today it is generally understood that its contents are non-binding, although, in 1948 Professor Cassin engaged in a nearly single-handed battle for the linking of the program to realistic enforcement,[1] and more recently a number of voices have been raised in his support. At most, the Declaration is a challenge, but surely not an achievement. This was clearly recognized by the then President of the General Assembly, Mr. Evatt of Australia, who said:

---

* President, Tel Aviv District Court; Professor of Law, Tel Aviv University

Millions of men, women and children all over the world will, in the future, turn to it for help, guidance and inspiration. The man in the street who appealed to the Declaration could support his protest with the authority of the unanimous decision of the peoples and governments of the United Nations.

True, the man in the street did turn to the United Nations for help. But he turned to a sphinx. Innumerable petitions, mostly unread, ended in the wastebasket. A glance at events in the world today affords plentiful proof that the challenge was not met. Not a single delegation voted against the Universal Declaration, but eight of them abstained, and the reasons for their abstention may provide us with a clue to its inadequacy. The abstainers were a motley crowd: the six eastern bloc countries (including Yugoslavia), Saudi Arabia, and the Union of South Africa. The motives of the Union are self-evident, and we shall content ourselves below with probing those of the other abstaining States.

Even at the time of the acceptance of the Universal Declaration it was obvious that it was no more than a cry in the wilderness. Therefore the General Assembly concomitantly instructed the Human Rights Commission, through the intermediary of the Economic and Social Council, to prepare a draft for a binding legal document. The result appeared after 18 years of drafting—in December 1966—in the form of the Covenant on Civil and Political Rights (including an Optional Protocol) and the Covenant on Social and Cultural Rights. While the Covenants were accepted unanimously, the Optional Protocol was carried against two votes, but with 32 abstentions. Among the abstainers were, again, the whole eastern bloc and four Arab countries.

These covenants in themselves are rather modest achievements. The so-called rights conferred by the Covenant on Social and Cultural Rights—the right to social security, to work, to just remuneration, to rest and leisure, to an adequate standard of living, to medical care, and to assistance to mothers, and the right to education—are not rights at all, but directive principles of social policy.[2] Their implementation on an international level is impossible. Moreover, the sole step to this end was the introduction of a system of reporting on progress achieved by individual States, with the very States who are parties to the Covenant being responsible for the reports.[3]

The Covenant on Civil and Political Rights, reiterating the classic liberties crystallized during the American and French Revolutions, is to be implemented by a Human Rights Committee where, again, reporting is the hard core of implementation.[4] True, the Committee may try conciliation if one state party claims that another State party does not fulfill its obligations under the Covenant. But action by the Human Rights Committee depends upon an explicit declaration of consent by the State against which the complaint is lodged, and such declaration may be withdrawn at any time until the case is actually pending.[5] The Committee's action is limited to the appointment of an *ad hoc* Conciliation Commission. In case of failure of conciliation, the committee is to prepare a report embodying the relevant facts and pointing out possible amicable solutions. With that the Committee's competence comes to an end.[6] The individual concerned has no standing under the Covenant. In case of an alleged human rights violation, he may apply to a State, which might take up the matter if it sees fit to do so, thereby converting a purely humanitarian problem into a political issue—certainly the worst possible solution.

Strivers for human rights hail the Optional Protocol appended to this Covenant as a breakthrough to human rights implementation. Here the right to individual petitions is recognized after all domestic remedies have been exhausted, though anonymous communications are not admissible. Now, surely, the important thing is not to receive complaints but to deal with them. What can the Committee do in this respect? It can consider the complaint, ask the State concerned to reply, examine the documents in closed meeting, and forward its views to the individual and to the State against whom the complaint is made. This again is the end of the matter. Though the protocol is optional and applies only to States which have expressly adhered to it, nearly one third of the United Nations Member States abstained from voting on it in the General Assembly, as said above.

As regards these Covenants and this Protocol—what is their true effect? Their acceptance by the General Assembly does not even bind the States that voted for them. In order to transform them into living law, they have to be signed by a given number of governments and ratified by their parliaments or other appropriate organs of the State, according to its constitution. It is perfectly possible that a certain State has voted for a Covenant in the General Assembly, but that the government of this same State withholds its signature or that its appropriate organ refuses ratification. Ratification is, therefore, the only test of efficacy, and talk of progress achieved in Covenants without dealing with the question of their ratification is pure shadow-boxing. The two Covenants under review must be ratified by 35 States each in order to become effective, and the Optional Protocol by ten. Though a sufficient number of governments have signed the covenants,[7] only three States have hitherto ratified them: Costa Rica, Cyprus, and Syria. The Optional Protocol has been ratified by Costa Rica only. The net result is that neither the Covenants nor the Optional Protocol are law.

The high water mark of the United Nations achievement in the Human Rights field is the International Convention on the Elimination of All Forms of Racial Discrimination, adopted unanimously on December 21, 1965, and since ratified. In condemning all forms of racial discrimination—this expression being used in a very general sense—the State Parties will establish a Committee of 18 experts acting in a personal capacity. Provision has been made for the usual reporting system; in addition, the Committee may be presented with complaints by other States, and with the consent of the State complained of, by individuals. When a complaint is brought by a State Party, the Committee may appoint an *ad hoc* conciliation commission which will, if conciliation fails, forward its actual findings and its recommendations to the Committee. If the States concerned do not accept the recommendations, the latter will be forwarded to all State Parties.[8]

In case of complaints brought forward by individuals, the Committee, after consideration of same, will communicate its suggestions and recommendations, if any, to the State Party and to the individual concerned. A summary of such proceedings will be enclosed in the Committee's annual report. Here again the matter rests.

But even this modest achievement was not dictated by concern for human rights as such, but is to be viewed as part of a certain political framework. Says a modern lawyer:

> That convention . . . would have been unthinkable were it not for its symbolic significance in the rising campaign against South Africa's racial regime and for self-determination in South West Africa, Southern Rhodesia and the Portuguese possessions in Africa.[9]

The convincing proof of this allegation is the dismal failure of the United Nations to produce a convention against religious discrimination.

In order to find out whether anything can be done for the progress of Human Rights, one must understand the reasons for its absence. Our thesis is that Human Rights are a Judeo-Christian conception which found its scientific expression in the natural law theory, and which is alien to Marxist-Leninist thinking, to the ideals of Islam, and to the preoccupations of the newly-created States of Africa and Asia.

The religious basis of human rights was thus most forcefully expressed by Schwarzenberger:

... human rights in the western sense are only secularized religious values. When man is no longer visualized in God's image, then he is no longer protected against being used as a means to merely human ends. Then his basic rights and fundamental freedoms have lost their metaphysical raison d'être.[10]

This credo was recognized by Socialists like Harold J. Laski[11] and by liberals like Georg Jellinek[12] at the beginning of our century.

The idea of the sanctity of mankind is already expressed in the first chapter of the first book of the Bible:

... God created man in His own image, in the image of God created He him ...[13]

The Hebrew Prophets were possibly the first articulate fighters for human rights, with Amos foremost among them. It was Hillel who compressed the essence of Jewish learning and morality into a nutshell, saying:

What is hateful to thee, do not do to another,

and there is probably only a verbal difference between his saying and Jesus' words:

Do unto others what you would wish others to do unto you.

Hardly is there a loftier expression for the recognition of the diversity of men, and, at the same time, of the equality of their rights, than this passage from the Talmud:

A man may coin several coins with the same matrix and all will be similar. But the King of Kings the Almighty has coined every man with the same matrix of Adam, and no one is similar to the other. Therefore every man ought to say "the whole world has been created for me."[14,15]

The dignity of man stands out in the western conception of human rights. Though at the end of the 19th century this idea was overshadowed by an exaggerated legal positivism, the experience of the Second World War renewed the natural law concept. Already at an early stage, the pre-eminence of human rights was pointed out by the then leader of the western world, President Franklin D. Roosevelt who, in his famous Four Freedoms speech, stated as the aims of the Allies the achievement of Freedom of Speech, Freedom of Religion, Freedom from Fear, and Freedom from Want.

It is not by chance that the clearest expression of this approach is to be found in the Constitution of the Federal Republic of Germany which declares that

> the Geman people recognizes human rights as the inviolable and unalterable basis of every human society, of peace and justice in the world,[16]

and that the legislator is not allowed to detract from the recognized fundamental human rights.[17]

The salient point is that these human rights are rights directed *against* the state in its executive and even in its legislative capacity, as a protection for the individual.[18,19]

The Western conception accords a territory to every individual, a sphere of immunity from the King's writ.

The Soviet conception of human rights, which led to the absention of the Eastern bloc when the Universal Declaration and the Optional Protocol to the Covenant on Civil and Political Rights were voted, is diametrically opposed to this idea. How can one explain that, during the preparatory work for the Universal Declaration, the U.S.S.R. representative in the Human Rights Commission, Mr. T.V. Tepliakov, demanded that the following be deleted from the list (of recognized rights):

> "the right of personal liberty, the prohibition against slavery and forced labor, the right to petition national governments and the United Nations, the right to own property and the prohibition of unlawful expropriation, the right to free movement across frontiers"?

Mr. Tepliakov maintained that these rights were either superfluous or beyond the power of the United Nations to defend or would violate national sovereignty or local laws.[20]

Such an attitude is only possible because Soviet philosophy is strictly opposed to transcendentalism and denies, therefore, the existence of Natural Law. Fundamental rights are those which the State, from time to time, deems necessary to accord to the citizens, in the same manner as other tools are put at their disposal, and may be withdrawn if expedient. Since in a classless society the interests of the State and of the citizen are presumably identical, no fundamental right may be used *against* the State. On the contrary, fundamental rights are accorded to the individual only in the interest of society and only to the extent of its interest.[21] It is presupposed that the State will take care of the individual, so that the necessity of safeguarding his rights against the State appears to be an atavism. For example, when speaking about the freedom of the press, a Marxist-Leninist author from Hungary arrives at the following paradox:

> . . . as far as the freedom of the press is concerned it would not suffice to introduce mere legal protection for its safeguarding and to define the scope within which the press is free for the working people; the state also has the duty almost to "create" a press to . . . contribute to its unfolding . . .[22]

Obviously, the use of the same term human rights for rights of both the western and of the Soviet type is misleading. It is one of the many exercises in semantics which characterize United Nations activities and are classified as successful diplomacy.[23]

We have already noted the abstention of Arab States at the time of the voting for the Universal Declaration and the Optional Protocol. Moslem religious law strives for a State

> wherein all relationships are regulated by the authority of the same religious command.[24]

In such a State the ruler's conscience is the sole arbiter in limiting his exercise of power. Mohammed is said to have stated

> that one has to submit to the will of the Sovereign (Sultan, Khalif), as one has to submit to the will of God, whether his acts are just or unjust; that armed resistance against the ruler is in no case permissible even if he is unjust.[25]

A leading scholar on Islam[26] thus sums up his examination of "Government in Islam":

> Islamic thought is authoritarian. Political absolutism parallels the theological absolutism of God's relation to His creatures . . .
> Ideally God is the head of the state.

Already Abu Yusuf, one of the heads of the Hanafi School of Moslem Law, was aware of one source of authority only:

> God's choice by which the caliph becomes a vice-regent of God on Earth.

He has rationalized the religious obligation of absolute obedience to existing powers by citing the following saying attributed to Mohammed:

> "Yield to and obey even a flat-nosed, shrunken-headed Abyssinian slave once he is appointed."[27]

The struggle for human rights has, so far, not made much headway in the young nations of Asia and Africa. Most of them have been liberated but recently from colonial rule. Their frontiers do not demarcate national entities and, though the State exists, the nation has yet to be formed. Democracy, as the prerequisite for the existence of human rights, requires political differences to yield to conscious consensus; otherwise Government and Opposition cannot live together. It is said that even the word "opposition" does not exist in many African languages.[28] In a country where tribal allegiance and kinship ties are infinitely stronger than the attachment to the nation as a whole, democracy cannot develop. Hence the pernicious tendency towards a one-party system which is enshrined as opposed to "football politics."[29]

We are therefore driven, however reluctantly, to the conclusion that, at present and probably for very many years to come, the search for universal human rights will have a chimerical character. For the time being the only means for progress is to search for international implementation of human rights wherever societies have integrated western political conceptions.[30] A hopeful beginning was achieved with the European Convention for the Protection of Human Rights and Fundamental Freedoms, signed in Rome on November 4, 1950. This Convention includes specifically defined undertakings of State Parties towards individuals. With their express declaration, State Parties may in future be made a party to proceedings before the European Commission on Human Rights, which includes a member of each of the States which have become contracting parties. Not only may a State Party apply to this Commission when it believes that a human right has been violated, but, having exhausted all domestic remedies, every individual may exercise the same privilege. Should the Commission not achieve a compromise, it may then apply within three months to the European Court of Human Rights, which consists of a number of judges equal to the members of the Council of Europe. No two judges may be nationals of the same State. The same application can be made by the defendant State or by the State of which the injured individual is a national, but not by the individual. Submission of the defendant State to the jurisdiction of the European Court of Human Rights is a condition precedent.

If no application to the European Court of Human Rights has been made within three months, the executive organ of the Council of Europe has to act. In this capacity, it is composed of the Foreign Ministers of the Convention Parties which were represented in the Commission, who may decide, with a two thirds majority, how the European Commission of Human Rights report shall be implemented.

While the European Court of Human Rights can afford compensation to the injured individual, the Committee of Ministers can expel a State member that does not conform to its decisions.[31] This, at least, is a degree of progress.

However, the real test of the European Convention's efficacy lies, of course, in the ratification and adherence to it by the member states. Here, too, it can be pointed out with satisfaction that 16 States have ratified the Rome Convention—in fact all Western European States, except France and Switzerland (Switzerland having acquired observer status).[32] Eleven States have declared their willingness to be made parties before the European Court of Human Rights, so that the Convention has come into force.

Though progress has been considerable in the European Community—and here only—a warning has to be sounded. Legal unity is impossible without a corresponding economic and political accord. The European Convention without the European Common Market (from which England is still excluded in an atavistic way) is a lifeless spectre.

The Convention has been successful, after all, because it is the expression of an awakening of a European spirit and of a European common economic interest. All human progress since the Stone Age has been made by broadening the entities to which man gives his allegiance.

Because of the wide gap between the cultures of North and South America and their widely divergent economic interests, the American Declaration of Rights and Duties of Man of April 1948, has remained a somewhat dead letter.[33] Thus the draft of the Convention has been voted on but not yet ratified, although it corresponds, roughly, to the two United Nations Covenants.[34]

During the period in which there may develop legal, economic, and political unity in Europe, the question will inexorably arise: is this union the transformation of smaller units into a greater one which is directed against the outer world, or is this union an open society, so that every nation that subscribes to its credo may find a place within its scope? In the latter case only will this regional beginning open the way to Universal Human Rights.

This is a possibility. But, as we said at the outset, it is also a question of survival. The possibility is at the same time a necessity. When engaged in such a cause "never surrender,"—to recall a thought of General Jan Smuts—"for you can never tell what morning reinforcements in flashing armor will come marching over the hilltop."[35]

ZEEV ZELTNER

NOTES

[1] D.P.O'Connell declared: "Should a notorious violation of the Declaration occur, it may constitute a situation affecting international order which will bring into play the peace enforcement provisions of the Charter" (INTERNATIONAL LAW, Vol. II, p. 821, London, 1965).
But already 14 years earlier, Schwarzenberger said most convincingly: "In the Charter, a clear distinction is drawn between the promotion and encouragement of respect for human rights and the actual protection, of these rights."

[2] Jenks: THE COMMON LAW OF MANKIND, London, 1958, p. 164.

[3] Articles 16 and 17 of the Covenant.

[4] Art. 40 of the Covenant.

[5] Art. 41 of the Covenant.

[6] Art. 42 of the Covenant.

[7] The Covenant on Civil and Political Rights has been signed by 38 States, the Covenant on Social and Cultural Rights by 37 (as per June 16, 1969).

[8] Arts. 8, 9, 11–14 of the Convention.

[9] Moskowitz: THE POLITICS AND DYNAMICS OF HUMAN RIGHTS, New York, 1968, pp. 98s.

[10] *Op. cit.*, at p. 712.

[11] Quoted from: *Auf dem Wege zu einer universellen Erklärung der Menschenrechte.* In: UM DIE ERKLÄRUNG DER MENSCHENRECHTE, EIN SYMPOSIUM (UNESCO), Zürich-Wien—Konstanz, 1951, S. 103.

[12] Antwort and Emile Boutny. Quoted from: ZUR GESCHICHTE DER ERKLÄRUNG DER MENSCHENRECHTE, Darmstadt, 1964, S. 20, *Cf.* Ritter: URSPRUNG UND WESEN DER MENSCHENRECHTE, *op. cit.*, S. 205.

[13] Genesis, Chapter I, 27.

[14] Sanhedrin 38, 1.

[15] Throughout the annals of history Jewish identification with the struggle for Human Rights never abated. It was reopened by Lauterpacht, following World War II, in his book: INTERNATIONAL LAW AND HUMAN RIGHTS, London, 1950. *Cf.* Nathan Feinstein: THE INTERNATIONAL PROTECTION OF HUMAN RIGHTS AND THE JEWISH QUESTION, in: Israel Law Review, Vol. III (1968), pp. 487–500.
Is it not surprising that, despite this Jewish record, the express mention of Anti-Semitism was suppressed in the International Convention on the Elimination of All Forms of Racial Discrimination and the final drafts of the Convention against Religious Intolerance?

[16] Bonner Grundgesetz, 1949, Art. 1, Abs. II: "Das Deutsche Volk bekennt sich darum zu unverletzlichen und unveräusserlichen Menschenrechten als Grundlage jeder menschlichen Gemeinschaft, des Friedens und der Gerechtigkeit in der Welt."

[17] *Ibid*, Art. 79.

[18] Georg Brunner: Die Grundrechte des Sowjetsystems, Köln, 1963, S. 106. Ritter: *op. cit.* S. 214. Ezijiofer: PROTECTION OF HUMAN RIGHTS UNDER THE LAW, London, 1964. p. 3. Moskowitz: *op. cit.,* p. 249, n. 4. Oestreich: DIE IDEE DER MENSCHENRECHTE, Berlin, 1963, S. 25, Krüger: ALLGEMEINE STAATSLEHRE, S. 536, Anm. 36, Stuttgart, 1964. Grassi: DIE RECHTSSTELLUNG DES INDIVIDUUMS IM VÖLKERRECHT, Winterthur, 1955, S. 123.

[19] The Israeli High Court of Justice stressed the protection accorded to the individual against the legislator—even in the absence of a written constitution—in annulling the Elections Financing Act, 1969, passed by the Knesset, as running counter to the principle of equality of voting by allotting public funds only to parties represented in the existing Knesset.

[20] Quoted from the Manchester Guardian of Feb. 13, 1947.

[21] Brunner: *op. cit.*, Ss. 46, 53, 62.

[22] Imre Szabo: SOCIALIST CONCEPTION OF HUMAN RIGHTS, Budapest, 1966, pp. 309ss.

[23] Laski, *op. cit.,* at p. 106, observes quite rightly that the word "democracy" does not have the same meaning for the Chairman of the National Committee of the U.S. Republican Party and for Generalissimus Stalin.

[24] N. Coulson: THE STATE AND THE INDIVIDUAL IN ISLAMIC LAW. In: The International and Comparative Law Quarterly, Vol. VI, part I, p. 49, at p. 60. A HISTORY OF ISLAMIC LAW (by the same author), Edinburgh, 1964, p. 134.

[25] Quoted from Tyan: INSTITUTIONS DU DROIT PUBLIC MUSULMAN, T.I, p. 393, Paris, 1954.

[26] G.E. von Gruenebaum: ISLAM, ESSAYS IN THE NATURE AND GROWTH OF A CULTURAL TRADITION, London, 1955, p. 135, and n. 23.

[27] Kitab al-Kharaj, 1346, p. 10. Quoted from S.D. Goitein: STUDIES IN ISLAMIC HISTORY AND INSTITUTIONS, Leiden, 1966, pp. 203–4.

[28] Rita Hinden: HUMAN RIGHTS IN AFRICA. In: Patterns of Prejudice, Vol. II, no. 1, p. 29, at p. 31.

[29] An expression used by President Nyerere; see Ezijiofer, *op. cit.*, at p. 251.

[30] Guradze: *op. cit.*, S. 124.

[31] A.H. Robertson: HUMAN RIGHTS IN EUROPE, Manchester, 1963. Guradze, *op. cit.*, Ss. 158f.

[32] The same status has been accorded to Israel.

[33] Resolution XXIV of the Second Special Inter-American Conference, of November, 1965, has so far yielded no results.

[34] The only original contribution being the duty to receive instruction and the duty to vote – achievements of rather doubtful impact.

[35] Advice given to students at Oxford. Quoted from Vanderbildt: MEN AND MEASURE IN THE LAW, New York, 1949, p. 118.

HUMAN RIGHTS AND HATE PROPAGANDA:

A CONTROVERSIAL CANADIAN EXPERIMENT

MAXWELL COHEN*

The human right not to be maligned, or not to be set upon through the incitement of third persons against the one to be harmed, has long had the general protection of the criminal and civil law of most civilized states. Defamation, assault or conspiracies to encourage or incite to harm, or to cause a more general breach of the peace that could injure individuals at random, and more recently legislation aimed at discrimination in employment, housing, education and so on, are now well-established rules of private and public law in many states.

Indeed, the concept of human rights in one sense may be regarded as an extension of norms of individual protection and social equality to which the laws of many countries already were moving, particularly after World War I—evidenced, for example, in the work of, and conventions sponsored by, the International Labor Organization (ILO).

What is new, however, has been the concern for finding a framework to protect the good name and social opportunities of identifiable groups, marked off from fellow majorities, or otherwise, by reason of color, race, sex, language, religion, nationality or ethnic origin. The impetus here came, of course, from the racial and religious horrors of World War II as evolved and applied by Nazi policy; and also through the general conviction that some broad international standards of decency in the treatment of the individual and minority groups now was required by a global conscience that had been bruised through the disclosures

*Macdonald Professor of Law and sometime Chairman of the Minister of Justice Special Committee on Hate Propaganda, 1965–66. The views are those of the writer only and not of the Committee.

of the inhumanity of totalitarianism, whether of the right or the left, but dramatized unforgettably by the genocide policies of the Third Reich.

The Canadian experience with hate propaganda, and the recent legislation enacted by the Parliament of Canada to prohibit such activities, should be seen therefore in this global context of a new, vital international concern with the application of human rights concepts and doctrines not only to individuals but to identifiable groups as well.

The controversial debate over the recent amendments to the Canadian Criminal Code to control hate propaganda ended with its passage by the Federal Parliament in May-June of 1970.[1] Few pieces of legislation in recent years have evoked or provoked such strong divisions of opinion, not only among those who might be expected to support or oppose such legislation, but, more significantly perhaps, among those who held in common their devotion to free speech in particular and civil liberties in general. That the latter should be strongly divided on grounds of both principle and legal technique makes it necessary to assess the nature of the controversy, the results hoped for in the legislation, and perhaps more important, the place of such controls within a relatively free society at a time when there are new threats to both freedom and "order." Indeed, it is the general social context of growing anxieties about the conflicting pressures to protect freedom, and yet to find new ways of controlling disorder—which themselves may or may not threaten basic freedoms—that undoubtedly contributed to escalating the controversy, perhaps beyond what it might have been in less troubled times.

The general history of the legislation has recently been summarized with considerable objectivity in a useful paper entitled "The Story Behind Canada's Anti-Hate Law" by Mr. B. G. Kayfetz.[2] No purpose would be served therefore in a detailed recounting of that story. Nevertheless, for a proper evaluation of the legislation it is necessary to examine at least the following:

1. What gave rise to the demand that such legislation be enacted?
2. What were the means used by the Government of Canada to determine the need for legislation and the scope of possible amendments to the Criminal Code?
3. How did Parliament approach the problem of deciding upon the legislation as it was finally enacted?
4. Does the legislation, overall, serve a constructive democratic purpose, and what are the unkowns which all civil libertarians may conscientiously be concerned about now that the legislation has been enacted?

What Gave Rise To The Demand That Such Legislation Be Enacted?

As Kayfetz points out, requests for legislation against religious and racial hate propaganda go back at least to March 1953, when representations were made by the Canadian Jewish Congress and other interested and classically "vulnerable" minority groups to a Joint Committee of the House of Commons and Senate dealing with revisions of the Criminal Code.[3] But the origins of anxiety in this area are a good deal older than this formal démarche. Indeed, as long ago as 1933–34 when Nazi-type propaganda began to make its appearance in various parts of Canada, the Province of Manitoba enacted a statute attempting to deal with the issue.[4] That legislation remains on the books of the Province to the present day—whatever the questions raised about its constitutionality, in the matter of jurisdiction.

The postwar years left in Canada, and among all the anti-Hitler allies, some continuing sensitivity to the Nazi-Fascist program, philosophy and political tactics aimed at the incitement to contempt and hatred— certainly by Germans, and of others as well—toward particular "target groups." Indeed, theories of racial superiority on the one side, and of conspiracy and inferiority on the other, were dominant features of Nazi ideology and were given the sanction and prestige of law both in Germany and often also in the areas occupied by the Third Reich and its allies.[5]

It may be said, therefore, that the "free world" emerged from World War II—apart from the special physical immunities of North America— scarred not only by the general effects of a global war of immense proportions, but also in a psychological sense by the introduction into the political and military conflict of a deep ideological division, one of whose principal elements was race theories expressed in a variety of forms, but most conspicuously and tragically in its denigration of many vulnerable minority groups, virtually "outlawing" them by specific legislation.[6]

While the anti-Semitic component of this period of heightened race propaganda in Germany and elsewhere may have been its most dramatic and publicized form of expression, these concepts, ideas and laws were by no means confined to anti-Jewish policies. The total effect was to create a tradition within the Third Reich, and the occupied areas, of open and official hatred toward particular groups on ground of race, religion, nationality or ethnic origin generally—to which, of course, should be added a parallel political and legal philosophy that was antiliberal, antifreedom, "antisocialist," as an overall objective of repressing antifascism and compelling conformity to the "new order."

It was significant, therefore, that by the middle of the 1950's a number of the West European countries which had been occupied by Hitler's Germany had enacted legislation forbidding varieties of hate propaganda directing an animus toward groups on racial, religious, ethnic or similar grounds.[7] Indeed, the Charter of the United Nations also reflected this broad determination to reject racism and advance individual and group human rights through the language of its Preamble and elsewhere—all buttressed later, of course, by the Universal Declaration of Human Rights of 1948, and by subsequent Conventions in this general field.[8]

Nevertheless, it was clear to many observers in the postwar years that patterns of prejudice, some of them long part of the Western tradition, had been both partly reinforced and officially rejected by the indirect results of prolonged German propaganda. Indeed, despite the massive defeat of Hitler and of Germany there was a spillover into the postwar period that was noticeable in the persistence with which certain types of racial propaganda, inciting hatred toward "target groups," and even advocating genocide for some, had become a reappearing phenomenon in otherwise democratic societies.

This spillover also affected Canada throughout this period and became quite acute in the late 1950's and early 1960's with the emergence of extreme right-wing groups, some natively Canadian, others recruited from a limited number of new immigrants, and all echoing in literature or public statements views not dissimilar from the Nazi approach toward Jews, Negroes, some Roman Catholics and other minority targets.[9]

Thus, it was not unexpected that the quite heavy distribution of hate propaganda materials between 1959 and 1966, in a variety of Canadian centers, notably in Ontario and Quebec, should give rise to strong reactions on the part of the target groups concerned. This was particularly so among members of such groups, often new Canadians, many in the Jewish community, who had experienced in Europe some of the warnings and final horrors that such propaganda had foretold in their own experiences. It was inevitable, therefore, that the anxieties created by the distribution of such materials through the mails and by hand, the making of public statements by speakers in open forums, and the often clandestine character of the new organizations (small in number though they may have been) devoted to such activity, all should prompt a vigorous response from those who were now Canadian "targets," whether as established or "new" Canadians.

The difficulty with the growing Canadian debate over this issue in the late 1950's and early 1960's was twofold. On the one hand, there was a new emphasis on individual freedom, expressed internationally through the symbolism of "human rights" and domestically in legislation dealing with nondiscrimination which seemed to emphasize increasing political and social rights for the individual, liberty of expression and other freedoms. On the other hand, there was a growing recognition that these very liberties could be dangerously abused through their use in attacking a sense of well-being and group security, and thereby threaten the good will and cohesion within the Candian democratic order itself.

Moreover, Canadians were made increasingly more sensitive on this issue because of the depth and danger of escalating Quebec and French-English tensions, and indeed the challenges to the Canadian federal system itself.

Substantial numbers of studies emerging from research in the field of social psychology and group relations increasingly supported the view that propaganda could influence materially the attitude of many otherwise reasonable people, to say nothing of its very direct effect on those already prone to extreme prejudice, and even more tragically such propaganda affected the self-image of the target groups themselves.[10] Finally, just as the Universal Declaration on Human Rights and all democratic legal systems recognized that liberty was not "absolute" if its tools and principles were employed to destroy the society itself, so there was already some public readiness to examine what balance should be drawn between freedom of expression and freedom from target exposure in a legal system and a social tradition already weighted in favour of the right to speak on, and to communicate about, almost any and all ideas as part of the democratic process itself.

Determining The Need For Such Legislation

In January of 1965 the then Minister of Justice, The Hon. Guy Favreau, P.C., appointed a Special Committee on Hate Propaganda to study the problems behind the increasing demands for action from several target groups and other national organizations not themselves attacked.[11]

In November 1965 the committee issued a unanimous report containing both specific recommendations in the form of a potential draft bill as well as other proposals not put in legislative form.[12] The Committee also included in its Report a number of appendices, the most important of which were a detailed study on "sedition" and "seditious libel" and related offenses in England, the United States and Canada; and a social-psychological analysis of hate propaganda in the form of a survey of the literature in the field amounting to a comprehensive overview of the postwar studies in this area.[13] And, finally, there was a considerable amount of documentation, both national and international, dealing with existing legislation, international and domestic,[14] together with a sample of the hate propaganda materials distributed in Canada, almost all of which were published there or imported from Sweden or the United States.[15]

Some of the debate over the Report concerned the technical competence of the membership of the Committee to deal with the legal and social-psychological issues involved.[16] It is difficult for the writer to comment on this aspect for obvious reasons. Sufficient to say, however, that to the best of the writer's knowledge, no single critic of the Report, or the subsequent legislation, has been able to demonstrate that the technical level of the research done on the legal or the social-psychological issues was less than that required by a Committee strongly aware of its need to determine for itself the essential legal and psychological issues, to evaluate the status of the law in Canada and elsewhere, and to measure the nature and effects of racist propaganda. It was and is possible for other generalists or specialists to deny in whole or in part the conclusions arrived at by the Special Committee—namely, that existing Canadian law was inadequate to contain hate propaganda activities or that the social damage to target groups and the community as a whole was not effectively demonstrated. But at least a serious reading of the Report cannot detract from the efforts made by the Committee to determine for itself whether protection was needed in this area and whether existing law afforded it. Finally, the Committee faced the difficult question of whether rules could be designed which might provide such protection with no reasonable threat to the existing Canadian traditions of free speech in their broadest sense.

Apart from these important technical-political questions, criticism of the Report and of the proposed legislation was also based on the minimal character of the hate propaganda problem, both in the volume distributed or the number of persons and organizations involved, whether as distributors or as makers of public statements in open meetings. Critics argued that very small numbers originally, and even fewer today, participated in the distribution of such propaganda or public incitement to group hatred. Equally, it was argued, the so-called target groups involved were few and supersensitive in a society which would have only contempt for such propaganda; and that therefore these materials were in the end not only marginal in their impact on public opinion but essentially irrelevant to the mainstream of Canadian social debate, and hence self-defeating by the very nature of their crudity and non-credibility.[17]

To this criticism the reply must be given that the volume of actual distribution between 1959 and 1966 in Toronto and Montreal particularly, and in several other centers was sufficient to disturb not merely the so-called small numbers represented by the main target groups (mainly Jews, Negroes and "communists") but also many organizations and members of majority groups who nevertheless felt keenly the destructive and vicious character of these materials or statements, and had urged the Government of Canada, several of the Provinces and the Special Committee itself to curb and eliminate such distribution or expressions of hate propaganda.[18]

Finally, the Committee had before it the views of the Attorney General of Canada, of several of the Attorneys General of the Provinces principally concerned, a number of leading counsel at the criminal Bar, and of the Royal Canadian Mounted Police,[19] asserting that existing law in the Criminal Code or elsewhere did not provide adequate legal tools for the elimination of these materials or of public statements.

Indeed, only in three areas did federal law appear to be effective: (1) the application, under Section 7 of the Post Office Act, of a Prohibitory Order which had the effect of depriving certain persons or organizations of the right to use the mails "for the purpose of transmitting or delivering writings that are scurrilous contrary to section 153 of the Criminal Code." In due course, one such order was supported by the opinion of Wells J. acting as a Board of Review appointed by the Postmaster General under the Post Office Act when he found that the materials dealt with in an Interim Prohibitory Order were "scurrilous" within the meaning of section 153 of the Criminal Code;[20] (2) the regulations under The Customs Act and (3) The Broadcasting Act dealing in the first case with materials of a "treasonable or seditious, or of an immoral or indecent character"[21] and in the second case, where radio broadcasting regulations prohibited "any abusive comment on any race or religion," while those dealing with television prohibited "any abusive comment or abusive pictorial representation on any race, religion or creed."[22]

While the studies made by the Committee dealt in detail with many other areas of the Criminal Code and the civil law, that conceivably might be thought to apply to problems of hate propaganda, it was clear from these views and from research of the Committee itself that the only specific and reliable protections were those referred to above, namely, section 153 of the Criminal Code, the Customs Tariff Regulations and the Radio and Television Broadcasting Regulations.

This analysis was particularly underscored by the very important changes that had taken place in the legal concept of "sedition" or "seditious libel." In its mid-nineteenth century definition, it might have covered several aspects of the problem, particularly the classical definition which included the notion of inciting or "creating ill will between one class of Her Majesty's subjects and other classes." That standard was qualified in a series of judgments culminating in Canada in the important civil liberties achievement represented by the *Boucher case*[23] which required for the effective application of the doctrine that the circumstances giving rise to the charge would have to amount to a challenge to constituted government itself.[24]

In view of the state of the law as the Committee found it, and as the various law enforcement agencies, federal and provincial, declared it to be from their enforcement point of view, there was no other conclusion to which the Committee could have arrived except that existing law was inadequate, but for the limited areas referred to above.

Here, some critics have argued that no attempt was made over the years to apply many of the provisions of the Canadian Criminal Code which conceivably could have been effective to control the distribution and publication of such materials or statements, inciting to hatred and contempt or amounting to group defamation.[25] The Committee found itself unable to be persuaded, in view of the opinions and information before it, that the failure was not a failure of law but a failure of the willingness to take the forthright risks of its application. On balance, the Committee, with the views and studies available to it, could not in all responsibility have come to any other conclusion–namely, that the law was incomplete in its coverage of most of the more pernicious aspects of the hate propaganda problem.

The Committee concluded that there were three main areas where the existing law simply did not supply effective answers:[26] (1) materials and statements "advocating" or "promoting" genocide in relation to "identifiable groups" on grounds of their religion, color, race, language, ethnic or national origin; (2) materials or statements inciting "hatred" or "contempt" against any identifiable group where such incitement was likely to lead to a breach of the peace; and (3) materials and statements willfully promoting hatred or contempt against any identifiable group, except where the statements communicated "were true or where if not true they were relevant to any subject of public interest, the public discussion of which was for the public benefit, and that on reasonable grounds the person charged believed them to be true."

In the Committee's view, none of these questions were dealt with either directly or indirectly by the existing Criminal Code or could be caught by any aspects of the civil law, e.g., defamation, or nondiscrimination legislation, federal or provincial.

Given the Committee's views on the state of the law and its enforcement possibilities; given the character of the psychological effects, with their individual and social damage to target groups not merely in the eyes of the public but in the destructive self-image often created for the target groups themselves by such propaganda; and given the Committee's conviction that no freedom is absolute except perhaps the freedom to exist itself (limited perhaps only by the disappearing rules governing capital punishment); the Committee inevitably concluded that it was justified not only in making its findings but in recommending that the criminal law be altered accordingly.

Finally, the Committee took into account the important criticism generally aimed at any such controls—namely, that such legislation cannot change the human heart and that fundamental change must come from within and that the most formidable enemy of prejudice was education and not punitive criminal law. As a general proposition, the Committee accepted this broad concept of the basic role of the educational process, and of the social environment in general, as the more desirable framework within which to alter and control prejudice. But it could not reject the double conclusion to which it came, that many of the community's most important, self-educating values were enshrined in statements of criminal law, and these in turn, once so enacted, had a continuing behavioral effect by their very formulation.

The Committee also held that the long-term process and goal of reducing or eliminating prejudice through educational and social action was not in conflict with, and could provide a necessary environment for the more direct administrative measures required for dealing with immediate problems. Far from being mutually exclusive, the criminal law and the educational process were here complementary and interacting. It was for these reasons that the argument for reliance upon the educational system's impact on general Canadian values, although fully accepted, had to be put in its proper perspective in relation to other systems of social control which themselves could have both regulatory and educational consequences.[27]

Parliament's Approach To The Problem

The legislation had a stormy parliamentary history.[28] Introduced first in November 1966 in the Senate where it did not reach the committee stage, it was reintroduced the following year in the Senate; but Parliament adjourned in the midst of Senate committee hearings after only two or three witnesses had been heard.

Again introduced into Senate after the 1968 Liberal election victory, with Mr. Trudeau now as Prime Minister, the Senate held detailed hearings by late winter-spring of 1969, with many witnesses and briefs before it representing a wide variety of pro- and anti-positions. The Bill eventually was passed by the Senate but with a number of changes and awkward clauses which, while reflecting the spirit and largely the letter of the Report's recommendations, nevertheless were open to criticism on a number of technical and policy grounds, particularly the omission of "religion" among the "identifiable groups" and the "police" power to seize hate propaganda materials independently of a trial on the merits.

But the hearings were a quite exhaustive canvass of policy problems—even though, in this writer's opinion, the arguments that existing criminal law was sufficient, and that the Bill could or would limit free speech to a serious degree in Canada, were unconvincing. The 1969 hearings, as those of 1968, reflected the concern on the one side for the defense of target groups against all forms of hate propaganda and, on the other, an equally powerful concern for the threat the amendments would pose to many forms of free expression in a democratic society.

Although the Bill passed the Senate in 1969, Parliament adjourned and the Bill died accordingly. But the hearings in 1969 were chaired by that remarkable nonagenarian, Senator A. W. Roebuck, who managed the proceedings with fairness, skill and the determination of an old civil libertarian who himself was convinced that such legislation was necessary. He had the support of his predecessor, the 1968 Committee Chairman, Senator J. H. Prowse, who also had given every indication of a determined sympathy for the measure and a broad understanding of its purposes, and of its possible but minimal risks.

The Bill was again introduced in the autumn of 1969, this time as a government measure in the House of Commons where before Second Reading it was referred to the House Committee on Legal Affairs. Here, vigorous debate took place, with very few witnesses but with strong advocacy by the Minister of Justice who had already made an effective and very clear address in the Commons when introducing the Bill itself. Some valuable suggestions were made in Committee which were adopted by the Government and the House. These were related particularly to the protection of private conversations.

In the voting on the Bill in the House, the Conservatives and the

Creditistes were mostly against the Bill, while some New Democratic Party (Social Democrats generally) and Liberals also were opposed; but significantly a very large proportion of the House was absent on the Third Reading where the vote was 89 to 45, with 127 not voting or absent from the Chamber[29]—a disappointing quantitative measure of the Bill's support, but a serious majority nevertheless.

In the Senate no hearings were held, but there was determined debate and a vigorous but unsuccessful effort was made to have the Bill referred, before enactment, to the Supreme Court of Canada on the ground that it might be in conflict with the Canadian Bill of Rights and possibly other constitutional or statutory principles.

In any event, although party lines were crossed in the voting, the Bill passed the Senate and received Royal Assent on June 11, 1970.

Canadian press opinion was strongly divided on the issues, with probably a majority of the editorials either definitely opposed or lukewarm, but equally there were some powerful editorial voices supporting the amendments.[30] Indeed, few pieces of legislation in recent years received such a thorough and detailed examination from the point of view of principle and technique as did these amendments.

The Bill as finally enacted retained the three classes of offenses described above and recommended by the Report; but there were notable changes in the definition of "genocide," in the definition of an "identifiable group"; in the role of the Attorney General of each Province by permitting, with his approval only, prosecutions dealing with advocating genocide and group defamation as well as in the matter of the seizure of hate propaganda materials; in removing the concept of "contempt," leaving "hatred" to stand alone in the offenses concerned; and finally in the special protection given to "private conversations." In this connection it is instructive to compare the recommendations of the Report and the Bill as enacted (see Appendices A and B).[31]

Does The Legislation Serve A Constructive Democratic Purpose?

In this writer's view, weighted of course as it is in favor of the Report and its recommendations, there seems no persuasive argument in favor of permitting the advocacy of genocide; or permitting the deliberate incitement to group hatred which is likely to lead to a breach of the peace; or permitting defamation of identifiable groups, holding them up to public hatred when there are very specific safeguards leaving wide opportunities for the tough debate necessary in a pluralistic, "anti-establishment" time within a democratic society.

No purpose would be served therefore in recapitulating here the issues or the debate about them already summarized above. The significant question to be asked is whether the amendments will achieve their preventive and deterrent objectives, and above all, whether these more refined standards for the legitimate scope of public utterances and published materials will not themselves have an educational impact in the long run more important than the immediate punitive aspects of the criminal law as such, while at the same time doing no damage to the fundamental freedoms of speech and expression.

In this writer's opinion, the legislation provides abundant protection both in the definition of the offenses and in the permission required from the Attorneys General in several instances, to render unlikely either harassing prosecutions or easy convictions. The weight, indeed, seems to be on the other side—namely, that the legislation is so seriously concerned to protect freedom from any serious limitations that it may prove very difficult to obtain prosecutions or convictions, except in the case of advocating genocide. Even here the offense is limited to "advocacy" and "promotion," and the definition of "genocide" has been narrowed to a degree that makes it far less comprehensive than that originally found in the Genocide Convention itself—which Canada now has ratified. It is obvious that the advocacy will have to be very clear from the evidence before a conviction is successful, limited again by the definition of "genocide" itself.

The most controversial aspects of the legislation, however, are those surrounding the new offense of "group defamation." But here, too, the defenses, both in the Report and in the legislation as finally enacted, as well as the role of the Attorney General, will make it very difficult for courts ever to have before them frivolous prosecutions, or situations that really involve serious debate over responsible questions relating to intergroup tensions or political party conflict—no matter how tough or abusive the language used.

It has always seemed to the writer very significant that relatively homogeneous and socially well-managed societies such as Denmark, the Netherlands, Norway, Sweden and Switzerland should have long ago enacted analogous provisions.[32] Equally important, societies with a much more divisive internal tradition, such as France and Italy, have also found it desirable to provide for protection against these forms of propaganda.[33] In the Commonwealth itself, Australia and the United Kingdom have adopted quite stringent legislation, which in the case of the United Kingdom may be said to go further perhaps than do the presently adopted Canadian amendments.[34]

70

Concluding Reflections

That organizations and individuals with unchallengeable credentials
in the areas of human rights and general civil liberties should have been
so seriously divided on this legislation, as was Parliament itself, suggests
that the argument is by no means all one way. However, the conclusions
of the Committee and its recommendations, as well as those of the majority of both Houses of Parliament, reflected authentic anxieties which
had to be faced, and faced by law specifically on an issue that could
not be dealt with only by the general educational process on the one hand
or by provincial nondiscrimination legislation on the other. Something
more was needed if the issues were to be treated seriously.

It was argued that the hate propaganda problem had diminished
markedly in Canada since its peak years of 1961 to 1966. That is no
answer to the general question of principle or to the practical question
of its sporadic reappearance in word and deed, however minimal the
volume may be at some moments, thereby leaving a deceptively optimistic
impression that the issue is no longer potentially dangerous.[35]

The Preface to the Report states the Committee's rationale, whether
dealing with large or small volumes of propaganda, peak or minimal
moments, maximum or minimum sensitivities over a period of time.
We might well conclude by relying upon that Preface as the justification
for the legislation, and we hereby quote it:

> This Report is a study in the power of words to maim, and
> what it is that a civilized society can do about it. Not every
> abuse of human communication can or should be controlled
> by law or custom. But every society from time to time draws
> lines at the point where the intolerable and the impermissible
> coincide. In a free society such as our own, where the privilege
> of speech can induce ideas that may change the very order itself,
> there is a bias weighted heavily in favour of the maximum of
> rhetoric whatever the cost and consequences. But that bias
> stops this side of injury to the community itself and to individual
> members or identifiable groups innocently caught in verbal
> crossfire that goes beyond legitimate debate.
>
> An effort is made here to re-examine, therefore, the parameters
> of permissible argument in a world more easily persuaded than
> before because the means of transmission are so persuasive. But
> ours is also a world aware of the perils of falsehood disguised
> as fact and of conspirators eroding the community's integrity

through pretending that conspiracies from elsewhere now justify verbal assaults—the non-facts and the non-truths of prejudice and slander.

Hate is as old as man and doubtless as durable. This Report explores what it is that a community can do to lessen some of man's intolerance and to proscribe its gross exploitation.

APPENDIX I

Report's Recommendations

Having in mind, therefore, the detailed evidence set out in Chapter II; the attitudes toward and the consequences of hate propaganda in all of its forms as described and analyzed in Chapters I and III; the deficiencies in the present Canadian law discussed in Chapter IV; and bearing in mind, too, the detailed conclusions expressed in Chapter V; the Committee believes it to be desirable now to draft a proposed series of amendments to the Criminal Code that would express as specifically and clearly as possible, these findings, conclusions and recommendations.

Principal Recommendations

Our principal recommendations therefore are incorporated in the following proposed draft amendment to the Criminal Code:

1) Every one who advocates or promotes genocide is guilty of an indictable offence and is liable to imprisonment for five years.

2) Every one who, by communicating statements in any public place, incites hatred or contempt against any identifiable group, where such incitement is likely to lead to a breach of the peace, is guilty of
   (a) an indictable offence and is liable to imprisonment for two years,
      or
   (b) an offence punishable on summary conviction.

3) Every one who by communicating statements, wilfully promotes hatred or contempt against any identifiable group is guilty of
   (a) an indictable offence and is liable to imprisonment for two years or
   (b) an offence punishable on summary conviction.

4) No person shall be convicted of an offence under subsection 3
   (a) where he proves that the statements communicated were true, or
   (b) where he proves that they were relevant to any subject of public

interest, the public discussion of which was for the public benefit, and that on reasonable grounds he believed them to be true.

5) In this section
(a) "Genocide" means any of the following acts committed with intent to destroy in whole or in part, any identifiable group:
  (i) killing members of such a group
  (ii) deliberately inflicting on such a group conditions of life calculated to bring about its physical destruction.
  (iii) deliberately imposing measures intended to prevent births within such a group.
(b) "Public place" includes any place to which the public have access as of right or by invitation, express or implied.
(c) "Identifiable group" means any section of the public distinguished by religion, colour, race, language, ethnic or national origin.
(d) "Statements" include words either spoken or written, gestures, signs or other visible representations.

We have several comments to make on the penalties and definitions in the above draft. In our view the advocacy of genocide is so serious that it requires a more severe sentence than the other offences proposed, and we therefore have recommended that it should be an indictable offence with a sentence of up to five years' imprisonment. As to the other recommended offences we believe that as they would vary considerably in seriousness depending on the circumstances we should provide for the option of prosecution by way of summary conviction or by indictment. Where the prosecution chooses to proceed by way of summary conviction, the accused will be faced with a less serious charge—which balances the fact that he will be deprived, as in the case of all summary conviction offences, of his right to trial by jury. Where, on the other hand, the prosecution chooses to treat the charge as indictable, the accused will retain his right to trial by jury in addition to the other options available to him. We feel that a maximum sentence of two years' imprisonment provides a sufficient upper limit range for most foreseeable situations.

The Committee also was governed by the desire to depart as little as possible from existing legal concepts and terms, and we therefore adopted the definition of "public place" now in section 130 of the Code. We have also retained the "hatred and contempt" formula traditional to criminal defamation, although we have omitted the word "ridicule" from the phrase for fear of inhibiting legitimate satire and out of a conviction that the kind of "hate" propaganda we are concerned with is much stronger than simple ridicule. The definition of "genocide" is taken (as explained in Chapter IV) from that used in the United Nations Convention on Genocide.

Supplementary Recommendations

In addition to the above specific recommendations involving legislative changes we also recommend the following as general policy guides in dealing with related aspects of the hate propaganda problem and its control of correction:

a. We recommend that the Minister examine the language of sections 153 and 160 of the Criminal Code in the light of our principal recommendations and our comments on these sections to determine whether they themselves may require amendment.

b. We recommend that the Minister examine the legislation and regulations governing the various Agencies and Departments of the Government of Canada in the light of our comments, particularly those that disclose some significant differences between postal and customs powers —as explained in Chapter IV.

c. We recommend that as far as may be possible, and with due allowance for the particular problems and responsibilities of each Agency and Department, statutes and regulations governing hate propaganda material or activities should be related to the general standard as set out in the Criminal Code rather than to a standard established independently by such agencies and departments, including Broadcasting.

d. We recommend that study be given to the matter of the seizure of hate materials and of their confiscation after conviction.

The Committee considered the advisability of requiring the consent of the Attorney-General of the Province or of Canada to each prosecution instituted under the legislation proposed in order to prevent frivolous or unwarranted prosecutions, and without making any recommendation, we draw the Minister's attention to this possibility.

APPENDIX II

THE HOUSE OF COMMONS OF CANADA
BILL C-3

An Act to Amend the Criminal Code

Her Majesty, by and with the advice and consent of the Senate and House of Commons of Canada, enacts as follows:
1. The *Criminal Code* is amended by adding thereto, immediately after section 267 thereof, the following heading and sections:

Hate Propaganda

267A. (1) Everyone who advocates or promotes genocide is guilty of an indictable offence and is liable to imprisonment for five years.

(2) In this section "genocide" means any of the following acts committed with intent to destroy in whole or in part any identifiable group, namely:

(*a*) killing members of the group, or

(*b*) deliberately inflicting on the group conditions of life calculated to bring about its physical destruction.

(3) No proceeding for an offence under this section shall be instituted without the consent of the Attorney General.

(4) In this section "identifiable group" means any section of the public distinguished by colour, race, religion or ethnic origin.

267B. (1) Everyone who, by communicating statements in any public place, incites hatred against any identifiable group where such incitement is likely to lead to a breach of the peace, is guilty of

(*a*) an indictable offence and is liable to imprisonment for two years; or

(*b*) an offence punishable on summary conviction.

(2) Everyone who, by communicating statements, other than in private conversation, wilfully promotes hatred against any identifiable group is guilty of

(*a*) an indictable offence and is liable to imprisonment for two years; or

(*b*) an offence punishable on summary conviction.

(3) No person shall be convicted of an offence under subsection (2)

(*a*) if he establishes that the statements communicated were true;

(*b*) if, in good faith, he expressed or attempted to establish by argument an opinion upon a religious subject;

(*c*) if the statements were relevant to any subject of public interest, the discussion of which was for the public benefit, and if on reasonable grounds he believed them to be true; or

(*d*) if, in good faith, he intended to point out, for the purpose of removal, matters producing or tending to produce feelings of hatred towards an identifiable group in Canada.

(4) Where a person is convicted of an offence under section 267A or subsection (1) or (2) of this section, anything by means of or in relation to which the offence was committed, upon such conviction, may, in addition to any other punishment imposed, be ordered by the presiding magistrate or judge to be forfeited to Her Majesty in right of the province

in which that person is convicted, for disposal as the Attorney General may direct.

(5) Subsections (6) and (7) of section 171 apply *mutatis mutandis* to section 267A or subsection (1) or (2) of this section.

(6) No proceeding for an offence under subsection (2) shall be instituted without the consent of the Attorney General.

(7) In this section,

(*a*) "public place" includes any place to which the public have access as of right or by invitation, express or implied;

(*b*) "identifiable group" has the same meaning as it has in section 267A; and

(*c*) "statements" includes words spoken or written or recorded electronically or electromagnetically or otherwise, and gestures, signs or other visible representations; and

(*d*) "communicating" includes communicating by telephone, broadcasting or other audible or visible means.

267C. (1) A judge who is satisfied by information upon oath that there are reasonable grounds for believing that any publication, copies of which are kept for sale or distribution in premises within the jurisdiction of the court, is hate propaganda, shall issue a warrant under his hand authorizing seizure of the copies.

(2) Within seven days of the issue of the warrant, the judge shall issue a summons to the occupier of the premises requiring him to appear before the court and show cause why the matter seized should not be forfeited to Her Majesty.

(3) The owner and the author of the matter seized and alleged to be hate propaganda may appear and be represented in the proceedings in order to oppose the making of an order for the forfeiture of the said matter.

(4) If the court is satisfied that the publication is hate propaganda, it shall make an order declaring the matter forfeited to Her Majesty in right of the province in which the proceedings take place, for disposal as the Attorney General may direct.

(5) If the court is not satisfied that the publication is hate propaganda, it shall order that the matter be restored to the person from whom it was seized forthwith after the time for final appeal has expired.

(6) An appeal lies from an order made under subsection (4) or (5) by any person who appeared in the proceedings

(*a*) on any ground of appeal that involves a question of law alone,

(*b*) on any ground of appeal that involves a question of fact alone, or

(*c*) on any ground of appeal that involves a question of mixed law and fact, as if it were an appeal against conviction or against a judgment or verdict of acquittal, as the case may be, on a question of law alone under Part XVIII and sections 581 to 601 apply *mutatis mutandis.*

(7) No proceeding under this section shall be instituted without the consent of the Attorney General.

(8) In this section,

(*a*) "court" means a county or district court or, in the Province of Quebec

(i) the court of the sessions of the peace, or

(ii) where an application has been made to a judge of the provincial court for a warrant under subsection (1), that judge;

(*b*) "genocide" has the same meaning as it has in section 267A;

(*c*) "hate propaganda" means any writing, sign or visible representation that advocates or promotes genocide or the communication of which by any person would constitute an offence under section 267B; and

(*d*) "judge" means a judge of a court or, in the Province of Quebec, a judge of the provincial court.

NOTES

[1] Actual passage in the Senate was completed in May, but Royal Assent was not given until June 11, 1970.

[2] Kayfetz, *The Story Behind Canada's Anti-Hate Law in Patterns of Prejudice* (Institute of Jewish Affairs, London), May–June 1970, pp. 5–8.

[3] *Ibid.*, pp. 5–6.

[4] Stats. Man. 1934, c. 23; R.S.M. 1954, c. 185.

[5] Shirer, *The Rise and Fall of the Third Reich* (1960) pp. 231–36.

[6] Report of the Special Committee on Hate Propaganda, 1966, pp. 24–25; App. II, p. 121. (Hereafter called Report.)

[7] Report, pp. 277–88.

[8] Art. 1, 55, 56, 57; Report, pp. 289–303.

[9] Report, Chap. II, pp. 11–25.

[10] Report, App. II, pp. 171–250.

[11] Report, pp. 1–3. The members of the Committee were: Dr. J. A. Corry, L'Abbé Gérard Dion, Mr. Saul Hayes, Q.C., Prof. Mark R. MacGuigan, Mr. Shane MacKay, Prof. Pierre Elliott Trudeau; and as Executive Assistant to the Chairman and Secretary of the Committee, Mr. Harvey Yarosky. The author was Chairman.
Prof. Trudeau is now The Rt. Hon., The Prime Minister of Canada; Prof. MacGuigan is now a Member of Parliament and Co-Chairman of the Joint Senate-House Committee on the Constitution.

[12] Report, Chap. VI, pp. 69–71; but see the limited reservation of Mr. Saul Hayes, Q.C., on the defenses to the group defamation proposals of the Committee.

[13] Report. App. I and II, pp. 73–251.

[14] Report, pp. 277–303.

[15] Report, pp. 253–71.

[16] See particularly the views of Prof. Alan Mewett, now of the University of Toronto, expressed on a number of occasions.

[17] This view is to be found in the statements of a number of witnesses testifying before the Senate Committees and in editorial opinion critical of the proposals.

[18] Report, p. 59.

[19] Report, pp. 1–3, pp. 59–60.

[20] Report, pp. 42–49; App. VI, pp. 319–27.

[21] Report, p. 50.

[22] Report, p. 51.

[23] 1951 S. C. R. 265; 1951 (2) D. L. R. 369.

[24] See the judgment of Rand J. in 1950 (1) D. L. R. at 680; in his decision on the first hearing of the case.

[25] These views were frequently stated in the Senate Committee hearings and elsewhere.

[26] Report, Chap. V, Conclusions, pp. 61–67.

[27] Report, pp. 8–9, pp. 66–67.

[28] Kayfetz, *op. cit.,* n. 2.

[29] *Ibid.,* p. 7.

[30] *Ibid.,* pp. 6–7.

[31] Report, pp. 69–71; Bill C-3, as passed by the House of Commons on April 13, 1970, and accepted in that form by the Senate and given Royal Assent on June 11, 1970. See Appendix I herewith for the Report's recommendations, and Appendix II for the Bill as enacted.

[32] Report, Denmark, p. 282; The Netherlands, p. 287; Norway, p. 288; Sweden, p. 288; Switzerland, p. 288.

[33] Report, France, p. 284; Italy, p. 285.

[34] Report, Australia, p. 277; the United Kingdom, pp. 96–97 (as amended).

[35] It is worth asking the interesting speculative question as to whether a Law Reform Commission beginning to draft a Criminal Code for Canada, *de Novo*, would or would not take into account the contemporary research into social-psychology and related areas, in drafting its provisions for the modern needs of Canada and its values, and its expectations for the future.

BEHIND THE CEASE-FIRE LINES: ISRAEL'S ADMINISTRATION IN GAZA AND THE WEST BANK

JULIUS STONE*

The legal relations arising from a cease-fire embrace, besides the military conduct of the parties *inter se*, and the possible reversionary rights of any ousted sovereign, also the relations between the local inhabitants of occupied territories and the State under whose control these have come. I pointed out in my recent study of "The November Resolution . . ." in the *Festschrift* for Josef L. Kunz forthcoming from the *University of Toledo Law Review*, that serious questions may affect any supposed reversionary rights of Egypt and Jordan in Gaza, East Jerusalem and the West Bank. If those questions were well-based, Israel's status in these territories might, correspondingly, be more than that of mere military occupation. For purposes of the present study, however, I ignore these questions and adopt the hypothesis less favorable to Israel's position, namely that she has only the rights and powers of a military occupant. The law governing the matter would then be the traditional law of military occupation as supplemented by the Fourth Geneva Convention, 1949, concerning the protection of civilian persons.

The administration of the territories under Israel control is (with the exception of East Jerusalem) vested in Military Governors, respectively of the West Bank, the Golan Heights, Gaza, Sinai, and South Sinai, this division corresponding also with the former Jordanian, Syrian and Egyptian areas of control. General civilian supervision has been secured, since October 1968, by the establishment of a special Committee of Ministers for the Administered Territories and there is also a special Minister appointed for economic development plans in the territories and employment of refugees. This structure, along with the

* Professor of International Law and Jurisprudence, University of Sydney

subordinate local military government, conforms to rather usual patterns found in military occupation.

The Israel administration, however, also manifests some notably unusual features. There is, first, a basic policy, carried to unusual lengths, of leaving all administration as far as possible in Arab hands, and of minimizing the ordinary governmental role of military personnel. Second, it has been the policy, again to an unusual degree, to preserve the basic law in force under Jordanian administration, as required by the fourth Convention. This is subject to necessary measures for security, and for ensuring the maintenance of order and the uninterrupted administration of justice in the changed conditions, all of which seem authorized under the traditional law or under Article 64 of the Convention. Third, considerable energy and ingenuity have been spent on encouraging maximum freedom of movement of the local inhabitants, consistent with military security, both within the territories, and between the West Bank and East Jerusalem, and Israel and Jordan respectively. Fourth, the administration has made considerable financial sacrifices to ensure the economic viability of the territories (including its 1948 "refugee" populations). These features, all of which are of benevolent tendency as contrasted with most earlier occupations, merit some elaboration.

According to Israel figures as of June 1968, only 313 Israelis (including military personnel) were involved in administering (apart from prisons, customs and police services) all the territories involved. By contrast, 9,395 local Arab officials had been maintained in office, with 12,000 other local Arabs employed in public and related works. This figure included 6,770 persons on the West Bank, of whom 3,855 were teachers and 282 police; but did not include 10,000 Arab casual workers on public works, about half of them on the West Bank. Low Jordanian salaries paid to officials and workers were quickly increased by 20%, and a system of family allowances introduced. Judicial personnel remain in office from the pre-war period, and law and order in the streets is still in the charge of *Arab* policemen. On March 27, 1970, no less than 780 local Arabs were serving as policemen, of whom 559 or 72% continued from before the 1967 War. There were also 79 Arab policemen in East Jerusalem. The ordinary laws enforced by the courts are (as already seen) mostly unchanged, the most notable exception being perhaps the abolition of the *mandatory* death penalty formerly prescribed in East Jerusalem and the West Bank by Jordanian, and in Gaza by Egyptian law, for certain offenses. (It may be interposed that this is despite the fact that Article 68 of the Fourth Convention still authorizes the death penalty for serious acts of sabotage, or homicidal acts, under the standing law.)

A strike of Arab lawyers was called by the Bar Council in Amman immediately after the 1967 War. It affected judges as well as advocates, the latter for a longer time. Five judges returned to their duties early in 1968, and others gradually as court business mounted towards the level of 36,000 cases. The number of judges on the West Bank and in East Jerusalem had been 22 before the War and is now 19, of whom only 4 have been newly appointed by the Military Administration. These new appointments were made from Arab lawyers applying for office. So that, in general, Jordanian-appointed judges continue in office and function, though of course some have been promoted, and some have retired. A new spate of promotions, returns to work, and new appointments followed the retirement early in 1970 of the President of the Court of Appeals in Ramallah, Judge Sabah al-Abassi.[1] The number of advocates in the region had been 80 in 1967, including 21 in East Jerusalem. Of the 80, 7 applied for judgeships, 5 being appointed. Another 5 practise in the civil courts and military courts and offices, and 3 more only before the military courts. Others continue to practise in the religious courts, and as corporate or municipal legal advisors. The main difference in Gaza was that Egypt had, by 1967, filled the higher judicial posts with Egyptians and left the administration of justice in Sinai to the Egyptian military. The Israel Administration restored the former non-Egyptian Arab judges to their posts, and 19 such judges now hold court in Gaza.

Judicial independence was respected even when Arab Judge H. El-Schajuchi, of Hebron, disallowed orders of the Military Governor permitting Israel lawyers to plead for Arab litigants, while Arab lawyers were boycotting the courts. The Hebron judge also claimed to continue to administer justice in the name of King Hussein rather than in the name of justice. Arab Judge T. El-Sakka, of Bethlehem, came to the opposed view on both points under the Hague Regulations, and the Fourth Geneva Convention, 1949, Article 64. A scholarly examination, as well as an overruling decision by the (Arab) Court of Appeals in Ramallah of June 17, 1968 (Civil Appeal 34 168), have exposed other errors of the Hebron judgment. But the point here is not who was right, but that the Israel authorities, in face of this direct challenge, and at a time when terrorist activities from Jordan kept tension high, left the local Arab judges in office to judge according to their consciences.[2]

No less significant is the support given by the Military Governor and the Government of Israel to the Arab authorities as against the claim of the Jewish religious community of Hebron (which had suffered virtual massacre in 1929 at the hands of the Arabs of Hebron) to re-establish

81

their community there. This was despite the great sensitiveness of this issue in Israel domestic politics. Only in late October 1968, after bomb outrages at the tombs, injuring both Arab and Jewish pilgrims, were proposals for Jewish settlement in Hebron seriously canvassed in order to strengthen local security. Even then Cabinet Ministers disagreed as to whether they would be implemented.

It took from that time until the middle of 1970 for the divergent views within the Israel Cabinet to come to a head on this matter, with vigorous public exchanges in March, April and May, 1970. In those exchanges Prime Minister Meir[3] stated that "no decision has been taken about the establishment of an urban center in Hebron." Foreign Minister Eban said[4] that "Jews cannot be cut off from Hebron, just as the Arabs cannot be cut off from the Old City", and he linked the decision with the Government's "open borders after peace" policy. Deputy Prime Minister Allon said on March 25, 1970, that Israel dare not let Hebron remain "*Judenrein*" because of the murderous pogrom of 1929.[5] The tiny existing community "must reach the sort of size . . . to maintain the minimal services of a settlement, small as it may be." The issue presented itself, not as one of international law, but as one of whether a limited Jewish settlement of 250 families would, as the Israeli "doves" and the United States and the United Kingdom thought, preempt "peace options". The most common grounds in the controversy regarding Hebron are that the Jewish community there was massacred by Arabs in 1929, and that the tombs which are the famed holy places in Hebron are those of the Hebrew patriarchs. So that Hebron, like Jerusalem, holds Jewish and universal, as well as Arab interests, despite its predominantly Arab population in modern times.

The Cabinet decision of May 1970 was to permit the settlement of 250 Jewish families in housing projects in Hebron, in view of its vital place in Jewish history, and also in order to render viable the tiny number of religious Jews who had already returned to Hebron to resume religious study there.[6] The Cabinet rejected the demand of the Gahal party (led by M. Begin and E. Weizman) for establishment of a Jewish urban center in Upper Hebron.[7] The majority decison was supported as having no political significance, but springing, as above indicated, from the special history and circumstances of Hebron. It is consistent with this that the Government did not yield to parallel pressures to allow settlement also in Battir, Nablus and Mt. Gerizim.

An outside observer, after commenting that "the fundamental principle underlying Israel policy is the restoration of local Arab administration", has pointed to the early difficulties in the field of education.[8] These arose from the policy of integrating educational curricula and administration in East Jerusalem with those of other Arab schools in Israel, and of removing deliberately anti-semitic and anti-Israel passages from existing schoolbooks. Here, too, no attempt was made to force the opening of the schools or replacement of teachers. Teachers and pupils in most schools have long since returned to their studies. The continuing problem of textbooks has been handled on both sides with a prudent give and take which is highly commendable. A committee of three scholars from the United States, Turkey and France was set up on the initiative of the Director-General of Unesco to classify textbooks used in UNRWA schools in the territories as either (1) usable as they are, or (2) not usable at all, or (3) usable subject to amendment, having regard to the anti-Israel incitement of their contents. Jordan agreed to print amended books for importation by the Government of Israel.[9]

As to the criminal and civil law to be maintained in force by the Administration, the basic principles seem to be prescribed by Articles 64 and 47 of the Geneva Convention. This is given a somewhat whimsical twist by the fact that in important segments of the law, the rules applicable are identical with those applicable in Israel, both having originated in the former British Mandatory's Defence (Emergency) Regulations, Regulation 119 (as to forfeiture and demolitions) and 112 (as to deportations), for the whole of Palestine.[10] This, interestingly enough, is the case even as to the most controversial measures used by the military authorities against terrorist activities, namely, the demolition of structures involved in such activities, and the deportations, limited in number, to Jordan. Whatever may be said shortly hereafter as to the consistency of this law with the Geneva Convention must therefore be said not only against Israel, but also against Egypt and Jordan, who left substantially the same law in force between 1948 and 1967 in the course of their own military occupations of the same territories. The main changes in the criminal law concern traffic, in order to conform with Israel traffic laws, and the liberalization of certain penal laws, e.g. as to capital punishment, and the introduction of the principle *non bis in idem*.[11]

The newly conferred freedom of movement of local inhabitants is, of course, most dramatic in East Jerusalem. The improvised post-1948 walls of division manned by sandbagged sniper detachments have disappeared; and life has been restored to the desolate stretches of no-man's land between the ravished halves of the city. Subject to the possession of identification cards, Arabs of the Gaza Strip and of the

West Bank moved freely, very soon after the war, from one territory to another without permits and (subject to holding freely available permits) to and from Israel, and across the River Jordan into the State of Jordan and back. In the summer of 1968, indeed, this liberty of Arab entry and exit was extended even to members of the families of local inhabitants who (for one reason or another—mostly for educational purposes, or to await the outcome of the Middle East troubles) had continued to reside elsewhere after the June war. It was subject only to security clearance and the obtaining of entry visas. A total of 15,304 Arabs, including 4,000 students, visited relatives on the West Bank in 1968 under this "summer visits" scheme program. Despite the freedom of movement allowed not a single visitor was detained in 1968 on security charges. The number entering under the "summer visits program" rose to 26,254 in 1969, and (according to Mr. Eban's speech to the General Assembly of September 28, 1970) to no less than 55,000 in 1970.[12]

This Israel policy of freedom of movement had a temporary setback after the heavy casualties caused by the treacherous detonation of a parked motor vehicle laden with explosives in the crowded Jerusalem Mahaneh-Yehuda Market, in December 1968. Restrictions were imposed on vehicles usable for such crimes and special permits were required for private passenger vehicles and trucks across the Jordan, as well as for vehicles crossing the pre-1967 demarcation lines ("the Green Line"). Nevertheless, the number of permits granted for movement into Israel for voluntary employment there continued to increase. As of April 1, 1970, 24,600 Arabs from the Administered Territories were regularly entering Israel for employment, 18,000 from the West Bank, and the rest from Gaza. To this figure should probably be added another 8,000 entering for more casual employment. A main reason for this movement is, of course, the higher wages and social security benefits prevailing in Israel for Jews and Arabs alike.

The movement of Arabs across the Jordan bridges between the West Bank and Amman reached the remarkable total of over 200,000 in 1968, but decreased to the (still considerable) number of nearly 100,000 in 1969.[13,14] In January 1970, in anticipation of Jordanian restrictions, the number of crossings dropped to 5,800, as compared with 8,800 in January 1969.[15] The Jordanian restrictions took the form of requiring all travelers to bear a valid Jordanian passport, and trucks a valid Jordanian licence, and barring absolutely entry by Gaza Arabs. The former restrictions were protested by a meeting of 500 West Bank Arab personages from Hebron and Jericho in Hebron Town Hall, as barring

all Arabs who were too young or too poor to have obtained
Jordanian passports before 1967.

It was defended by Jordan as a measure against use of forged documents (denied by the West Bankers), and also to secure surrender and
cancellations of passports containing Israel entry endorsements and the
like. Imposition of the restraints was accompanied by Arab League
pressure to limit the stay of West Bank Arabs who went to work in
Kuwait, Jordan or other Arab countries. The background motive appears
to have been one of unsettling West Bank acceptance of the clear advantages to them of the "open bridges" policy, and to make difficulties
for Israel's policies of economic development of the territories. As
regards Gaza Arabs, a further purpose was, no doubt, to prevent the
easing of the refugee problem there. Rumors were spread that the Israel
authorities were in some way bringing pressure on the Gaza Arabs to
leave Israel-held territory. The Israel answer was that the Government
was neither promoting nor preventing their emigration. On principle,
too, it *could not* exclude the Gazans from free movement without
emulating the lamentable Egyptian policy from 1948 to 1967, of virtually
closing Gaza off as a kind of concentration camp.[16]

That the resulting reduction in travel was not due to any new fear for
Arab safety under Israel administration is clear. For there was a steady
concurrent *rise* of Arab visitors to Israel-held territories under the
"summer visits program", from 15,000 in 1968 to over 26,000 in 1969,
and an even higher figure in 1970.

It is, indeed, paradoxical that the more serious restrictions in the
administered territories have been on the movement of Israelis who
wish to establish or re-establish themselves in the territories, as with
the remnant of the Arab-massacred Jewish community of Hebron.
As regards movement for the purpose of tourism or shopping, which
is[2] beneficial to the local inhabitants (and, of course, competitively
harmful to corresponding business in Israel), no such restrictions have
been imposed. Money thus spent by Israelis is an important support
for the local economies, as well of East Jerusalem, as of Gaza and the
West Bank. Obviously, this two-way mobility has also ensured, to the
common benefit of both peoples, stirring recognition of the common
humanity too long overlaid by warlike Arab political propaganda,
and Israel defensiveness. No one who has moved by day or night in
the centers of Arab population can fail to conclude that day-to-day
relations between Jews and Arabs (usually requiring not even police
supervision, or only background supervision by local Arab police) have
already substantially redrawn the Arab image of Israeli soldiers and

civilians, and the Israel-held image of Arabs. This, indeed, has been an explicit objective of the Minister of Defense. And, all in all, this cardinal policy of freedom of movement would appear to respect the spirit and letter of the Geneva Conventions, as well as the rights of the populations concerned, well beyond the minima there demanded. It can scarcely, at this stage of history, be a military occupant's duty to discourage peaceful relations between the populations concerned, or to continue pre-war policies of promoting hatred, prejudice and alienation between them.

Some of the respects in which the legality of Israel measures in the territories has been questioned concern restitution of traditional rights of Jewish and other religious denominations which had been violated under Jordanian administration, for instance, in the Jewish Quarter of East Jerusalem, and on the Western Wall of the Temple Mount (Moriah). The legality of such measures depends on the Geneva Conventions only in due relation to the preceding Jordanian illegalities which they attempt to undo. Those illegalities, *vis-a-vis* Israel, included Jordan's refusal to honor the provisions of the Jordan-Israel Armistice Agreement, 1949, as regards free access to the Hadassah Hospital and the University on Mount Scopus, and the desecration of the holy places in East Jerusalem.

But those *vis-a-vis* various Christian churches were also serious. Among many such measures, one was the Jordanian Ordinance of 1965, imposing an embargo on acquisition by juridical persons (including Churches) of land or property within municipal boundaries, a measure preventing building of new Church institutions, but not of numerous mosques in the city. Another was a law of 1958, requiring all members of the Brotherhood of the Holy Sepulcher to become Jordan nationals, despite their traditional enjoyment of Greek citizenship since the fifth century. By contrast, leading Christian denominations have taken occasion publicly to acknowledge the restoration of freedom of religion under the present Israel administration.[17]

As to the Jewish Quarter of East Jerusalem, where Arab States charged the heartless expulsion of 3,000 Arabs, the Israel answer was that 160 families were moved *out of the ruins of synagogues pillaged and stripped after the Jordanian seizure of the Old City in* 1948. Israel further contends that alternative accomodation as well as compensation to the amount of IL120,000 was provided for these families, and that 3,500 Arabs still remain in the Jewish Quarter quite unmolested. This answer has not been contradicted.

Other measures have been taken for the beautification of Jerusalem

by freely negotiated agreements with Church owners of the lands involved. They can scarcely prejudice the interest of any other authorities,
since they merely add to the assets and amenities of the city; and they
would seem legally unexceptionable. Complaints have also been made,
however, concerning certain measures of requisition of land in East
Jerusalem, which may not be justified on any such particular grounds.

Their legality will depend, therefore, on the legal meaning and effect of
the measures taken after the June War for the "unification" of
Jerusalem.[17]

II

The positions of the Israel administration, as compared with the minimum norms set by international law, are even more dramatically seen
in the details of economic activity. In the first year of the military ad-
inistration about IL180 million (IL3.5 = $1) were poured by
Israel into the territories to maintain and improve public utilities and
health and welfare services, as well as to repair the losses resulting
from hostilities. From the end of the war to March 31, 1968, the Israel
authorities had subsidized the economy of the Gaza Strip alone (and
notably its citrus growing and fishing industries) to the extent of $10
million, the already hazardous local economy having been placed in
crisis by Egypt's wartime removal to Cairo of deposits in Arab banks
there. Israel undertook, in this situation, to redeem the Egyptian currency
at its nominal value of IL6.00, though it could be purchased in
Switzerland at the equivalent of only IL3.00. A million and a half
Israel pounds were spent on repairing and refurbishing the schools.
By April 1, 1968, the Gaza economy had received the further
support of Israel tourism and shoppers to an amount of $2½ million.
The 1968–69 budget for unemployment relief in the territories was
IL21 million.

East Jerusalem was provided for the first time with a continuous
water supply, and hospitals, child welfare, sanitary and health services
were extended to its 60,000 inhabitants on an equal basis with all other
inhabitants of the city. This was without levying commensurate charges
on East Jerusalem taxpayers, in view of hardship arising from their
lower income levels. Even three years later, in May 1970, after great
extension of such benefits, taxes on the Arab citizens of East Jerusalem
had not been raised commensurately, and the attempted adjustments
of that month led to a business strike, followed by further negotiations
to coordinate assessments.[18] Water and electricity supplies were

extended in main townships, and irrigation flow was improved. To meet post-war needs of West Bank agriculture, regulated marketing was introduced, with outlets to Amman, to Israel's food processing plants, to Israel Army and welfare institutions, and experimentally to Europe and Africa. Budgetary provision was made to buy up to 100,000 tons of crop surpluses, but it did not need to be used. Exports to Amman by May 1968 amounted to $19.6 million. All this obviously testifies to the co-operation between Israel, local West Bank officials and farmers, and also Amman, for the mutual advantage of the West and East Banks. Instruction in cultivation techniques, irrigation systems, agricultural implements, fertilizers, insecticides and seeding was also provided for no less than 8,000 farm workers. The Administration also dealt by a variety of measures with the financial crisis caused by the Jordanian transfer of cash balances to East Jordan on the eve of the war.[19]

Three years are a sufficient period to allow assessment of the tendencies of Israel's administration. This may be stated first in terms of employment, which presented such grave problems in June 1967. In the improved economic situation in the territories, and with the voluntary flow of workers to employment in Israel itself, the number of Arabs employed in public works in the territories had, by April 1, 1970, decreased to 7,650 persons, of whom 1500 were in Gaza and the rest on the West Bank. As of February 13, 1970, all but 4% (2,000) of the employable population of 55,000 in Gaza and Sinai had found jobs.[20] The correlation of the fall in unemployment and relief employment figures with the preference of the local inhabitants for jobs in Israel, is clear from the statistics of December 1969. By that time 32,000 Arabs had applied for work; 27,000 had been found jobs, 9,000 within the administered areas and 17,900 in Israel. The strength of the preference is indicated by the fact that the December figure of 17,900 was an increase of 3,500 over the previous month. It is also clear that this preference is not limited to unskilled men. Of the 17,900 Arabs thus working in Israel, 10,000 were in skilled work, mostly construction, and 3,300 in unskilled work. Of the same total, 5,000 were from Gaza, and the rest from the West Bank; and 1500 women were included.

In terms of living standards, consumption and investment, a Survey Report of the Bank of Israel of July 1970, found that there had been a rapid rise in living standards on the West Bank and Gaza and North Sinai, private demands in real terms having risen 19% in one year. Israel imported 17% of the total export of the areas. Imports into the areas which had run at the rate of IL130 million per annum in the second half of 1967, rose to IL240 million in 1968, and IL295 million in 1969. Investment in the areas rose in 1969 from IL33 million to IL67 million, half from the public sector. Gross national product rose by 25 per cent. Public projects in Gaza and Sinai included a major four-lane highway between Gaza and Khan Yunis (opened in February 1970), the completion of a well-equipped free medical clinic for the 20,000 welfare recipients in the Gaza Strip, costing an initial IL1.1 million and maintenance of IL800,000 annually. [21]

This is the background of facts for weighing charges such as that made by the "Front Line" Arab Conference of December 1969, that Israel policies were "exploiting and converting" the resources and wealth of "the Arab nation" into "weapons for Israel". The *legal* background is the law of military occupation under which, far from having any duty to *advance* the welfare of the areas and their people, and to divert her own scarce resources to this purpose, Israel would have been entitled to limit her activity to military security requirements and to levy the costs of this on the inhabitants themselves. The fact that, *instead of this*, she has heavily subsidized the welfare and economic advancement of the inhabitants sufficiently disposes of such charges.

The problems of welfare and economic development of Arab refugees confined in Gaza by Egypt, or living in camps on the West Bank, in 1967, also bear on the present matter, for these constitute an important segment of the local inhabitants. According to a report in the Knesset of February 18, 1970, given by the Minister for Civilian Affairs in the Administered Territories, Shimon Peres, the earnings of refugees willing to work averaged $100 per month, as compared with UNRWA rations valued at about $30. This figure of $100, though much higher than before 1967, he regarded as still too far-behind the prevailing average of $250 for West Bank Arabs, a much higher average for Arabs and Jews living in Israel. He outlined the Government's programs up to that time of vocational training and job placement, the improvement of camps by provision of water, electricity, drainage, roads and dwelling renovation, the provision of new homes outside the camps, and improved health and education facilities. All this, while producing important improvements, did not solve the basic problems of long-term rehabilitation. The Government considered that any long-term rehabilitation planning by Israel would provoke sharp opposition in the Arab world. The dimensions of the problem also placed it beyond Israel's sole resources. [22] But the Government in 1969 (and again on February 19, 1970) affirmed its readiness to participate in a world conference on this question, in advance of the settlement of other outstanding questions. [23]

The basic principle that the military occupant is entitled to take measures reasonably necessary to maintain his military hold of the territories, and to draw the cost from the territories themselves, is also relevant to other controversies. Some of these concern the Government of Israel's policy of establishing strong defensive positions along the cease-fire line, for example, on the Golan Heights and in the Jordan Valley. The mere fact that these *nahalim*, or military-type settlements, have been established by Israel investments designed also to initiate fruitful agricultural or other development can scarcely bring their legal propriety into doubt.

The uncertainty as to when the Arab side would enter upon peace negotiations impelled the Israel authorities, in the third year of occupation, to enter on a five-year plan for the settlement of the Golan Heights, with an investment of IL280 million, calling for 17 new settlements of 3,500 settlers, in 1,600 dwellings with related road, power and water supply developments. About 28 million cubic metres of water per annum have been allocated to Golan. This plan was initiated by the Jewish Agency Settlement Department,[24] but it must obviously be regarded as relevant to the security program of the Government of Israel. It is only indirectly related to the defense of the area. Yet insofar as these activities go beyond defense needs, for instance in extending the cultivated area from 45,000 to 105,000 *dunams* they are obviously of permanent benefit to the territories, whatever their ultimate disposition turns out to be.

III

For fair assessment, all this must be compared with the less benevolent standards set by international law. Article 55 of the Fourth Geneva Convention requires the occupant within his means to assure the availability of food and medical supplies, and Articles 59–62 require him to agree to relief schemes and admit relief supplies from outside. But beyond this, there is no duty to be economically bountiful. On the contrary, Article 49 of the Hague Regulations would permit the exaction of substantial contributions from the local inhabitants for the maintenance of the administration and the occupying army, and also requisitions of goods and premises against "fair" (but in practice more or less arbitary levels of) compensation. Article 55(2) preserves the right of requisition subject to the requirements of the civilian population. Certainly international law imposes no duty on an occupant to devote his skills and resources to redeeming an economy which the predecessor has, for his own ends, stripped and left in a parlous condition. Nor does it oblige him to improve the level of welfare, public utilities and other services. Even if the Israel administration was seeking long-term goodwill, this objective can rarely have been so sincerely pursued by an occupant who had such grounds for resentment. Certainly fairness requires specific complaints against Israel to be seen in the overall context of an administration whose humanity and constructiveness has gone well beyond what international law demands.

Israel's handling of the occupied Arab territories, reported the British *Daily Telegraph* on April 30, 1968, has been "the most humane and generous in modern history. . . . On its record so far, Israel can have a clear conscience before the United Nations or any other international bar on its handling of the occupied Arab territories." Mr. J.D.F. Jones, Foreign Editor of the *Financial Times* on May 20, 1969, about a year later, reported that "the Military Administration on the West Bank, for example, still strikes me as being one of Israel's most impressive achievements." Six months later another English observer, Raymond Gunter, a Minister in the former Labor Government, thought that Israel's occupation was "unique in the history of humanity", there being no signs of pressure or suffering "of the kind one expects to find in areas of occupation".[25]

Nor has the tenderness on the economic and welfare side been counter-balanced by repression in other respects. There has been a scrupulous regard for the integrity of family life, including facilities for the reunion of families across the cease-fire lines, and even admission of 4,000 Arab students from abroad. In view of present tension, and the participation of many Arab students abroad in terrorist groups, refusal to readmit them would have been warranted. Neither Article 134 of the Fourth Convention, nor the more exacting Stockholm Draft, envisage any scheme for return until after the conclusion of peace or the end of the occupation. Freedom of speech, whether for officials or for private individuals, has been generally assured, with proper limits set to incitement to violence, terrorism or other forceful subversion. Defense Minister Dayan, indeed, publicly commended the criticism of the occupation regime as a proper (even if unjustified) way of opposing the Israel administration.

It is significant in this regard that the Israel authorities have reversed the pattern of draconic law-making usually associated with military occupants. They have abolished, in all the territories, the mandatory death penalty formerly imposed by Egypt, Jordan and Syria for a wide range of offenses.[26]

These new Israel Orders substituted life imprisonment for death as the mandatory punishment. Even under the special security legislation the death penalty is permitted only in respect of premeditated causing of death or sabotage of a military installation (Proclamation No. 3, Annex, section 44). This is clearly within the authority of the Fourth Geneva Convention, Article 68(2). And despite the terrorist toll on civilians, including women and children, even this power to impose the death penalty had not* been exercised against either local inhabitants or even infiltrating terrorists, even when these have been convicted of grave offenses liable to it, and for which the Geneva Convention clearly permits the death penalty. The Order Concerning Security Regulations was amended in Article 47(A)(6) to *forbid* imposition of the death sentence "except when at least two . . . judges are officers of legal training, and the sentence is imposed unanimously". Article 27 in any case forbids acceptance of a plea of guilty where the death penalty *could* be inflicted. The prosecution in practice has not asked for a death sentence, and the punishment imposed is imprisonment, up to life. A death sentence for murder passed by a *local* court in Gaza on a local resident was commuted by the area commander, and the local courts now in practice also refrain from using the death penalty. The small number of cases of unrest (much less disorder and violence) originating with local inhabitants up to October 1968 is also notable. This may, of course, reflect dissatisfaction with the earlier regimes, as well as acceptance of the Israel administration: it would be speculative to guess at the proportions. The level of cooperation of the inhabitants with the authorities is, at any rate, notable in view of the pressure to which they are obviously subjected by the terrorist organisations to shelter or assist the infiltrators. Despite this, and despite the fact that most local governmental duties (including police duties) are in Arab hands, and the leeway for conspiracy against the Israel authorities is thus considerable, no activist local underground hostile to Israel established itself. The case of Abdul Latif Arshid indicates that very calculated risks have to be incurred to sustain these rather relaxed policies as to Arab official personnel and the open bridges policy. The accused, a former resident of Jenin, was in the Jordanian police in the Nablus Area, and then in the Jordanian army, before the 1967 War. After that War, when a West Bank resident, he crossed into Jordan and was recruited to organize terrorist activity for El Fatah on the West Bank, which he did with substantial success in the Haifa area, before being convicted and imprisoned by a military court.[27]

Cooperation of local residents with terrorists is reported to be rare, a fact to which no doubt the improved living standards under Israel

* Up to summer 1970

rule, as well as the penalties for active cooperation with them, have contributed. (The military law does *not* require such cooperation *with* the Administration in handing in terrorists, but it does forbid positive assistance to terrorists by way of harboring and the like.) Terrorist attacks on local Arabs aim to check the current degree of peaceable living and mutually beneficial cooperation of Arabs with the Military Administration, and with their employers in Israel.

The terrorist groups outside Israel seem, indeed, increasingly worried by the great number of Arabs seeking better conditions of work in Israel, leading to increasingly vicious intimidatory measures. Lamentably, favorite targets have become labor exchanges, offices where work permits are issued, and buses carrying people to and from work, as well as schools and particular individuals in their homes. [28]

Up to April 1970, 95 local Arabs had been deliberately attacked by terrorists; this is apart from 666 killed or injured incidentally to terrorist attacks on Israelis. These casualties were mostly in the Gaza Strip where, in March 1970 alone, 103 Gaza inhabitants were wounded and seven killed by Arab terrorist attacks, five killings being deliberate murders. [29] According to reports of August 1970 [30], there had been 15 political murders by terrorists between mid-July and mid-August, "apparently trying to liquidate Arabs suspected of collaborating with the Israel authorities". In these circumstances, it was not surprising, though still sad, that the 12 East Jerusalem citizens who, after two and a half years, agreed to become members of committees of the Municipality of Jerusalem, all withdrew within a week of the publication of their names. [31]

Despite all this, the pattern of cooperation for local welfare, and of frank and peaceable discussion of differences, has largely persisted. Almost as cogent is the inference which must be drawn from the remarkable freedom of movement to and from Jordan. If West Bank Arabs were *really* oppressed, they would scarcely, once they had escaped to Jordan, return daily and so willingly to "the oppressor's" yoke. Yet this is happening every day across the River Jordan, as will be seen from the massive figures given in Section I above. As of October 1968, an average of 1,500 persons were crossing the Allenby Bridge every day. The number of crossings by Arabs in both directions in 1968 was no less than 203,000. It was by virtue of restrictions *imposed by Jordan* on Gaza and also on West Bank residents, mentioned in the last Section, that this number fell in 1969 to 96,000. The 1969 figures detailed in Section I as "summer visits" suggests that these restraints were very severe. They were the subject of protest by West Bank Arabs, leading to some relaxation. The truth appears to be that local Arabs, though no doubt hoping for some form of independence in a more stable Middle East, probably see the chief obstacle to this in the uncertainties due to the Arab States' refusal to negotiate (or allow others to negotiate) a peace with Israel. Meanwhile they prefer to live their lives and conduct their affairs under the protection of an orderly Israel administration, even when "staying put" is presented, as it sometimes also is, as part of the Palestine Arab's patriotic duty.

Since no restrictions (except their ineligibility to serve in the Israel Defense Forces) have been imposed on Arab citizens of Israel, the low level of security offenses among these is also noteworthy. A report was given on June 8, 1970 to the Knesset on this matter, three years after the war. It showed that out of more than three hundred thousand, no more than 200 Israeli Arabs had been tried or awaited trial for security offenses, and that only 34 of them were under administrative detention for related activities.[32] A rare but notable exception to this record had been the terrorist network of Israel Arabs centered at Acre, affiliated with El Fatah, which operated in 1969 in the Haifa-Acre area. Its members were captured in October 1969, and tried in May 1970 before a military court.[33] There has been no serious activity of this sort since the uncovering of this network. There were virtually no incidents among Israeli, or East Jerusalem, West Bank or Gaza Arabs on the Third Anniversary of the Six Day War, despite vigorous incitement from Amman, and the various terrorist groups outside Israel.[34]

IV

The most difficult legal questions surround Israel's security measures involving demolition of buildings implicated in terrorist activities, and of deportations to Jordan, as means of dealing with persons guilty of activities against security. For convenience, preventive detentions, though not raising such questions, will here also be mentioned.

As to demolitions, a number of preliminary points need to be made before approaching the question of their consistency with Geneva Convention IV for the protection of civilian persons. These demolitions are carried out under the British Mandatory Government's Defence (Emergency) Regulations 1945, Regulation 119, which was continued in municipal legal force in the State of Israel throughout its existence, and in the West Bank after its seizure in 1948 by Jordan.[35] Regulation 119 provides for forfeiture and destruction of a building from which shots are fired, or which has been used for a security offense (that is, an offense triable in a military court). It follows that this legislation was part of the existing penal law on the West Bank in June 1967 and was not introduced especially by the occupant against the population of the occupied territories. Similar existing provisions are, as already seen, applicable throughout Israel, as well as in the occupied territories. Their relation to the Geneva Convention will shortly be considered. But it can be said immediately that *complaints by Jordan* of the continued application under Israel military occupation of legal provisions maintained *by Jordan* throughout her own military occupation of the same territories can scarcely be taken seriously. A similar point can be made as to Gaza, where the relevant continuing law is Order No. 6 of June 1, 1948. In the almost three years up to April 1, 1970, throughout the Administered Territories, Regulation 119 had been applied to 654 buildings.

Yet of course, this practice still has to be tested by the Fourth Geneva Convention of 1949, to which the States concerned are all parties, and by the Hague Regulations considered as now declaratory of customary international law.[36] Under Article 4 all persons in the hands of an occupying power of which they are "not nationals" are "protected persons" under it. It would appear therefore that, for the purposes of the present discussion, the inhabitants of all the occupied territories are "protected persons" within Article 4, not being nationals of Israel and yet in its hands as an occupying power. Equally clearly armed bands continuing acts of war after the cease-fire are not protected persons.[36] And, since the main part of the Convention (Articles 27–141) also seems inapplicable to active participants in war, questions also arise as to local inhabitants who aid and abet such combatants. Side by side with the safeguards for the persons, honor, property and beliefs of protected persons to which most of the Fourth Convention is devoted, the Convention reserves to the occupant necessary powers for maintaining orderly government and securing his military situation, by administrative judicial and even legislative action.

The legality of demolitions would appear to turn primarily on Article 53, which prohibits destruction of property, but always subject to the important exception "where such destruction is rendered absolutely necessary by military operations". M. Pictet[37] observes that "it will be for the Occupying Power to judge the importance of such military requirements". Pointing to the vagueness of the term "military necessity", and the danger of abuse, he offers the precept that "occupying authorities must try to keep a sense of proportion in comparing the military advantages to be gained with the damage done". In this light the legality of the demolitions here in question would depend on estimation of the military dangers from the actions of terrorist infiltrators, and of the importance of destroying the rendezvous or caches as a measure for controlling these dangers, and the dangers of casualties from "booby traps" unless the structure is summarily razed. Obviously these are highly debatable questions. No doubt the Israel case would stress the heavy loss of life caused by terrorist activity, and that the Arab States themselves have declared this to be a chief method of conducting hostilities against Israel. As against this it can be argued, in turn, that mere infiltration action and counteraction to it do not constitute "military operations" within the reservation to Article 53. Even if they are, it may be said that demolition rather than mere posting of permanent guards is not "absolutely necessary" as part of them; but this is subject to the above objection that the occupant should not have to risk loss of lives from traps set within the implicated premises. Significantly, a high level official of the Arab League who testified in 1969 before the Special Working Group of the Commission of Human Rights with reference to the above exception to the prohibition of Article 53 stressed the fact that "military operations continue to take place, which is the prevailing situation along the cease-fire line and inside the occupied territories."[38]

Insofar (and only insofar) as the exception for military necessity is not invoked (as it usually has not been), or may be held inapplicable, problems would arise under Article 33. This Article (deriving from Article 50 of the Hague Regulations) forbids collective penalties, and measures of "intimidation or terrorism", and all punishment except for an offense "personally committed" by the accused. It is, of course, highly unlikely that premises would be in use for terrorist activities without the owner being in fact implicated. So far as he is, the demolition practice would not violate Article 33; and it is the rule not to demolish premises if the family concerned shows that it was not aware of the sabotage activity.[39] According to the Israel authorities, therefore, Regulation 119 is administered by way of individual, not collective, punishment, procedures being designed to determine guilt before demolition. Erroneous demolition of the house of an innocent person would be followed by compensation, though it was claimed in October 1968 that there had been no such case. The required practice would still be on this view, to observe the provisions of Articles 71–74 concerning regular trial and conviction after due notice to the accused and other requirements.

All the above legal complexities are simplified, and indeed probably removed altogether, by the peremptory provisions of Article 64, paragraph 1, that "the penal laws of the occupied territory shall remain in force". For this casts additional doubt on the applicability of Article 33. As already seen, the demolitions in question have taken place under provisions of local penal law in force when Israel entered into occupation. Article 64 thus seems even to *require* continuance of this law. Moreover the same paragraph permits repeal of such a law in force which is a threat to the occupant's security. It would thus be very strange indeed to hold that the occupant was forbidden to *maintain* the existing law when *this* was necessary for his security. The paragraph also authorizes him to repeal a law which obstructs the application of the Convention; but it does not *oblige* him to do so. (Related inferences also arise from Article 47.) It would thus appear that the entire practice of demolitions (like that of deportations shortly to be mentioned) under the unaltered local law in force is legally justifiable under Article 64, paragraph 1. Such demolitions *within Israel territory*, moreover, would have still another *additional* legal basis, Article 5, paragraph 1, depriving persons "definitely suspected of activities hostile to the security of the State" of the protection of the Convention where this would prejudice the security of the State.

As to internment, Article 78 authorizes the occupant, where the security situation makes it imperatively necessary, to detain protected persons in internment or in assigned residence. When it is so necessary is "very largely" at his discretion, with no judicial procedure required, though each case should be decided separately.[40] The main specific duty in respect to internment or assigned residence, apart from those as to personal treatment (Part III, Section IV of the Convention), is the duty of the Detaining Power to reconsider each individual case at indicated intervals (Article 78). The required procedural arrangements, including those for reconsideration at least twice a year by a committee presided over by a Justice of the Supreme Court of Israel, are made by Israel.[41] There appears to be no legal substance, accordingly, to complaints concerning preventive detentions by the Israel authorities.

Police Minister Shlomo Hillel, on April 4, 1970,[42] categorically denied any practice of torture or even "face slapping" by investigators, and reaffirmed that any report of such practices from any source was strictly investigated. He declared that it was the policy of the Government to use detention only against hostile *activities*, not mere hostile opinions; and also to release detainees as soon as it is clear that they will not resume the activities leading to detention. There is also provision for release on bond in certain cases.[43] As of that date, 3,200 persons were in detention, and their cases were reviewed twice a year by the above Committee.

As to deportations, it should be noted at the outset that the total number of cases involved, from the beginning to April 1, 1970, is 15 from East Jerusalem and 56 from all the other territories; and one of these, a woman, has been readmitted for humanitarian reasons. All were cases of deportations of individuals from the West Bank to Jordan on grounds of sabotage and active incitement of the population to disobedience on behalf of Jordan. The family of the deportee may choose to accompany him, and in that case they may take their property with them. So few cases being involved, the issue is, in any case, not a major one.

The question of legality nevertheless arises, and involves consideration of three provisions. Article 78 seems to allow discretionary measures of "at the most" assigned residence or internment for such activities, implying that other less severe measures may also be permissible. Article 45 permits transfers of protected persons to Powers party to the Convention, and repatriation in any case, but this figures in Part III, Section II, of the Convention under the heading "Aliens within the Territory of a Party". M. Pictet comments that Article 45 provides for "transfer" for internment, or repatriation, or return to the country of residence, and (moreover) "would not appear to raise any obstacle to the right . . . to deport aliens in individual cases when State security demands such action." (P. 266.) Finally, in Part III, Section III, under the heading "Occupied Territories", Article 49 forbids "individual or mass forcible transfers, as well as deportations of protected persons from occupied territory to the territory of the Occupying Power or to that of any other country, occupied or not . . . regardless of their motive".

Deportation to Jordan from the occupied territories, therefore, is warranted under Article 78 if it is not more severe than internment. This would certainly cover any cases where the deportee was allowed to choose this in preference to internment.[44] Former Gaza judge Adel Shorrab, for example, after conviction for spying for Egypt, repeatedly applied while serving his four-year sentence to be allowed to emigrate. At his request he was allowed to cross into Jordan with his family in April, 1970. According to the *Jerusalem Post* of April 22, 1970, these facts did not prevent him from announcing the same night over Amman television that the Israelis had "expelled" him. Deportations could also, if made from Israel territory, be warranted under Article 45 if the transfer were to the home State, or to a Party to the Convention, and there was no reason to anticipate that he would be persecuted. The relation of these Articles to the literal words of Article 49 is rather complex. This last Article was inspired by the hideous Nazi practices of the Second World War, involving mass transfers for slave labor or extermination of millions of persons.[45] Such transfer by the Nazi occupant, whether to his own territory or to that of the State of nationality or to that of a third State, was always still, *in the conditions then, to Nazi-controlled territory.* It left the persons concerned equally at the tender mercy of the Nazi tyranny, which then dominated all of continental Europe.

Applying these provisions together to the comparatively few deportations here in question, common sense suggests that in most of the cases deportation to Jordan would be a less severe measure than internment, and within the license of Article 78. For the hostile activities in question have invariably been on behalf of Jordan, to which they were deported, and where they might expect to be welcomed and even rewarded, sometimes by high public office. Such cases include, though not exhaustively, Ruhi Al-Hatib, ex-Mayor of Jerusalem, who was appointed Chairman of the "Committee to Save Palestine" on his arrival in Amman; Nadim Zaru, ex-Mayor of Jerusalem, who became Jordanian Minister of Municipalities; Abdul Hamid Al-Sayach, a former Cadi, who became Minister for the Waqf in the Jordanian Government.

Insofar as Article 49 conflicts with this meaning of Article 78, it seems reasonable to limit the sweeping literal words of Article 49 to situations at least remotely similar to those contemplated by the drafters, namely the Nazi World War II practices of large-scale transfers of populations, whether by mass transfer or transfer of many individuals, to more hostile or dangerous environments, for torture, extermination or slave labor (see M. Pictet's commentary on Article 49) would suggest this. Obviously, the present deportations to Jordan have no similarity to these. To hold them within Article 49, despite the above inconsistencies with Article 78, would subject to the letter of Article 49 conduct which lies completely outside the evils at which it was aimed. It is to be recalled, in support of this view, that Article 45 would explicitly permit all these deportations *if made from Israel territory, and if the Israel authorities allowed wide freedom of movement to and from occupied and Israel territory to the population of the West Bank.* And the above discussion is also apart from the debatable scope of the exceptions to Article 49 itself, on grounds of "security of the population or imperative military reasons" (Paragraph 2).

Here again, as with demolitions, the apparent complexities seem to be resolved in favor of Israel by the basic principle of Article 64, paragraph 1, of the Convention. This Article, as already seen, not only authorizes but requires the military authorities to maintain in force the pre-existing criminal laws. Among these pre-existing laws were the provisions of Regulation 112, under the former British Mandatory Government's Defence (Emergency) Regulations 1945, maintained in force by the Jordanian and Egyptian measures referred to in Section I above. Regulation 112 authorizes deportations on grounds of certain activities against security, and the limited deportation policy under discussion held by the Israel authorities seems to be within the scope of the law in force.

The question that is of course different from all of these is whether it is prudent for Israel in terms of her own security to leave such persons at liberty, and facilitate their engaging in further hostile activity, sometimes in positions of power and leadership, under the aegis of the State of Jordan.

It is to be added, finally, that the major difficulty for Israel's security administration has proved to be that of overcrowding in the jails. And it is but fair in this regard to observe that it is a difficulty much aggravated by the Government's adamant stand on humanitarian principle against imposition of the death penalty, even for the gravest and most murderous offenses. On March 27, 1970, Minister of Police Hillel had to report that overcrowding had become the rule, due to the fact that in addition to the normal jail population of only 1600 before 1967, 3142 Arabs from the administered territories or infiltrators from Arab States were now in custody, 90% of them (2866 persons) for terrorist and security offenses.

V

The *relative* even-handedness manifest in June-July 1967, when both the General Assembly and the Security Council withstood formidable Communist and Arab pressures to require withdrawal of Israeli forces, or to declare Israel an aggressor, faded rapidly in 1968. Taking advantage of the tendency of opinion to favor the "underdog" regardless of the merits, and to disengage concern once the immediate crisis was over, the Arab and Communist States have steadily campaigned to charge Israel with violation of human rights in the administrered territories.

Among the few resolutions adopted by the Security Council immediately after the Six Day War were S/Res. 237 (1967), A/Res. 2252 (ESV), each of which contained two identical paragraphs. One of these paragraphs was addressed to the State of Israel, concerning the safety, welfare and security of persons in the occupied territories. The other recommended to the Governments concerned "to respect humanitarian principles in the treatment of prisoners and civilian persons." Of the resolutions the Secretary-General's representative, in his report on the condition of civilians in the aftermath of the war, observed that they "might properly be interpreted as having application to the treatment, at the time of the recent war, and as a result of that war, of *both Arab and Jewish* persons in the States which are directly concerned because of their participation in that war".[46] And, of course, unless this were so, it would be impossible to understand why the Resolution in relation to humanitarian principles referred to "Governments", in the plural.

Nevertheless, the General Assembly was persuaded at the end of its 23rd Session on December 19, 1968, to adopt Resolution 2443, obviously departing from the impartial concern with human rights envisaged in Resolution 237. Resolution 2443 established a Committee of Three Member States "to investigate Israeli practices affecting the human rights of the population of the occupied territories." Discriminatory as this was between the States to which Resolution 237 had been addressed, barely half the Members of the General Assembly voted fo its adoption, 22 Members voting against it, and 37 Members abstaining. The ground had been laid for this one-sided approach by a surprise campaign at the 1968 International Conference on Human Rights at Teheran, extraneous to that Conference's agenda. A resolution of that Conference of May 7, 1968, passed without any show of impartial inquiry, in effect *asserted* the existence of "violation of human rights in Arab territories occupied as a result of the June 1967 hostilities . . . ." Whatever the truth of this assertion, it was to be expected that enough Soviet bloc, Arab, and African and Asian votes would be available to rally 40 or 50 votes. The Resolution was indeed carried by 42 votes, as against 5 negative votes and 25 abstentions.

The next Arab initiative, taken in the Commission of Human Rights at its 25th Session on March 6, 1969, built on this dubious unexamined assertion of the Teheran Conference. Only 13 members, a minority of the Commission, were prepared to vote for the establishment of a Special Working Group of Experts to inquire concerning "Israel's violations of the Geneva Convention IV", 16 members abstaining, and Israel voting against. Of the 13 members who voted for the Resolution, 9 did not maintain diplomatic relations with Israel, so that little weight can be given to their votes. This now doubly tainted judgment was in due course included in Resolution 2546 at the 4th Session of the General Assembly on December 11, 1969. That Resolution set up a Special Committee of Three ostensibly to inquire into practices in Israel-administered territories; but *in advance of the very inquiries* the Resolution instructed the Committee to take cognizance of the General Assembly's condemnation of them. The device was so patent that less than half (52) of the

Members of the General Assembly voted for the Resolution. 49 abstaining and 13 voting against.

The first ground given by the Government of Israel for boycotting these inquiries was the unilateral nature of these Resolutions. It was ready (it declared) to facilitate inquiries as to treatment of Arabs in its territories, but only if parallel inquiries were directed, and permitted by the States concerned, concerning Jews in Arab countries. Grave charges concerning forfeitures, arbitrary detentions, concentration camps, and other restraints on their Jewish citizens, had long been leveled against the Governments of Syria, Egypt and Iraq. At about the time of the proposed United Nations investigations (Prime Minister Meir pointed out), innocent Iraqi Jews were being publicly hanged in Baghdad after secret "trials", and the "small and persecuted" residue of 3,000 souls from the former Iraqi community of 150,000 lived under constant threats. After being invited to register for exit, their exit was barred, and they were held as prisoners of Iraqi hostility to Israel.[47] (On March 4, 1970, General Ammash, Iraqi Minister of the Interior, announced "some" easing of the "restrictions" on Iraqi Jews.) Four thousand Syrian Jews (Mrs. Meir said) were living "under a regime of terror which can be likened only to that of the Nazis", reporting several times daily to the police, barred from trading, and from overseas contacts, and under constant security police surveillance. In Egypt, too, local Jews were imprisoned on the outbreak of the Six Day War, and (at the date of her speech to Parliament on January 20, 1970) the heads of families of half the small remaining Jewish community of Egypt were still in the repressive Toura Gaol in Cairo. In July 1970, between 800 and 1000 Jews were said still to be held in Egypt under varying degrees of restriction.[49] The United Nations and the Commission of Human Rights (concluded Prime Minister Meir) "which display sensitivity to baseless accusations about what is happening in the areas, display total impotence regarding the danger hanging over Jews in Arab lands."[49]

Second, the Israel Government also denounced the prejudicial nature of the terms of reference drawn so as to condemn it in advance of the inquiries authorized. Third, as to the matters referred by the Commission of Human Rights to its "Special Working Group" concerning Geneva Convention IV, the Government of Israel objected that these were within the functions of the International Red Cross, which already maintained in Israel (with that Government's ready cooperation) its largest Delegation in the Middle East. The relevant reports of that Delegation were received and considered by the Government of Israel, and no other authority was competent or necessary under the Convention.[50]

Finally, in the Israel view, the work of the three-member Special Committee of the General Assembly under Resolution 2443 was affected by other serious irregularities. The President of the General Assembly, Dr. Arenales of Guatemala, whose function it was to nominate its members, had expressed the view, on March 6, 1969, that the appointment of the Committee would add "further causes of friction to the already tense situation in the Middle East." On the death of Dr. Arenales during his term of office, the Secretary-General, by an unprecedented procedure in an admittedly rare situation, had purported to confer the task of forming the committee on the representative of Peru (as one of the *previous* General Assembly's Vice-Presidents). Of the three members thus "nominated", Somalia was a State which had always refused to recognize the State of Israel; Yugoslavia was closely aligned with Egypt both politically and through the personal friendship of Presidents Tito and Nasser, and had severed diplomatic relations with Israel in 1967; and Ceylon had voted steadily on the Arab side in the current dispute, having only limited diplomatic relations with Israel which she in due course terminated in 1970. The Chairman, H.S. Amerasinghe, vigorously rejected Israel's suggestion that the Committee was biased by its very composition.

The work of both Committees is subject, in any view, to the serious comment that it took almost all its evidence from witnesses living in Arab countries, or volunteering to testify there. Since, for the above reasons, the Government of Israel felt unable to cooperate, the testimony remains *ex parte* and untested, often emanating from politically motivated persons. They included for example, Emil El Ghouri, the aide of Haj Amin El-Husseini, the former Grand Mufti of Jerusalem, whom the Polish delegate at the Special Committee on Palestine of the General Assembly in 1947 described as one of "the former Nazi collaborators whose very political record makes Arab-Jewish cooperation impossible and precludes any real cooperation with them by the United Nations".[51]

So far as the rather untested evidence alleged torture and other ill-treatment of persons under administrative detention, a rather wry light is cast on it by the application made on May 14, 1970 by administrative detainee Sabri Jera (an attorney by profession) to a three-judge panel of the Supreme Court of Israel. His complaints against his Israeli custodians were that he was not allowed to bring a radio and his own books to his place of detention, and that weekly visits by relatives and friends were not allowed. He also complained that he was not provided with other work, after he refused to do the kinds of work offered to him. He based his complaints on the principle that while in detention he should be allowed to lead a normal life and enjoy the same rights as other citizens.[52] The fact that these were the gravest complaints that the detainee wished to put before the court obviously implies that his experience as an Arab, and as a detainee, and what he heard from his fellow-detainees, led him to expect very high standards of consideration from his wardens.

The evidence received by these Committees was, of course, also distorted by the lack of testing and correction of accusations hostile to Israel, due to that State's refusal to permit their formal entry into its territory unless they also enquired into the conditions of Jews in Arab countries. Yet it is also *unlikely* that this refusal deprived the Committees of any substantial evidence which might have been *unfavorable* to Israel. Not only (as already noted) does the International Red Cross carry out its functions in the areas concerned, with the goodwill and cooperation of the Government of Israel, but many hundreds of officials of international organizations, and foreign States, and of the international press, move freely each year throughout the administered territories, talking to Arab and Israelis alike. High-level editorial staff of the London *Times*, for example, toured the areas and wrote more than one series of articles in 1969, which manifested sharp divergencies between praise of the alleged liberality and concern of the Israel administration for the welfare of the inhabitants, on the one hand, and criticism of its alleged oppressiveness, on the other.

Not only were such eye-witness sources of information available outside Israel to the Committees, but the Special Committee under Resolution 2546 was permitted *by the Israel authorities* freely and prominently to advertise in the Israel press, invitations to any persons in Israel to testify before the Committee in "open or private session". The Committee, for example, had a 5" × 5" notice in the *Jerusalem Post* of March 8, 1970, of this import, indicating its impending visits to Beirut (April 5–9), Damascus (April 9–13). and Amman (April 13–19).[53]

It is well known, moreover, that movement of Arabs abroad, even to enemy Arab countries, is not prohibited by the Israel authorities. On February 24, 1970, no less than 258 Arab students of Gaza were allowed to cross the Suez Canal to study in Egypt, part of a larger movement of 2,000 students. Obviously, such persons could (and some no doubt did) testify to United Nations Committees overseas with just as much freedom and security as if they had testified in Israel. The same applies to the 16,000 students and other "summer visitors" from enemy Arab countries admitted by Israel to visit the administered territories in 1968, the 26,254 in 1969, and the still larger number in 1970.

The fact, indeed, that ever-increasing numbers of Arabs deliberately choose to come to Israel from surrounding Arab States for summer visits contradicts the whole tenor of the charges made against the Israel Administration. The parallel fact that the number of crossings of the Jordan in both directions in 1968 was no less that 203,000, and that even after drastic restrictions by Jordan in 1969 (vigorously protested by West Bank Arabs), the number was still 96,000 in that year, even more sharply contradicts it. Arabs living under Israel rule would certainly be aware of oppressions from which they suffered. If the charges given currency in these manipulated United Nations procedures had substance, it would pass belief that so many West Bank Arabs, after escaping from allegedly inhuman oppression would so regularly return to it.

The proof of the pudding is in the eating. The readiness of so many thousands of Arabs to come and live under Israel administration, supports rather the views quoted in Section III of impartial observers who have gone to see for themselves. The trust of the local Arab population supports the picture there painted of an administration which is "the most humane and generous in modern history", as a "most impressive achievement", rather than that painted in these so-called United Nations inquiries. Yet the important thing is the factual and legal record, which it has been the present purpose to set down.

It has to be recalled, finally, that the first United Nations Human Rights mission to the Middle East after the 1967 War inquired, also without discrimination, into allegations concerning the treatment of Jews in Arab lands. It was readily permitted to fulfill its mission in Israel from July to September 1967. If the Israel Government had any motive of concealment in 1969, it would certainly also have had such motives in 1967, in the immediate aftermath of the disorders of war.

NOTES

[1] For details see *Jerusalem Post* (hereafter referred to as "*J.P.*") Jan. 13, 1970.

[2] One exception, I must add, is Judge A.M. Shara, convicted on October 3, 1968 of working with El Fatah terrorists. He pleaded guilty, but that he acted under pressure.

[3] *J.P.*, April 20, 1970.

[4] *J.P.*, March 31, 1970.

[5] *J.P.*, March 26, 1970.

[6] *Cf.* the statements of Mr. Eban, *J.P.*, March 26, 1970, and Y. Allon, *J.P.*, March 26, 1970.

[7] *Cf.* Mr. Begin, *J.P.*, April 24, 1970, with Mr. Eban, *J.P.*, March 31, 1970.

[8] Don Peretz, "Israel's Administration and Arab Refugees" (1968) 46 *Foreign Affairs*

336, 342–43. The author is Director of the South-West Asian Program at the State University of New York at Binghamton.

⁹ *J.P.*, May 7, 1970.

¹⁰ These Regulations are unchanged in the October 1969 Amendments and Consolidation of the Order Concerning Security Regulations.

¹¹ See e.g. Modes of Punishment (Miscellaneous Provisions) Judea and Samaria (No. 206) Order, 5728–1968, *Kovetz Ha-Minsharim*, No. 10, p. 404.

¹² *Jerusalem Post Weekly* (hereafter referred to as "*J.P.W.*") June 29, 1970, p. 4, and October 5, 1970, p. 11.

¹³ *J.P.*, March 6, 1970.

¹⁴ *J.P.*, March 3, 6, 9, 16 and 19, 1970.

¹⁵ *J.P.*, April 1, 1970.

¹⁶ *J.P.*, issues already cited.

¹⁷ See for other examples, and generally, the materials and quotations collected in *Barbed Wire Shall Not Return to Jerusalem*, Israel Information Service, N.Y., being excerpts from Israel statements in the General Assembly April 27 and May 21, 1968. For statements of relative Arab complaints, see S.S. Jones, "The Status of Jerusalem . . ." (1968) 33 *Law and Contemporary Problems* 169, 171; M.H. El-Farra, ". . . The Palestine Question" *id.* 68, 75.

¹⁷ See Stone, *No Peace-No War in the Middle East* (1969, repr. 1970) 17–24; E. Lauterpacht, *Jerusalem and the Holy Places* (1968) esp. 44–53; Y. Blum, "The Missing Reversioner . . ." (1968) 3 *Israel Law Review* 279–302, esp. 281–295; S. Schwebel, "What Weight to Conquest?" (1970) 64 *A.J.I.L.* 344–47.

¹⁸ *J.P.*, May 31, June 1, 1970.

¹⁹ For detailed Israel statements, see Israel Information Service (N.Y.), *Where Arab and Jew Meet . . .* (1968), Ministry of Defense, *The Military Government's Civil Administration . . . June 1967-June 1968* (1968).

²⁰ *J.P.*, Feb. 13, 1970.

²¹ See report of Governor of Bank of Israel, *J.P.W.*, July 27, 1970, p. 4. For other Projects see Anan Safadi, *J.P.,* March 1, 1970, and news items *J.P.,* Febuary 13, 1970, and March 1, 1970; and on child welfare, see Susan Bellos, "Health on the West Bank" *J.P.*, March 9, 1970.

²² Peres, reported *J.P.*, February 19, 1970.

²³ *J.P.*, February 20, 1970.

²⁴ See *J.P.*, June 1, 1970.

²⁵ *Cf.* among similar reports, *Neue Zürcher Zeitung*, June 7, 1968.

²⁶ For Gaza and Sinai, see the Local Courts Death Penalty (Gaza Strip and Northern Sinai) no. 239 Order, of 5728–1968; for the West Bank, the similarly named Order (Judea and Samaria) No. 268; and for Golan similarly by the Golan Heights, No. 246 Order.

²⁷ See *J.P.*, February 23, 1970.

²⁸ See for recent reports, *J.P.*, January 28, 1970, March 4, 1970, *J.P.W.*, July 13, 1970. A statistical survey of terrorist activities was published by the Israel Army authorities on January 19, 1970.

²⁹ H. Ben-Adi, "Gaza's Bloodiest Month" *J.P.*, April 6, 1970.

³⁰ *The Australian*, August 13, 1970, *J.P.W.*, August 3, 1970.

³¹ *J.P.*, February 2, February 4, February 13, 1970.

³² *J.P.*, June 10, 1970. Recent trials for espionage and terrorist activities are reported in the *J.P.*, January 10, 1970, February 5, 11 and 22, and March 30, 1970.

³³ *J.P.*, May 20, 1970.

[34] *J.P.*, June 5 and 7, 1970.

[35] Concurrently by the Law for the General Administration of Palestine, No. 17 of 1949, Section 2, Off. Gaz. No. 1002, p. 380, and by the Royal Law No. 28, of 1950, alongside the General Defence Regulations No. 2 of 1939, under the Transjordan Defence Ordinance of 1935, of similar purport as to demolitions.

[36] See, as to Israel, *A.G.* v. *Sylvester* (1948) *Annual Digest . . . of International Law Cases* 573, and (1949) *id.* 466.

[36] See T. Meron, "Some legal Aspects of Arab Terrorist Claims to Privileged Combatancy" in S. Shoham (ed.), *Of Law and Man (Festschrift for Justice Haim Cohn,*1971, Faculty of Law, Tel Aviv) pp. 1–44.

[37] M. Pictet, *The Geneva Conventions,* vol. ii (1958), p. 302.

[38] Doc. E/CN. 4/AC 26/RTI, pp. 16, 21.

[39] Minister of Defence Dayan, statement in the Knesset, October 29, 1968, *J.P.*, October 30, 1968.

[40] M. Pictet, *op. cit.* 257,367.

[41] See the order Concerning Security Detentions, Section 67, esp. s. 4 as to the Committee for appeals and reviews.

[42] *J.P.*, April 5, 1970.

[43] Salah Muhammed el-Masser was so released on May 13, 1970: *J.P.*, May 14, 1970.

[44] J.P. reported on July 2, 1970, the deportation of 12 "administrative detainees" to Jordan, but without indicating whether this was the preference of the detainees.

[45] See Pictet, *op. cit.* 278–79.

[46] Report of Nov. 2, 1967, U.N. Doc. S/8158 or A/6797. (Italics supplied.) Resolution S/237(1967) and A/2252(Esv) both carefully distinguished in separate numbered paragraphs between the assurance of the safety, welfare, and security of the inhabitants of the war zones (on the one hand), and (on the other), the scrupulous respect of humanitarian principles "governing prisoners of war and protection of civilian persons". The latter concern it drew to the attention not of the Israel Government alone, but of "the Governments concerned", that is, of the Arab States as well as the State of Israel, as regards their respective inhabitants liable to oppression or ill-treatment in the circumstances of war. (Texts in *International Legal Materials*, 1967, Vol. 6, 608, 833.)

[47] On March 4, 1970, General Ammash, Iraqi Minister of the Interior, announced "some easing" of the "restrictions" on Iraqi Jews.

[48] However, 90 families are reported to have been recently allowed to leave in secret after surrendering all their property. (*J.P.W.*, July 27, 1970, p. 13.)

[49] *J.P.*, January 21, 1970.

[50] See the Report of the Working Group (E/CN.4/1016) which also reproduces the Israel Note of 25 June, 1969, in paras. 9 and 22. And see the full Statement by Israel Ambassador Leshem to the Commission on Human Rights on March 19, 1970.

[51] U.N. Doc. A/C. 1/PV. 54, p. 43.

[52] *J.P.*, May 14, 1970.

[53] *J.P.*, March 4, 1970.

LAW OF NATIONS

THE FUTURE OF INTERNATIONAL LAW IN AN UNRULY WORLD

Arthur J. Goldberg*

If there is a single theme that runs through the distinguished career of Justice Cohn, it is that of the application of law and ethics to the problems of contemporary society. Justice Cohn is not merely a renaissance man of the law itself, he is also the exemplar of a humane tradition which views the law as embodying the highest moral values of Judaism.

When I left the Supreme Court of the United States to enter on my new duties at the United Nations, I made a statement which may have sounded to some like a mere rhetorical flourish; but it was entirely serious. The statement was that I was moving from one area dedicated to the rule of law to another dedicated to the same principle; and that, to my mind, the effort to bring the rule of law to govern the relations between sovereign states, is the greatest adventure in history.

These beliefs come naturally to me from a lifetime in the law and in the pursuit of the just resolution of conflicts through due process. The rule of law among nations is obviously more difficult than at home; but it is even more necessary, and we have ample proof that it is possible—indeed, in some measure it is an accomplished fact.

I am well aware that there are other views of this subject, even among people who have wide experience of diplomacy and world politics. We hear it said that what nations really respect is not law but political power. Besides, we are told, this is an age of revolutions, of deep splits of values between East and West and between North and South. And since law derives from values, this revolutionary era is said to be going through what one distinguished critic calls "a withdrawal of the legal order," in which sheer power is more decisive than ever in international

* Former United States Ambassador to the United Nations

affairs, and laws have become little more than a mockery. My own reading of the facts leads me to a very different conclusion.

First, we must beware of framing the argument in such a way that law and power become antithetical. In real life, law and power operate together. Power not ruled by law is a menace; but law not served by power is a delusion. Law is thus the higher of the two principles; but it cannot operate by itself.

My second broad point is that law cannot be derived from power alone. Might does not make right. On the contrary, law springs from one of the deepest impulses of human nature. No doubt the contrary impulses to fight and dominate often prevail; but sooner or later law has its turn. In one of the decisive moments in the history of law, King John thought he could impose his arbitrary will by force; but the barons who mustered superior force preferred to substitute an agreed rule—Magna Carta—for any man's arbitrary will. Thus, the King became subject to the law, and new proof was given of the strong human impulse toward law and the peace that law brings. In the history of my country, this impulse has been especially strong from the beginning, and found its highest expression in our written Constitution.

My third point flows from the second. Because law responds to a human impulse, it rests on much more than coercion. Law must have the police power, but it is by no means synonymous or coterminous with police power. It is much larger in its conception and in its reach. It builds new institutions and it produces new remedies. It tames the forces of change and keeps peace. People obey the law not only out of fear of punishment but also because of what law does for them: the durability and reliability it gives to institutions; the reciprocity that comes from keeping one's word; and the expectation, grounded in experience, that the just process of law will right their wrongs and grievances. All the police power in creation could not long uphold a system of law that did not meet these affirmative expectations.

Our hope for world peace depends on our ability to extend to the international sphere a dual concept of law, both creative and coercive.

This extension of law into the international realm is not going to be achieved in one great Utopian stroke of the pen. In the United Nations Charter, and in age-old norms of international law, the community of nations already has a set of fundamental rules which do not need to be rewritten so much as they need to be observed. Our task, therefore, is to make greater use of existing machinery and existing norms—to build on them and to broaden out the areas of international relations that are susceptible to them.

To keep the matter in perspective, let us first recall that the areas of international law and order are already very broad—and they are constantly broadening to fit the emerging common interests of nations. Without law, international mail would not be delivered; ships and aircraft would collide in the night; international business contracts could be violated with even greater impunity than now; infectious diseases and insect pests would cross frontiers all the time; there would be no extradition of criminals; weather information would not be exchanged; radioactivity from nuclear testing would jeopardize our lives and those of our posterity; the Antarctic and the moon would be subject to competing claims of sovereignty and rival armaments; the safety and return of astronauts accidentally landing on foreign earthy soil would not be guaranteed; and even diplomats—who are supposedly full-time practitioners of power politics—would be unable to carry on their business.

Many functions of the international order are so familiar as almost to be taken for granted. Some of them long antedate the United Nations. But it would be a great mistake to underrate them or to dismiss them as merely "technical" and "nonpolitical." They are bridges of common interest among nations, and the sum of these common interests is one of the great unseen inhibitors of political conflict and international violence.

The United Nations and its agencies, through their economic, technical and social programs, continue to add to this system of bridges. In doing so, they serve not only the technical convenience of nations but also their desperate need to cure the evils from which lawless action springs: poverty, illiteracy, hunger, disease and deprivation of human rights. I believe that this multilateral system must be strengthened further whenever possible.

With all its weaknesses, and they are many, I believe the existence of the U.N. during the past twenty-four years, beset with the dangers of war and the persistent pressures of revolutionary change in every continent, has been a decisive blessing to mankind. It has been a meeting ground between East and West, and when hardly any common interests could be perceived save the interest in sheer survival. And today it affords a coherent framework and a place of dignity and influence to more than fifty nations, newly born from the colonial age. It is their international home, their badge of legitimacy, their disinterested helper and adviser, their training ground in the arts of diplomacy—the visable sign of their stake in the community of nations.

There are still some who dream of an international Utopia in which a few civilized states could use their power to settle the affairs of the world, much as the major powers of Europe did in the century after the Congress of Vienna. But we should remember that when the rule of the concert of Europe finally fell apart, world war ensued. This happened in great part because, in large areas of the world, the international order of the nineteenth century did not redress grievances but merely submerged them—until in our own century they erupted in revolution and world war.

The world law we should seek should be different. It should extend impartially to white and black, north and south, old and new. It will still be imperfect; it will still depend for its effectiveness on the willingness of the stronger nations to put their power at its service. But it should embrace in a spirit of equality all the races and cultures of the world—and it should address itself to the real troubles of mankind: poverty, inequality and the deprivation of rights. If it does, it will surpass even the hundred years' peace of the Congress of Vienna which was based on the subjection to impotence of half the world's peoples.

It must be acknowledged that the United Nations is not yet the agency to achieve such a world order based on the law of the Charter; thus far the members lack the common will to make it so. But, despite its weaknesses, it is still the best instrument for peace and law among nations that our unruly world possesses. There is no realistic alternative to it. No country in its own interest can afford to slacken its support of this world organization, or to diminish its efforts to make the United Nations more effective. All nations must rededicate themselves to the unfinished task of perfecting the world organization so that in our time, and to insure our survival, it will extend the benefits and restraints of the rule of law to all peoples and to all governments.

What Justice Benjamin Cardozo said of the law is equally true of the United Nations: "The inn that shelters for the night is not the journey's end. The law, like the traveler, must be ready for tomorrow."

PROBLEMS OF TREATY-MAKING COMPETENCE

REFLECTIONS ON THE VIENNA CONVENTION OF 1969 AND THE *KAMIAR* CASE

SHABTAI ROSENNE*

The Vienna Convention on the Law of Treaties of May 23, 1969,[1] devotes no less than five articles directly to different aspects of the relationship between the treaty-making authority as a matter of domestic[2] law and government and the treaty as a transaction between two States governed by international law.[3] This testifies to the intricacy of the question. The relevant provisions of that Convention (see Appendix to this article, p. 135) are found in Article 7, on full powers; Article 8, on subsequent confirmation of an act performed without authorization; Article 27, on internal law and observance of treaties; Article 46, on provisions of internal law regarding competence to conclude treaties; and Article 47, on specific restrictions on authority to express the consent of a State.[4]

The complexity of this issue is illustrated by the fact that the International Law Commission between 1962 and 1966 devoted in all no less than 29 meetings in whole or in part, and the Vienna Conference 17 meetings in whole or in part, to the elaboration of these texts, not counting the work of their respective drafting committees; furthermore, they excited much governmental comment in the preparatory phases. An indication of the difficulties can be seen in a procedural discussion at the Commission's 780th meeting in 1965, when there was little consensus on the question whether what were then Articles 4 and 31 (now Articles 7 and

---

* Ambassador, Deputy Permanent Representative of Israel to the United Nations. The views expressed herein are personal to the writer

46) were two sides of the same coin (as we thought) or two separate and distinct topics. Much, indeed, can be said for both points of view.

All the major issues which the Vienna Convention attempts to solve on the international level arose in one form or another as a matter of domestic law in the *Kamiar* case.[5] This exercised the Jerusalem District Court twice and the Supreme Court of Israel three times, in its capacity of High Court of Justice and of Court of Criminal Appeals, between 1965 and 1968 and led to a series of significant judicial pronouncements.

The principal issues in this aspect of *Kamiar* are easy to state. On a request by the Swiss Government for his extradition on the basis of the Israel-Swiss Extradition Treaty signed at Berne on December 31, 1959 (the existence of a treaty providing for reciprocity being a pre-condition for extradition, under the law of Israel), Kamiar contended that no such treaty was in existence since *(a)* the Ambassador of Israel at Berne was not legally empowered under the law of Israel to sign the treaty, and *(b)* by the law of Israel the Government was not empowered to ratify it.

In preliminary proceedings, the President of the Jerusalem District Court, Judge Baker, upheld the objection to the Ambassador's power to sign the treaty, but rejected the objection to the Government's power to ratify it, holding also that the ratification cured any antecedent defect. In the view of many, the decision on the second objection rendered unnecessary the decision on the first point. Moreover, that part of the decision, aside from certain aspects of the reasoning on the second objection, caused considerable confusion in the conduct of the country's foreign relations since it seemed to endorse doubts on the extent to which the Government acting alone could exercise the treaty-making power. Doubts of this nature had been expressed both in the Knesset and in the literature, and they were fed, naturally, by the fact that the Government's position was based on its interpretation of an admittedly unclear legal situation which had not, prior to *Kamiar,* been tested judicially.

According to figures given during the hearing, up to the date of the case something like 780 treaties had been concluded by Israel since May 15, 1948, of which 356 had been subject to ratification and the remainder had entered into force on signature. The latter category included some of the most important treaties to which the country was a party, among them the General Armistice Agreements of 1949 and the Agreement of March 30, 1950 with the United Kingdom for the settlement of financial matters outstanding at the end of the Mandate for Palestine.

Since the decision on the signature issue did not affect the disposition of the case (and if relevant could always have been tested on appeal should extradition have been ordered), many felt that all that part of the judgment was an unnecessary *obiter dictum*—a view echoed in some of the pronouncements in the Supreme Court. As for the Supreme Court itself, in effect and by implication it overruled the lower court's decision on the first objection and upheld it on the second. In that respect the Supreme Court has created more certainty regarding the exercise of the treaty-making power in Israel than had previously been the case. However, the multiplicity of opinions rendered by the Justices, and the difficulty of establishing clearly the *ratio decidendi* of the Court itself, detracts from the jurisprudential value of this case, by inducing a philosophical confusion on why the position is what it is. Nevertheless, the embarrassment caused by the District Court's decision in the end converted what should have been a routine case into one of high constitutional importance.

The percentage of Israel's treaties requiring ratification given above appears to be considerably higher than the current international average which seems to be about 25 per cent, and is closer to the average in the inter-war period, which was just over 50 per cent. This is probably explained by the fact that as a new State which in the area of State succession and treaties adopted the so-called *tabula rasa* approach, Israel has probably had to conclude a large number of treaties which are of a type normally requiring ratification, such as extradition treaties, which older States had concluded in an earlier period.

The general significance of the question raised in *Kamiar* for the constitutional law of Israel was acknowledged by the Supreme Court which took the unusual step of determining the case through a Bench composed of five instead of the customary three Justices. The case relates exclusively to the domestic law of Israel, and any tendency to read more into it should, as always when domestic judgments deal with legal problems having some affinity with rules of international law, be resisted. Nevertheless, considerable though perhaps not always fully relevant use was made of the final report of the International Law Commission on the law of treaties (though not of its antecedents), and there is a remarkable parallelism between some of the underlying considerations which led to the final consensus embodied in the Vienna Convention and some of the reasoning of the Israeli judges to uphold the validity of the treaty. In each case the end-product—the text of the Convention and the upholding of the validity of the treaty—embodies a healthy entelechy itself giving expression to two time-honored factors of particular value and proven worth in public law and administration, namely: *quieta non movere* abd *ut res magis valeat quam pereat*. That these two end-products prevailed over strongly held minority views reflecting fundamental differences of ideological approach to basic questions of State-organization evidences the strength of the public interest—on the international level as on the national level—in the stability, at least relative, of international treaty law and of the national foreign policy as it is enshrined in treaties to which the country is a voluntary party.

The five articles of the Vienna Convention are deliberately spread through the three principal parts of that instrument. Articles 7 and 8 belong to Part II (more particularly, Section 1 on the conclusion of treaties) which deals in essentially formal terms with the conclusion and entry into force of treaties. Article 27 belongs to Part III on the observance, application and interpretation of treaties, and more particularly to Section 1 on the observance of treaties. It raises many problems only indirectly of concern to us here, and therefore beyond this mention no further reference will now be made to it. Articles 46 and 47 are placed in Part V, on the invalidity, termination and suspension of the operation of treaties (more particularly in Section 2 which covers the invalidity of treaties as a matter of international law).

Except for Article 27, which was introduced by the Vienna Conference (after the International Law Commission had in effect decided that an article on that question was not necessary, the rule being self-evident), these articles were similarly located by the International Law Commission, an aspect of which no specific mention is made in *Kamiar*. This matter of the *location* of the articles is not one of intellectual sophistication (in the earlier stages what is now Article 8 was placed in part of what became Article 47). Adopting the classification of Chief Justice Agranat in *Kamiar*, this is not for the general law of treaties a procedural-external question but one of an integral-material character. As such it reflects above all on the addressees of the rule, and the consequences of its observance or non-observance, and it follows that if the issues of the *Kamiar* case are considered in the context of the law of treaties, domestic or international, there is obvious advantage in placing the relevant rules in a similar classification, so far as possible.

The Vienna Convention is not an abstract statement of general principles of international law but an agreed statement of ground rules of international conduct positively applicable *only* in the mutual relations of States. As is stated in Article 1, "The present Convention applies to treaties between States"—a formula corresponding exactly (with drafting changes only) with the carefully drawn general limitation on the scope of the draft articles postulated by the International Law Commission.

Thus in all cases the addressees of the rules contained in the Vienna Convention are States—and more particularly the States which are parties to treaties to which the Vienna Convention applies.[6] What is more, for the rules to apply, a minimum of two States on "opposing" sides are needed—which was not the case in *Kamiar*.

An attempt will now be made to enumerate the various principal phases in the currency of an international treaty, with special reference to the consequences of the non-observance of the rules laid down.

The first stage is the formation of the will of the State to be bound by the treaty. Obviously and in the nature of things this is an internal matter and not one of international law. Furthermore, whatever the manner in which that will is formed and whatever the requirements of domestic law which have to be observed, the carrying out of that intent is exclusively a matter for the executive branch. Here international law and diplomatic practice, outwards looking and with the object of facilitating the transaction of international business and stabilizing international relations, provide a number of non-obligatory guidelines for the international procedures to be followed in the negotiations. But looking inwards, the domestic law is relevant at this stage only as a matter of the relations between the executive branch and its constituency. The substantive provisions regarding *what* may be done relate to the formation of the will of the State, not to the manner in which the treaty is negotiated. It is believed that on the whole this aspect escaped notice in *Kamiar* (except perhaps obliquely, in the merits phase in the Jerusalem District Court, in connection with the highly technical examination of the relationship between the stipulations of the Extradition Treaty regarding evidence and those of the Extradition Law and the general rules of evidence in Israel on the same matter).

The second phase consists in the negotiation and establishment of the text of the treaty giving expression to the will of the States concerned. Whatever be the requirements of domestic law, they are irrelevant on the international level in this phase. Here the dominant, though not the exclusive, role is played by the diplomatic service, which enjoys a recognized standing in international law and relations.[7] There is a presumption—that the higher the diplomatic rank[8] that members of the diplomatic service are endowed with, the stronger their representative capacity for their State, and this embraces fairly extensive general powers to carry forward negotiations for a treaty, although not necessarily to give final and binding expression of the consent of their State to be bound by the treaty. Where this presumption does not operate, for whatever reason, the production of an instrument of full powers may be required. Whether or not such an instrument is in fact produced *and examined*, a statement to that effect is almost invariably included in a formal treaty, and generally the instrument of full powers of the re-presentative of the counter-party is archived with the party's original copy (in the *alternat*) of the signed treaty.

The examination of the instrument in those circumstances is exclusively formal and is limited to establishing that it was signed by one of the three dignitaries who by general international law are exempt themselves from producing full powers—the Head of State, Head of Government or Minister for Foreign Affairs— and relates to the treaty about to be signed. It does not go so far as to inquire into whether the signatory of the instrument was himself authorized to perform that act.

That problem has two aspects, the one formal and the other material. A formal defect can be cured by subsequent confirmation by a competent authority of the State. This is a commonsense rule reflected in Article 8 of the Vienna Convention, and substantively its application in the Jerusalem District Court rendered unnecessary all that Court's investigation into the legal aspects of the signature of the Israel-Swiss Extradition Treaty. There is some discussion in *Kamiar* of the implications of the production and examination of the instruments of full powers, but the reader may gain an impression that the courts were not familiar with the real techniques of these procedures.

Of course, already at that stage the material question of the power of the Government concerned to bind itself by the proposed treaty, or more frequently the extent of the Government's power to enter into the proposed commitment, will form part of, if not the negotiation proper, then at least its preparatory stages, and the elementary requirement of good faith obliges the negotiators to indicate to each other any unusual specific legal requirements of their domestic law relevant to the negotiation, or at least not to conceal them. When the Israeli and Egyptian delegations arrived at Rhodes in February 1949, the first matter examined by the U.N. Mediator, Dr. Ralph Bunche, was whether they were each em-powered, both as a matter of domestic law and as one of formal full powers, to conclude an armistice agreement which entered into force on signature.[9] (The fact that agreements enter into force on signature need not today cause any serious concern, and the word "plenipotentiary" is something of an ornamental overstatement, though not without its conveniences. There is no difficulty in telexing the most complicated texts from one end of the world to the other in a very short time. This is frequently done, and domestic and international political processes have shown that they are quite capable of adapting themselves to these new diplomatic and administrative techniques).

In the case of a non-urgent treaty like an extradition treaty, the text of which is normally elaborated by experts, with only nominal participation of diplomatic personnel, the complete text is carefully studied before instructions are given to an ambassador to sign it, and production of an instrument of full powers will invariably be required.[10] In matters such as extradition, judicial assistance, reciprocal exemption from taxation, or in general where the subject matter of the treaty is governed by domestic law and is thus subject as a matter of application to close scrutiny by the domestic courts, no Government can give absolute answers to questions put to it by the co-contracting party. But if it has acted in good faith and the treaty subsequently becomes inapplicable through changes in the law or in judicial interpretation of the law—*tant pis*! The reasons were well explained by Justice Halevi in *Kamiar*. Judicial evolution of the domestic law may well produce a fundamental change of circumstances or lead to an impossibility of performance, both of which are recognized grounds of treaty termination.

If any consequences of an international character follow from failure to require the production of an instrument of full powers in cases where it would, in accordance with usual practice, be appropriate to require one, it is doubtful if they would in any way affect the legal situation produced by the formal conclusion of the treaty on the international plane. In international law, there is a presumption that once concluded, a treaty remains in force unless its validity is impeached on one of the recognized grounds, a rule now embodied in Article 42 of the Vienna Convention. The invalidity of the treaty is not dependent upon external factors relating to the manner of its conclusion, but upon material factors relating to non-compliance with known provisions of domestic law. If it is accepted that the purpose of these provisions of the Vienna Convention is to establish presumptions for determining where the risk lies in cases of absence of a request for the production of an instrument of full powers, surely this is to leave the realm of the law of treaties for that of State responsibility.

The opinion is sometimes expressed that the conclusion of a treaty *ultra vires* the domestic law gives rise to a case of State responsibility, but does not affect the international validity of the treaty. Beyond saying that there seems to be excessive simplification in this way of presenting the matter, we would wish to reserve our position on this issue. Nevertheless, there is attraction in the conclusion that the *only* consequence of failure to require the production of an instrument of full powers, formal though that requirement may be, is that the State adopting such a nonchalant attitude has to take the consequences, whatever they are. At all events, those consequences can only run as between State and State.

The third phase in the currency of a treaty consists in the expression of the consent of the State to be bound by the treaty—the actual conclusion of the treaty. How this consent is expressed—by signature alone, by signature followed by ratification, acceptance or approval, by accession or by any other method—depends upon the terms of the treaty or the understandings reached between the parties in the course of the negotiation, or even upon indications appearing in the instruments of full powers (very frequently the requirement of ratification is formally stipulated in the instrument of full powers, especially for conferences at which multilateral treaties are to be drawn up).[11] If signature alone is to have this effect, the third phase becomes merged in the second.

Domestic law has nothing to do with the *manner* in which that final consent is expressed on the international level: for its part international law has no mandatory rules on the subject, particularly no residuary rule giving preference to ratification or to signature alone, in cases where the treaty itself is silent and it is not possible to establish the intention of the negotiating States *aliunde*.[12] Therefore, if there are mandatory rules of domestic law on the topic, international law has no difficulty in absorbing them. On the other hand, domestic law is decisive on the question whether and how the treaty is to be ratified on the domestic level. Ratification as an international act and ratification as an internal act are quite distinct as acts, although their general characteristic is similar and there is a real inter-connection between them. The International Law Commission formulated the position in the following terms:

> "The word 'ratification', . . . is used here and throughout these draft articles exclusively in the sense of ratification on the international plane. Parliamentary 'ratification' or 'approval' of a treaty under *municipal* [*sic.*; italics in original] law is not, of course, unconnected with 'ratification' on the international plane, since without it the necessary constitutional authority to perform the international act of ratification may be lacking. But it remains true that the international and constitutional ratifications of a treaty are entirely separate procedural acts carried out on two different planes.[13]

As in the case of the second phase, Article 7 of the Vienna Convention deals with the formal authority to perform the international acts of ratification (and its equivalent); and, as before, it is couched in the form of non-obligatory guidelines for the States. Following the same approach, Article 8 again supplies a commonsense rule for the cure of formal defects, although its employment is likely to be rarer in the cases where the signature has to be followed by some other act to express the final consent of the State to be bound by the treaty, than in the cases where the signature alone is sufficient for this purpose. In the first case, the legal consequences of signature are minimal.

When a treaty includes the standard formula—as does the Israel-Swiss Extradition Treaty—that it "shall be subject to ratification and shall enter into force on the date of the exchange of the instruments of ratification," it formally acknowledges the two procedures of ratification just described. The word "ratification" as it first occurs refers only to ratification as a domestic procedure: the word as it occurs in the phrase "instruments of ratification"—in a broader and more accurate context—refers to the international procedure which normally consists of the exchange or deposit of the instruments of ratification in the manner agreed between the parties. As Justice Cohn, who emphasized the intention of the parties (which is always the dominant element in treaty interpretation) stated in *Kamiar,* "obviously it was the intention of the parties that the Swiss ratification would be done in the form which the Swiss Government had in mind and that the Israel ratification would be done in the form which the Israel Government had in mind." On the other hand, it was equally the intention of the parties that the exchange of the instruments would be done in the customary international diplomatic form, and would be evidenced by the usual protocol or other identification. Israel domestic law could have nothing to say about that. Sometimes a broader formula is found, such as in the present treaty—"shall be ratified by the signatory States in accordance with their respective constitutional processes." An example is Article 110 of the United Nations Charter. There is no form of international control over the constitutional processes of States—indeed the concept of domestic jurisdiction would preclude this—and these words, which may serve some political purpose, are legally self-evident and therefore pleonastic. The only way in which a State can ratify a treaty is in accordance with its constitutional process in the first domestic step, and the notification of that act to the other States concerned, in accordance with the established international practice. Furthermore it is only with the completion of the international procedure that the treaty is "ratified" as a matter of international law.

It is usual in the negotiating phase, especially for a bilateral treaty, for the States to acquaint themselves with the nature of the domestic constitutional ratification processes. It is immaterial whether this is done as part of the negotiation, or independently of the negotiation through diplomatic channels, or through private legal advisers retained by Governments to assist them in matters of local law. At all events, it is unlikely that a Government be under any obligation in normal cases to advise its co-contracting party of the nature of the domestic ratification process in general (subject to the general duty of good faith in negotiation). But in cases where several procedures exist in the domestic system, it may be necessary for the negotiation to clarify which one is intended. The relatively new international practices of "approval" and "acceptance" are a reflection of these differences in domestic practices.[14] Furthermore, it may be mentioned that the old idea, that there should be perfect reciprocity (mirroring the principle of the equality of States) regarding the ratification procedures to be observed by each of the contracting parties, is no longer followed.

A question on which there was a serious division of judicial opinion in *Kamiar* was the following: When the Israel Extradition Law, 5714–1954,[15] speaks of "an agreement providing for reciprocity . . . between Israel and the State requesting . . . extradition," does that mean an agreement according to international law or one according to the law of Israel? In Israel, as elsewhere, such a question, apart from its legal interest, possesses important ideological undertones, and caution is required in answering it. It raises the spectre of the well-known doctrinal controversy between the various dualist and monist schools regarding the relationship between the international and the internal legal systems. One may assume that the legislature—any legislative body—would not lightly or unthinkingly take a position on a question of this nature, and that the attribution of a position only through the processes of interpretation of a statute would place the legislative organ in an unlikely posture. In passing the Extradition Law the Knesset was concerned with specifying precisely the parties to and some aspects of the contents of an extradition agreement requisite for the invocation of the Law. This shows that whatever agreement is reached, and howsoever it is reached, it must be one which is binding on Israel and upon the other State concerned, by whatever legal system is acknowledged by them both to be applicable in the circumstances. Instinctively one would assume this to be international law, but there is no reason of principle why this should not be some other system of law (including Swiss law or Israeli law) if that is what the parties wanted. Be that as it may, the Israeli legislature certainly had in mind that, apart from the material law governing the substance of the agreement, the law of Israel would be controlling as regards the procedure by which Israel would become a party to that agreement. This, it may be assumed, is about as far as anybody went in thinking about the legal system to govern the agreement.

That being so, it is submitted that a tenable answer to this problem of interpretation would be that it be according to both systems of law, depending upon the forum in which the question were raised. It is not believed that such a vacillating answer would cause any prejudice to any party's case in domestic litigation, for reasons more fully explained in the course of this article.

* * * * *

Kamiar exhibits some confusion between the external evidence that the Government of Israel thought and maintained that it had concluded a valid international agreement, and the internal-material proof that an agreement had been concluded according to the law of Israel (at least as the Government interpreted it). Amongst elements of the former, reference was made to various notices (a matter to which we will return later) published in the *State Records* on behalf of the Ministry for Foreign Affairs regarding the signature and entry into force of this treaty, the text of which was also published in the *State Records*[16], and to the registration of the agreement by Israel (Switzerland was not a member of the United Nations) with the Secretariat of the United Nations, in accordance with the obligations undertaken in Article 102 of the Charter.[17] The relevance of these acts in domestic litigation in which the other contracting State was not a party is negligible and oblique; and the Judges were obviously justified in not regarding them as in themselves decisive of the question of the validity of the treaty-making acts according to the law of Israel, but only as an indication of what the Government of Israel thought to be the legal position. On the other hand, had the issue arisen in any litigious relationship between Israel and Switzerland, whether in international or in domestic law, acts of this nature could well have been of considerable if not of decisive importance, if only on the basis of the well established principles of good faith and fair dealing—as valid in international law and relations as in private law and relations.

Amongst the elements of internal-material proof, reliance was placed upon a series of public notices duly published in the *State Records* concerning the exercise of the treaty-making power in general and upon specific and previously unpublished formal decisions of the Government regarding the conclusion and ratification of the treaty in question.

The validity of those acts raises no question whatsoever of international law, but the issue of domestic law that arose in *Kamiar* concerned in fact their validity.

One of the "red herrings" drawn across the trail in this case was the possibility of a contradiction between the rules of international law regarding the representation of the State for the purposes of treaty-making and those of internal law. The curious argument was advanced that, since according to international law *only* the Head of State is recognized for this purpose, no validity can attach to international acts in which the Head of State did not participate. This is not a rule known to any international lawyer, and all the judges who dealt with the point rightly gave it short shrift. As has been seen, international law has no mandatory rules on the subject—indeed, this would constitute a quite unwarranted interference in the internal affairs of States—but has only a series of rebuttable presumptions. Least of all does it determine that *only* the Head of State can exercise the representative functions associated with the conclusion of international treaties. It contents itself with laying down a number of non-obligatory general guidelines, themselves based on wide international experience and practice, all of which are couched in extremely flexible terms. Fundamental in all of this is the assumption that full faith and credit must be given to the official statements made by a State's diplomatic representatives of the intention of their State. The subjects of international law are not minors or other persons whose interests require complete protection by the law in regard to everything which they do. As a colleague in the International Law Commission was wont to say, "les Etats ne sont pas des bèbès."

The International Law Commission, on which such heavy reliance was placed by many judges in *Kamiar*, approached the question of the influence of the domestic law not in terms of making the international *validity* of the treaty depend upon compliance with the internal law (a phrase which is somewhat broader than "constitutional law," which had earlier been current in this context), but of making certain non-compliance with the internal law invocable as a ground for the invalidity of the treaty in international law. This is now embodied in Article 46 of the Vienna Convention. In thus introducing the concept of the voidability of the treaty in these circumstances, the Commission broke with the famous Harvard Research,[18] with much *doctrine*,[19] with the Havana Convention on the Law of Treaties of 1928[20] and with an earlier approach adopted by the Commission itself in 1951,[21] when it had followed the lead of its first Special Rapporteur, the late Professor Brierly.[22] The intervening Special Rapporteurs, the late Sir Hersch Lauterpacht[23] and Sir Gerald Fitzmaurice[24] had shown, in their lengthy investigations, the weaknesses and instability which would ensue from too close an adherence to this rigid constitutionalist theory in this aspect of the international law of treaties. This opened the way to the compromise proposed by Sir Humphrey Waldock,[25] and despite prolonged discussions and many governmental observations on the topic, the final proposals of the International Law Commission, those repeatedly cited in *Kamiar,* had been adopted on both readings in the Commission with no negative votes (although with a few abstentions in each case), and in the Vienna Conference no attempt was made to go back to the full constitutionalist theory as it had been adopted by the Commission in 1951, or to annul the compromise.[26]

By dealing with this substantive problem in the context of the invalidity of the treaty, the Vienna Convention places the matter within a complex framework. That context determines at one and the same time who may invoke this invalidity, the procedure by which it may be invoked, on what grounds, and what responses may be made. To revert to terminology employed elsewhere in this paper, it determines the addressee of the rule which the Convention lays down, the material conditions for its exercise, and the modalities by which the rule may be invoked. The addressee, of course, is the State whose internal law has not been complied with, and is only that State. In fact, this limitation is written into the text of Article 46, as it had been likewise written into the International Law Commission's text of Article 43 as adopted in 1966. None of the opinions delivered in *Kamiar* which dealt with this aspect appear to have captured this nuance, although Chief Justice Agranat, doubting whether Article 43 was really applicable when the plea of invalidity was raised by "a person who is not a party to the treaty," pointed out that the case did not raise the question of the validity of the Extradition Convention in international law.

The invocation of this ground of invalidity by the addressee may be met with the contention that by reason of its conduct it must be considered as having acquiesced in the validity of the treaty[27]—a general rule which here parallels the more specific rule of Article 8 of the Vienna Convention previously cited. Furthermore, even if the ground for the invalidity is upheld, the consequence may relate not to the whole treaty but to the affected clauses only, if they are separable from the remainder.[28] Above all, the grounds cannot be effectively invoked by a State unilaterally, but only in accordance with the procedure laid down in Articles 65–68 and the Annex of the Vienna Convention. That means that the invalidating procedure operates only as between

States which are parties to the treaty. The International Law Commission, and following it the Vienna Conference, did not consider the hypothesis which lay at the root of the *Kamiar* case, that the invalidity would be invoked in domestic litigation by a private litigant who was not in any way party to the treaty in question, and was even a national of the only State entitled to invoke the invalidity under international law. (The significance of this is that it excluded the element of diplomatic protection leading to possible international litigation at a later stage.) Accordingly, it is doubtful if anything in the work of the International Law Commission is directly relevant to the problem which the learned judges faced in *Kamiar*. To that extent, therefore, reliance on the Commission, whether by the parties (although everything would be grist to their mills) or by any member of the Court, however interesting a consideration, may have been misplaced. Indeed, the exceptional quality of the rule laid down in Article 46 is stressed by the negative formulation of the rule in its "unless . . ." clause.[29]

In principle, what has been said regarding Article 46 of the Vienna Convention is applicable to Article 47. That article, in the form adopted by the Vienna Conference, raises other problems which are not relevant to this paper.

* * * * *

In 1953 the United Nations Secretariat, acting on the basis of a general recommendation made by the International Law Commission, published a volume entitled *Laws and Practices concerning the Conclusion of Treaties*.[30] This too was to play quite a significant role in *Kamiar*. It contains (p. 67) a memorandum dated 11 March 1951, from the Government of Israel. That memorandum, which started with a statement that the law in Israel was then characterized by the absence of clear and specific provisions of a legislative character, went on to explain in some detail why in the Government's view the Government alone was competent to exercise all the treaty-making power in Israel, and that the intervention of neither the President of the State nor the legislative body, the Knesset, was a positive requirement of the law.[31]

One of the questions which was considered in *Kamiar* was the effect of that publication on the validity of the treaty. This meant, of course, its validity as between Israel and Switzerland, as a matter of international law. This is an aspect of the "manifest" character of the rule of the domestic law, to which Article 46 of the Vienna Convention specifically refers. Justice Cohn put it this way: "In the absence of evidence to the contrary and in the absence of any other authoritative international publication, it must be assumed that States which negotiate with Israel for the conclusion of treaties obtain their information on the treaty-making processes under the laws in force in Israel, including the processes of ratification, from the information conveyed to the United Nations by the Government of Israel."[32] A similar position was adopted by other judges who expressed themselves on this aspect.

As far as we are aware, this is the first occasion on which a domestic court has considered the validity o a construction placed by a Government on its domestic law in an international document of this character. In international litigation it is quite common for international tribunals to take into consideration the legal position thus stated by litigating Governments, and there is a certain amount of international jurisprudence on the topic.[33] This innovation by the Israel courts is a welcome development. It must be stressed, however, that it imposes an extremely high standard of care on the authors of such documents, as well as on the courts themselves, to indicate with maximum accuracy whether in the circumstances the document is being written *de lege lata* or *de lege ferenda*. This *caveat* is entered because of the frequency with which the United Nations as well as other international organizations invites Governments to submit comments on questions of a legal nature.

The relevance of the 1951 memorandum to the problems of Israeli constitutional law which the judges faced in *Kamiar* was indirect. However, written and published independently of any litigation, it gave notice to the whole world of what the Government believed to be the law of Israel. To that extent it embodied the essence of the contentions of the Government in *Kamiar*. *Grosso modo* the construction there advanced, or at least the operative conclusions, were upheld in the Supreme Court (and partly upheld in the District Court), thus terminating one phase of what has already been a prolonged internal controversy in Israel.

* * * * *

The President of the Jerusalem District Court reached his decision essentially on the basis of his reading of the internal law of Israel, and it will be obvious by now that we share the view that in this way the problem was correctly "sited." Because of this approach, too, his references to international law sources were incidental and minimal, a disciplined approach which is very frequently more satisfactory than attempts to solve private law problems on the basis of the doctrines of public international law when those doctrines are at most of marginal interest.

In upholding the power of the Government to ratify the treaty, the ratification curing antecedent defects in the signature (a natural consequence having regard to the nature of ratification today in the case of a treaty which specifically provides for a connection between its ratification and its entry into force),[34] Judge Baker added that it was immaterial whether the Government knew or not of the earlier imperfection. "Determining, in my opinion, was the Government's intention, and I have not the slightest doubt that it intended to ratify the treaty and that it did so." In so deciding, the learned President was disposing of an argument which had been advanced on behalf of Kamiar.

This *dictum* has been criticized on the ground that it deals too laconically with the question of why under the law of Israel this should be so.[35] The criticism relates to the issue of the nature of ratification in modern law—a matter which had also been considered by the International Law Commission.

Whatever the historic origins of the institution of ratification, today it is not the signature which is ratified, or some other act of an agent of the sovereign, but the treaty itself, as indeed was pointed out by the Justices of the Supreme Court who found it necessary to deal with the point— particularly the Chief Justice. In that sense, neither on the plane of international law nor, it is submitted, on the plane of internal law, does the ratification of a treaty resemble in any way the ratification of the act of a person's agent, so that analogies or interpretations derived from domestic law conceptions of agency are unconvincing. The domestic act of ratification of a treaty is not characteristically different from the international act, from which, indeed, it cannot be conceptually dissociated. Both on the international plane and on the domestic plane, when a treaty enters into force on ratification, the formation of the will of the State to be bound by the treaty is expressed *only* through the processes of ratification. It is for that material reason that the validity of the antecedent acts is irrelevant, just as the acts themselves are irrelevant for this purpose. Only an express provision on the domestic law could justify any other conclusion.

* * * * *

A somewhat technical point of domestic law—but one of potential significance to private litigants—relating to the promulgation of the treaty in the *State Records* produced some contradictory judicial pronouncements in *Kamiar*.

It is the practice of the Israel Ministry for Foreign Affairs to publish, over the signature of its Director General, a notice regarding the signature and the entry into force for Israel of all international treaties to which Israel is a party. This publication is effected in *Yalkut ha-Pirsumim,* or Collection of Notices, the principal section of the *State Records (Reshumot).* After the treaty has entered into force, the text of the treaty together with a Hebrew version is published in the *Kitvei Amana,* or Treaty Series, section of the *State Records.* Article 34 of the Interpretation Ordinance provides *inter alia* that a copy of the *State Records* containing a public notice constitutes for every court and for every purpose *prima facie* evidence of its contents. On that basis it was argued that the notices regarding the entry into force of the Extradition Treaty were conclusive of the validity of the treaty.

None of the judges was prepared to accept this contention in the form in which it was presented by the representatives of the Attorney-General, and on the whole the fundamental reasons, relating to the proper construction of the Israeli statute, are convincing, especially since, as we have seen, the validity of an international treaty must depend in part at least upon proper compliance with the domestic law, and a Government notice in the *State Records* cannot in all fairness be held to establish that which has to be proved.

However, discussion on this issue evidences some confusion between the notices published in the *State Records,* the formal status of which derives from a provision of the domestic statute law, and what is called a Foreign Office Certificate, which has found its way into Israeli domestic litigation practice from its common law (Anglo-American) origins.[36] This, as is known, is a document by which the executive, normally the Minister for Foreign Affairs, brings a state of fact to the notice of the Court in a form which is conclusive, not in the sense that it itself dictates the decision to the Court, but in the sense that the Court is not entitled to go behind the certificate in determining the facts upon which its decision is to be given. There can be detected in the opinions in *Kamiar* a view that the notices published in the *State Records* are the equivalent to Foreign Office Certificates in the technical sense. With respect, that view is erroneous.

The conclusion can be accepted that the notice in the *State Records* did no more than convey that the Government of Israel regarded itself as bound by the Convention, as Justice Cohn put it, and in most cases, where no substantive issues of Israel law arise, that would be conclusive. The same information could have been conveyed by a Foreign Office Certificate had one been asked. It is doubtful whether the notice, or the certificate, which is external evidence and not material proof, could go beyond that.

Since what was at issue in *Kamiar* was the notice in the *State Records* and not a Foreign Office Certificate in the strict sense, it follows that what was contended by the parties or stated by the judges on the matter of Foreign Office Certificates was *obiter*. In some of the opinions of the Supreme Court, doubt is expressed as to whether the Foreign Office Certificate can be employed to answer questions concerning the validity of international treaties or regarding the content or application of international law in general. Insofar as concerns the *fact* that Israel is a party—in the international law sense—to any international treaty, there can be little doubt that a Foreign Office Certificate would be a proper vehicle to bring the facts to the notice of a court, at all events if for some reason no notice has appeared in the *State Records*.[37] That is a question of fact. On the other hand, the question of domestic law relating to the validity of the acts by which the treaty was concluded cannot be disposed of only by a Foreign Office Certificate.

During the International Law Commission's second reading of the draft articles on the law of treaties, the question arose of whether to include a provision obliging the parties to a treaty to give it publicity in their territories. However, the Commission did not pursue this idea after Sir Humphrey Waldock pointed out that the proposal raised wide issues concerning the responsibility of a State for the application of treaties to which it is a party, and thus came within the sphere of the topic of the responsibility of States which was a separate item on the work program of the Commission, and which had been formally excluded from the law of treaties.[38] Discussion of the issue of promulgation in *Kamir* suggests that the Commission did well to omit this matter, for obviously it would have raised a host of problems, not only of State responsibility, which could not be approached with any degree of confidence without further detailed study of all the implications of the promulgation of treaties in the different legal systems.

* * * * *

The pleas raised by Kamiar and his Counsel and their disposal opened the way to a full airing in the Supreme Court of an issue which has aroused very strong emotions in Israel ever since the establishment of the permanent organs of the State, especially the Presidency and the Knesset. That issue concerns the respective rights and duties of the President, the Government and the Knesset in the treaty-making power. In brief, as explained, the Government has taken the view that *de lege lata* the whole of the treaty-making power is vested exclusively in the Government, without the interposition of either the President or the Knesset (beyond the Knesset's normal powers to debate the Government's policies and actions), and from that point of departure it has opposed any attempt to change the situation. Against this it has been argued either that this is not the position *de lege lata*, or, if it is, that this is an unsatisfactory position which must be changed, on the one hand by introducing the Presidency for the performance of the ceremonial acts connected with treaty-making and on the other by associating the Knesset with the substantive process by which the will of the State to be bound by the treaty is formed. This issue has been raised in the Knesset itself several times, the most famous instance being on the occasion of the ratification of the Convention for the Prevention and Punishment of the Crime of Genocide.[39] Formal attempts to change the law have all been abortive.

Commenting on this the President of the District Court said:

> ". . . [I]t seems to me desirable that the matter should be settled by a law of the Knesset, since the road leading to [the] conclusion [that the Government possesses the exclusive power to ratify treaties] is tortuous, and recourse must be had to British law and to the Mandate [for Palestine], which is not appropriate for the status of Israel as an independent State . . . Furthermore, it is in my view undesirable that there should remain any doubt in Israel or abroad as to the authority which in Israel is authorized to make and ratify treaties between Israel and foreign States."

The view that it was necessary to have recourse to British law and the Mandate in order to reach the conclusions reached in the Supreme Court was contested. Justice Cohn expressly said:

> "These are the consequences of the establishment of the State and its authorities and of the constitutional structure as laid down in the Law and Administration Ordinance [5708–1948] and the Transition Law [5709–1949]. I do not share the view that as far as concerns the general and fundamental powers of the organs of the State it is either appropriate or necessary to fall back on interpretations of the corresponding powers vested in British or mandatory authorities in the pre-State epoch and to construct some theory of inheritance from them. Indeed, in that approach there is something distasteful."

Be that as it may, there is little doubt that as a result of *Kamiar*, whatever uncertainty may have existed *de lege lata* has been set at rest, both for the Government of Israel and for other Governments which may wish to enter into treaty relations with it.[40]

On the major doctrinal division between the learned judges who tried this case, we share the views of those who think that as far as concerns the domestic litigation in the domestic courts, only the law of Israel is relevant. This seems to be the construction of international law itself, which will assume the validity of a treaty according to the domestic law and leave it to the State affected to raise the matter with its co-contracting party, if it is so inclined. The object of the exercise in interpretation in *Kamiar* was an Israel statute. It would be an unusual example of legislative technique if the legislature intended words used in an Israeli statute to be interpreted exclusively by reference to international law, at all events when the context in which the words were used in the statute did not absolutely impose such a *renvoi*. There is sufficient in the decisions in *Kamiar* to show that this is not a necessary conclusion from the language of the Extradition Law.

In the same way that the question reduced to its fundamentals did not raise any question of international law, it likewise avoided the issue of the relationship between international law and the domestic law of Israel. On this point, several references can be found in *Kamiar* to the following principle of interpretation: that it is presumed that the legislative organ does not intend to enact that which is incompatible with the international obligations of the State, so that, unless absolutely unavoidable, domestic statutes are to be interpreted in a manner that will not conflict with the international obligations of the State. That position did not arise in this aspect of *Kamiar,* since the Extradition Law, as stated, refers simply to an agreement between Israel and the State requesting the extradition, not to an international agreement. Moreover, it was implicit in the Extradition Treaty that its application comprises judicial application, and this of necessity embraces the possibility that the courts might find it impossible as a matter of law to apply the Treaty.

In reality this important case, which constitutes a significant milestone in the evolution of that limited aspect of Israeli constitutional law which concerns the formal treaty-making power, has the minimum of significance for the evolution of international law, for which it hardly constitutes any authority. On the other hand, given current interest in the codification of the international law of treaties, it constitutes a vivid illustration of the frontiers of that branch of international law, and the extraordinary parallelism between the international and the domestic law of treaties. It goes further, and brings out the risks of drawing analogies too hastily from one legal system to the other.

APPENDIX

Relevant articles from the Vienna Convention on the Law of Treaties

Article 7. Full powers

1. A person is considered as representing a State for the purpose of adopting or authenticating the text of a treaty or for the purpose of expressing the consent of the State to be bound by a treaty if:
   (a) he produces appropriate full powers; or
   (b) it appears from the practice of the States concerned or from other circumstances that their intention was to consider that person as representing the State for such purposes and to dispense with full powers.

2. In virtue of their functions and without having to produce full powers, the following are considered as representing their State:
   (a) Heads of State, Heads of Government and Ministers for Foreign Affairs, for the purpose of performing all acts relating to the conclusion of a treaty;
   (b) heads of diplomatic missions, for the purpose of adopting the text of a treaty between the accrediting State and the State to which they are accredited;
   (c) representatives accredited by States to an international conference or to an international organization or one of its organs, for the purpose of adopting the text of a treaty in that conference, organization or organ.

Article 8. Subsequent confirmation of an act performed without authorization

An act relating to the conclusion of a treaty performed by a person who cannot be considered under article 7 as authorized to represent a State for that purpose is without legal effect unless afterwards confirmed by that State.

Article 27. Internal law and observance of treaties

A party may not invoke the provisions of its internal law as justification for its failure to perform a treaty. This rule is without prejudice to article 46.

Article 46. Provisions of internal law regarding competence to conclude treaties

1. A State may not invoke the fact that its consent to be bound by a treaty has been expressed in violation of a provision of its internal law

regarding competence to conclude treaties as invalidating its consent unless that violation was manifest and concerned a rule of its internal law of fundamental importance.

2. A violation is manifest if it would be objectively evident to any State conducting itself in the matter in accordance with normal practice and in good faith.

Article 47. *Specific restrictions on authority to express the consent of a State*

If the authority of a representative to express the consent of a State to be bound by a particular treaty has been made subject to a specific restriction, his omission to observe that restriction may not be invoked as invalidating the consent expressed by him unless the restriction was notified to the other negotiating States prior to his expressing such consent.

NOTES

[1] For the full text and notes on its history, see Rosenne, *Law of Treaties: Guide to the Legislative History of the Vienna Convention* (1970).

[2] The expressions "domestic" or "internal" as the antithesis of "international" are to be preferred to the misused and ambiguous "municipal"—a term redolent of the administrative system of Imperial Rome, quite inappropriate to legal terminology current in the modern independent State-system.

[3] Vienna Convention, Article 2 (1) (*a*).

[4] Article 27 was inserted by the Vienna Conference (originally as Article 23 [*bis*]). The others were previously Articles 6, 7, 43 and 44 of the International Law Commission's final draft articles, and are so cited in *Kamiar* (next note). For the draft articles, see U.N. document A/6309/Rev.1. Reprinted in Yearbook of the International Law Commission (hereafter Yearbook), 1966–II, at 172. Also in the work quoted in n. 1 above.

[5] *Attorney-General v. Kamiar*, 51 *Pesakim Mehoziim* 13 (1966); 20 *Piskei-Din* 608 (1966); 57 *Pesakim Mehoziim* 184 (1967); 22 *Piskei-Din* 132 (1968). A consolidated English translation by the present writer will be published in a forthcoming volume of *International Law Reports*. Citations in this article are taken from that translation.

[6] This unusual wording is adopted because of the provisions on non-retroactivity contained in Articles 4 and 28 of the Vienna Convention.

[7] Cf. for permanent diplomatic missions, Article 3 of the Vienna Convention on Diplomatic Relations of 1961; for temporary diplomatic missions, see the Convention on Special Missions, opened for signature by General Assembly resolution 2530 (XXIV) of December 8, 1969, *passim*; and for permanent missions to international organizations, see Articles 7 and 14 of the draft articles on Representatives of States to International Organizations adopted on first reading by the International Law Commission in 1968, doc. A/7209/Rev.1; and Articles 53, 58 and 88 on the same topic adopted on first reading by the Commission in 1970, doc. A/8010/Rev. 1. Israel has ratified the Vienna Convention of 1961 and is a signatory of the Special Missions Convention of 1969. It has recently (January, 1971)

commented favorably on the latest proposals for Representatives of States to International Organizations, which the International Law Commission hopes to complete this year. In all cases these provisions are supplemented by Article 7 of the Vienna Convention of 1969. International law, in this general context, accords a special place to the Head of State, Head of Government and Minister for Foreign Affairs.

[8] This writer was once engaged in some delicate negotiations involving strenuous intercontinental travel, in the course of which his instrument of full powers was badly damaged, being engulfed in some spiritous odor. When asked to produce it, he persuaded the other side that diplomats having the personal rank of Ambassador Plenipotentiary and Extraordinary did not really need to produce an instrument of full powers, especially when they were negotiating at the invitation of the other side. This was accepted. The present author does not wish to condone what was probably a breach of diplomatic propriety and has always been grateful to his opposite number for acquiescing in this doubtful law. He does not advise others to emulate him as a general practice! The problem does not arise in respect of persons accredited *en poste* to another capital; their *lettres de créance* would normally be sufficient at least to negotiate a treaty, an aspect which appears to have escaped notice in *Kamiar*. At all events, despite an unusually voluminous citation of documents, Ambassador Linton's *lettres de créance* are not mentioned.

[9] For further details see Rosenne, *Israel's Armistice Agreements with the Arab States* (1951), p. 30, n. 1.

[10] This writer recollects one instance where, when he was legal adviser of the Ministry for Foreign Affairs, he happened to be in a foreign country on official business when the Israeli Ambassador received instructions to sign a treaty subject to ratification, which both Governments regarded as urgent. The other Government refused to accept an undertaking by the Ambassador and by the present writer that the instrument of full powers had been signed and was in the diplomatic pouch, but insisted on waiting either until it was physically produced or until telegraphic full powers had been received before proceeding to the signature. This is probably a matter of local chancellery practice—chancellery practice being notoriously conservative.

Nevertheless, it is a fact that save perhaps in cases of exceptional urgency, even when a bilateral treaty is subject to ratification and regardless of the terms of the full powers, instruction to sign is normally only given to an Israeli plenipotentiary after close study by the competent authorities. Signature, even in these circumstances, is by no means merely a ceremonial act. Different considerations may apply as regards multilateral treaties, depending upon the circumstances of their conclusion.

[11] Vienna Convention, Articles 11–17 inclusive.

[12] This aspect was thoroughly clarified in the course of the codification of the law of treaties. See the work cited in n. 1 above, on Articles 12 and 14 of the Vienna Convention.

[13] Paragraph (1) of the Commentary on Article 11 adopted in 1966, n.4 above. Reflected in Article 2 (1) (*b*) of the Vienna Convention.

[14] There is considerable discussion in *Kamiar* on whether the Hebrew word *ishur* in the 1949 constitutional legislation is the equivalent of "ratification" or of "approval." I have little hesitation in stating that for a long time the Ministry for Foreign Affairs assumed it to be the equivalent of "ratification" in the current international law sense. It was only later, when the necessity for greater precision in terminology was clarified and the Government had at its disposal appropriate linguistic bodies with more clearly defined competences, that the neologism *ishrur* came to be used for "ratification", leaving *ishur* for "approval." As the internal law of Israel stands at present, there is no substantive difference between the procedures in either case. The necessity for precision in language

derived above all from the need to produce accurate Hebrew versions of treaties to which Israel is a party. In many bilateral treaties, the treaty is signed in Hebrew as well as in some other language. If Israel treaty practice itself at present is indifferent as regards the procedures of ratification, acceptance or approval, this may have considerable significance for the other party.

[15] 8 Laws of the State of Israel, authorized translation from Hebrew, p. 144.

[16] 10 Kitvei Amana, No. 309, at 391.

[17] 377 United Nations Treaty Series, 305.

[18] Research in International Law under the auspices of the Faculty of the Harvard Law School. Draft Convention on the Law of Treaties. Reporter, James W. Garner. 29 American Journal of International Law, Special Supplement 653 (1935). See Article 21.

[19] See survey in Holloway, *Modern Trends in Treaty Law* (1967), particularly at 123 ff. In Israel, this view of the law underlies the works of Ruth Lapidoth, especially her *La conclusion des traités en Israël* (1962). In the Jerusalem District Court proceedings in *Kamiar*, the President complained that this work had not been cited before him by either party. Nevertheless Judge Baker disagreed with certain views expressed by that learned author. More surprising, perhaps, is the fact that apparently neither party in the Court proceedings drew attention to the observations of the Government of Israel, in its *note verbale* of 15 May 1964, on Article 31 of the draft articles on the law of treaties adopted by the International Law Commission in 1963, corresponding to Article 46 of the Vienna Convention. Implicit in those observations, which related exclusively to matters of drafting (and which contained a specific reference to extradition treaties) was acceptance of the approach which had been adopted by the Commission in 1963. The text of that note appears as No. 12 of the Annex to the Commission's Report for 1966, n. 4 above. For the 1963 text, see document A/5509, also in *Yearbook*, 1963–II, 187 at 190.

[20] 22 American Journal of International Law, Supplement 138 (1928). See Articles 1 and 6.

[21] Article 2 of the articles tentatively adopted by the Commission in 1951 provided that a treaty becomes binding in relation to a State by signature, ratification, accession or any other means of expressing the will of the State, in accordance with its constitutional law and practice through an organ competent for that purpose. Document A/CN.4/L.28, *Yearbook*, 1951–II, at 73.

[22] [First] Report on the Law of Treaties, document A/CN.4/23, *Yearbook*, 1950–II, 223 at 230. The opinion has since been expressed, however, that on that occasion the Commission had apparently acted less on the basis of legal principles than on a belief—subsequently proved to have been mistaken—that States would not accept any other rule. Sir Humphrey Waldock, Second Report on the Law of Treaties, document A/CN.4/156, Article 5, Commentary, paragraph 3, *Yearbook*, 1963–II, 36 at 42. This view was adopted by the Commission in paragraph (3) of its final commentary on Article 43 as adopted in 1966.

[23] In Article 11 of his [First] Report on the Law of Treaties, Sir Hersch proposed voidability at the option of the party concerned in case of disregard of the limitations of its constitutional law and practice. Document A/CN.4/63, *Yearbook*, 1953–II, 90 at 141. This is close to the final text of Article 46, which is not, however, limited to "constitutional law and practice."

[24] Third Report on the Law of Treaties, Article 10, Document A/CN.4/115, *Yearbook*, 1958–II, 20 at 33.

[25] See n. 22 above.

[26] All the amendments submitted at Vienna related essentially to the drafting. An

attempt to introduce the "Head of State rule" contained in an amendment by Iran (A/ CONF.39/C.1/L.280) was withdrawn by its sponsor in the Committee of the Whole (43rd meeting) after the discussion had shown that there was no support for it. For the Israel reservation on the final text of Article 43 in the Committee of the Whole, see United Nations Conference on the Law of Treaties, *Official Records,* volume I at 464. At the final vote in the 18th plenary meeting, the present text of Article 46 was adopted by 94 votes (including Israel) to none, with three abstentions. That seems to be a decisive indication of the current direction of State practice.

[27] The basis of the rule that a party is not permitted to benefit from its own inconsistencies is the principle of good faith and fair dealing (*allegans contraria non audiendus est*). The Commission wisely refrained from introducing even into its commentaries such technical terms of domestic law as the "estoppel" of the common law or the "forclusion" of the civil law. In some of the earlier texts of the Commission a word which looks like a French word appears—*preclusion*—but it is found in none of the standard dictionaries of the French language. Cf. discussion at the 891st meeting of the Commission in 1966.

[28] Vienna Convention, Article 44.

[29] Note the exchange of views between the Algerian and Italian members of the Commission, MM. Bedjaoui and Ago, at its 841st meeting in 1966. At the Vienna Conference, an amendment by Venezuela to word this clause positively (A/CONF.39/C.1/L.252) was withdrawn by its sponsor at the 43rd meeting of the Committee of the Whole.

[30] United Nations Legislative Series, document ST/LEG/SER.B/3.

[31] That memorandum was prepared at the time by the Ministry for Foreign Affairs, in consultation with the Attorney-General's office.

[32] Incidentally, the Swiss Government has drawn precisely the opposite conclusions. In 1927 it did not approve the idea of the League of Nations' making a comparable collection of the provisions of national constitutions, on the ground that such a publication might be taken to imply, in certain cases at least, that a Government could plead non-observance of some part of its constitution in order to avoid an international obligation to which it had subscribed. "The result would be that, in order to make sure of the absolute regularity of the undertaking to be concluded, each of the contracting States would have to ascertain whether the other State or States had proceeded correctly in accordance with their own constitutional law, and they would consequently be entitled to raise objections if, in their opinion, some formality had been omitted. The security of international relations seems to render it necessary for us to maintain the principle, which today is generally admitted, that agreements ratified by the executive power of a State are definitely binding on the latter." League of Nations, Committee of Experts for the Progressive Codification of International Law, Report . . . on the Questions which appear Ripe for International Regulation (Questionnaires Nos. 1 to 7), document C. 196. M. 70. 1927. V. [C.P.D.I.95(2)], at 253. A similar view was expressed by the representative of Switzerland at the Vienna Conference. According to Ambassador Ruegger at the 43rd meeting of the Committee of the Whole, conclusion of a treaty *ultra vires* would raise a question of State responsibility. As stated, the present writer wishes to reserve his position on that point.

[33] For an example, taken from the jurisprudence of the International Court of Justice, see *Fisheries* case, I.C.J. Reports [1951] 116 at 134 (interpretation of Norwegian law contained in a memorandum to the Secretary-General of the League of Nations, in connection with the codification of a topic of international law).

[34] "The ratification of a treaty which provides for ratification . . . is an indispensable condition for bringing it into operation. It is not, therefore, a mere formal act, but an act of vital importance." The International Court of Justice in the *Ambatielos* case (jurisdic-

tion) [1952] I.C.J.28, at 43. This concept of the function of ratification is as applicable in domestic law as it is in international law.

[35] Blum, *The Ratification of Treaties in Israel,* 2 Israel Law Review 120 at 127 (1967). That case-note deals only with the decision of the President of the District Court, not with the case as a whole, or with the whole problem of ratification of treaties in Israel.

[36] Rosenne, *Teudot Misrad ha Hutz* [Foreign Ministry Certificates], 11 ha Praklit 33 (1955). The practice there laid down has been consistently followed by the Israel Foreign Ministry. It may be doubted whether a Foreign Office Certificate would be issued if the effect would be merely to duplicate something already easily available elsewhere, such as in the *State Records.* Since Foreign Office Certificates are in principle conclusive, unless deliberately worded in a temporizing way, care is normally exercised to issue one only when there is no other way in which the question of fact can be satisfactorily elucidated for the Court.

[37] In our article cited in the previous note, we have given some examples to show where Foreign Office Certificates should have been used for the purpose of establishing that Israel was *not* a party to various international treaties in which the Court was interesting itself. There is some Anglo-American authority for the proposition that the Certificate can be used to establish the fact that the Government considers itself a party to a given treaty.

[38] Sir Humphrey Waldock, Fifth Report on the Law of Treaties, document A/CN.4/177, Section entitled New Proposal—Entry into force of treaties within the territories of the parties. *Yearbook,* 1965–II, at 57. For the reservation of State responsibility, see Article 73 of the Vienna Convention.

[39] See *Divrei ha Knesset (Official Records* of the Knesset), vol. 3, p. 313, (1949). The Chief Justice referred in his opinion to the Israeli instrument of ratification of that Convention, cited from Blix, *Treaty-Making Power* 202 (1960). Copies of the instrument would, of course, have been available from the Archives, and since the citation in Blix is only partial, we have given the full text in our translation of *Kamiar,* above, n.5.

[40] In connection with this view of the treaty-making authority in Israel, it should be emphasized that it has as its counterpart the axiom that an international treaty duly ratified and brought into force is not *per se* part of the law of the land, let alone the supreme law of the land, and that if the proper application of the treaty requires changes in the internal law, those changes have to be enacted in an appropriate manner. This is because the constitutional law and practice of Israel establish the Knesset as the legislative authority, and the Government has shown no wish to exercise legislative powers in the guise of the treaty-making power, except of course where that form of legislative power is conferred upon it by statute, as is the case under the Extradition Law. Questions relating to that aspect arose in the merits phase of *Kamiar,* in both instances, but space prevents us from examining them here. As a general proposition it can be stated that on the matter of the relationship between international treaty law and the internal law of Israel, Israel follows the British rather than the American constitutional practice and precedents.

THE NORTH SEA CONTINENTAL SHELF CASE*

Isi Foighel**

I. History

On September 28, 1945 President Truman issued a proclamation in pursuance of which the United States declared that it had an original, natural and exclusive right to the continental shelf off its shores known to contain exploitable natural resources. The continental shelf constitutes the part of the seabed which slopes from the coast—or, more accurately, from the outer boundary of the territorial sea—towards the deep ocean to the sudden drop in the seabed which usually occurs in ocean depths of approximately 200 metres.

The U.S. declaration—though not the first official statement to display an interest in the riches of the seabed and the subsoil—became the starting point of a number of similar declarations from other coastal states. There is very little doubt that the concept that a coastal state has a sovereign right, independent of other states, to its continental shelf dates back to the initiative of President Truman.

It was to be expected that the extension of the territorial rights of a state to its continental shelf would give occasion to a delimitation between opposite states (*e.g.* Great Britain and Denmark) and adjacent states (*e.g.* The Federal Republic of Germany and Denmark). With regard to delimitations of this nature, the Truman Proclamation merely stated that as far as the United States were concerned such boundaries shall be determined "by the United States and the state concerned in accordance with equitable principles".

In 1951 the matter of the interpretation of the right of a state to the continental shelf was referred to the International Law Commission[1].

The International Law Commission dealt with the question of the continental shelf during the years 1951/1956 and prepared a set of

---

* Judgment by the International Court of Justice of February 20, 1969
** Professor of Law, University of Copenhagen

draft articles which contained not only a definition of the term but also a precise formulation of the sovereign rights of a coastal state to the exploration and exploitation of the natural resources in its shelf. It furthermore established that the boundary between opposite states and adjacent states shall be determined by agreement between the states concerned. In the absence of agreement and unless another boundary line is justified by special circumstances, the boundary shall be the median line every point of which is equidistant from the nearest points of the baselines from which the breadth of the territorial sea of each state is measured.

A perusal of the International Law Commission discussion discloses that the problem of delimitation caused difficulties. Many possibilities were discussed, among them that of leaving it to the parties to reach an agreement, possibly with recourse to a judicial body. This thought was dropped, however, and when in 1953 the problem of delimitation had been submitted to a committee of experts which proposed the application of the principle of equidistance as answering the purpose, agreement was reached on the formulation cited above.

On the basis of the ILC proposal, the United Nations summoned a Conference on the Law of the Sea in 1958 where the draft articles were submitted to the member governments. The Conference which took place in Geneva adopted four Conventions on the Law of the Sea, one of them on the Continental Shelf.

Article 6 of the Continental Shelf Convention provides as follows:

1. Where the same continental shelf is adjacent to the territories of two or more states whose *coasts are opposite each other*, the boundary of the continental shelf appertaining to such states shall be determined by agreement between them. In the absence of *agreement*, and unless another boundary line is justified by *special circumstances*, the boundary is the *median line*, every point of which is equidistant from the nearest points of the baselines from which the breadth of the territorial sea of each state is measured.

2. Where the same continental shelf is adjacent to the territories of two *adjacent* states, the boundary of the continental shelf shall be determined by agreement between them. In the absence of *agreement*, and unless another boundary line is justified by *special circumstances*, the boundary shall be determined by application of *the principle of equidistance* from the nearest

points of the baselines from which the breadth of the territorial sea of each state is measured.[2]

The Convention was signed by 46 states (amongst others Denmark, the Netherlands and Germany) and has subsequently been ratified by 39 states (including all the Great Powers, Denmark and the Netherlands). Germany, however, has not ratified the Convention, although the Federal Republic, in a Government Declaration of 20 January, 1964, signified its intention to produce a bill in the near future to enable it to become a party to the Geneva Convention and to ratify the Convention. Nevertheless, no such bill has ever been passed.

II. The Relationship between the Parties

On 27 June 1963, the Danish Ministry of Public Works issued a Decree concerning the question of delimitation of the continental shelf appertaining to Denmark which contained, *inter alia,* the following provision:

> 2. (2) The boundary of the Continental Shelf in relation to foreign states whose coasts are opposite the coasts of the Kingdom of Denmark or which are adjacent to Denmark shall be determined in accordance with Article 6 of the Convention. Accordingly, in the absence of any special agreement the boundary shall be the median line, every point of which is equidistant from the nearest points of the baselines from which the breadth of the territorial sea of each state is measured.

In October, 1964 negotiations were opened with Germany on the delimitation between the two countries of the continental shelf areas situated in the immediate vicinity of the coast. On the 9th of June, 1965 the boundary was determined by a Treaty to extend from the outer boundary of the sea territory to a point approximately 50 kilometers out in the North Sea. The terminal point of the partial boundary was equidistant from Denmark and the Federal Republic.

The parties, however, failed to agree on the further demarcation of the boundary. Denmark contended with reference to Article 6 of the Geneva Convention that the Boundary should be the equidistance line; the Federal Republic contended that it was not bound by the equidistance line and that the boundary should be drawn according to other principles. During these negotiations, a shelf demarcation was proposed in accordance with the principle of an equitable division of the shelf area in proportion to the length of the North Sea coast-lines of the two parties; another proposal was that the shelf might be divided into sectors. At this stage, the Federal Republic also proposed that the parties might abstain from a division altogether and establish a joint exploitation of possible resources.

The negotiations between the Federal Republic and the Netherlands were not much different. The Netherlands, too, claimed that the principles embodied in the rules of the Geneva Convention were applicable and in the course of tripartite negotiations in 1966 it became clear that a deadlock had been reached.

III. The Court Proceedings

On 2 February 1967, Special Agreements were concluded between Denmark and the Federal Republic and between the Netherlands and the Federal Republic to submit the dispute to the International Court of Justice and an agreement was furthermore reached about the questions to be submitted to the Court.

In their Special Agreements, the parties requested the Court to decide what principles and rules of international law were applicable to the delimitation of the areas of the continental shelf in the North Sea which appertain to each of the parties beyond the partial boundary determined by the Treaty of 9 June, 1965 (relating to the areas in the vicinity of the coast). The Special Agreement also stated that the parties shall determine the delimitation by agreement in pursuance of the decision requested from the International Court of Justice.

During the court proceedings Denmark and the Netherlands contended that the respective boundaries should be drawn in conformity with the principles and rules of international law expressed in paragraph 2 of Article 6 of the Geneva Convention: in the absence of agreement between the parties and as no special circumstances exist in the North Sea, the boundary shall be governed by the principle of equidistance. Alternatively, Denmark and the Netherlands contended that the boundary must be determined on the basis of the exclusive rights of each party over the continental shelf adjacent to its coast and on the principle that the boundary is to leave to each party every point of the continental shelf which lies nearer to its coast than to the coast of the other party.

Although these two contentions are identical in content the sources of law upon which they rely differ widely. The first presupposes the existence of a rule of international law, which in 1958 found its codification in Article 6 of the Geneva Convention. The second contention derives the principle of proximity (the principle of equidistance) from the very right to the continental shelf which had been acknowledged by all states a long time before the Geneva Convention. It relies upon the conception that if states find support in international law for a claim to the continental shelf adjacent to the coast, the shelf must then belong to the state which lies nearer to this shelf than to any other state.

The Federal Republic contended that the delimitation of the North Sea continental shelf between the parties shall be governed by the principle that each coastal state is entitled to a just and equitable share of the shelf and that the criterion of equidistance—not only as formulated in the Geneva Convention but generally—does not form part of international customary law. Although the rule embodied in Article 6 of the Geneva Convention might apply, "special circumstances" do exist in the North Sea—owing to the "bend" in the German North Sea coast—which rule out the application of the criterion of equidistance. The contention also stated that the equidistance method is not applicable unless it has been established through agreement or arbitration. As the principle of equidistance does not achieve a just and equitable apportionment of the North Sea areas between the parties, the latter should agree on a division to that effect, based on criteria relevant to the special geographical configuration of the North Sea.

IV. The Judgment

Both the Danish/Netherlands and the German contentions were rejected in the Judgment of the Court of 20 February, 1969 by 11 votes to 6.

The Court did not feel able to accept the contentions of Denmark and the Netherlands holding that it had not been proved that the principle of equidistance forms part of customary international law; nor could the Court accept that the state concerned should have a right to the shelf area nearer to it than to any other state. The fact that a shelf area had to be adjacent to a coastal state in order that the state might exercise sovereign rights over it did not necessarily imply that the shelf area must be the one situated closest to the state.

The rejection of the contention of the Federal Republic was due to the reluctance of the Court to accept the theoretical foundation of the German concept of the rights of a state to the continental shelf. According to the Judgment, the continental shelf is not an area which must be apportioned between states. The shelf, *i.e.* the area which constitutes a natural prolongation of the land territory, belongs to a state *eo ipso*. The only problem which may arise is that of delimitation in cases where the shelf areas of two or more states overlap. The method of solving this problem of delimitation differs in principle from the problem which occurs when an undelimited area is to be divided—or apportioned—among several states.

The Judgment finds the following two rules applicable to the North Sea continental shelf:

> 1. Delimitation is to be effected by agreement in accordance with equitable principles, and should take into account all the relevant circumstances, in such a way as to leave as much as possible to each party all those parts of the continental shelf that constitute a natural prolongation of its land territory into and under the sea, without encroachment on the natural prolongation of the land territory of the other.
> 2. If, in the application of these criteria, the delimitation leaves to the parties areas that overlap, they should be divided between them in agreed proportions or, equally, unless they decide on joint jurisdiction, use, or exploitation of overlapping zones.

In the opinion of the Court, this rule is in conformity with the Truman Proclamation of 1945, the provisions of which contain the very elements reflected in the Judgment, namely that the boundary shall be determined by an agreement which should be governed by the principle of equity. The Judgment likewise establishes that there is no single criterion of delimitation the application of which is obligatory under all circumstances.

The Court thus does not commit itself as to where the boundary shall be drawn between the parties. The rules laid down by the Court are chiefly procedural. The parties must attain a delimitation by agreement which becomes an accepted rule of international law regardless of its content, provided it is not contrary to the rights of a third state.

In accordance with established practice in other cases[4] the Judgment contains directions as to how the present problem between the parties should be solved. The Judgment specifies the following factors to be taken into account by the parties in their negotiations, "(1) The general configuration of the coasts of the Parties, as well as the presence of any special or unusual features; (2) so far as known or readily ascertainable, the physical and geological structure, and natural resources, of the areas involved; (3) the element of a reasonable degree of proportionality, between the extent of the continental shelf areas of the coastal state and the length of its coast measured in the general direction of the coastline, account being taken of the effects, actual or prospective, of any other continental shelf delimitations between adjacent states in the same region."

The enumeration of these factors in the Judgment does not prevent the parties from invoking other elements in their negotiations as being of significance in the delimitation. The factors are in the nature of a framework for the negotiations but it is left to the parties themselves to reach an understanding as to whether, and to what extent, the individual elements shall form part of the ultimate solution. None of the parties can enforce a boundary determined by these factors unless the other party accepts it or it is established, possibly through another court case, that the boundary or the criterion invoked by one of the parties is in conformity with equitable principles.

The Judgment was presumably phrased in this manner because the Court considered the parties as still conducting negotiations which merely have broken down temporarily. The Court viewed its task in the matter as part of these negotiations, claiming in its conclusion that it has aided the parties in overcoming the obstacle which held up the negotiations. That the negotiations when resumed will be intricate— probably more so than foreseen by any of the parties—is simply the consequence of the Court's rejection of the contentions of both parties.

In consideration of the criticism which has been raised against the Court from many quarters to the effect that it seeks to evade complex questions, it is only fair to point out that in the present Judgment the International Court of Justice has given a direct answer to the question which the parties agreed to submit to it.

In the part of the Judgment which enumerates the factors to be taken into account in the coming negotiations, the Court seems to have stepped beyond the contentions of the parties. The fundamental appropriateness of this procedure is a moot point since it is the contentions of the parties which define the questions subject to controversial negotiations between them in the course of the written and oral proceedings. However, the Judgment is clearly in conformity with precedent[5, 6]. It may be presumed that in exceeding the contention, the Court endeavored to aid the parties in reaching a solution which it deemed appropriate in the present case.[7]

V. The Premises of the Judgment

The Court's conception of recognized international law obviously concurs with the positivistic school which maintains that no state can be bound by the rules of international law unless the state itself has expressed its recognition of those rules. A state may, of course, interpret the rules of international law in a manner which seems to it most appropriate[8]. A case in point is the Royal Decree of the Government of Denmark of June 7, 1963 on the principle of equidistance. This interpretation is not binding upon other states. Autointerpretation confers no right to autodecision unless it is recognized that the interpretation is in conformity with customary international law.

It has been generally assumed that the rules of customary law also require the presence of both an objective and a subjective element, namely that a course of conduct must have been adopted uniformly, consistently and over a considerable period of time and that it must express a legal obligation.

The question the Court was requested to decide was whether a rule of customary law has been created through the development of the rules on the continental shelf as crystallized in Article 6 of the Geneva Convention.

At this point, the Judgment touches on the important and central issue in modern international law, namely whether multilateral treaties in themselves are evidence of the existence of customary international law. A notable example—but not unique—is the Hague Convention of 1930 on the Conflict of Nationality Laws which the International Court of Justice accepted as customary law in the Nottebohm case even if none of the parties to the dispute had ratified the Convention.[9]

The law-creating character of a multilateral treaty may manifest itself in several ways. First, the treaty may be a codification of general customary law and thereby serve the purpose of defining a previously accepted but imprecise rule of international law. Second, a miltilateral treaty may form part of the progressive development of international law. Finally, if acceded to by a large number of states, the treaty may prove the existence of a uniform and constant usage displaying thereby a legal obligation.

The Judgment strongly dismisses the argument that the Geneva Convention of 1958 may have declared the customary law in the issue under consideration.

With regard to the view that the equidistance principle might have achieved the stature of customary international law prior to 1958— and that the Geneva Convention, in conclusion, constituted a codification of a pre-existing rule of law—the Judgment stated that the rule found its first embodiment in juridical doctrine through the International Law Commission. The recommendation of this Commission relating to the principle of equidistance took place—on an experimental basis *de lege ferenda* or as a proposition to the states without the Committee assuming the role of law-makers. Although the proposal of the International Law Commission was adopted practically unaltered by a large number of States at the Geneva Conference in 1958, its adoption does not constitute evidence that the participant states were of the opinion that the rules of the Convention amounted to a codification of previously established customary international law.

The Judgment equally rejects that the Geneva Convention purported to create a new rule of law by formulating a principle of equidistance binding on states other than those which had ratified the Convention. This statement was based on the following considerations:

First, the principle of equidistance is merely proposed in Article 6 as a subsidiary delimitation method to be effected by "agreement". Second, Article 6 contains a provision to the effect that another boundary than the equidistance line may be justified by special circumstances. While emphasizing that it does not attempt to interpret the meaning of this rather fluid exception to the main rule, the Judgment finds that the ambiguity of the exception throws doubt on the character of the equidistance principle as a precise rule of law. Third, the Judgment stated that Article 12 of the Geneva Convention conferred a right upon the states to enter a reservation to Article 6 when becoming parties to the Convention. The argument appears to be that it would be illogical to establish a rule which as customary international law would be binding on every state, at the same time permitting a state not to be bound by it. All this is incompatible with the opinion that the treaty is evidence of the intention that Article 6 should be binding on other states than those which ratified the Convention.

In its reasoning the Court conforms with the traditional concept of international law in presupposing that to declare customary law, a treaty must signify either in its preamble, its text or in its *travaux préparatoires* that its draftsmen purported it to create a rule of customary law.

By refusing to accept that the Geneva Convention has declared customary law, the Court had to reject the arguments put forward by Denmark and the Netherlands that the rule of equidistance is subsidiary to the rule that delimitation shall be determined by agreement. Nor has the Court committed itself in relation to the argument between Denmark and the Netherlands that the rule of special circumstances as formulated in the treaty is an exception to the principle of equidistance, an exception which may be interpreted as a rule of law, by its nature of restricted content. Eventually, the Court has found it necessary to disregard a number of treaties which were undeniably of a declaratory nature;

for instance, the Convention on the Law of the Sea which was also adopted by the Geneva Conference in 1958 and which states in its preamble that it is "generally declaratory of established principles of international law".

In addition, the Judgment stated that the number of States which have become parties to the Convention is insufficient in itself as evidence of the existence of an accepted customary rule of international law on the mandatory character of the equidistance principle. The Court was aware of the fact that other reasons than disagreement relating to the content of a treaty may cause the failure of a state to ratify it but—says the judgment—these reasons are speculative whereas the facts (*i.e.* the nonratification) are real.

Nearly all the dissenting judges repudiated this argument. Some forty states is a sizeable number when account is taken of all the states which do not, within a span of years or ever, have an interest in the rules of law relating to the continental shelf. Also, other states which did not ratify the Convention accepted the principle of equidistance. Finally, all the Great Powers and the different political systems were represented in the Convention. It is necessary to award The Convention, stated the dissenting judges, the stature of a declaration of international customary law. It would be appropriate here to draw attention to another interesting aspect of the Geneva discussions, *viz.* that the equidistance principle encountered practically no censure from the delegates present and that there was nothing to indicate that disagreement on this specific point might have caused the states to abstain from ratifying the Convention.

The Judgment, however, finds added support for its argument in the circumstance that state practice subsequent to the Convention has been insufficient as evidence that accepted international law was created by virtue of the number of states which became parties to the Convention.

The Judgment does say—that it is not an indispensable requirement that a course of conduct must have been followed over a considerable period of time to have generated a rule of customary law. However it is necessary that within the period in question—short though it may be—state practice should be both extensive and virtually uniform in the sense that the potential rule must occur whenever the proper occasion arises and manifests a legal obligation.

No evidence to that effect has been put forth by Denmark or the Netherlands. The two countries have merely cited 15 cases in which states since 1958 have delimited their continental shelves according to the equidistance principle. Either Denmark or the Netherlands were parties to four of these cases which were consequently of doubtful value as precedents. It may be presumed that in some cases the equidistance principle was applied only because the states concerned were or shortly became parties to the Convention and not because the equidistance principle attained the status of customary law. As regards those states, which were not parties to the Convention, there was not a shred of evidence that they considered the equidistance principle to be a rule of customary international law. They may simply have applied the method because it was convenient.

The Court attached great importance to the fact that Denmark and the Netherlands have provided no evidence that the practice of states— amounted to an *opinio juris sive necessitatis*. The Court followed the view adopted by the Permanent Court of International Justice in the *Lotus case*,[10] namely that the abstinence of a state from acting does not allow one to infer that the state felt an obligation to abstain.

Even if it was not self-evident that the requirements of proof of *opinio juris sive necessitatis* by abstention must correspond to evidence of the positive conduct of a state, it should be acknowledged that the mere fact that the Court demanded evidence of a subjective *opinio juris* is in conformity with the traditional conception of international law. The question which hitherto has caused doubt—and according to the Judgment will continue to do so—is the nature and strength of the evidence required to prove that a state is acting under legal obligation. Normally, states hesitate to make superfluous declarations and evidence of the *opinio juris* which motivated a specific conduct will practically always be a matter of opinion or an interpretation of the act in question. It would be appropriate at this point to follow the example of Judge Sørensen in his dissenting opinion by citing Sir Hersch Lauterpacht on this issue:

> Unless judicial activity is to result in reducing the legal significance of the most potent source of rules of international law, namely, the conduct of states, it would appear that the accurate principle on the subject consists in regarding all uniform conduct of Governments (or, in appropriate cases, abstention therefrom) as evidencing the *opinio necessitatis juris* except when it is shown that the conduct in question was not accompanied by any such intention.[11]

Finally, the Judgment stated that the majority of the cases of delimitation cited by Denmark and the Netherlands as instances of the application of the equidistance principle did not apply to the present case because the delimitations concerned were median lines between opposite states and not lateral delimitations between adjacent states as in the present case. The Court stressed that a median line delimitation between opposite states will always be an equitable shelf division whereas this is not so in a delimitation between adjacent states governed by the equidistance principle. Moreover, a delimitation between opposite states will always allot each of the states a shelf area which is a natural prolongation of the land territory, whereas a delimitation between adjacent states, *e.g.* where the coastline is concave such as between Denmark, the Federal Republic and the Netherlands, may allot a state a shelf area which more accurately could be described as the natural prolongation of the neighbouring state.

This conclusion is hard to understand. The question of identifying the natural prolongation of the land territory has no immediate answer, depending as it does on whether the delimitation is to be at right angles to the coast or otherwise. It applies equally to opposite states and adjacent states that delimitation problems arise solely where areas overlap, namely where either state may be justified in considering the disputed area a natural prolongation of its land territory.[12] In order to establish juridically a distinction between the median line principle and that of equidistance the Court has had to disregard cases (*e.g.* the Gulf of Bothnia) in which a boundary line constitutes a delimitation between adjacent states and, simultaneously, between opposite states. Also a median line delimitation between opposite states may produce inequitable results as it was shown during the proceedings by means of the median line delimitation of the Baltic between the Federal Republic and Denmark which awards the Federal Republic a shelf area considerably larger than that of Denmark. Finally the rule of equidistance is warranted by a number of conventions on related subjects such as the Conventions on the Territorial Sea, on the Contiguous Zone, and on the Conservation of certain Fishery Zones. These Conventions make no distinction regarding delimitations between adjacent states and between opposite states. Both delimitation methods express precisely the same principle, namely that the areas which lie nearest to a state belong to it.

By its reasoning, the Court made it plain that it did not concur in the fundamental aspect of the contention of Denmark and the Netherlands that the state practice since the Truman Proclamation in 1945 was an expression of how they have interpreted the declaration that delimitation shall be made in accordance with equitable principles.

In itself the term is of little value insofar as it is impossible to derive from it the meaning of the abstract equitable principle. Does it imply that states of the same size shall be entitles to equal shares of continental shelf in proportion to their own size? If so, how is the area concerned to be measured? By population? Or land area? Or coastline? Does the equitable principle mean that a continental shelf must be divided equally according to requirements or possibilities of exploitation? The precise definition and formulation of the general juridical principles as embodied in the Truman Proclamation were the very questions referred to the International Law Commission for consideration. As mentioned earlier, the Commission had the problem under consideration for years after which, having obtained statements from governments and cartographic experts, it rejected a number of delimitation proposals and decided to adopt the principle of equidistance as the only applicable principle of delimitation which consequently was accepted by the Geneva Convention.

This signifies that the equidistance principle was quite widely accepted and that no other principle has attained general theoretical and political recognition. Inherent in the equidistance principle is the traditional concept of equity based upon proximity, as acknowledged in international law. A state situated nearer to certain areas than other states acquires the title to those areas. This definition of the rule of equity in which the decisive factor is that of equidistance is not a mere invention on the part of the International Law Commission. It has found expression in a number of divisions relating to the so-called accessories to land territory: superjacent airspace, territorial sea, contiguous zones, rivers, lakes, etc. By far the greater part of the delimitations effected in these fields have been determined by the equidistance principle unless special circumstances were present. The outcome has not always been an equitable division in the sense of equally large or equally valuable areas. After all, the geographic configuration, the geological qualities and political circumstances of individual states vary to such an extent as rendering an equitable division impractical. *Per contra* a delimitation governed by the equidistance principle which also takes special circumstances into account has always fulfilled the purpose aimed at by the rules of international law, that of avoiding or settling the disputes which may occur between states.

It is a well-known fact that an analogy requires a decision as to whether there is a causal relation between the two cases. The Court has made it clear that it has not found the required analogy between the hitherto acknowledge accessories to the land territory of a state and the continental shelf; consequently, the Court has had to reiterate the entire debate which has taken place since 1951 for the purpose of defining and crystallizing in rules of law the equitable principles.

VI. Conclusion

The Judgment delivered in the present case is a significant contribution to the permanent discussion whether the International Court of Justice is a court whose sole task it is to pronounce positive law or whether it should also contribute to the progressive development of international law.

In theory, this is an easy question. In practice, it presents considerable difficulties. By applying the rules of international law in the Anglo-Norwegian Fisheries case (1951), the Court contributed to the development which less than ten years after its decision has led to a general enlargement of the territorial sea to the benefit of local fishing and other social interests.

In the present Judgment the Court has proved extremely restrictive in its attitude towards the progressive development of international law. Viewed abstractly as a theoretical proposition the restrictive concept of international law appears highly justified. It is not to be expected that the states will esteem a court which by its judgments imposes obligations which the states have not expressly or tacitly accepted as legally binding.

The Court might with reason have attached more importance to the fact that the Geneva Convention came into being through the efforts of the United Nations to codify and develop international law, the very field in which the United Nations has had and may come to have considerable influence upon the creation of law.

It seems as if the Court has hesitated to intervene in the deliberations on the problems, lately much discussed in the United Nations, concerning the exploitation of the seabed outside the continental shelf in ocean depths.

By merely referring the parties to delimit their respective shelf areas by an agreement founded upon equitable principles, the Court has not contributed to a clarification of how to effect the delimitation of shelf areas existing in various parts of the world, the exploitation of which is growing steadily more urgent.

NOTES

[1] The International Law Commission is a body set up by the United Nations General Assembly in pursuance of Article 13 of the United Nations Charter and was originally composed of 15 lawyers of recognized competence in international law. They were elected chiefly on the basis of their scholarly qualifications whereas their nationality was of importance only insofar as the International Law Commission was always to be composed in such a manner that the principal legal systems of the world should be represented. It is the objective of the ILC to encourage the progressive development of international law and its codification. The number of members has now been raised to 25.

[2] Italics added.

[3] The Court was composed as follows: *President* Bustamante y Rivero; *Vice-President* Koretsky; *Judges* Sir Gerald Fitzmaurice, Tanaka, Jessup, Morelli, Sir Muhammad Zafrulla Khan, Padilla Nervo, Forster, Gros, Ammoun, Bengzon, Petrén, Lachs, Onyeama; *Judges ad hoc* Mosler and Max Sorensen.

[4] Cf., e.g., *Lotus case,* Series A/10 1927, p. 30. *Right of Nationals of the USA in Morocco.* ICJ Report 1953, p. 209. *Anglo-Iranian Oil Company case*, ICJ Report 1951, p. 53.

[5] See Rosenne, *The Law and Practice of the International Court* (1965) p. 586.

[6] See *Lotus case*, Series A/10 p. 12, *Serbian Loans case*, Series A 20/21, p. 47, *Free Zones case*, Series A/B 46, p. 114 and *Minquiers and Ecrehos* case, Report 1953 p. 53.

[7] See H. Lauterpacht, *The Development of International Law by the International Court* (1958) p. 205.

[8] Cf. the principle of "autointerpretation" as laid down and formulated by Leo Gross in "States as organs of international law and the problem of autointerpretation" in Lipsky, *Law and politics in the world community* (1953) pp. 59–89, see also Judgment in the *Asylum case,* ICJ-Report 1950 pp. 274–275.

[9] *Lichtenstein v. Guatemala*, ICJ Report 1955, p. 4 and p. 22 ff.

[10] PCIJ Series A/10 1927, p. 28.

[11] Diss. Op., p. 380.

[12] In stressing that the continental shelf constitutes the natural prolongation of the land territory, the Judgment concurs to the views set forth by Denmark in particular (especially regarding interpretation of the term "special circumstances"). But as stated in the text the "element of prolongation" does not solve the problems which arise when several states claim that the continental shelf is a natural prolongation of the land territories of all the states concerned. At this very point the equidistance principle assumes its independent role as a convenient and precise method of delimitation.

SUBSTANCE OF LAW

CONSCIENCE, NATURAL LAW AND CIVIL DISOBEDIENCE IN THE JEWISH TRADITION

Milton R. Konvitz*

1

In the first chapter of Exodus it is related that the new ruler of Egypt, alarmed by the increase in the number of Israelites, spoke to the "Hebrew midwives" and directed them to kill all male infants born to Hebrew women. "But the midwives feared God," the Bible goes on to relate, "and did not as the king of Egypt commanded them, but saved the men-children alive." (Exodus 1:15–17). Thereupon the king issued a new decree, directed not to the midwives but to the people generally, who were ordered to kill all new-born Hebrew males by throwing them into the river Nile. (Exodus 1:22).

These events, which may have happened some thirty-four hundred years ago, relate to what may well be the first recorded instance in history of what is today called non-violent civil disobedience.

From the biblical text it is not clear that the midwives were themselves Hebrews; for they acted as they did, not because they were Hebrews, but because they "feared God." The text twice mentions the fact that they "feared God"—or, as we say today, that they listened to the voice of conscience rather than to the law of the state or the voice of the king.

In the first book of Samuel there is another clear and dramatic instance of non-violent civil disobedience. It is related that when King Saul learned that a certain priest had given David food and other assistance, he ordered the priest to appear before him and decreed his death and the death of all his kin. The crucial words of the biblical text are as follows:

> And the King said to the guard who stood about him, "Turn and kill the priests of the Lord; because their hand also is with David, and they knew that he fled, and did not disclose it to me." But

* Professor of Law and Professor of Industrial Labor Relations, Cornell University

the servants of the king would not put forth their hand to fall upon the priests of the Lord. I Sam. 22:17)

This may be the first recorded instance of non-violent civil disobedience by military men's refusal to obey superior orders. It is not clear why the men of the guard refused to lay hands on the priests and their families whether because the victims belonged to the priestly class, or because they were civilians. Whatever the reason, their action was a clear case of civil disobedience.

In the book of Daniel we find the first instance of what became a pattern in Jewish life and history: the worship of God without regard to the fact that such worship had been prohibited at the price of one's life. The book relates (in Chapter 6) that Darius the king had appointed Daniel chief of his officers. The officers then conspired to bring about the fall of Daniel, and to this end they contrived an ingenious trap. They induced Darius to issue a decree that for thirty days no man was to offer petition to any man or god except to the king, on pain of death in the lion's den. Daniel, however, went on to pray (i.e. petition) to God three times daily, with the window of his chamber open toward Jerusalem. His enemies came upon Daniel when he was thus petitioning God rather than Darius, and then went with their report to the king. After trying to find a way out, the king felt compelled to order his law to be enforced, and Daniel was put into the den of lions. The following morning, however, the king found Daniel unharmed, saved by an angel.

The case of Daniel, it should be noted, differs from our two previous instances in two important respects, as follows:

(a) In the case of the Egyptian midwives and in the case of Saul's guards, there was simply a refusal to commit an act which was deeply felt, by the persons ordered to perform it, to be inconceivable. In the case of Daniel, however, there was a positive act: he did not merely *refuse* to perform an act; he *performed* an act in violation of a law.

(b) The first two cases involved moral conscience—in the face of orders to commit murder. In the case of Daniel, however, we have an act that is not in the realm of the moral conscience but in the realm of religious worship. While these differences are significant, the concept of non-violent civil disobedience is broad enough to accommodate these as well as additional types of conduct.

The four books of Maccabees in the Apocrypha offer numerous instances of civil disobedience during the period of the Hellenization of Judea, when the second Temple was defiled and was dedicated to Zeus Olympius. Some Jews assisted in the work of Hellenization and even in the persecution of fellow Jews who tried to obstruct the process. The Syrian overlords forbade the Jews to offer sacrifices and to observe the Sabbath and festivals. They were compelled to make and to worship idols, to sacrifice swine, and to leave their sons uncircumcised. Disobedience meant death. But 1 Maccabees records (Chapter 1) that:

> Nevertheless, many in Israel were firmly resolved in their hearts not to eat unclean food. They preferred to die rather than be defiled by food and break the holy covenant, and they did die.

When the king's officers came to Modi'in, to enforce the decrees against religious observances, Mattathias answered them in these resounding words:

> ... yet will I, my sons and my brothers, walk in the covenant of our fathers ... We will not listen to the decrees of the king by going astray from our worship, either to the right or to the left.

And then he issued his call: "Let everyone who is zealous for the Law, and would maintain the covenant, follow me." (1 Macc., Ch.2)

The second book of Maccabees records many dramatic instances of martyrdom when Jews resorted to civil disobedience: women who had violated the law on circumcision, hurled from the city wall with their infants held to their breasts; men who had secretly observed the Sabbath day in caves, burned alive. Special mention may be made of the case of Eliezer, one of the foremost scribes, whom the authorities tried to compel to eat swine's flesh which apparently had been used in a forbidden sacrifice. The officers tried to induce him to bring his own meat but pretend that he was eating meat of the sacrifice as ordered by the king. But he refused, saying that if he were to comply, the young would say that old Eliezer had been converted to heathenism and would thus be led astray by his example. He died on the rack. (Cf. 4 Macc., Ch.5.)

The second and fourth books of Maccabees relate the story of the martyrdom of a mother and seven brothers who refused to eat forbidden food which was associated with idolatrous sacrifices. The position of non-violent civil disobedience is stated unambiguously by them as they cry out to the king's officers: "It is certain that we are ready to die rather than transgress the laws of our fathers." (2 Macc. 7:2.)

The seven brothers, who were called Maccabees by the Church, became models for Christian martyrs; and though the rabbis rejected the books of the Apocrypha from the canon of Sacred Scripture, they,

161

too make a great deal of the story of the seven brothers. (4 Macc., p.129, Moses Hadas trans.)

What may be the first recorded instance of mass non-violent civil disobedience is found in Josephus' *Antiquities of the Jews* (Bk. 18, Ch. 8). The incident he relates occurred during the reign of the emperor Caligula, 37–41. The incident revolved around the decision of Caligula (referred to as Caius) to place his statue in the Temple in Jerusalem. He appointed Petronius as his agent. Petronius was given a large army, but was instructed to try, in the first instance, to persuade the Jews to permit the installation of the statue peacefully. If however, the Jews were to refuse, then Petronius was to move with his army and install the statue with force. Petronius prepared an army of Romans and auxiliaries to carry out this mission, and in due course arrived at Acre (referred to as Ptolemais). What happened after that is graphically reported by Josephus:

> But there came ten thousands of the Jews to Petronius at Ptolemais to offer their petitions to him that he would not compel them to violate the law of their forefathers. "But if," they said, "you are wholly resolved to bring the statue and install it, then you must first kill us, and then do what you have resolved on. For while we are alive we cannot permit such things as are forbidden by our law and by the determination of our forefathers that such prohibitions are examples of virtue."
>
> Petronius, however, was angry at them, and said: ". . . Caesar has sent me. I am compelled to observe his decrees . . ." Then the Jews replied: "Since, therefore, you are so disposed, O Petronius, that you will not disobey Caesar's orders, neither will we transgress the commands of our law . . ."
>
> When Petronius saw by their words that their determination was hard to be removed, and that . . . he would not be able to be obedient to Caius in the dedication of his statue, and that there must be a great deal of bloodshed, he took his friends and servants and hastened to Tiberias, to see how the Jews there felt about the affair; but many ten thousands of Jews met Petronius again when he came to Tiberias . . .
>
> Then Petronius came to them [at Tiberias]: "Will you then make war with Caesar, regardless of his great preparations for war and your own weakness?" They replied: "We will not by any means make war with Caesar, but we will die before we see our laws transgressed." Then they threw themselves down on their faces and stretched out their throats and said that they were

ready to be slain. And this they did for forty days, neglecting to till their soil, though this was the season which called for sowing. Thus they continued firm in their resolution and proposed to die willingly rather than see the statue dedicated.

When matters were in this state . . . Petronius determined to listen to the petitioners in this matter. He called the Jews together in Tiberias, who came many ten thousands in number . . . Said Petronius: "I do not think it just to have such a regard to my own safety and honor as to refuse to sacrifice them for your preservation, who are so many in number and who endeavour to preserve the regard that is due to your law . . . I will, therefore, send to Caius and let him know your resolutions, and I will assist your cause as far as I am able, so that you may not suffer on account of your honest designs, and may God assist you . . . But if Caius should be angry and turn the violence of his rage on me, I would rather undergo that danger and affliction on my body or soul than see so many of you perish . . ."

When Petronius had said this and had dismissed the assembly of Jews, he asked the principal men among them to look after their fields, to speak kindly to the people and to encourage them to have hope . . . He then wrote to Caius . . . to entreat him not to drive so many ten thousands of these men to distraction; that if he were to slay these men, he would be publicly cursed for all future ages.

Philo, recording the same incidents, reports the Jewish plea to Petronius in essentially the same words as those of Josephus. The core of the plea, according to Philo, was in the following words:

"We are evacuating our cities, withdrawing from our houses and lands . . . We should think ourselves gainers thereby, not givers. One thing only we ask in return for all, that no violent changes should be made in this temple . . . But if we cannot persuade you, we give up ourselves for destruction that we may not live to see a calamity worse than death. We hear that forces of cavalry and infantry have been prepared against us if we oppose the installation [of the image of Caesar]. No one is so mad as to oppose a master when he is a slave. We [therefore] gladly put our throats at your disposal."[1]

II

With the instances before us— from the Hebrew Scriptures, the Apocrypha, and Josephus—it is now possible to state the essential elements for a case of civil disobedience:

a) There was a law or an official decree.

b) Those whose obedience was commanded considered the law to be unconscionable.

c) They refused to obey.[2]

d) They resorted to no violent resistance.

e) They showed a readiness to suffer for their conscience, and they stood ready to put their lives on the line.

f) The incident in Josephus discloses an additional element; i.e. civil disobedience, in which the above five elements are manifested, and which includes also an effort to convert the opponent, to achieve reconciliation by the assertion of the force of truth and love in the place of fear, hate, and falsehood.

The ancient texts before us do not formulate a principle of civil disobedience in abstract terms. The ancient Hebraic mind did not tend to conceptualize. That mind moved in an existential way, within a specific configuration of facts and forces. It did not become engaged in philosophic analysis beyond the small range disclosed by the Wisdom Literature. But with our hindsight it is not difficult to see the modern philosophy of civil disobedience prefigured in the incidents we have selected from the Hebrew Scriptures, the Apocrypha, and Josephus. Neither Thoreau nor Gandhi, nor Martin Luther King, Jr., detracted from or added to the elements of civil disobedience as formulated above. Each of them, because of his own situation, tended, however, to emphasize one element or another. Thoreau emphasized the duty of conscience to assert itself against evil law or state action. Gandhi emphasized the need of resistance to be non-violent, and to seek by this means, and the practice of humility, to penetrate to the heart of the enemy, to transform him into a friend. Dr. King emphasized the need to be non-violent and the readiness to submit to the penalty of the law for its wilful breach. But what element is singled out for stress at any one time is not decided abstractly but by circumstances of time, place and people.

In the light of some of the events in the late 1960's—in the demonstrations by black students, by opponents of the Vietnam War on college campuses, by welfare recipients and others making demands on government officials—perhaps the element in non-violent civil disobedience that most needed emphasizing, apart from stress on non-violence, was the willingness to submit oneself to the penalty of the law that had been broken. Such submission is important for the following reasons:

(a) It clearly marks off the civil disobedient from the ordinary criminal, who tries to suppress evidence of his action and to escape punishment.

It also marks him off from the person who seeks to *evade* a law, which he considers unconscionable, by flight to another jurisdiction—e.g., the thousands of American draftees who went to Sweden or Canada because of their opposition to the Vietnam War, but who feared that they could not prove their conscientious objection to the satisfaction of the Selective Service authorities or the courts. This is not the place to consider the moral arguments for or against *evasion* of a law considered unconscionable; all that is meant is that there are significant differences between civil disobedience and evasion.

We should also note that readiness to submit to legal punishment does not preclude a willingness to appeal one's conviction through a hierarchy of courts. This was the practice of Dr. King, and at times he succeeded in persuading the Supreme Court that the law under which he and demonstrators associated with him were convicted was in fact unconstitutional. A willing submission to the penalty implies a valid judgment of conviction under a law sustained by the Constitution.

(b) The posture of readiness to suffer the punishment prescribed by the law demonstrates the seriousness with which the defendant considers the law that he has knowingly violated and the response of his conscience to the demands of that law; for in effect the defendant says that he would rather lose his liberty or even his life than obey the law which is against his conscience. In the words of the second book of Maccabees, he says: "It is certain that I am ready to die rather than transgress the law of my conscience." To break the law and to fail or refuse to submit to its sanction may lead to the inference that the defendant wants to have the best of both worlds: to break the law for the sake of his conscience, but at the same time to treat the law as if it were a mere scrap of paper and not a test of his conscience.

By willingly submitting to the law's penalty the defendant shows to himself—as well as to the community—that he had faced his conscience squarely. A member of society accepts or tolerates the burden of countless laws which he does not approve of or like. He makes no claim that he has the power to veto or nullify laws which he, for one reason or another, dislikes. By resorting to civil disobedience and submitting to the sanction of the breached law, the defendant shows that he has deliberated, that he has weighed and measured, that he is not acting on a mere impulse or whim, that he has made a decision that is of supreme importance to himself.

(c) By showing his willingness to accept the punishment, the defendant declares or affirms his membership in the community and his respect for the rule of the law. This will mark him off from the radical revolutionary and the anarchist who may wish to subvert the whole social order.

This was the position taken by Gandhi and Dr. King, and they could have looked to Socrates as the classical model of this argument. When Socrates was in prison awaiting his execution, his friends urged him to make the escape which they had arranged. But Socrates spurned the suggestion. He himself, he argued, would *do* no wrong; but it was not against his conscience to *suffer* a wrong. It was his duty, he said, willingly to accept the punishment even if the verdict of guilty was an injustice. For he was not, Socrates in effect said, an anarchist. He respected profoundly the legal order. It had its imperfections—witness the unjust judgment against him; but it is a citizen's duty to respect the legal order in general, for without it life as a human being would be impossible. Who, he asked in the *Crito*, would care for a city without laws? Goodness and integrity, institutions and laws, he said, are the most precious possessions of mankind.

This must be, indeed, the position if civil disobedience is to be differentiated from the acts of the anarchist and the social revolutionary who wish to subvert the entire legal and social order.

It was in the spirit of this insight that Gandhi wrote that he who resorts to civil disobedience:

> ever obeys the laws of the state to which he belongs, not out of fear of the sanctions, but because he considers them to be good for the welfare of society. But there come occasions, generally rare, when he considers certain laws to be so unjust as to render obedience to them a dishonour. He then openly and civilly breaks them and quietly suffers the penalty for their breach. (Gandhi, *Non-Violent Resistance,* p.7.)

It was in the same spirit of submission to the rule of law that Martin Luther King, Jr., wrote from his cell in the Birmingham jail:

> I submit that an individual who breaks a law that conscience tells him is unjust, and willingly accepts the penalty by staying in jail . . . is in reality expressing the very highest respect for law.

(d) Finally, breaking the immoral law openly and standing ready to pay the price demanded by the very law that was broken will, it is hoped, have the effect of opening the eyes of others to the way the law in question offends the conscience. This happened, according to Josephus, as the Roman General saw the anguish and suffering of the Jews, and their fixed determination to face torture and death rather than permit the perversion of their religion. This is the appeal that non-violent civil disobedience is supposed to make to the instincts of truth, justice and peace as it pushes out ignorance, prejudice, and hate.

III

Leaving out for the moment the incident from the book of Daniel, the biblical instances of civil disobedience that we have cited—the case of the Egyptian midwives and that of Saul and his guards—involved orders to commit murder. The cases cited from the books of the Maccabees and from Josephus involved orders to commit the sin of idolatry. Now a man of conscience may readily agree that he would prefer martyrdom rather than commit murder or practice idolatry. But what of laws or decrees that call for acts not so heinous as murder or idolatry though against the conscience? In the course of the war that Hadrian waged to destroy Judaism and the Jewish nation, countless Jews stood ready for martyrdom. But the rabbis saw that indiscriminate martyrdom might itself be a peril to Jewish survival. With this consideration before them, the rabbis decreed that the duty to prefer martyrdom shall be restricted to three transgressions: murder, idolatry, and incest (or adultery or gross unchastity). The rabbis attached this legal principle to Leviticus 18:5, which reads as follows: "And ye shall guard my statutes and my ordinances, by doing which a man *shall live*." They concluded from this passage that the Torah was given to enhance life rather than to induce death. The emphasis of the Torah is on holy living and not on holy dying. The rabbis also pointed to the fact that the passage stated that the statutes and ordinances are such that by observing them "a man" shall live—not an Israelite, but "a man." With these two highly significant interpretations in mind, the rabbis felt that martyrdom had to be limited to instances that involved laws that transgressed the most basic principles of what came later to be called natural law or the laws of nature. (There can hardly be any question about murder and incest falling into this category. Idolatry was so closely associated with grossly immoral practices that it could rank with the transgressions of the basic precepts of natural law, and that association was made and stressed by the prophets of the Bible and the rabbis of the Talmud.)[3]

The *locus classicus* of the legal formulation of the principle concerning martyrdom is in the Babylonian Talmud:

> For every law of the Torah the rule is that a man may transgress the commandment rather than suffer death—excepting idolatry, incest and murder ... Murder may not be committed [even] to save one's life. ... For example, someone came to Raba and told him: "The general of my town has ordered me to go and kill a named person, and if not, the general will kill me." Raba said to him: "Let the general kill you rather than that you should commit murder. Who knows that your blood is redder? Maybe his blood is redder!" (Sanhedrin 74a)

In the face, then, of laws or orders that command idolatry, incest or murder, the above-stated Halachic (legal, jurisprudential) principle calls for the *duty* of civil disobedience, even at the cost of one's life.[4]

Now what of the incident from the book of Daniel? As the story is related, Daniel was not called on to perform any act at all. If he had not petitioned (prayed) at all for thirty days, he would have complied with the king's decree. Why, then, did he resort to civil disobedience? Was his conduct consistent with the Halachic principle later formulated by the rabbis?

It seems that the incident may be interpreted consistently with the above principle. The Persians believed that their king was a god; accordingly, they set a trap for Daniel, for they suspected that he would refuse to pray to the king as one prays to God. Had Daniel failed to offer prayers to anyone for thirty days, his enemies could have used this as evidence of a rejection by him of a belief in the king as a divinity. From this point of view, the story in its essentials is not significantly different from the story in Josephus, of Caligula's desire to have his statue installed in the Temple on Mount Moriah. By praying to God while looking out the window that faced toward Jerusalem, Daniel acted out his rejection of Persian idolatry. Accordingly, the story of Daniel is not only an instance of civil disobedience, but is also an instance of the later legal formulation of the *duty* of civil disobedience to avoid the commission of idolatry, incest or murder.

IV

Going beyond the three-fold principle of the duty of civil disobedience, the Halacha formulated a duty of civil disobedience that is operative even when the act that is commanded falls short of constituting idolatry. This second principle applies only in times of persecution, when the government seems determined to destroy Judaism. In such circumstances, when one is ordered to violate a commandment in public (i.e., in the presence of ten adult Jews), he must refuse to comply with the order, even at the cost of his life. This is the principle of *Kiddush Ha-Shem* (Sanctification of the Name). To violate a commandment under these circumstances would be a desecration of the name (*Chillul Ha-Shem*). The principle applies, under these circumstances, even if the religious commandment is a relatively minor one—even if it involves merely the deviation from an established custom in Jewry. In such a case, the principle that applies is the same as that when idolatry is commanded: "Let yourself be killed but do not transgress the law of the Torah."

While the three-fold principle involving the duty of civil disobedience applies to any man, for it is based on the demands of natural law, the second principle, limited to the persecution of Judaism, applies only to Jews.

While the case of Eliezar and the case of the mother and the seven brothers, as related in Maccabees, could be interpreted as involving the ban on idolatry, as we have seen, they could also be interpreted, more simply perhaps, as falling under the second principle. For they were ordered to violate a detary ban in a time of religious persecution, and under circumstances which would have given their compliance publicity within the Jewish community. Their death was, therefore, a martyrdom, a *Kiddush Ha-Shem*.

The second principle may at times appear to run counter to the thinking of the rabbis when they decided to limit the duty of civil disobedience to idolatry, incest and murder. For was not the time of the Emperor Hadrian a time of religious persecution? If in such a time the second principle is also operative, may not its operation itself be a threat to Jewish existence and survival? The contradiction was probably resolved by Jewish community leaders *ad hoc* in the light of the facts and circumstances as they were known and interpreted at the time. It may thus be that the nature of the Hadrianic persecution, and the character and temper of the people called for the additional principle of *Kiddush Ha-Shem*, as well as for the first principle.

V

The relations in classical Jewish thought between law and conscience—conscience in which civil disobedience is rooted—are extremely subtle and complex.[5] For the purposes of the present discussion we shall limit our exploration of this matter to three aspects:

(a) Conscience, as a specific concept of value, does not appear in the Hebrew Scriptures. It is, however, clearly implied. The story of Cain and Abel would have no point unless conscience were assumed; for there had been no supernatural revelation of a law against murder before one brother killed the other, nor was there at that time an enacted criminal code. The same may be said of the judgment on Sodom and the other cities of the plain; and so, too, of Noah and the judgment on his generation; and so, too, of the judgments on Egypt and on the people of Canaan. Much of the Bible, including many passages of the prophets, assumes that there are laws written on the tablets of the heart (Prov. 7:3), that there is a law in the heart (Deut. 30:14).[6]

The words of Jeremiah (31:32), "I will put my law in their inward parts, and in their hearts will I write it," were not only a promise but also a statement of basic belief as to the nature of man. Without this belief in a law written by God on the tablets of the heart of every man, God could not be the judge of all the universe, of all peoples and nations. Without this belief, God would be only the tribal God of Israel, and he could not have been their judge before the revelation of the Ten Commandments at Sinai; without this belief, the commandments not to kill, not to commit adultery, or not to commit theft would have binding force only on Israel. Indeed, it may be argued that the conception of man made in the image of God means primarily that man is made with a moral conscience—and with the freedom to act against it. It is this that the Bible means when it states that the Egyptian midwives "feared God;" that Amalek, when he acted cruelly, showed that "he feared not God" (Deut. 25:18); that Abraham pretended to be the brother of Sarah, because when they came to Gerar he thought: "Surely the fear of God is not in this place; and they will slay me for my wife's sake" (Gen.20:11).

Indeed, in Biblical contemplation, there may be said to be a special category of sin which is an act committed "against the Lord," that is, a sin which implies the denial of the existence of God, or atheism. This applies to a wrong done to another person secretly, under circumstances where there are no witnesses—no witnesses but God. In Leviticus this type of sin is referred to as follows: "If any one sin, and commit a trespass against the Lord, and deal falsely with his neighbor in a matter of deposit, or of pledge, or of robbery, or have oppressed his neighbor; or have found that which was lost, and deal falsely therein, and swear to a lie; in any of all these that a man doeth, sinning therein; . . ." (Lev. 5:21,22.). Rabbi Akiba attached great significance to the phrase "against the Lord," for he believed it points up the fact that the guilty man denies that God was a witness to the deposit or the other acts, and thus by implication he denies God's existence or presence. This, it seems to me, gives the phrase in Leviticus the same meaning as the phrase "feared God," and it is a meaning based on what we generally speak of as conscience.

It was with such views in mind, and especially the story of Noah and the flood, that the rabbis of the Talmud formulated what they called "the seven commandments given to the descendants of Noah" (Sanhedrin 56a). These commandments prohibit idolatry, murder, theft, incest, blasphemy and the eating of flesh taken from living animals, and require the establishment of courts of justice.[7] How were these seven commandments "given" and to whom? They were "given" on the "tablets of the heart," and to every man everywhere, since Noah was a kind of second Adam. These commandments spell out, therefore, a natural law, a law binding on the conscience of every man, and from which no man, nation, or generation can claim exemption.

(b) This principle of a law of nature, elaborated into the seven commandments given to the descendants of Noah, is obviously the source from which the Jewish tradition selected the three-fold principle of civil disobedience: that a man must choose to die, if necessary, rather than obey a law or decree that he commit murder, incest, or idolatry.

One significant aspect is that the duty of civil disobedience is not extended to all of the seven commandments but only to these three. Thus, if the order is to commit, e.g., theft, on the pain of death, the person should commit the theft.[8]

Suppose that the sanction for a refusal to commit theft, however, is imprisonment, not death. May a person, then, resort to civil disobedience and choose to go to prison rather than commit the wrong? The principle is silent as to such cases. The principle only states *explicitly* that one *must* choose to suffer a wrong rather than commit it when the wrong to be committed is idolatry, incest, or murder. And the principle *implies* only that when the wrong to be suffered is *death* as a penalty, one *must* commit the wrong ordered—except idolatry, incest, or murder—and avoid death. A great deal is, therefore, left open—when the wrongs commanded are other than the three cardinal ones, or when the penalty threatened for disobedience is something other than death. Exploration of this open territory is beyond the reach of this essay.

(c) Finally, our discussion should have demonstrated the distinctly Halachic approach to the problem of conscience *versus* law that is an expression of the genius of classical, normative Judaism. The legal order provides a constitutional or higher law by which a man is commanded to disobey certain orders, even when they are made by the king or other high officers of the state. Halachic normative Judaism thus speaks not of a right, but of a duty, a legal duty, of civil disobedience. Thus, while it recognizes conscience, or "the fear of God," or the laws written on the tablets of the heart, it converts morality into law by demanding that, given proper circumstances, the higher law became the living law—a living law that contradicts, and even nullifies, the enacted law—or what wrongly pretends to be the law.

The dialectic of the conceptual relationship between the demands of conscience (or of the inner or natural law) and those of enacted law or orders of the state, is probably impossible to express with any precision, or in the terms of logical consistency. The ancient Jewish authorities were wise not to make the attempt but instead resorted to existential terms by conjuring up the case of the governor of the town ordering X to go and kill Y. What did Raba say to X? "Let the governor slay you rather than that you should commit murder. Who knows that your blood is redder? Perhaps Y's blood is redder than yours." Thus, as is often the case in Hebraic-rabbinic thought, an example symbolizes a principle,[9] the commentary becomes the text—as if there were a fear of making the word into a thing, of accepting the notion that in the beginning was the *Logos*, the word. For the ultimate sanctity is life, God's creation, and not what is said about it in some abstract formula. Yet life, sacred as it is, is given and sustained for certain ends. If these ends are threatened —by coerced idolatry, immorality, or "the shedding of blood"—life becomes worthless and must well be given up. But the ends are such only because they enhance life. It is "holy living" and not "holy dying" that is sought and hoped for and cherished.

But the values for which life itself must be sacrificed, if the tragic need arises, are very few. This perhaps explains the silence of the Talmud regarding the 960 men, women and children who defended Masada, the fortress on the Dead Sea, in the course of the Judean revolt against Rome. Especially repulsive to the rabbis must have been the agreement among the members of the garrison's council, as their final act of defiance, to kill the members of their own families and to put one another to death. As against the nationalist zealots, the rabbis stressed the need to save the lives of Jews from fruitless martyrdom; the value of non-violent, nonmilitary action; and, of supreme importance to them, the winning of the right to continue to study and to teach Torah without distraction or fear.[10]

172

In the light of the Talmudic principles of non-violent civil disobedience, the attitude of the rabbis to Masada and its defenders, led by Eliezar ben Yair, is entirely understandable. To them, what was indispensable for life was not political independence but the independence of their religious life and the values it contained and sustained. This included, of course, as a minimum, life in conformance with the natural law, as formulated in the seven commandments to the descendants of Noah—a natural law which, it could have been reasonably assumed, the Roman overlords would respect and observe.

The unsympathetic critic may say that we have constructed a rather heavy and imposing superstructure on a meager foundation of small incidents, like that of the Egyptian midwives and Saul's bodyguards. Until our own tumultuous days, one would not have thought of such incidents as implying and foreshadowing a principle so momentous for the human spirit as that of civil disobedience. But often it takes many centuries and a great deal of history to disclose the existence of an ideal, theory or principle. In the Preface to his *Poems* (1853 edition), Matthew Arnold glibly wrote that

> An action like the action of the *Antigone* of Sophocles, which turns upon the conflict between the heroine's duty to her brother's corpse and that to the laws of her country, is no longer one in which it is possible that we should feel a deep interest.

One may be sure that when read in 1853 this judgment seemed to be eminently to the point. But would Arnold have made this judgment in 1953—after the Nürnberg Tribunal judgments, after the other many war crime trials, after the Eichmann trial? Would he have made this judgment in the light of Gandhi's civil disobedience struggle to end untouchability in India? Would he have made this statement in the 1960's in the light of the lunch-counter sit-ins led by Martin Luther King, Jr.? Indeed, in the 1960's perhaps more people read or saw *Antigone* as written by Sophocles or in the version prepared by Anouilh than in the hundred years from 1853.

Great actions, whether they be those of a young, bereaved girl, or of midwives, or of young soldiers engaged to protect their king, have a way of surviving the ravages of time, and demonstrate, when the time is appropriate, their relevance and significance for that which is "permanent in the human soul." That demonstration can be made by Antigone or Socrates, by Thomas More or Bronson Alcott or Thoreau, by Gandhi or Martin Luther King, Jr., or by thousands of nameless Jews not afraid of a Roman general nor of the Roman Emperor who sent him, nor of death, but who did have the "fear of God"—a "fear" that gives boundless courage to a spirit that suddenly discovers itself as boundless. These men and women found it easy to act but impossible or difficult to give a rational account of their actions. But this is natural, for conscience demands that the act be justified before God, and not necessarily before men; God knows the heart, and its inner thoughts and secrets.

And God does not demand great sacrifice when the occasion is not one of transcendent importance; God makes his demands only when man is called upon to perpetrate murder or commit immorality or idolatry. Only then does the law of God demand violation of the law of man at the cost of one's life. Civil disobedience is not offered as an every-day method for meeting unwelcome situations, for the amelioration of which society and individuals must find other methods and agencies.

Beyond this, however, Jewish tradition and the Halacha, as we have seen, place the highest value on martyrdom that is the price paid for defiance of a tyrant whose policy it is to destroy the Jewish religion. In the solemn service of Yom Kippur, a prominent place is given to a recital of the heroism and martyrdom of the ten great scholars who, during the Hadrianic persecutions, steadfastly refused to accept the pro-hibitions on observances and the ban on the study of the Torah. At the risk of their lives they acted in defiance of imperial edicts and gladly suf-fered torture and death in order to sanctify the Name of their God *(Kiddush Ha-Shem)*. Within the Jewish tradition of non-violent civil disobedience, these ten martyrs have played a role, in the education of the Jewish conscience, that is at least comparable to that of Socrates for Western society: the role of witnesses to the force of the moral and religious conscience and its imperious claims to obedience—claims that are more pressing than those of any state or emperor.

NOTES

[1] Philo, *De Legatione ad Caium*, in Loeb Classical Library, vol. X, 232 ff.

[2] It may be noted that while the Egyptian midwives refused to assist in the proposed genocide of the Israelites, they did not openly avow their intent knowingly to violate the king's decree. They resorted to a subterfuge by claiming that the Hebrew women did not really require the services of midwives. (Exodus 1:19.)

[3] Compare the Oedipus cycle in Greek drama for a similar feeling of revulsion against an incestuous act.

[4] In post-Talmudic Judaism, authorities did not all agree that the Halacha imposed an absolute duty freely to choose martyrdom under the circumstances in view of the great degree of duress. They also stressed the question whether the cardinal sin was required

to be committed publicly or secretly. The post-Talmudic discussions are not considered in this essay. See Samuel Belkin, *In His Image,* pp. 210–211.

Cf. David Daube, *Collaboration With Tyranny in Rabbinic Law,* especially pp. 26–27, 31, 35–36, 40, 83, for discussion of related questions.

[5] See *Law and Morals: In the Hebrew Scriptures, Plato and Aristotle,* by Milton R. Konvitz, 23 Conservative Judaism 44 (Winter 1969).

[6] Cf. Romans 2:14–15.

[7] Cf. Jubilees 7:22; Acts 15:20, 29.

[8] See Maimonides, *Hilchot Yisodei Ha-Torah,* 5,4. Cf. Belkin, *op. cit.,* 102, 132.

[9] Cf. Daube, op. cit., at pp. 99–100.

[10] Cf. Bernard Heller, *Masada and the Talmud,* 10 Tradition 31 (Winter 1968).

THE NATURE OF PURE EQUITY

Ralph A. Newman*

It has been said that the history of law is the record of the slow emergence of the idea of ethical right to explicit consciousness.[1] The advance from relative to absolute justice, from strict law to equity, is necessarily intermittent. The stages of legal growth may be regarded as so many halts along a road which leads to justice.[2] At certain periods, as in the time of Coke in the sixteenth century, of Mansfield in the eighteenth, and of Holmes before and after the turn of the nineteenth, there will be sudden leaps forward. Sometimes, as in England during the transition from medievalism to the Age of Reason, and during the past hundred years, except for occasional advances due largely to the influence of Lord Denning, the progress is slow. The importance of equity in the structure of law has been recognized since classical antiquity and beyond, but its precise nature, like the nature of law itself,[3] has proved difficult to define. The tissue of equity is woven of ideals, and ideals are not easily reduced to formulae. There are those who have despaired of arriving at a definition,[4] and it has been suggested that it may be more desirable to describe equity than to attempt to define it.[5] The principles of equity, as Lord Evershed has aptly stated, illustrate, but never precisely define, the concepts which lie behind, understood but unexpressed.[6] Equity in the general sense of what is fair and just is synonymous with law, as is implicit in Celsus' definition of law in the opening sentence of the Digest, as *ars boni et aequi.*[7] Cardozo has said that the progressive humanization of the law has been an almost universal phenomenon of man's search for justice.[8] Another great legal philosopher has described equity as one of the names under which is concealed the creative force which animates the life of the law.[9] The difficulty of defining equity is increased because it is always in transition, and equitable doctrine is being constantly absorbed into the law.[10] Yet if equity is

* Professor of Law, University of California, Hastings College of the Law

to perform its creative role in the evolving law of today and tomorrow we must try to find explicit expression for the basic moral values which constitute its source.

The earliest historical record of a distinction between right and wrong appears in the *Maxims* of Ani, which date at least back to 4266 B.C.E., and which include prohibition of intentional infliction of harm, recognition of the inviolability of rights of property, and reference to rudimentary types of fraud.[11] Intimations of a general concept of justice, *maat*, are to be found in the *Maxims* of Ptahhotep in the twenty-eighth century,[12] but there is as yet no recognition of a moral order based on compassionate justice. There is a reference in the Prologue of the Code of Hammurabi (which recent research places in the seventeenth century) to the mission of the King as including the obligation to prevent the strong from oppressing the weak, but the Code is permeated by the principle of revenge.[13] By the time of Ikhnaton (roughly estimated to be a contemporary of Moses), in the fourteenth century, there begins to emerge from the mists of the past a fleeting recognition of a God of benevolence, but the concept of the fatherhood of God was not extended to include a concept of the brotherhood of men. Out of Judea was to come the first formulation of the moral conscience based on brotherly love.

Across the vast panorama of the history of the law it is possible to trace the various streams by which the law has been progressively enriched by the introduction of moral principles. The remarkable spiritual development which took place from the fourteenth to the sixth centuries before the Christian era is vividly expressed in the Book of Leviticus,[14] the Psalms of David,[15] and the teachings of Hosea,[16] Amos[17] and the authors of the Book of Isaiah.[18] In Leviticus appears the earliest expression of the obligation to love one's neighbor as one's self, and to love even the stranger within our gates.[19] In the sixth century the great unkown Isaiah said that when righteousness (*nekohah*) stands afar off, justice (*mishpat*) cannot enter the marketplace.[20]

Two centuries later Aristotle defined *epieikeia*, which we translate as equity but which to the Greeks meant compassion, as a force external to *nomos*, strict law, and by which the injustices of strict law were corrected.[21] Greek philosophy was unable to effect a reconciliation between equity and strict law through the mediation of religion, because of the extremely tenuous connection between religion and morality. The Greek gods, like the personal gods of Egypt, hated and killed, and were as immoral as the human beings after whose image they were modelled. Jewish law recognized, from the beginning, that law is composed of both justice and mercy, and the reconciliation between law and equity came about not through the correction of law by an external force but through the operation of moral ideals within the law itself. The vision of righteousness and brotherhood of the Prophets of the Old Testament was carried, under the name of charity,[22] into a new religion, by a Jewish rabbi who became a god.

Until the middle ages the Judaic-Christian ethic of human brotherhood remained insulated from western jurisprudence because by the time of the Christian Emperors the moral principles of Roman law had taken definitive form. Morality was to enter into Roman law from a different source, the law of nature. In the twelfth and thirteenth centuries natural law, which during the dark ages had lain buried and forgotten, was revived by the scholastic philosophers. In the thirteenth century Saint Thomas combined the fundamental ideal of the brotherhood of man which had been preserved in the teachings of the Church Fathers (principally Saint Augustine) with natural law,[23] Roman law, institutions of canon law largely derived from Roman law, and institutions of Germanic customary law[24] largely derived from natural law. The swelling stream, shaped by the medieval scholastic philosophers and augmented by institutions of the customary law of Gaul[25] became the source of the civil law systems of Europe. In this stream natural law carried the Judaic-Christian concept of justice, based on brotherly love, into western jurisprudential thought.[26] The European sources beat with less success on the cliffs of Albion, but in the thirteenth century the influence of the *Decretal of Gratian*, embodying the fundamental moral doctrines of Roman law but with important canonical innovations, was carried by the Dominican and Franciscan canonists to England.[27] There these concepts became the basis of the legal system which was to be administered in the following century in the English Court of Chancery.[28]

"Every system," as Del Vecchio has said, "even apparently closed has in reality its safety-valves and its natural means of renewal, of transformation and increase. Justice may proclaim itself as valid and effective even against a legal system actually in force, when the rules of the system in force are in irreconcilable conflict with those elementary requirements of justice which are the primary reason for its validity."[29] The introduction of the principles of equity into the written law is sometimes facilitated by express provision,[30] but whether or not the need for such supplementation of the written law is explicitly recognized, the inevitable *lacunae* in the codes are filled from the same source, however that source is identified. In the legal systems of the Orient and in Scandinavian and Hungarian law the principles of equity were incorporated directly into the main body of the law. In some parts of the world auxiliary systems of commutative justice which paralleled systems of strict law were administered in separate courts. In canon law the rules of strict law and the doctrines of mitigation were administered at the Holy See at Rome in two courts, the *Signatura Justitiae* and the *Signatura Gratiae*.[31] In the fourteenth century a series of Papal decretals transferred the function of mitigation from the *Signatura Gratiae* to the *Signatura Justitiae*, and in the course of the following two centuries the *Signatura Gratiae* disappeared. In other legal systems the two functions were administered in the same court. In Roman law from 357 B.C.E., the *praetor peregrinus* provided extraordinary remedies in exceptional cases.[32] In the reign of Hadrian the praetorian equity, after nearly five centuries of administration, as a separate system in the same court as the *ius civile,* became merged with it.[33] Modern civil law, which gradually took form from the early part of the twelfth century until the end of the eighteenth, fell heir to a system of Roman law in which law and equity had already become completely fused.

A transition somewhat comparable to that which occurred in praetorian equity seems to be taking place in our own time in the French *Conseil d'Etat*, in which an evolving body of equitable doctrine is being administered alongside the Civil Code, which does not permit of equitable supplementation.[34] The apparent duality of the system of law which is administered in the *Conseil d'Etat* through its open recognition of equity as a source of law independently of the Civil Code is perhaps less significant than it seems at first impression. The Court has merely made explicit the principles of equity which, by reason of their integration into the Civil Code have been a part of the law administered in the *Cour de Cassation* and which have underlain the decisions of that court ever since it was established. In Anglo-American law, although the separate courts of equity have been abolished except in a few jurisdictions, equity has persisted as a separate inner system, even if in some areas of law its principles have permeated only imperfectly into the general law.

Why has equity appeared in so many parts of the world as a concept separate from law, although a part of it? The phenomenon appears to be due to the fact that law has dual objectives which conflict with one another. The objectives of law may be described as the establishment of the basis for an effective social order, and the humane adjustment of individual relations. In the beginnings of social life the paramount considerations are peace and security, to be attained by a small number of simple rules designed to cover ordinary situations. When the facts of a case do not fall within the kinds of situations for which the rules were designed, the cases must be fitted to the rules, even at the sacrifice of justice to the persons immediately concerned in the dispute. Only later, as the social group feels itself more secure, can the law afford to take into account moral considerations, which depend so much on the particular facts and which may require a departure from the general rules. When the principles of equity are introduced into the relatively unfriendly environment of strict law the principles disintegrate, leaving in their wake only fragments of the principles. This phenomenon, although most pronounced in Anglo-American law, exists in all legal systems because of the conflict between the objective of social order, which requires rules that are certain and inflexible, and the objective of individual justice, which requires the relaxation of the rules in order to meet the need for justice to the litigants. There exists in all legal systems a *malaise* arising out of the conflicting objectives of strict law and of equity, leading to an unevenness in the application of equitable doctrine.

Justice, in the words of a philosopher who was a poet, "emerged from social life and soared above it, categorical and transcendent."[35] Like all other moral elements of law, the principles of equity originate outside the law in the moral convictions of the place and time. Law, as Pound has said, is experience tested by reason, and reason tested by experience.[36] In the beginnings of law it is reason which determines impersonally the shape of the legal norms. As law becomes humanized in the course of the moral growth of mankind, justice requires that the law be not only reasonable but also humane. The rules of law open to receive the principles of equity, and reason and justice together shape the legal norms.

Plato said that he who could discover a source of virtue agreeable to truth would be as a living man among shades.[37] Since the time of Homer many men have believed that the rules for the ordering of virtuous conduct can be derived from the laws of nature. It is true that the laws which govern physical phenomena are made by nature the law which drives the planets on their course and which manifests itself in the cycle of growth, death and regeneration of living organisms. Men merely interpret such laws. Not all natural laws, however, are appropriate for the guidance of human affairs, since nature can afford to be lavish with the lives of its subjects. Men must therefore choose among the laws which have been established by nature for the accomplishment of its purposes; and the choice must be determined by human reason. Nevertheless, men have found in the ecology and self-regeneration of nature the prototype for cooperation in achieving the goals of human existence. It may not be by chance that the gods of the Greeks dwelt in the forests and mountains, or that Saint Louis administered justice under an oak at Vincennes, as did the possibly mythical Emperor Shun, in the same century and at the opposite end of the earth, under a flowering pear tree. Others have turned to human nature rather than to the physical world for the source of moral law. This theory finds strong corroboration in the presence, in widely scattered countries and widely different cultures, of what prove on analysis to be substantially similar moral concepts which have gradually permeated into the law. As Sorokin has noted, "There have been certain universal and perennial moral and legal norms that are required to be practiced in all societies in regard to their members and which are quite necessary for the maintenance of a good life in any society of individuals. The main moral commandments of all great religions, of all legal codes, of all mores and folkways . . . are very similar, often identical."[38]

The most probable explanation of the similarity of basic equitable doctrine in different legal systems is that equity is based on a sense of social solidarity which is innate in human nature, however diverse may be the explanations of its presence there. Henri Bergson's analysis of the source of morality and religion is relevant to the problem of the source of altruism.[39] In animals the goal is physical survival of the species through nourishment, shelter and propagation. At the human level of evolution the goals are not only physical survival but also psychological and spiritual fulfillment. Psychological fulfillment is obtained from a sense of participation in social progress. Spiritual satisfaction is obtained by aiding other members of society to fulfill their own aspirations. The satisfaction of men's spiritual goal is achieved through altruistic concern for one's fellowmen. Julian Huxley has given to this fundamental impulse of human nature the name of Evolutionary Humanism. In the case of human beings there is not only a biological compulsion to promote the interests of society but also the power of choice of ends which conduce to the fulfillment of the social goals. Concern for one's fellowmen is thus not only the result of biological compulsion but is also the result of deliberate choice, which can be influenced by education. Plato maintained that only a just man is happy, and our experience tells us that few men are thoroughly content who are concerned only with themselves. Whatever may be the origin of the sense of social solidarity, a comparison of the evolution of law in various societies brings us to the irresistible conclusion that the goals of society, and therefore the goals of law, tend to approach each other, among peoples in corresponding stages of social development. There is thus good reason to conclude that the sense of social solidarity is deeply rooted in instincts which are common to all humanity.

It is clear that not all moral principles which are to be found in the law fall within the exclusive province of equity. With the progressive humanization of the law we can no longer, as Aristotle could, speak of strict law as law without moral content. The distinction in modern times is not between law and morals but between the moral standards of legal norms in which the standards of equity are either irrelevant or into which they have not been completely absorbed, and the moral standards of legal norms into which complete absorption of equitable principles has taken place. When we compare the moral content of the principles of equity which have become clearly identified in Anglo-American equity with the moral content of the legal norms of all legal systems, we find two different levels of moral standards. At one level are standards aimed primarily at establishing the conditions of an effective social order, as contrasted with the fulfillment of individual interests. The laws which are required for social order often necessitate the sacrifice of individual interests to the interest of society as a whole. In the laws which are less essential to the social order, the social interest yields to the need for individual fulfillment. Examples of standards of social order are the rules of criminal law and of many areas of administrative law such as taxation and the regulation of trade practices; the rules of contract law governing offer and acceptance, of property law governing the ownership and transfer of property, and of the law of torts forbidding infliction of harm on persons or property intentionally or by reason of lack of care. In these and other legal norms the urgent social need for certainty ordinarily precludes their modification on equitable grounds. The objectives of these rules are identical with the objectives of equity in the general sense of what is fair and just. It seems that men have reached in almost all legal systems, fairly similar solutions to problems which give rise to the need for stable juridical institutions. Surface distinctions disappear when the practical results are compared, and the jural solutions differ only slightly from one system to another, regardless of differences of conceptual approach.

There is a second level of moral standards which, to distinguish them from equity in the general sense of what is fair and just, might be called standards of pure equity. The norms where this level of duty is required apply higher ethical standards of conduct than those which are found at the first moral level. In the norms lying at the second moral level the social need for certainty yields to the demand for individual justice. The standards at this level are those which have been shown by experience

RALPH A. NEWMAN

to be enforceable at law. In the application of the rules which permit
a wide latitude for the exercise of judicial discretion, the solutions
differ widely from case to case, but most of the differences in the solutions
can be reconciled within the pattern established by the fundamental
principles upon which the rules of application—the decisions in each
case—are based. Beyond this second level are ethical standards which
must be left for enforcement to religion, public opinion or the individual
conscience. It is at the intermediate level that law, through the mediation
of pure equity, "provides ethics with explicitly expressed content as
formulated by the people themselves of a given culture."[40] Equity may
be defined as a force which gives shape to the ideal of decent and honorable conduct in the relations of man. In our search for the nature
of equity we must recognize its moral origin, and must look at the nature
and purpose of the moral doctrines from which the principles of equity
have been derived. Any workable system of equity must relate equitable
rights and duties to concepts which have already received well-recognized
interpretations in systems of ethics and morals.

The Golden Rule, which is exemplified in the Parable of the Good
Samaritan, is the basis of Stammler's theory of *richtige Recht* (just law).
Rules for the solution of conflicting interests must recognize the rights
of all members of the social community, not only the rights of one who
has been harmed, but also the rights even of one by whom the harm has
been inflicted. Stammler considers the moral basis of law to be the concept of "the community of men of free volition;"[41] that is, of a society
in which everyone makes the objects of others his own, as soon as they
permit of an objective justification. "The person subject [to legal norms]
must be respected as an end in himself, and treated as a participant in
the community. He must be regarded as a means . . . and may still
remain his own neighbor . . . Thus it may happen that he is required to
offer a sacrifice, even a sacrifice of himself, provided it is done to realize
the idea of the community and of the common rights. What the principles
of just law forbid is for the one party to treat the other according to his
own arbitrary desires . . But . . . every member of the community must
be loyal to the rest."[42] There is a parallel between Stammler's idea and
that of Spinoza, who says that "the mental intellectual love toward God
is the very love of God with which God loves himself."[43] Stammler
concludes that "we should [then] have to conceive of the party excluding
and the party injured thereby as united in a separate community, and
see how this community must be worked out and adjusted in accordance
with the principles of just law . . . Each of the parties must be treated
in such a manner that whatever his position he may remain his own

184

neighbor ... The disadvantage arising from a passive attitude or an active exercise must not be one-sidedly set to the account of the one party only. The loss must be divided; this is the social ideal."[44]

It is probable that the reluctance of the Positivists, from the time of Herbert Spencer in England and James Bradley Thayer in the United States, to recognize morals as a source of law, stems from the long history of the struggle to emancipate law from theological control. The conflict over the applicability of moral standards to legal norms has crystallized in the major clash between natural law and positivism. It has been thought in the past that to question moral principles is itself immoral; that our concepts must remain unchangeable because, as Saint Thomas and Spinoza thought, they are either inspired or self-evident, and an appeal from absolute value edicts to logic might lead to moral anarchy. Thus the identification of morality and religion discourages a pragmatic approach to the problem of determining the validity of rules of conduct expressed in either morals, religion or law, and adds nothing to the simple proposition that law and morality, as Del Vecchio[45] and Henri Bergson[46] have pointed out, have a common source in human nature. Ideas of justice ceased to be absolute in the Age of Pericles, when the rights of the individual became recognized.

It has been said that "ethical science involves an analysis of ethical judgments, a clarification of ethical premises ... There can be no edifying controversy among the current legal crypto-idealisms since there is no recognition of the moral issues to which their differences reduce. One looks in vain in legal treatises and law review articles for legal criticism conscious of its moral presumptions."[47] The principles of equity which have gradually worked themselves pure in biblical law, in the codes and systems of customary law of European, Latin-American and Asiatic countries and in Anglo-American equity enable us, by tracing the principles to their moral sources, to make explicit the concepts which Lord Evershed felt lie behind the principles. These can be succinctly stated:

(1) The law is concerned with substance and not with form
(2) The law will not permit the unscrupulous to carry out their plans
(3) Agreements made with full awareness of the circumstances must be carried out specifically, if this can be done without harmful effect on cotrolling public or private interests
(4) Conduct must conform to the legitimate expectations of others
(5) Benefits obtained by accident or mistake must be relinquished to those who are better entitled to them

(6) The law will give relief for mistake if this can be done without undue hardship to others

(7) Hardship resulting from human encounters must be shared, if necessary, by the whole social community.

These principles express what have been called the evolving ideals of decent and honorable conduct that mark the progress of a mature society. They are commonplace facts of all systems of ethics, morals and religion, of nearly all legal systems, and of Anglo-American equity. When we reduce these principles to their common elements, we find these elements to be good faith, honesty and generosity.

The equitable standard of good faith forbids any form of cunning, including failure to disclose; in equity, cheating is as reprehensible as it is in morals, without regard to the way the cheating is done. The bargaining process is looked upon as a transaction between persons who are aware of all material facts and neither of whom need bargain under the pressure of controlling economic compulsion exerted by his adversary. The obligation of good faith extends to strangers, with whom there is no consensual relationship. It applies not only to the formation of contracts but also to their enforcement.

The equitable concept of honesty is relevant whenever benefits have been obtained gratuitously, in bad faith, or by accident or mistake under circumstances in which the acquirer would be unjustly enriched at the expense of another person if the acquirer were permitted to retain the benefits.

The equitable concept of generosity requires the relinquishment of, or compensation for, benefits acquired or positions of advantage arising from services rendered or consensual agreements or from ownership of property, and requires compensation for unsuccessful efforts to provide assistance. The concept also applies to situations which require affirmative action (where a slight effort would prevent loss to another person); the principle of mitigation of damages by reducing the loss. The concept of generosity also explains the requirement of relief for mistake or frustration of the contractual expectation resulting from subsequent occurrences.

The precepts of good faith, honesty and generosity, embodying the ideal of decent and honorable conduct, provide, when applied in law, the legal counterparts of the precepts which express the ethical and moral experience of mankind. It is undoubtedly true that the descriptions of moral conduct which appear in legal norms are not precise equivalents of the moral standards, since what are standards of voluntary conduct in ethics and morals, enforced only by public opinion or the individual conscience, become, in law, obligations which are subject to penalties for their violation; but the solid core of the corresponding legal standards has been so often defined, especially as, in Anglo-American law, brought into sharp contrast with the principles of the inner common law system, that their meaning is unmistakable. The first four principles rest on the precept of good faith. The fifth principle rests on the precept of honesty. The sixth and seventh principles rest on the precept of generosity. Behind the principles and precepts lies the concept of human brotherhood.

Sir Henry Maine has said that "equity is a stage in the growth of the law by which it is expanded and liberalized;"[48] but the process continues forever. Julius Stone has emphasized the relation between man's engagement with ethical and religious experience and his search for peace.[49] In institutions such as the Truman Center for the Advancement of Peace, in Jerusalem, may lie the hope of world peace based on a common understanding between nations of the role of equity in law. For hundreds of years a *pax Romana* rested largely on the *ius gentium,* composed of principles of law common to the nations grouped around the rim of the Mediterranean Sea. Can we disregard as utopian a vision of a world law, based on a *corpus aequitatis,* a body of principles of equity, which will serve as a means of common understanding among nations? May we not dream of a vision of world peace through a world legal order based on principles of decent and honorable conduct between men? The continuing need for equity arises out of the lag between the recognition of such standards in systems of ethics, morals and religion, and the acceptance of such standards in law. It is in the broad intermediate area between strict law and ideal morality that the principles of equity serve to narrow the gap between law and morals by incorporating into the law the standards of essential morality. Equity will never cease to be necessary in the progressive unfolding of our destiny, as man advances toward his Unknown Goal, glimmering faintly just beyond the horizon of his dreams.

It seems especiallly appropriate, in an essay honoring Justice Cohn, to recall his reference, in one of his essays, to the statement in Deuteronomy which says of God's Law that "it is not hidden from thee, neither is it far off."[50] God's law, the embodiment of righteousness, has been the directing force of Justice Cohn's life. Equity, too, is not far off; it lies in the conscience of mankind.

RALPH A. NEWMAN

NOTES

[1] Hocking, *The Present Status of the Philosophy of Law and of Right*, p.2 (1926).

[2] Henri Bergson, *The Two Sources of Morality and Religion*, p.76 (17th ed. 1956).

[3] Kantorowicz, *The Definition of Law*, pp.2, 53 (Campbell ed. 1958).

[4] H. de Page, *A Propos du Gouvernement des Juges; l'Equité en Face du Droit*, p.161 (1931); Hanbury, *The Field of Modern Equity*, in *Essays in Equity*, p.23 (1934).

[5] 2 Bryce, *Studies in History and Jurisprudence*, p.181 (1901).

[6] Evershed, M.R., *Aspects of English Equity*, p.17 (1954).

[7] D. l.i.l.

[8] Cardozo, *The Nature of the Judicial Process*, p.50 (1921).

[9] Puig Brutau, *Juridical Evolution and Equity*, in *Essays in Jurisprudence, in honor of Roscoe Pound*, pp.82, 84 (Newman ed. 1962).

[10] Millar, *Historical View of English Government*, quoted in Pound, *The Decadence of Equity*, 5 Colum. L. Rev., pp.20, 22 (1905).

[11] Budge, *The Egyptian Book of the Dead*, p.14, Intro. lxxxvi (1895, ed. 1967).

[12] Breasted, *The Dawn of Conscience*, pp. 138, 364–380 (1934).

[13] Durant, *Our Oriental Heritage*, p.219 (1935). See Kent, *Israel's Laws and Legal Precedents*, Intro., p. 4 (1907); *Code of Hammurabi* sec. 210.

[14] Lev. 19.15; 19.18; 19.34.

[15] Psalms 119.64; 25.10; 96.10; 19.9.

[16] Hosea 6.6; 10.12; 12.6.

[17] Amos 5.24.

[18] Isaiah 59.14.

[19] Lev. 19.15; 19.18; 19.34.

[20] Isaiah 59.14.

[21] Aristotle, Nich. Eth. Bk. 5, c. 10.

[22] 1 Cor.13.13.

[23] Petranzycki, *Law and Morality*, in 7 Twentieth Century Legal Philosophy Series, pp. 283–284 (1955).

[24] See Ehrlich, *Fundamental Principles of the Sociology of Law*, p. 421 (Moll transl. 1913), cited in Stone, *Human Law and Human Justice*, p. 61 (1965).

[25] Savigny, *Geschichte des Rpmischen Rechts im Mittelater*, p. 11, App. I (a) (ed. 1934).

[26] See Buchanan, *Natural Law and Modern Society*, pp. 82–153 (Cogley ed. 1963), cited in Stone, *Human Law and Human Justice*, p. 36, n. la (1965).

[27] Fabentinus, *Summa on the Decretum* (A.D. 1171). See William of Longchamp, *Practica Legum et Decretorum* (12th century), a manual of procedure based on civil law and canon law; Coing, *English Equity and the Denunciatio Evangelica of the Canon Law*, 71 L. Quar. Rev. 223 (1955); 1 Pollock and Maitland, *The History of English Law*, p. 116 (2nd ed. 1898).

[28] See Vinogradoff, *Reason and Conscience in Sixteenth Century Jurisprudence*, p. 24 L. Quar. Rev. 379 (1908); Bolland, *Eyre of Kent*, Seldon Society vol. 21, 22.

[29] Del Vecchio, *Justice*, p. 152 (ed. 1952).

[30] Natural law: Argentine Civil Code, Art. 16; Austrian Civil Code, sec. 7; Constituent Assembly Law of Ghana, Art. 4. Honesty and Good Faith: Swiss Civil Code, Art. 2. Treu und Glauben: German Civil Code, sec. 157, 242. Courtezza: Italian Civil Code, Art. 1175. The general legal system of the State: Italian Civil Code, Art. 12. The General Principles of Law: Spanish Civil Code, Art. 6; Chinese Civil Code, Art. 1; Portuguese Civil Code, Art. 16. Equity and Justice: Egyptian Civil Code, Art. 4.

[31] See Lefèbvre, *Le Role de l'Equité en Droit Canonique*, p. 7; *Ephemerides iuris canonici*, pp. 137, 151 (1951); Lefèbvre, *Recours à l'Office du Juge, Dictionnaire de droit canonique*, Fas. xxxl, col. 208 (1954).

[32] Munroe Smith, *Problems of Roman Legal History*, 4 Colum. L. Rev. 523, 525 (1904).

[33] See Lenel, *Das Edictum Perpetuum* (3rd ed. 1927); Pringsheim, *The Legal Policy and the Reforms of Hadrian*, 24 Jour. of Roman Studies, pp. 141, 143 (1934)

[34] Drago, *The General Principles of Law in the Jurisprudence of the French Conseil d'Etat*, 11 Am. U. L. Rev., pp. 126, 127 (1962).

[35] Bergson, *op. cit.* 76 (17th ed., Aufra and Brereton transl. 1956).

[36] Pound, *Toward a New Jus Gentium*, in *Ideological Differences and World Legal Order*, pp. 1, 4 (1949).

[37] Plato, *Menon*, pp. 99–100.

[38] Sorokin, *The Basic Trends of Our Times*, pp. 149, 150 (1964).

[39] Bergson, op. cit., p. 85.

[40] Northrop, *The Complexities of Legal and Ethical Experience*, p. 183 (1959).

[41] Stammler, *Wirtschaft und Recht*, p. 600 (2nd ed. 1906).

[42] Stammler, *Lehrbuch von dem Richtigen Recht*, vol. 2, sec. 5, pp. 152–155 (1919); *The Theory of Justice*, 8 Modern Legal Philosophy Series, pp. 217–218 (1925).

[43] B. Spinoza, *Ethics*, p. 36 (transl. 1949).

[44] Stammler, *The Theory of Justice*, pp. 247–248 (ed. 1925).

[45] Del Vecchio, *Mutability and Eternity of Law*, in *Humanity and Unity of Law, Essays in Legal Philosophy*, p. 262 (1963); *Man and Nature: Transcendental Parallelism*, in *Man and Nature*, p. 8 (Newman ed. 1969, transl. Campbell).

[46] Bergson, op. cit., p. 85.

[47] Felix Cohen, *Ethical Systems and Legal Ideals*, ch. 1, *The Ethical Basis of Legal Criticism*, pp. 3–5 (1933).

[48] Maine, *Ancient Law*, p. 27 (3rd Am. ed. 1887).

[49] Stone, *Research for Advancement of Peace*, p. 10 (1968).

[50] Haim Cohn, *Prolegomena to the Theory and History of Jewish Law*, in *Essays in Jurisprudence in Honor of Roscoe Pound*, pp. 44, 81. The citation to Deuteronomy is 30.11, 14.

"LIFTING THE VEIL" OF A CORPORATE ENTITY

SMADAR OTTOLENGHI*

The subject of "lifting the veil" of a corporate personality is being discussed more and more frequently in the courts and by jurists.[1] The academic question is whether it is undermining the long-established doctrine of the separate legal entity of the company. At the same time, there arises the practical point—when ought the veil to be lifted? Both these questions assume that the term itself, "lifting the veil", is already clear and well defined.

However, a close examination of the instances, statutory or in case-law, in which the veil is, and has been, lifted, reveals that the term "lifting the veil" has several meanings. It includes four different forms of approach to the company and its shareholders: glimpsing behind the veil; penetrating beyond the veil; extending the veil; and disregarding the veil or tearing it apart. This distinction offers an answer to the first problem, and it seems that it may have implications on the other question, too.

In assessing the category of "glimpsing behind the veil", the veil of the corporate entity remains intact: it is only the legal character and personality of its shareholders that is uncovered.

"Lifting the veil" is usually regarded as having originated in the Daimler case[2], where the main issue was the enemy character of the company. This case is cited as identifying the company's character with that of its shareholders. The justification of lifting the veil is, indeed, dealt with there in a lengthy discussion, but it is all *obiter* (as Lord Parker himself describes it). And even so, can this passage be considered as identifying the company with its shareholders for the purpose of affixing the company with an enemy character, when Lord Parker points out that "the character of individual shareholders cannot of itself

* Lecturer on Civil Law, Tel Aviv University.

affect the character of the company"?[3] The only lifting of the veil, by way of glimpsing only, is in an indirect form: "The enemy character of individual shareholders and their conduct may, however, be very material on the question of whether the company's agents or the persons in *de facto* control of its affairs are in fact adhering to, taking instructions from, or acting under the control of enemies."[4] This means that it is only the nature of its organs and agents that can decide the enemy character of a company[5], not the character of its shareholders as such.[6]

However, special statutory provisions relating to companies as enemies require glimpsing behind the veil, so as to establish the nationality of its shareholders.[7] Having taken a glimpse, the court then once more lets the veil fall, directing itself to the company as a legal person.

The courts in Israel have glimpsed behind the veil in order to determine the character of a company for the purpose of Business Tax also. The question that arose was: ought a family investment company, or a company established *ad hoc* to construct a single building, to be regarded as "carrying on business" for tax purposes? The Tel-Aviv District Court relieved a family investment company of liability for business tax, "in particular because of the private and family nature of the company." The Supreme Court reversed the decision, holding that "the shareholders are, after all, the persons interested in the carrying on of the activities, but nevertheless they are not identical with the company."[8] (The concluding words in this passage are an indication of the widely-held error, which always sees in the lifting of the veil the extinction of the company's legal personality, identifying it with its shareholders.) In another instance, a company tried to make use of the lifting of the veil for its own benefit, in reliance on this passage. The argument was that, since its shareholders (the Government and the Jewish Agency) are not in business for their own profit, the status of the company ought to be determined by the status of its shareholders. In rejecting this argument, the Supreme Court held that if the Government elects to act through the medium of a commercial enterprise, when it could have acted by administrative means, then it must bear the burden of the appropriate tax.[9]

The most common examples of the request to glimpse behind the veil, are the statutory definitions of companies as a holding, a subsidiary company[10], or as a "company of a few."[11] The definition itself necessitates consideration of the company's shareholders in order to determine whether the company answers any of these descriptions. Many statutory provisions are directed at people in control of the company, and to disclose them, a glimpse must be taken behind the veil.

Glimpsing behind the veil for the purpose of obtaining information only is to be observed also in those cases where there was some fault in the adoption of a resolution in a company (for instance, insufficient notice of the intention to propose the resolution), or an error in selecting the forum qualified to pass such a resolution (a directors' meeting instead of a shareholders' meeting). The court will, in such cases, lift the veil and examine, in the first case, whether all the shareholders have signed the resolution, in which case they are deemed to have dispensed with notice[12]; and in the second case, whether all the shareholders are also the directors, in which case the resolution can be deemed to have been signed by the competent organ.[13] This must not, it seems, be regarded as lifting the veil "so as to equate a decision of the members with a decision of the company."[14] This is rather a case of glimpsing behind the veil, examining the members making up the various organs, the result of which is the validation of the resolution, considering it to have been taken by the appropriate organ, and not by the members as such.

There is also a tendency to regard as a kind of lifting of the veil the investigation of a company's place of registration or place of central control of the company's business, in order to determine its residence for tax purposes.[15] This would appear to be an unwarranted extension of the veil-lifting procedure. An investigation of the place of registration or of the place the company's business is controlled from does not necessitate drawing aside the curtain. In the last case, it refers to the company's organs or agents only, and it is simply unrelated to the personality of the shareholders. In the Income Tax Ordinance (New Version), for example, the definition of "resident in Israel" as applied to a body of persons is "any body of persons the control and management of whose business are exercised in Israel", thus disconnecting it from the identity and character of its shareholders. On the other hand, where there is a specific statutory provision, that "the residence of a corporation is the place of residence of the majority of its members"[16]—glimpsing behind the veil does become necessary.[17]

There are quite a few instances where this glimpsing behind the veil has been made needlessly, one might say, out of sheer judicial curiosity. For example, descriptions are found in judgments of, say, "the X company, the shares of which are owned by Mr. and Mrs. AB", although the identity of the shareholders is irrelevant to the matter in question. Such references to the shareholders may be purely *obiter dicta,* but they may be indicative of an increasing, though hesitant, tendency to blur the otherwise clear-cut distinction between the company and its shareholders.

In the category "penetrating beyond the veil", the legislator or the courts concern themselves directly with the shareholders, by reaching through the veil. This attitude, again, does not involve the extinction of the company's legal personality. It only attributes a direct and personal interest of the shareholder in the property and affairs of the company.

Thus, a full statutory liability for a company's debts and obligations will be incurred whenever the number of the members of the company drops below the minimum number required by law. After six months, the remaining members who carry on business in the name of the company knowingly will become personally liable for all of the company's obligations, and each of them may be sued for the total amount, without the other members even being joined as defendants.[18] This is, again, only penetrating beyond the veil and not tearing it aside, for the debts and obligations remain the debts and obligations of the company, and the company continues to function as a separate legal entity, notwithstanding this adjoint liability imposed on its shareholders.

In most cases, penetrating beyond the veil is directed at one or more of the persons in control of the company. The "control" in a company is not a generally defined concept,[19] and different laws referring to the subject, and even individual sections within those laws, adopt different definitions. Thus one finds in the Income Tax Ordinance (New Version), that a person may be recognized as holding the controlling interest in a company only if he has at least 90% of the voting power therein,[20] or if he has 51% of the shares[21]; but even 10% of the shares may be deemed control of the company.[22] The power to appoint directors, being also considered as a factor of control[23], varies from the power to appoint the majority of the directors[24] to the power of nominating one director only.[25]

Other laws, not restricting themselves to the controlling shareholders only, provide that a person may be deemed to be the owner of the company's rights even if he holds as little as 26% of the shares[26], or that he is regarded as having a direct interest in the company's property, proportionate to his part in its share capital.[27]

The concern for excluding the possibility of favoritism or undue influence in bodies engaged in public services may be found in the laws concerning public officials, with a difference of degree in the importance attached by the legislator to the shareholding in the company. In one such law, a person having an interest, directly or by means of a controlled company, in a plan under consideration by the competent authority of which he is a member, is precluded only from participating in the meeting at which such a plan is to be considered.[28] Another law totally disqualifies from membership of the Plenum a person who is linked with the Authority by an agreement involving a commercial or contracting transaction, or a person controlling a body corporate so linked.[29] A third law regards a person as having a direct interest in contracts between a company and the Municipal Corporation of which he is a member if he holds only 5% of the shares in that company.[30]

The proceeding of penetrating beyond the veil is generally thought of as being detrimental to the shareholders or to the company. In point of fact, there are quite a number of instances, both statutory or in case-law, where it works to their benefit or the benefit of the company itself. The Income Tax Ordinance (New Version) provides some illustrations of both kinds.

A classic example of what is generally thought to be a statutory lifting of the veil, which is in reality a penetration beyond the veil, is s. 76 of the Ordinance, which provides that the shareholders of a "company of a few" may be liable to pay tax on the undistributed profits of the company, as if those profits had been distributed by way of dividend. The direct interest of the shareholders in the company's profits, recognized as such by the legislation, functions here to their disadvantage.

Penetrating beyond the veil to the detriment of the company itself may be found in ss. 24–26 of the said Ordinance, which deal with depreciation allowances on immovable property. These sections provide, *inter alia,* that such depreciation shall not be allowed where a person who has transferred property to a company retains control thereof, whether directly or indirectly, by virtue of his control of the company.

The same approach sometimes tends to result in an advantage for the shareholders or the company. Thus, a person selling his assets to a corporation in his control will not be liable for capital gains tax[31] and shareholders who consider that it would be fairer to tax them personally on the profits of their "company of a few" from the letting of its immovable assets—can ask the Income Tax Commissioner to do so, thus relieving the company from paying income tax on its own profits.[32]

In another law[33], the direct interest that a person has in a company's property has led to his being held liable to pay land appreciation tax, even where he has transferred only his shares in that company, if the latter constitutes a "real-estate association" controlled by not more than five persons.[34] On the other hand, a transfer of land from individuals to a "real-estate association", where the association right vested in the person who sold the real estate right to the association is co-extensive with the real estate right sold by him—will be exempt from land appreciation tax[35].

The attitude of the courts in penetrating beyond the veil has been stricter. The courts preferred to follow the decision in the Macaura case[36], in which the doctrine of Salomon v. Salomon[37] prevailed, particularly, as in that case, where the shareholders themselves have sought recognition of their direct interest in the company's property.[38] The rule is that "if persons choose to conduct their operations through the medium of a limited company with the advantages in respect of responsibility for debts thereby conferred, they cannot really complain if they have to face some disadvantages also."[39]

However, where the request to lift the veil is made by a stranger to the company, especially in the case of one-man companies where there is a confusion between the affairs of the company and those of its shareholder, the court will regard the assets and property of the company in the same light as the person in control has regarded it, namely, as his own private property. Therefore, the court will not permit the person in control of a company to evade performance of contracts signed by him personally in respect of the company's property, and it will oblige him to perform them and see to it that the company performs them, as the case may be.[40]

This form of lifting the veil is frequently employed to prevent tax evasion. In some cases, penetrating beyond the veil is an exceedingly useful weapon in the hand of the Income Tax Assessor, treating the profits of the company as the direct profits of its controlling shareholder.[41] In other cases, the lifting of the veil has enabled the Assessor to justify his opinion that a certain transaction was fictitious or artificial.[42]

Not in all cases has the penetration beyond the veil proved to be consistent. In one case, such a penetration led the court to regard the sale of the assets of an estate by the administratrix to a company under her control as a sale of the property to herself. But the court did not continue that reasoning to its logical end, namely, declare the sale to be invalid, on the ground that the company, being a separate legal personality, was not a party (not even a formal one) to the proceedings.[43] In another case, the veil was penetrated twice, with an interesting result: here a person fraudulently transferred land (including a part of which he was only a trustee) to a company in his control. Therefore, basing itself on the lifting of the veil, the court pronounced that the transfer had to be declared invalid. But in the meantime, the control of the company passed on to another, and "the new master" (as called there) was *bona fide* in respect of the former transaction. Accordingly, the court declined to void the sale, since such a decision might have injured the present shareholder only.[44] Thus, the first form of lifting the veil, by disregarding it, was to the detriment of the controlling shareholder; the second one, by penetrating beyond it, acted to his benefit.

"Lifting the Veil" of a Corporate Entity

As noted, direct penetrating beyond the veil is made especially in respect of companies with a limited shareholding, where the full control in the hands of the shareholders enables them to continue their control of the property. But penetration is also found in respect of holding and subsidiary companies, where the courts, after having investigated the relationship between the companies, attribute to them a relationship of principal and agent.[45] Having found that the subsidiary company was actually fully owned and fully controlled by its holding company, the courts have then treated the subsidiary's business as that of the holding company (and taxed it accordingly[46]). Now, must the shareholding be considered as the primary factor in determining the relationship between the two companies? The mere control of the company by way of shareholding (a fact which can be clarified by only glimpsing behind the veil of the subsidiary company) does not mean the existence of an agency relationship between the controlling shareholder and the company, where no other circumstances support it.[47] The attempts to attribute agency relations (being only "constructive agency") between the two companies, basing it on lifting the veil, proves the difficulty in which the courts find themselves, seeking to achieve a certain purpose: trying to avoid a direct lifting of the veil as the basis for their judgments, they base them on some generally accepted rules of law; and these rules cannot be applied in all circumstances. Indeed, in these cases, the desired result may be achieved best by lifting the veil by way of extending it.

The category of "extending the veil" refers primarily to a situation in which a number of companies are engaged in the same enterprise, horizontally (i.e., in the same branch of industry or services) or vertically (i.e., the same product, from manufacture through marketing).[48] Wherever companies are inter-related, whether through holding or subsidiary companies or as "sister" companies (the controlling interest in which is in the hands of the same shareholders or holding companies), the courts—more in U.S. than elsewhere—tend to ignore the separate personality of each of the companies, and regard the entire arrangement as one large single concern.

This approach has enabled the courts to prevent the circumvention of statutory prohibitions by the use of subsidiaries or other inter-related corporations.[49] Because of this attitude of the courts none of the companies escape liability, alleging that the property and the business in question were those of one of the other companies[50], or that the action in question was one for which one of the other companies is responsible.[51] The courts will lay hold of the individual veil and draw it across all those legal bodies, so that they are all hidden by the same veil.[52]

In that event, they are a single economic and legal unit, mutually responsible for the acts of every component company thereof.[53]

Thus three "sister" companies, which had offices in the same room and the same officials working for all three of them for the same purposes, were directed to pay rent to the landlord, notwithstanding frequent transfers between them of the lease of the premises, in order to avoid such payment.[54] In the same way, a holding company was held liable for the acts of its subsidiary company[55]; so also a claim by a subsidiary company was dismissed because the damage sustained by it was caused only as a result of the activities of its own holding company[56]; and a holding company's proof in the bankruptcy of its subsidiary was rejected.[57]

Evidence of such an all-embracing approach is to be found, in Israeli law, on the part of the legislator. A modern definition in this direction may be noted in the Mining Ordinance, as far back as 1925. S. 2 of that Ordinance states, that a company includes "a single company and a group of companies of which one or more companies may be controlled by, or affiliated or subsidiary to, another company of the same group."

A more detailed and even more extensive definition is to be found in the Restrictive Trade Practices Law, 5719–1959, which provides that
"The following shall be regarded as one person:
1. A company and its subsidiaries;
2. The subsidiaries of one company;
3. Companies most of the directors of which are the same persons;
4. A company and the person controlling it;
5. Companies controlled by one person"[58]

In the Land Appreciation Tax Law, 5723–1963, a person includes himself and a relative of his; and "a relative", as defined thereby, includes "an association controlled by that person"[59]

A certain trend of this intention of the legislator, i.e., to allow companies to extend their veil, is expressed also in the Industry Encouragement (Tax) Law, 5729–1969, which encourages the merger of interrelated companies.

In the few occasions that the courts have had to deal with enterprises carried on by a complex of companies, they have pointed out that, although two companies were concerned in the action, in practice they ought to be considered as one body, having regard to all the circumstances.[60]

Generally speaking, courts and jurists are disposed to use the term "lifting the veil" solely in reference to one category, namely, totally disregarding the company as a legal entity. The formula used by Judge

Sunborn is widely quoted as the *locus classicus*: "When the notion of legal entity is used to defeat public convenience, justify wrong, protect fraud, or defend crime, the law will regard the corporation as an association of persons".[61]

This category of veil lifting is the most fatal one, from the point of view of the separate legal entity of the company. It is a handy weapon in the hands of judges who wish to ignore what they term "bubble companies".[62] It is most frequently employed in respect of companies set up for fraudulent purposes, the majority of which are attempts at defrauding creditors. The debtor transfers all his property to a company in his control, so that the creditors desirous of suing him find themselves faced with an empty coffer; whereas they have no recourse to the company, it not having been privy to the transaction that is the subject of the claim. In such cases, the coutts have held that the company was no more than a "sham", "scheme", "instrumentality", "mask", etc.[63]

Now, is it really necessary to cancel out the legal personality of a company in such a case? Does such an attitude achieve the desired object? The answer to both questions should be in the negative. The property is now in the hands of the company. To declare a company as no more than a mere mask, bubble and so on, is to do away with the actual owner of the property. Does the property then, for that reason only, become restored to its former owner?

It is the actual transfer that is tainted with fraud, not the personality of the transferee. A transfer of property fraudulently vis-a-vis the creditors is what has to be invalidated. In fact, in the bulk of the cases, the problem arises within the framework of bankruptcy proceedings, in respect of which there are statutory provisions to avoid transfers of property *mala fide* and without valuable consideration.[64] The transferor is generally, by the very nature of things, also the director of the transferee company. It is he, therefore, that causes the company to be regarded as acting *mala fide* in respect of the same transfer, since whether by agency law or by the organic theory, his knowledge and intentions are attributed to the company, especially if they concern the company itself. Accordingly it is the transfer itself that ought to be attacked, not the personality of the transferee, whether an individual or a company controlled by the transferor.

Another form of fraud is the use of a company in order to evade the carrying out of contracts. A party, having contracted to sell land but going back on the contract before performing it, transfers the land to a company in his control. The court, in one such case, actually made an order against him for specific performance, remarking that the company was no more than "a device and a sham, a mask which he holds before his face in an attempt to avoid recognition by the eye of equity."[65]

Is this device of canceling the company's legal personality the only solution? Might it not have been possible, having regard to the seller's position in the company (investigation of which would necessitate glimpsing behind the veil only), to oblige him to carry out his undertaking, by simply having the necessary resolutions passed by the company, as the courts did, indeed, in other cases?[66]

Contracts in restraint of unfair competition are another example of the use of a company in an effort to avoid obligations. A party has personally undertaken by contract to refrain from competing with the other party, and then set up a company and run it in competition with the other party. Can he escape liability under that contract on the ground that it is not he who is in breach of the contract, whilst his company is not bound by contracts privately made by its shareholder? On facts similar to these[67], the court once more heaped deprecatory epithets on the company, such as "a device, a stratagem"[68], or "a mere cloak or sham"[69], and then issued an injunction both against the company and against its controlling shareholder. The remedy granted does not appear in line with the rationale of the decision. If the company is not a legal entity of its own, how could an injunction be issued against it? And if the injunction was made against the company as such, this means that it was regarded as a fit object for making orders against; which being so, how could it be treated as non-existing?

The legal approach to this problem could have been somewhat different. The court could have examined the relations between the contracting party and the company, in order to decide whether those relations might not be regarded as those of principal and agent. The extent of the defendant shareholder's control of the company could have been clarified by merely glimpsing behind the veil, if this constitutes a consideration in this respect. In this way, an injunction may be issued against both principal and agent, without in any way affecting the status and personality of the company.

In competing through the medium of a corporate body, the question is not in what kind of body was the competitive business being conducted—a partnership or a corporation[70]—but the degree of activity of the party, who has contracted not to compete, within the framework of that body.

In general, therefore, it seems, that the device of a separate legal entity in order to avoid contractual obligations or to circumvent a statutory prohibition, must be faced by reference to the circumstances of the case and the general rules of law.

One other matter ought to be mentioned in brief, namely, the practical problem. When would the courts lift the veil in one of the ways outlined above?

Various classifications of the cases where the veil would be lifted have been made, both by courts and by jurists.[71] The following rules have been accepted by both:

1. The veil will be lifted to prevent fraud;
2. The veil will be lifted to prevent circumvention of laws;
3. The veil will be lifted whenever the enemy character of the company is in question.[72]

It seems that there is a confusion between the grounds for lifting the veil and the objects of it. The first two mentioned are objects, purposes that the lifting of the veil should achieve. The third is only one example of the need to lift the veil (in this case by glimpsing only), so as to comply with statutory provisions. (Affixing the company with an enemy character is not very different, in this sense, from regarding it as a holding company or a company of a few.)

On the other hand, one can observe certain common considerations for the lifting of the veil. These considerations are generally for penetrating and extending the veil, because these are the more operative types of veil lifting. Such considerations are the kind of company (one-man company[73], a family company[74] or holding and subsidiary companies[75], as against a large public company); the way in which the company is managed (intermingling of private business with the company's affairs[76] or not performing the formal statutory requirements incumbent upon a company[77]); the under-capitalization of the company[78] (in order to increase the profits of those in control of it); the motives for setting up the company[79] (tax avoidance or tax evasion, fraud upon creditors, etc); the intention of the parties to a contract[80] (which there is now an attempt to circumvent or avoid); the identity of the person seeking the lifting of the veil in his favor[81] (a third party, the company itself, or the holder of the controlling interest in it); and perhaps yet others.

At all events, whatever may be the purpose for which the lifting of the veil in one or other of its different forms takes place, there is no reason why it should involve having an adverse effect on the doctrine of the separate legal entity of the company. The lifting of the veil need not constitute an antithesis to that doctrine. Lifting the veil is in itself not a doctrine, nor even a theory. It is the process by which the courts or the legislator may approach a company, for the particular purpose relevant to the case or the object of the legislator. At the same time, it does not ignore legal reality, which recognizes the fact that a company acts, and is in fact controlled, by physical agents, having a separate legal personality, so that for certain purposes recourse must be had to those self-same agents.

Such recourse does not of necessity mean that the company must be ignored. On the contrary, this recourse, in the form of glimpsing behind the veil for the purpose of information only, is used to adjudge the company itself. Or the lifting of the veil may be done by way of penetrating beyond the veil, in order to discover the direct property link between the shareholders and the company; or by way of extending the veil, to cover a complex of companies. It is only the fourth category, namely, disregarding the veil or tearing it apart, that is considered "lifting the veil" *par excellence;* and this kind of lifting runs counter to the doctrine of the legal personality of the company. Yet it is the one category of veil-lifting that is, in effect, mostly unnecessary, in the sense that the results obtained thereby can be achieved by other well established and better known legal methods and procedures.

The legal entity of the corporation is reserved, then, even though the veil is being lifted. The process of law is to seek the reality behind the formal forms, leaving the legal theories untouched.

NOTES

[1] For the main sources, see Grower, Modern Company Law, 3rd ed., Ch. 10 (1969); Friedman, Legal Theory, 4th ed., Ch. 33 (1960); Wormser, The Disregard of the Corporate. Fiction and Allied Corporate Problems (1927); Powell, Parent and Subsidiary Corporations (1931); Latty, Subsidiaries and Affiliated Corporations (1936); Ballantine on Corporations, rev. ed., Ch. 10 (1946); O'Neal, Close Corporations (1958); and Cohn-Simitis, "'Lifting the Veil' in the Company Law of the European Continent (1963) 12 International & Comparative L. Q. 189.

[2] Daimler Co. Ltd. v. Continental Tyre & Rubber Co. Ltd. [1916] 2 A.C. 307, H.L.

[3] Ibid., p. 345.

[4] Ibid., ibid.

[5] See Fink, "That Pierced Veil—Friendly Stockholders and Enemy Corporations", (1953) 51 Mich. L.R. 651.

[6] Indeed, in a later case, Lord Cozens-Hardy, M.R., directed himself only to the character of the directors of the company, the character of its shareholders being, in his opinion, irrelevant. See in re Hilches. Ex parte Muchesa Rubber Plantations Ltd. [1917] 1 K.B. 48.

[7] See s. 4 of the Trading with the Enemy Ordinance, 1939. And cf. s. 2 of the German Property Law, 5710–1050; s. 2 of the Absentees' Property Law, 5710–1950.

[8] Civ. App. 56–57/53, The Mayor and Corporation of Tel-Aviv-Jaffa v. Ahuzat Harari Ltd. & Ahuzat Nahum Ltd., 9 P.D. 892. Similar instances are to be found in the judgments in Motion 476/58, Batei Roni Haifa Ltd. v. The Mayor and Corporation of Haifa, 17 P.M. 38 (D.C.) and Civ. App. 367/58, 13 P.D. 1396, (S.C.) under the same name.

[9] Civ. App. 127/64, Rural Industries Ltd. v. The Mayor and Corporation of Tel-Aviv, 18 (III) P.D. 298. And see, conversely, Berger, "Disregarding the Corporate Entity for Stockholders' Benefit", (1955) 55 Col L.R. 808, 824.

[10] Four different definitions are to be found now in Israeli legislation for a holding or a subsidiary company: s. 107(8) of the Companies Ordinance, 1929–1936; s. 76 of the Income Tax Ordinance (New Version); s. 9 of the Restrictive Trade Practices Law, 5719–1959, as amended in 1963; and, lately, s. 22 of the Industry Encouragement (Tax) Law, 5729–1969.

[11] The name by which the Israeli legislator denotes a company in the control of not more than five persons, which is not a subsidiary company and in which the public has no interest. See definition in s. 76 of the Income Tax Ordinance (New Version).

[12] Re Oxted Motors Co. [1921] 3 K.B. 32

[13] Re Express Engineering Works [1920] 1 Ch. 466, C.A.; and cf. Civ. App. 135/48, Beer v. Rubin, 4 P.M. 182 (D.C.); Civ. File 1630/62, Goldbarth v. Halperine, Water & Co., 38 P.M. 307 (D.C.).

[14] Gower, op.cit., p. 209.

[15] Ibid., p. 207. And see Goldstein, "The Residence and Domicile of Corporations with Special Reference to Income Tax" (1935), 51 L.Q.R. 684, and see analysis of judgments therein.

[16] R. 3 of the Property Tax and Compensation Fund (Compensation Payments) (Drought Damage) Regulations, 5725–1965.

[17] See, for Federal Court jurisdiction, Judge Marshall, in Bank of U.S. v. Deveaux (1809) 9 U.S. (5 Cranch) 61, 81, which is still cited today.

[18] S. 112 of the Companies Ordinance, corresponding to s. 31 of the British Companies Act, 1948. Naturally, this problem would not arise in those countries which—unlike Israel and Great Britain—recognize one man as constituting a company. For a list of these states, see Hornstein, Corporation Law and Practice, p. 261.

[19] See Berle & Means, The Modern Corporation and Private Property, Chap. 5 (1950). And cf. Pickering, "Shareholders' Voting Rights and Company Control" (1965) 81 L.Q.R. 248.

[20] S. 95(a) of the Income Tax Ordinance (New Version), as amended in 1965.

[21] Ibid., s. 24.

[22] Ibid., s. 32(9), (as amended in 1968).

[23] S. 22 of the Industry Encouragement (Tax) Law, 5729–1969, not specifying the number of directors the appointment of which is considered as "control" in that company.

[24] S. 24 of the Income Tax Ordinance (New Version).

[25] Ibid., s. 9(2).

[26] S. 56(b) of the Petroleum Law, 5713–1953.

[27] E.g. in the Land Appreciation Law, 5723–1963. One of many other examples is also the Compulsory Loan Law, 5713–1953, s. 8(b) of which provides that "A person shall be regarded as the lessee of immovable property . . . by virtue of his membership in a company".

[28] S. 47 of the Planning and Building Law, 5725–1965.

[29] S. 7(c) of the Broadcasting Authority Law, 5725–1965.

[30] S. 122 of the Municipal Corporations Ordinance (New Version). And see also s.

13(2) of the Bank of Israel Law, 5714—1954; and s. 7(a) (2) of the State Comptroller Law, 5718–1958.

[31] S. 95(a) of the Income Tax Ordinance (New Version).

[32] Ibid., s. 64.

[33] The Land Appreciation Tax Law, 5723–1963, levying betterment tax on land upon its transfer.

[34] Ibid., ss. 7, 9(b), 12, 14(a).

[35] Ibid., s. 70.

[36] Macaura v. Northern Assurance Co. [1925] A.C. 619 (H.L.).

[37] Salomon v. A. Salomon & Co. [1897] A.C. 22 (H.L.), regarded as establishing the legal personality of the company, including a one-man company, as distinct from the personality of its shareholders. Actually, this had already been decided before, although not by the House of Lords. See, for example, Farrar v. Farrars, Ltd. (1888) 40 Ch. D. 395; Re Sax, Barned v. Sax (1893) 62 L.J.Ch. 688; John Foster & Sons v. C.I.R. [1894] 1 Q.B. 516.

[38] See the severe judgments in The Unitas [1948] P. 205, and Re International Telephone & Telegraph Corp., 343 U.S. 156 (1952).

[39] Tunstall v. Steigman [1962] 2 All E.R. 417, at p. 420, per Ormerod, L.J.

[40] Civ. App. 44/53, Barnowitz Ltd. v. Zimerman, 8 P.D. 1245 (S.C.); Civ. App. 147/63, Agib v. P.&B. Ltd., 17 P.D. 2169 (S.C.); Civ.App. 310/64, Goldstein Bros., Construction & Development Co. Ltd. v. Jacob, 19 (II) P.D. 72 (S.C.). And cf. Gilford Motor Co. v. Horne [1933] Ch. 935, C.A.; and Elliott v. Pierson [1948] Ch. 452.

[41] Civ. App. 137/56, Shor v. I.T.C., 11 P.D. 436 (S.C.); Civ. App. 4/63, Anzelievitz v. I.T.C., 17 P.D. 1302 (S.C.).

[42] I.T. App. 6/65, Ephraim Ltd. v. Director of Land Appreciation Tax Haifa, 50 P.M. 3 (D.C.), and Civ. App. 546/65, 20 (II) P.D. 176, under the same name; Civ. App. 356/61, Rosenfeld v. I.T.C., 16 P.D. 715; Civ. App. 34/61, Vadia v. Director of Land Appreciation Tax, 15 P.D. 2255 (S.C.); and Civ. App. 310/62, I.T.C. v. Ron, 16 P.D. 2751 (S.C.).

[43] Civ. File 430/51, Bar Shira v. Vernikov, 23 P.M. 381 (D.C.).

[44] Civ. App. 124/61, The Administrator General of Israel v. Heussman, 38 P.M. 347 (D.C.). And see the same reasoning in I.T. App. 204/62, Himpa Ltd. v. I.T.C., 41 P.M. 194 (D.C.). But in other cases, the courts refused to hear such arguments on the part of the new controlling shareholders: Civ. App. 127/63, Ahuzat Rahamim Ltd. v. Cristal, 17 P.D. 1929 (S.C.); Civ. App. 455/65, Givat Hacarcomim Ltd. v. Iamnik, 20 (I) P.D. 355 (S.C.).

[45] See, for example, Kodak, Ltd. v. Clark [1903] 1 K.B. 505; The Gramophone & Typewriter, Ltd. v. Stanley [1908] 2 K.B. 89; Re F.G. Films (Ltd.) [1953] 1 All E.R. 615; Rirestone Tyre & Rubber Co. v. Llewellin [1957] 1 W.L.R. 464, H.L. And see the survey "Liability of a Corporation for Acts of a Subsidiary or Affiliate", (1958) 71 Harv. L.R. 1122.

[46] Like in the breweries cases: The St. Louis Brewe Ltd. v. Apthorpe (1898) 79 L.T. 551 (Q.B.); Apthorpe v. Peter Schoenhofen Brewing Co. Ltd. (1898) 79 L.T. 98 (Q.B.); Apthorpe v. Peter Schoenhofen Brewing Co. Ltd. (1899) 80 L.T. 395 (C.A.).

[47] I.R.C. v. Sansom [1921] 2 K.B. 492 (C.A.), for a private company; Smith, Stone & Knight, Ltd. v. Birmingham [1939] 4 All E.R. 116; Canada Rice Mills Ltd. v. R. [1939] 3 All E.R. 991 (P.C.), for two companies. And see also Civ. App. 9/57, Mekoroth Ltd. v. Tel-Aviv Corporation, 12 P.D.. 278; I.T. App., 1015/65, Pi Gliloth Ltd. v. I.T.C., 52 P.M. 367 (D.C.).

[48] See the strict definition of "line of production" in this sense, in the Industry Encouragement (Tax) Law, 5729–1969.

[49] See, e.g., as to the attempt to avoid s. 1 of the Hepburn Act (known as the Commodities Clause), the following judgments: U.S. Delaware, L. &. W.R.R., 238 U.S. 516, 35 Sup. Ct. 873; U.S. v. Lehigh Valley R.R., 254 U.S. 255, 41 Sup, Ct. 104; U.S. v. Reading Co., 253 U.S. 26, 40 Sup. Ct. 425.

[50] Ross v. Pennsylvania R.R. Co., 106 N.J.L. 536, 148 Atl. 741 (1930); Berkey v. Third Avenue Ry. Co., 244 N.Y. 84, 155 N.E. 58 (1926).

[51] Constan v. Manila Electric Co., 24 F. (2d) 383 (1928).

[52] Berle, "The Theory of Enterprise Entity", (1947) 47 Col. L.R. 343.

[53] " 'Merger' or Agency of a Subsidiary Corporation as Grounds of the Liability of the Parent Corporation for Acts of its Subsidiary", (1927) 27 Col.L.R. 702.

[54] Higgins v. Cal. Petroleum & Asphalt Co., 147 Cal. 363 (1905).

[55] See ref. n. 50, supra.

[56] Rapid Transit Subway Construction Co. v. City of N.Y., 182 N.E. 145 (1932).

[57] Taylor v. Standard Gas & Electric Co., 306 U.S. 307 (1939). For other references on this subject, see Latty, op. cit.

[58] S. 30 of the Restrictive Trade Practices Law, 5719–1959.

[59] Land Appreciation Tax Law, s. 2. Other Laws refer to, and adopt, this remarkable definition: e.g. the Planning and Building Law, 5725–1965, s. 47(b).

[60] Motion 132/59, H.L.P.A. (Import & Agencies) Ltd. v. Johnson Joung & Co. Ltd., 13 P.D. 2195 (S.C.); H.C.J. 292/61, Packaging House Rehovoth Ltd. v. Minister of Agriculture, 17 P.D. 20 (S.C.). See, similarly, Re London Housing Society's Trust Deeds 1940 Ch. 777.

[61] U.S. v. Milwaukee Refrigerator Transit Co., 142 Fed. 242, 247.

[62] In re Carl Hirth. Ex parte Trustee [1899] 1 Q.B. 612. And see Civ. File 216/48, Janai Orchard Ltd. v. Ramat-Gan Corporation, 6 P.M. 380 (D.C.).

[63] First National Bank of Chicago v. Trebein Co. (1898) 52 N.E. 834; In re fasey. Ex parte Trustees [1923] 2 Ch. 1; and The Administrator General of Israel, supra.

[64] S. 42 of the Bankruptcy Ordinance 1936, which is closely based on the corresponding provisions in the British Act.

[65] Jones v. Lipman [1962] 1 W.L.R. 832.

[66] Elliott v. Pierson, supra; Agib. v. P.B. Ltd., supra.

[67] Gilford Motor Co. v. Horne, [1933] Ch. 935, C.A.

[68] Ibid., pp. 956, 961.

[69] Ibid., p. 969.

[70] Connors, Ltd. v. Connors [1940] 4 All E.R. 179, P.C.

[71] Gower, op. cit., pp. 189 et seq.; Friedman, op. cit., pp. 515 et seq.; Wormser, "Piercing the Veil of Corporate Entity", (1912) 12 Col. L. R. 496 et seq; and others.

[72] In the Israeli judgment of the Administrator General v. Heussman, another consideration was mentioned, namely, the concentration of the shares in the hands of one person. It seems that this argument cannot, of itself, justify the lifting of the veil, as discussed above. The second consideration mentioned above is restricted there to the Tenant Protection Laws. Yet, in the majority of cases where the parties tried to lift the veil in order to obtain the benefit of the law, the attempt failed. See Reidy v. Walker 1933 2 K.B. 266; Hiller v. United Diaries (London) [1934] 1 K.B. 57, C.A.; Lee v. K. Carter, Ltd. [1949] 1 K.B. 85; Pegler v. Craven [1952] 2 Q.B. 69, C.A.; Tunstall v. Steigman [1962] 2 All E.R. 417. So also in Israel—Civ.App. 117/47, Sharl v. Magdan Ltd., 2 Psakim 189 (S.C.).

[73] Cataldo, "Limited Liability with One-Man Companies and Subsidiary Corporations (1953) 18 Law & Contemporary Problems 473; Rice, " 'One Man' Company or One Man 'Company'?," (1964) 115 Journal of Business Law 36; Schmitthoff, "The

Companies Bill and Company Law Reform," (1966) 117 J.B.L. 106; and Fuller, "The Incorporated Individual: A Study of the One-Man Company," (1938) 51 Harv. L.R. 1373.

[74] Civ.App. 250/54, Cramer v. Director of Estate Tax, 11 P.M. 195 (D.C.); Civ. App. 413/62, Rosenzweig v. Rosenzweig Brewery Ltd., 16 P.D. 2548.

[75] Rembar, "Affiliated Companies Claims," (1939) 39 Col. L.R. 907; and see references there at p. 908.

[76] Douglas & Shanks, "Insulation from Liability Through Subsidiary Corporations", (1929) 39 Yale L.J. 193. And see Civ. App. 298/56, Rivlin & Ahuzat Reuven Ltd. v. Valis, 12 P.D. 85, (S.C.).

[77] O'Neal, op. cit., s. 8.02, p. 83; Baker & Cary, Cases and Materials on Corporations, p. 374.

[78] See the survey in 71 Harv. L.R. 1122; Krotinger, "The 'Deep Rock' Doctrine: A Realistic Approach to Parent Subsidiary Law," (1942) 42 Col. L.R. 1124, 1146.

[79] Elenkrieg v. Siebrecht, 238 N.Y. 254, 144 N.E. 519 (1924); Arnold v. Phillips, 117 F. 2d 497 (1941); Corpus Juris Secundum, Vol. 18, s. 6.

[80] Gonville's Trustee v. Patent Caramel Co. [1921] 1 K.B. 599; Hall' Safe & Lock Co. v. Herring-Hall-Marvin Safe Co., 146 Fed. 37; Moore & Handley Hardware Co. v. Towers Hardware Co., 87 Ala. 206.

[81] Tunstall v. Steigman, supra; Berger, op. cit., 824.

PROCESSES OF LAW

THE MORALITY OF ADVOCACY

HELEN SILVING*

In a volume dedicated to honoring Mr. Justice Haim Cohn of the Supreme Court of Israel, it behooves us to take notice of the connection between the "high dignity of the judicial office"[1] and the personal dignity of those holding it. Mr. Justice Cohn merits his Judicial Office by the wide range of his learning, by his humanism and humanity, as well as by the courage of his convictions. It is also fitting to emphasize his greatness as a lawyer, a quality achieved by a combination of legal talent and experience. Where judicial office is reserved to those who have first proven themselves to be exceptionally gifted lawyers—as is the case in Israel—it should be equally appropriate to keep in mind the dignity to be attributed to the profession of law practice, the "lawyer's office." The present paper will deal with that dignity and the privileges and responsibilities attaching to it in a free society based on rule of law. I believe this topic to be appropriate in honoring Mr. Justice Cohn, a distinguished lawyer as well as a prominent judge.

As a corollary to judicial independence, which constitutes a major ingredient of the dignity of the judicial office, there ought to be recognized the attorney's independence of equal scope.[2] The dignity resulting from such recognition of independence imposes upon the bearer a general duty of respect for the law that grants such recognition—if indeed it does grant it—balanced against the demands of conscientious service to the client.

For reasons rooted in historical legal philosophy, little appreciation is being expressed, even in those countries in which the law-creative function of judges is now taken for granted, of the law-creative function of lawyers. When judgments are handed down which reflect a spirit of innovation and progress, we praise our judges, forgetting all too readily that quite often the moving spirit behind such judgment is the

* Professor of Law, University of Puerto Rico

209

lawyer who formulated the cause of action or defense and wrote the the briefs; for judges neither bring actions nor consider claims beyond the scope of demand. In the United States we frequently find that an important judicial pronouncement is a *verbatim* copy of a passage in an attorney's brief. Since in countries in which judges are recruited from lawyers' ranks there is a close connection between the judicial and the lawyer's office, often in judicial pronouncements there may be detected a note of passionate plea for a chosen course, reminiscent of the role once performed by the writer in arguing a client's cause. Quite frequently also judges will pursue an argument of their choice when the latter is least expected, given the total context of a case.[3] "Argument" and "judgment"[4] are thus by no means clearly separable. With this feature there also coincides the practice of dissenting opinions, in which the lawyer's personality of a judge is perhaps best reflected. In countries of common law tradition the judge and the lawyer complement each other in the difficult process of administering the elusive concept of justice—the ideal of justice that is never deemed to be rigidly settled, yet always remains a chosen goal.[5]

However intricate may be the task of circumscribing with precision the scope of judicial independence, that of defining the attorney's independence is even more difficult. The term is now prominently used in reference to the lawyer's freedom to accept representation of "unpopular clients," in the sense of immunity from social repercussions, that might be reflected in legal or disciplinary action.[6] Occasionally it is also used in connection with the attorney's determination of the policy to be pursued in the course of proceedings.[7] The scope of the present essay does not permit an exhaustive study of the various meanings that might be attributed to the attorney's dignity or independence. I must confine myself to *ad hoc* observations relative to events now in the limelight of interest in the United States. On the one hand, there is noticeable a very unusual type of court conduct exhibited by some attorneys while representing clients or causes that are assumed to be "unpopular," though in certain circles they have ceased to be such, the "establishment" having turned "unpopular."[8] On the other hand, an effort is being made to formulate rules for proper conduct by attorneys, that are at best dubious in the light of the total philosophy of legal defense in a free society. I am referring particularly to the American Bar Association's proposed *"Standards Relating to The Defense Function."*[9] The overall picture of "defense" bears the imprint of certain peculiar features of Anglo-American procedure which to a lawyer of Roman-civil law background would appear puzzling, indeed, outrageous, such as the oath of the accused or guilty pleas.

Assuming the "attorney's independence" to mean his freedom to interpose an effective defense, there is a minimum scope beyond which, clearly, restriction should be barred. Politically motivated government intervention with attorneys' defense strategy belongs to this category of reprehensible state action.[10] Beyond such obviously improper restrictions on the attorney's independence there are those imposed by general law indiscriminately for all cases, that tend to frustrate the attorney's role. To these belong—as viewed by an attorney of common law tradition today—rules such as those of the recent Yugoslav Code of Criminal Procedure, permitting defense counsel to communicate with the defendant in detention only after the latter has been interrogated, and, if the Judge Investigator so decrees, only under circumstances of judicial scrutiny.[11] Such far-reaching intrusion into "defense rights" is not being contemplated in this country even by the most vigorous critics of Escobedo and Miranda.[12] The question remains as to the proper reach of the "attorney's independence," given the Anglo-American system of "defense rights."

How independent should a lawyer be of government goals, on the one hand, and of his client's wishes and instructions, on the other? Indeed, how independent should he be of the dictates of his social conscience, transcending government goals? How true should he be to his client, when the latter's interests as seen by the attorney differ from those the client himself professes? These questions press themselves upon our attention as changes in social structures call for resolution of ever new conflicts confronting the attorney.

In an "adversary system" of procedure counsel for the defense certainly has no obligation and no privilege to collaborate in any course of action that he considers detrimental to his client. While he must not knowingly aid and abet his client's lies, he has no obligation to expose or to discredit them explicitly or by conduct; indeed, he is prohibited from doing so. Should he resign when the client persists in a course of falsehood after being confidentially warned that in such event he could not count on counsel's cooperation and would, in fact, have to face the latter's withdrawal from the case? One might argue that this should be the attorney's duty, unless such withdrawal may under the circumstances be interpreted as an act of discrediting the client. However, if such duty were imposed upon the attorney, any withdrawal by him would arouse a strong suspicion of the client's lying. Thus, not requiring withdrawal facilitates it and resolves a serious conflict of legal conscience.

The attorney's conflict of conscience when facing a lying client is particularly acute in a system of law which admits putting the accused on oath. In such system, indeed, it could be argued that failure to resign renders the attorney responsible for aiding and abetting perjury. The *Standards* suggested by the American Bar Association for such event[13] are far from satisfactory. Where the client persists in lying, according to these standards, "the lawyer may not engage in direct examination of the defendant as a witness in the conventional manner." Notice that in Ferguson v. Georgia,[14] the Supreme Court of the United States held that denying the accused the right to be questioned by his counsel was tantamount to depriving him of his constitutional right to legal assistance. One might rejoin that, by lying, the defendant waives this right. But the Supreme Court of the United States "has always set high standards of proof for the waiver of constitutional rights,"[15] and to presume such waiver from the mere fact of his lying is imposing upon the defendant an added perjury punishment. The attorney's conflict of conscience in cases of this type may serve as a further demonstration of the irrationality of placing the accused under oath.[16]

There is an outright inconsistency between the American Bar Association's suggestion that counsel refuse the full scope of his assistance to a lying client and its intimation that he "should seek to establish a relationship of trust and confidence with the accused," explain to him "the necessity of full disclosure of all facts" and "the obligation of confidentiality which makes privileged the accused's disclosures relating to the case."[17]

Under no circumstances should counsel for the defense be called upon to cooperate in depriving the client of his personal freedom, whether under the label of imprisonment or under that of security measures. However "dangerous" a client may appear to be, persons other than defense counsel are charged with the responsibility of meeting such danger. Arguments to the contrary may be rebutted by invoking analogy to instances in law where privileges of silence are conceded and inaction imposed in the face of danger, indeed, clear and present danger.[18]

The American Bar Association has firmly rejected the so-called *alter ego* concept of a defense lawyer, which "sees him as a 'mouthpiece' for his client." It said that such concept is "fundamentally wrong, unethical and destructive of the lawyer's image."[19] While not a mere mouthpiece for his client, counsel for the defense should not be deemed the ultimate decision-maker where the life or personal freedom of the client is at stake. This would seem to apply to questions of trial strategy, where the latter may determine the outcome, as may well occur.[20]

Moreover, the extent to which concern for the general image of lawyers should be deemed paramount to service to the client's specific interest is much less obvious than one might wish it to be. Must the lawyer sacrifice his client's life, which might be at stake, in order to preserve an abstract "lawyers' image" for future cases, when his particular "image of lawyer" as evolving in the concrete case is not likely to affect the verdict or judgment in that case? If the answer is negative, what interest of the client ought to be thus sacrificed?

An especially intricate problem arises for defense counsel where his client exhibits self-destructive tendencies affecting his judgment as to matters properly within the range of his determination, e.g., whether to plead guilty. Phenomena of this type are by no means rare, and the course to be taken by the attorney confronted with such a suicidal client is as yet undefined.

In the United States "the overwhelming percentage of criminal cases in all state and federal courts, something on the order of 90 per cent, are disposed of by pleas of guilty."[21] This includes cases involving serious felonies, even capital cases. My crusade against these pleas[22] has passed completely unnoticed. Of course, any attempt at eliminating them would cast the total system of administration of criminal justice into chaos. The courts, overburdened as they are, cannot possibly face a 90 per cent increase of their case load. I believe the answer to be reducing crime categories to an absolutely necessary minimum and trying the remaining legitimate crime with the honesty and earnestness upon which in a free society the depriving an individual of his personal freedom should be predicated. The fact is that the institution of guilty pleas is a lineal descendant of the "oath of purgation."[23] Especially when appearing on such a gigantic scale, as it does in this country, it reduces the function of a criminal trial to an absurdity. The very essence of a criminal trial is visibility of justice done. Production of evidence is crucial in this process. The public is entitled to know how criminal justice is dispensed. Placing an individual behind bars on the basis of secret negotiations, is a bizarre spectacle in a system of rule of law. The rationalization advanced for admission of guilty pleas in such a system is awkward: the defendant himself, on whose behalf the trial is purportedly held, is taken to "waive" his right to it. With this, he allegedly "waives" three constitutional rights: the privilege against compulsory self-incrimination, the right to trial by jury and the right to confront one's accusers.[24] Ordinarily, of course, the plea is the result of a "deal" evolving in the course of "plea bargaining" between the "adversaries," defense counsel and prosecutor, which should secure some advantage to the defendant, such as reduction of the charge or of the penalty. The judge is carefully and hypocritically kept out of this process of "negotiation." It is considered not to be fitting for him to participate in them. Later he is expected to ascertain whether the plea has been voluntary. But what does the term "voluntary" encompass in this context? The plea does not imply a commitment with regard to the specific sentence to be passed.[25] The defendant gambles on its being advantageous to him. In this sense, the plea is not voluntary, for it is made in ignorance of the crucial circumstance—the actual sentence to be rendered. In a capital case the defendant may, indeed, be thus permitted to gamble, the stake being his own death.[26]

In this process of travesty of justice, defense counsel is assigned a crucial function: he acts as the defendant's negotiator. This is supposed to assure that negotiations are carried on "among professional equals."[27] While counsel must "keep the accused advised of developments at all times" and promptly communicate to him "all proposals made by the prosecutor," [28] it has been said that "it is usually undesirable for the accused to be present during the actual discussions in most cases."[29] Not being present obviously deprives him of the only opportunity he has of participating in his own adversary quasi-trial. As is the oath of the accused, so is the guilty plea a crucial obstacle to a fair administration of criminal justice, carrying with it a distortion of the so-called adversary system and of the role of defense counsel within it.

That "considerations of personal and professional advantage should not influence [the lawyer's] advice or performance"[30] is rather clear. Less clear is the answer to the question as to what extent it is proper for the attorney more or less indirectly to serve interests other than those of his immediate client by accepting representation at the instance of persons or groups whose interests in justice being done to the particular defendant are somewhat peripheral, their principal concern being either demonstration of prevailing social injustice, litigation of a specific point in issue, attack upon the "establishment," political propaganda, etc. An attorney thus hired may, nevertheless, be quite effective and it may be difficult to prove that the method of his employment had prejudiced the client's interests.[31] It is submitted that such employment of counsel actually does prejudice the client's interests, even where the prejudice is not clearly visible and that it mars the "lawyers' image," so that such employment should be generally prohibited. It is difficult enough to spot a lawyer's personal prejudices, of which he himself may not be conscious but which may well interfere with his wholehearted dedication to his client's best interests. Any feature that may generally affect that dedication, such as employment by persons pursuing goals, however lofty, that may conflict with the concrete best interest of a client, should constitute reversible error; the defendant in such case does not realis-tically have the assistance of his own counsel. Though undoubtedly great advances have been made in providing indigent defendants with legal assistance,[32] the present situation is far from satisfactory. Only recently we have witnessed the sore spectacle of a defendant in a pro-minent case selling "evidence" in order to secure legal assistance.[33] The fact is that nothing short of a complete equality in matters of legal assistance in criminal cases between the rich and the poor will do. This implies that fees for legal services in criminal cases must be equalized as nearly as may be.[34]

Do "considerations of personal advantage" mentioned in the Ameri-can Bar Association's *Standards* include those of higher values which the lawyer professes or which he may be believed to profess? Conflicts of conscience arise where the client's case may be promoted by a strategy that would adversely affect such higher values. Potential conflicts of this nature should certainly be taken into account by a lawyer when he considers accepting representation of a particular client. This issue is sufficiently intricate and important to deserve elaboration. It may best be clarified by use of an example.

The moral decision of a Jewish lawyer to defend an Arab nationalist— State of California v. Sirhan Bishara Sirhan[35]—is a delicate matter of personal conscience. For the purpose at hand, narrowly interpreted in order to preserve as much as possible the policy of abstaining from passing judgment upon the choice of conduct of a distinguished col-league,[36] it is sufficient to point out that such decision entailed the lawyer's total commitment: in a conflict, likely to arise in this type of trial, between the cause of the Jewish people and that of Sirhan, a lawyer serving Sirhan, a defendant admittedly motivated by Arab nationalism, was required to give preference to his client's cause.

In her testimony of March 3, 1969,[37] Sirhan's mother related an alleged event intended to support the contention of her son's attorneys of their client's diminished responsibility. That event was an alleged childhood experience of Sirhan. I am quoting Mrs. Sirhan's testimony as reported in the New York Times:[38]

> [Once a] "Zionist truck drove through our street carrying a number of young Arab girls whose breasts had been slashed. . . . I was out walking with Sirhan, who was about 4 years old at the time, and our attention was drawn to the truck by the sound

of Zionist soldiers aboard it who were clapping and shouting 'This is what we'll do to you.' 'Look at the blood, Mama, look at the blood,' Sirhan said . . . And he began to shake all over."

For the benefit of readers in countries of a Roman-civil law background, it is significant to mention that under our Anglo-American system of practice a lawyer is mostly well informed in advance of the contents of his witness's prospective testimony. It may be assumed that Sirhan's Jewish defense counsel, Emile Zola Berman, knew in advance what Mrs. Sirhan would say in court. As a lawyer representing Sirhan, Mr. Berman could not even as much as deny the veracity of the witness, Mrs. Sirhan, or question her capacity to observe or to recall or to interpret faithfully or to relate significantly the alleged event as described by her. Nor could he contest the objective truth content of her testimony, that is, deny that such an event actually occurred as she claimed it had occurred. It was utterly inconceivable that he cross-examine Mrs. Sirhan for any purpose adverse to Sirhan's interests. Thus, by force of law and of the Code of Legal Ethics binding American lawyers, the statement of that witness remained undenied and untested. To a layman, a Jewish lawyer representing Sirhan may appear to have admitted the veracity of that statement or, indeed, the actual occurrence of the described event as allegedly witnessed. By a clever trial strategy whereby Mrs. Sirhan was not subjected to any cross-examination at all, inquiry into the question of whether "Zionist soldiers" indeed did slash Arab girls' breasts was barred.

Of course, it would not have been in the utilitarian interest of Sirhan to produce at his trial evidence of sadistic actions of Arab militants against "Zionist" girls, which he may have witnessed in his childhood, even though such experiences might, in the light of psychological insight, have supported the contention of his diminished responsibility quite as much as did those of alleged "Zionist aggression". Nor would it be in Sirhan's utilitarian interest to show that often the victim of an aggression is seen by a properly conditioned observer as the aggressor. Sirhan's interest was served rather by producing a proper atmosphere in court and conditioning the jury emotionally in such a manner as to make an enemy of Sirhan appear to it to be the evil-doer. That this is the type of mental process many lawyers expect from jurors is regrettable. However, it is undeniable that lawyers base on such evaluation of the jurors' probable reactions their so-called trial strategy. The Jewish defense counsel of Sirhan could not disregard this generally prevailing ideology of jury trial.

Within our ideology of the attorney's function, it is counsel's duty to shed tears for his client.[39] Tears, of course, may have a variety of motivations and the unconscious determinants of some of these may be such as to render doubtful the usefulness of the tears to the client. An accused person is best served by a dispassionate professional performance on the part of his lawyer. Emotional responses such as self-denial, nobility, compassion, have no place in a criminal case.

Even more dubious from the standpoint of the morality of advocacy is an attorney's total identification with his client's person or cause. A classic example of such identification is Mr. Kunstler's controversial statement, "I only represent those I love."[40] Let us visualize what would be our attitude toward a member of the medical profession in possession of a special skill were he to declare, "I only treat those I love." One might argue that in the doctor's case ethical and political issues are not involved, whereas they are involved in law cases. However, a doctor too might choose not to treat, for example, a member of an "enemy" nation. Yet, it has been settled a long time ago that medical ethics require him to do so in much the same manner as he would treat a co-national. I submit that except in emergency situations, neither a doctor nor an attorney should be compelled to serve a person or a cause where he experiences a strong repugnance to do so. In the last analysis, an attorney can render the best legal service to a client if he can manage neither to love nor to hate him. Part of legal education should be directed to developing this quality in the student. An attorney cannot be said to be truly independent unless he can emotionally detach himself from the causes he represents. This, of course, does not mean that he must be indifferent to them.

Ability to achieve an emotional detachment from persons or causes at bar, which is one of the several meanings of the "attorney's independence," should also help him to meet a major challenge of our times, that of coping with disruptive practices in court. In the United States in recent years discruption of trials has been more common than ever before, and courts have proved to be unprepared to control defiant defendants, whom the Constitution has armed with an elaborate scheme of protection. A lawyer who enjoys the confidence of his client is best equipped to impress upon him the need for decorous behavior in court. Is it his duty to do so?

Sanctions against the attorney for failure to control a client who engages in disruptive or indecorous conduct in court do not seem to be tenable.[41] It may be argued that requiring the attorney to withdraw in such cases constitutes depriving the client of legal assistance at a stage when he needs it most.[42] However, the very fact that an attorney is not free to withdraw in such a situation may serve as an encouragement to the client to persist in his chosen course of conduct. Also, where the attorney-client relationship is attended by an atmosphere of trust and confidence, the client may interpret his lawyer's silence as acquiescence, indeed, as encouragement. Prominently to be considered is the question whether the client's concrete interest in the case at bar is objectively advanced by disruptive or indecorous behavior. All too often trials are being used as forums for political propaganda, for protest against general social injustices, for advocacy of general principles, rather than for vindication of the concrete rights of the concrete defendant. Indeed, the attorney may be faced with the need for protecting his client's concrete interest against exploitation of the trial for purposes other than those at bar—an exploitation which may well be practiced by the client himself.

I submit that unless disruption of the trial is the only means of safeguarding a concrete, proper, not otherwise pursuable interest of his client,[43] an attorney should have the duty, if the judge calls for his assistance, to make a *bona fide* attempt at controlling the client's disruptive behavior. In a country where any [male] citizen may be called upon to assist a police officer in catching an offender—a duty to this effect is imposed by penal code[44]—it is not too much to expect from an attorney, as officer of the court, that he help preserve order in court. The fact is that judges are much less free today to exercise authority over obstreperous defendants than they were before the civil disobedience movement became rampant. Moreover, there is a widespread belief among liberals that the judicial contempt power should be curtailed; that it should be reduced to "the least possible power adequate to the end proposed"[45] and, except in situations where it is used to prevent on-the-spot further disruption of proceedings, it should be subject to all the procedural safeguards of a fair trial within general constitutional standards.[46] Likewise, the authority of bar associations to impose sanctions upon attorneys should be limited, so as to secure to attorneys the widest possible independence in the discharge of their function.[47] Obviously, if there is substantial curtailment of those features of our system that serve as a potential deterrent to an attorney who is tempted to condone or, indeed, to abet a client's disruptive activities, we must seek for other available methods of maintaining peace and decorum in courtrooms.

In our system courts are the watchmen of the system's constitutional functioning. To be sure, as long as justice is human, there can be no ultimate solution to the eternal problem of "Who watches the watchmen?"[48] In a way, the task of supervision over judges is realistically in the hands of the legal profession as a whole, since lawyers are best equipped to evaluate judicial conduct. This task, in turn, imposes corresponding duties.[49] No matter what we may think of violence as a method of social change, by all means let us keep our courtrooms free of violence and intimidation. In the last analysis, courts must remain the bulwark of the attorneys' independence and the defenders of their dignity.[50] The courts' freedom and independence must be preserved, so that the attorneys' freedom and independence may survive.

NOTES

[1] See Rümelin, *Die hohe Würde des Richteramtes,* Rektoratsrede.

[2] Compare my Address to the First Bar of Korea on the Occasion of my Admission to its Membership in 1964, Korean version published in Seoul, Korea, by the Bar Association.

[3] A classic example of this practice may be found in Mapp v. Ohio, 367 U.S. 643, 81 S.Ct. 1684, 6 L.Ed.2d 1081 (1961). There, the Supreme Court of the United States overruled Wolf v. Colorado, 338 U.S. 25, 69 S.Ct. 1359, 93 L.Ed. 1782 (1949), which had held evidence illegally seized by State agents admissible in a State court under the federal Constitution. As pointed out by Mr. Justice Harlan, in dissent, while the issue of admissibility of the illegally seized evidence was raised "among appellant's subordinate points," . . . "the new and pivotal issue brought to the Court by this appeal [was] whether . . . making criminal the *mere* knowing possession or control of obscene material . . . is consistent with the rights of free thought and expression assured against state action by the Fourteenth Amendment. That was the principal issue . . .." The majority of the Court was obviously anxious to overrule Wolf and it seized upon the slightest opportunity for doing so.

[4] In the United States we use the term "opinion" rather than "judgment."

[5] As pointed out in Radbruch's famous attack upon National Socialist law (cited in my article, *In re Eichmann: A Dilemma of Law and Morality,* in *SOURCES OF LAW* [1968], pp. 354–355), the salient point in "justice" is the search for it.

[6] On this see *Controlling Lawyers by Bar Associations and Courts.* Comment in 5 Harvard Civil Rights and Civil Liberties Law Review 301 (1970); compare also Slovenko, *Attitudes on Legal Representation of Accused Persons*, 2 American Criminal Law Quarterly 101 (1964); also Sacks, *Defending the Unpopular Client,* The National Council on Legal Clinics, American Bar Center (1961).

[7] See American Bar Association, *Standards Relating to The Prosecution Function and The Defense Function,* Tentative Draft (1970) [hereinafter referred to as ABA Standards], at pp. 239–240, on allocation of decision-making power as to strategy and tactics to defense counsel. The term "independence" is not used here, but is obviously implied.

[8] Notice the vigorous critique of the Bar Associations' "harassment" of lawyers appearing in unpopular cases in *Controlling Lawyers by Bar Associations and Courts,* see above, at 308–333. It may be interesting to note the report in The New York Times (March 18, 1969, page C 17) on the contempt trial of one of the attorneys whose "harass-

ment" was prominently mentioned in the cited comment, see above, at 301–302. We read in this report that Daniel T. Taylor was "accused of showing contempt for a pistol-packing judge from Louisville." Among the subtitles of the report there appears a particularly colorful one, "A Judge and a Pistol." Under this subtitle there appears first prominently displayed a statement that on adjournment, "the judge lost his grip on the pistol and juggled it in the air before a gasping courtroom, finally catching it against his chest." Only thereafter is it mentioned that the judge "had received threats against his life." I should not like to be understood as critical of the lawyers' acceptance of the defense of so-called "unpopular cases" or of zeal in advancing all available means of defense. It is desirable, nevertheless, that lawyers do so without trying to arouse passionate responses from "anti-establishment" groups. It is at best doubtful that appeal to such groups actually serves the concrete interests of the client.

⁹ Cited above, n. 7.

¹⁰ In our times we have witnessed the sad phenomenon of a reprimand by the Polish Minister of Justice and a temporary suspension of lawyers for the manner in which they defended accused persons in a capital charge for corruption on the ground that this was contrary to so-called "decisive tendencies of political life." See Adolf Arndt, *Umwelt und Recht,* 9 Neue Juristische Wochenschrift 399 (1961).

¹¹ Text as adopted by the Legislative Commission of the Federal Assembly of Yugoslavia, December 9, 1967, translated by Mirjam Damaska, in Institute of Comparative Law Collection of Yugoslav Laws, vol. 19 (Beograd 1969), Article 73.

¹² In Escobedo v. Illinois, 378 U.S. 478, 84 S. Ct. 1758, 12 L.Ed.2d 977 (1964), the Supreme Court of the United States held that as soon as a criminal "investigation is no longer a general inquiry into an unsolved crime but has begun to focus on a particular suspect, the suspect has been taken into police custody, the police carry out a process of interrogations that lends itself to eliciting incriminating statements, the suspect has requested and been denied an opportunity to consult with his lawyer, and the police have not effectively warned him of his absolute constitutional right to remain silent, the accused has been denied 'the Assistance of Counsel' in violation of the Sixth Amendment to the Constitution as 'made obligatory upon the States by the Fourteenth Amendment,' [citation], and that no statement elicited by the police during the interrogation may be used against him at a criminal trial."

In Miranda v. Arizona, 384 U.S. 436, 86 S.Ct. 1602, 16 L.Ed.2d 694 (1966), the Supreme Court of the United States held that "when an individual is taken into custody or otherwise deprived of his freedom by the authorities in any significant way and is subjected to questioning, . . . [h]e must be warned prior to any questioning that he has the right to remain silent, that anything he says can be used against him in a court of law, that he has the right to the presence of an attorney, and that if he cannot afford an attorney one will be appointed for him prior to any questioning if he so desires. Opportunity to exercise these rights must be afforded to him throughout the interrogation." Unless the warning is given, admission in evidence of any confession made in the course of the interrogation is reversible error.

These two decisions have been special targets of attack by "law and order" advocates who claim that they impede the work of the police in pursuing criminals. But it is at least doubtful that they have this effect. Compare on this Silving, *On "Police Brutality,"* Statement prepared at the request of the Commission of Civil Rights of the Commonwealth of Puerto Rico, printed in 37 Revista Juridica de la Universidad de Puerto Rico 279, at pp. 286–289 (1968).

¹³ Cited above, n. 7, §7.7 (c): "If withdrawal from the case is not feasible or is not

permitted by the court, or if the situation arises during the trial and the defendant insists upon testifying falsely in his own behalf, the lawyer may not lend his aid to the perjury. Before the defendant takes the stand in these circumstances, the lawyer should make a record of the fact that the defendant is taking the stand against the advice of counsel in some appropriate manner without revealing the fact to the court. The lawyer must confine his examination to identifying the witness as the defendant and permitting him to make his statement to the trier or the triers of the facts; the lawyer may not engage in direct examination of the defendant as a witness in the conventional manner and may not later argue the defendant's known false version of facts to the jury as worthy of belief and he may not recite or rely upon the false testimony in his closing argument."

[14] 365 U.S. 570, 81 S.Ct. 756, 5 L.Ed.2d 783 (1961). For discussion of this case see Silving, *Essays on Criminal Procedure* (1964), pp. 273–274.

[15] Miranda v. Arizona, above, 384 U.S. at 475.

[16] In countries where the accused is not admitted to oath and, in fact, is often said to have a "right to lie," a conflict of this type may also arise, but in an attenuated form. Though the accused himself may have a "privilege to lie" based on his special state of necessity, his attorney does not necessarily share in this privilege. However, since the accused is not subject to prosecution for perjury, it would require creation of a special crime to prosecute the attorney for aiding and abetting the client's lying.

[17] ABA Standards, §3.1.

[18] It may be sufficient to mention the husband and wife privilege, and the privilege of a priest as regards matters revealed to him in confession.

ABA Standards, §3.7(d) require a lawyer to reveal the expressed intention of his client to commit a crime where the contemplated crime is one [among others] which would "corrupt the processes of the courts and the lawyer believes such action on his part is necessary to prevent it." Thus, according to the comment to this section, the lawyer should report to the authorities his client's "intention to bribe . . . a juror or witness." It would seem that it is one thing to withdraw from the case and another thing to inform against a client. Where withdrawing suggests suspicious dealings of the accused, it is still more acceptable than an outright report to the authorities.

[19] ABA Standards, §1.1(c), and Comment at p. 174.

[20] The ABA Standards, §5.2, reserve certain decisions to the accused: (i) what plea to enter; (ii) whether to waive jury trial; (iii) whether to testify in his own behalf. So-called "strategic and tactical decisions are [said to be] the exclusive province of the lawyer after consultation with his client."

[21] ABA Standards, comment at p. 244.

[22] Compare Silving, *op. cit.*, above, n. 14, at pp. 249–255; for argument in favor of elimination of all types of confessions, compare also Silving, *A Plea for a New Philosophy of Criminal Justice*, 35 Revista Juridica de la Universidad de Puerto Rico 401, at 403–404 (1966).

[23] See Silving, *op. cit.*, above, at 245–249.

[24] Boykin v. Alabama, 395 U.S. 238, at 243 (1969).

[25] The ABA Standards, comment at pp. 252–253, have this to say on the subject: "A critical factor is that the defendant not commit himself irrevocably to a guilty plea without knowing approximately what the consequences will be. The prosecutor and defense counsel may have 'agreements' but there can be no agreement binding on the judge, since he must retain his independent posture at all times. Confusion in treatment of this subject which exists among lawyers and among judges stems from failure to distinguish between agreements between two lawyers and tentative, preliminary expressions from a

judge." Notice in this context the tremendous range of possible sentences in the American system of criminal law. Obviously, the defendant does not "know" in any significant sense what exactly he is contracting for.

[26] See, e.g., Boykin v. Alabama, above, where defendant was sentenced to die on each of the five indictments for robbery, on the basis of guilty pleas. Assuming that such a plea can be conceivably entered "voluntarily," the defendant should be taken as either insane or as suicidal.

[27] ABA Standards, comment at 244.

[28] *Id.*, §6.2 (a).

[29] *Id.*, comment at 249–250.

[30] *Id.*, §1.6.

[31] See, In re Ades, 6 F. Supp. 467 (D.C. Md., 1934).

[32] Legal aid in the United States has been in operation for a century. Last year marked the fiftieth anniversary of the involvement of the American Bar Association in it. On the history of the advances made see Voorhees, *Legal Aid: Past, Present and Future*, 56 American Bar Association Journal 765 (1970).

[33] James Earl Ray, later convicted on his guilty plea of the assassination of the Rev. Dr. Martin Luther King Jr., had sold his rights to his life story to William Bradford Huie, and received an advance of $25,000, which he signed over to Mr. Hanes as part of his legal fee. See The New York Times of March 13, 1969, p. 22 C.

[34] There ought to be no difference in this matter between rich and poor. For recommendations of a system of equalization see Silving, *op. cit.,* above, n. 14, at 340–343.

[35] Sirhan was charged with first degree murder for killing Senator Robert F. Kennedy and was defended during his trial by several attorneys, one of whom was Emile Zola Berman, trustee and former president of the International Academy of Trial Lawyers, who entered the case at the invitation of chief defense counsel Grant B. Cooper. Mr. Berman was chosen to deliver the opening statement. Mr. Cooper explained that choice by saying, "because he's recognized as the top lawyer in the country at this. No one's better than Berman." See The New York Times of Feb. 9, 1969, p. 33. Some controversy arose regarding Mr. Berman's acceptance of the defense. On the one hand, criticism came from Arab quarters, on the ground that the function of the trial was to convey to the world "an understanding of the Arab cause" and that "consciously or subconsciously . . . it would be very difficult for a Jew to present some of this." The New York Times of Feb. 2, 1969, at p. 45. On the other hand, the contention was made that Mr. Berman was "betraying his own heritage." To the latter contention, Mr. Berman replied: "I'm not required to adopt Sirhan's philosophy in order to defend him. I'm not defending his crime, only his rights." The New York Times of Feb. 23, 1969, at p. 7 E (comment by Lacey Fosburgh).

[36] I wish to stress as emphatically as I can that I am not criticizing this choice, but only wish to present the type of "conflict of conscience" that may arise in a situation of this nature and to indicate my very personal preference for a choice of conduct in a comparable situation.

[37] See The New York Times of March 4, 1969, at p. 22 M.

[38] *Ibid.*

[39] Ferguson v. Moore, 98 Tenn. 342, 343, 39 S.W. 341 (1897).

[40] When asked whether he would defend the Minutemen on the same grounds that he defended the Panthers, meaning, the right to violent "self-defense," Kunstler answered: "No, I wouldn't defend them at all. I only defend those whose goal I share. I'm not a lawyer for hire. I only defend those I love." Quoted from The New York Times Magazine, April 19, 1970, p. 92.

[41] This view has been expressed by Marshall Beil in *Controlling Lawyers by Bar Associations and Courts*, above, n. 6, at p. 385: "Although a lawyer is an 'officer of the court,' he is not a bailiff or marshal whose job is to restrain physically potential contemnors [citing Cammer v. United States, 350 U.S. 399, 405 (1956)]."

[42] The recent case in which the United States Supreme Court laid down the ground-rules for judicial control over a defendant's disruptive conduct, State of Illinois v. Allen, 90 S.Ct. 1057 (1970), abundantly demonstrates the need in such cases for expert, efficient legal assistance. The conduct of the accused in this case was indeed outrageous. One of his remarks to the court was: "When I go out for lunchtime, you're [the judge] going to be a corpse here." His final remark before being ordered by the judge to be removed from the courtroom was: "There is going to be no proceeding. I'm going to start talking and I'm going to keep on talking all through the trial. There's not going to be no trial like this. I want my sister and my friends here in court to testify for me." Above, at p. 1059. As pointed out by Mr. Justice Douglas, in his concurring opinion, above, 1064, at 1065, there was "more than an intimation in the . . . record that the defendant was a mental case." Presumably, the judge himself should have taken appropriate steps to protect this defendant and the record. But the defendant had been found competent to stand trial and beyond such finding we have no answer to "the difficult questions as to what a trial judge should do with an otherwise mentally ill defendant who creates a courtroom disturbance." *Ibid.* Apart from potential mental illness, this defendant demonstrated by the choice of his language a total lack of education, a primitive attitude, that in itself called for protection.

[43] It is here assumed for the purpose of argument that there may be some legitimate interest of the defendant that can be protected only by disruptive conduct. It is being argued (*Controlling Lawyers by Bar Associations and Courts*, Comment, above, n. 6, at pp. 390–391) that order and decorum in court exist only for the protection of the defendant and that his counsel may waive that protection. This position, to the extent that it assumes an overriding interest of a defendant that cannot be vindicated except by disruption of court proceedings, overlooks public opinion transcending legal remedies. The philosophy of law prevailing in the United States interprets "law" to consist of predictions of what courts will do in fact (Holmes), and courts undoubtedly, whether consciously or unconsciously, take into consideration public response to courtroom conduct. In this sense, whatever advantage may accrue to a defendant from subversion of court proceedings in terms of legal resources may well be overridden by the harm suffered by him in terms of public opinion. There will always remain at least a suspicion that such subversion is intended to serve interests other than the immediate ones of the concrete defendant.

[44] Compare §195.10 of the Penal Law of New York, L. 1965, c. 1030, eff. Sept. 1, 1967 (McKinney's Consolidated Laws of New York 1967); §150 of the Penal Code of California, as amended by Stats. 1968, c. 1222 (West's California Codes 1968 Supplement) (neglect or refusal "to join the posse comitatus"); art. 139 of Penal Code of Puerto Rico, 33 L.P.R.A. §497. This duty to assist in making an arrest is one of the few instances of a positive duty imposed by the criminal law by way of a statutory implementation of a common law obligation to join a sheriff's posse upon request.

[45] Anderson v. Dunn, 6 Wheat. 204, 227 (U.S. 1821).

[46] The most impressive argument to this effect may be found in Justice Frankfurter's dissenting opinion in Sacher v. United States, 343 U.S. 1, 23 (1952). See also the persuasive article by Harper and Haber, *Lawyer Troubles in Political Trials*, 60 Yale L. Journ. 1 (1951).

[47] Such curtailment is desirable to prevent assertion of "harassment" of attorneys or prospective attorneys who might serve unpopular causes or clients.

[48] It is most essential that the "watchman" not be permitted to act as a judge in his

Helen Silving

own case. Thus, since any subversion of court proceedings may be interpreted as an offense to the judge, he should be permitted to impose a sanction only for the immediate safeguarding of the concrete proceedings. It is, in fact, doubtful that a sanction in such a case should take the form of "punishment." As suggested by Harper and Haber, above, at p. 5, "There is little doubt that in most, indeed, perhaps all cases, the administration of justice can be adequately protected by means other than punishment, as for example, by warnings, prompt use of the marshal, the ejection or threatened ejection of the offender from the courtroom, temporary recess or adjournment."

[49] In the recently recommended *Principles as to Disruption of the Judicial Process of the American College of Trial Lawyers,* July 1970, Standard II (c) declares it to be a lawyer's professional obligation "to conduct himself in such a way as to avoid disorder or disruption in the courtroom;" subdivision two of this article provides that "[A] lawyer is not relieved of these obligations [those enumerated in subdivision one] by any shortcomings on the part of the judge, nor is he relieved of them by the legal, moral, political, social or ideological merits of the cause of any client."

[50] It is quite true, of course, that a judge's conduct may provoke a defendant or his counsel, and this might be considered in the process of determining whether a conduct was contemptuous. For example, in one case defendants refused to plead unless they had lawyers of their choice paid for by the state. The Judge was reported as remarking: "These boys wouldn't know a good attorney from a good watermelon," which was regarded as an "out-and-out racial slur." See The New York Times of Feb. 22, 1969, p. 16 C. However, restraint in the face of provocation should be expected from an attorney as well as from a judge. On the other hand, provocation of the defendant should constitute an exemption ground.

SOME LEGAL ASPECTS OF ARAB TERRORISTS' CLAIMS TO PRIVILEGED COMBATANCY

THEODOR MERON*

INTRODUCTION: THE PROPER FRAME OF REFERENCE

Claims are often advanced, by Arab terrorist organizations, Arab jurists and others that captured terrorists should be given prisoner-of-war status. The object of this paper is to examine some of these claims.

The first, and a very fundamental question which arises in this respect is that of the frame of reference within which the above examination should be undertaken. The very question of the proper frame of reference is in dispute. For example, Dr. Clovis Maqsud, an Arab journalist and jurist, recently claimed that "the non-aligned States are requested to break out of the strict, literal interpretation of international law and to assist in the [elaboration] of a concept of international law which grasps the fact stressed by the fight of the nations of the third world, i.e., what is legitimate from the political point of view, ought to be legitimate also in the eyes of the law."[1] This is of course a purely political-subjective criterion advanced as justification for the modification of the law.

Other Arab jurists attempt to justify their claims that captured terrorists are entitled to prisoner-of-war status by unilaterally defining the Arab-Israel conflict as a "war of liberation," to which—so they argue—special rules of international law should apply. Still other Arab jurists invoke the "cause" or "motive" of the fighting. Such subjective presentation makes impossible an objective legal analysis of the problem.

The question of the so-called wars of liberation will be considered at greater detail below, but it is necessary from the outset to determine that in a *legal* discussion of the claims of the Arab terrorists to prisoner-

* Legal Adviser, Israel Ministry for Foreign Affairs

of-war status, the only possible frame of reference is that provided by the Geneva Convention Relative to the Treatment of Prisoners-of-War (hereafter "the Third Convention"), of August 12, 1949, to which as many as 126 States are Parties, and which should be regarded as a truly universal convention.

The governing text which must guide our examination is that of Article 4 of the Third Geneva Convention, which reads, in the part relevant to us:

> A. Prisoners-of-war, in the sense of the present Convention, are persons belonging to one of the following categories, who have fallen into the power of the enemy:
> . . . .
> (2) Members of other militias and members of other volunteer corps, including those of organized resistance movements, belonging to a Party to the conflict and operating in or outside their own territory, even if this territory is occupied, provided that such militias or volunteer corps, including such organized resistance movements, fulfill the following conditions:
> (a) that of being commanded by a person responsible for his subordinates;
> (b) that of having a fixed distinctive sign recognizable at a distance;
> (c) that of carrying arms openly;
> (d) that of conducting their operations in accordance with the laws and customs of war.[2]

Article 4 itself already reflects an adaptation to post World War II circumstances, especially in matters of "resistance movements," of part of Article 1 of the Regulations respecting the Laws and Customs of War on Land, annexed to the Hague Convention concerning the Laws and Customs of War on Land, and adopted at the Second Peace Conference, at The Hague, on October 18, 1907. That Article reads, in part:

> The laws, rights, and duties of war apply not only to armies, but also to militia and volunteer corps fulfilling the following conditions:
> 1. To be commanded by a person responsible for his subordinates;
> 2. To have a fixed distinctive emblem recognizable at a distance;

3. To carry arms openly; and

4. To conduct their operations in accordance with the laws and customs of war.[3]

The following examination will bear on the question of the extent to which certain essential facts concerning the nature, relationships and activities of the Arab terrorist organizations correspond to Article 4A(2) of the Third Convention. Indeed, with all due respect for political, sociological and other considerations, there is no other way to undertake a legal analysis of the subject. In other words, the discussion must revolve around the existing law, not on individual views as to a possible change of the law in order to make it conform to certain partisan interests. The study will not be exhaustive and will concentrate on certain major questions arising from Article 4 of the Third Convention. (No attempt will be made to compare the status of Arab terror organizations with other groups involved in conflict-situations elsewhere in the world, as each group and each situation merits an exhaustive examination of all the applicable considerations. This would fall outside the limited scope of this paper.) It may be pointed out, however, that there exists a rich literature on Article 4, and on the World War II resistance movements.[4]

In an article in the *International Review of the Red Cross,* Ford concludes an exhaustive study as follows:

> The present laws of war as they bear upon this matter can be summarized as follows:
>
> 1. The laws of war (*jus in bello*) must be applied regardless of the cause of war. The question whether a war is lawful or not is therefore irrelevant with respect to the legal status accorded to members of resistance groups.
>
> 2. Articles 1 and 2 of The Hague Regulations and Article 4 of the Geneva Convention Relative to the Treatment of Prisoners-of-War 1949 lay down the conditions which members of the resistance groups must meet in order to be treated as privileged combatants.
>
> 3. Members of resistance movements who do not conform to the requirements mentioned in 2 above cannot be considered as privileged combatants. In case of capture they will be treated as common criminals and not as prisoners-of-war. They may claim a certain amount of protection by virtue of the Fourth Geneva Convention and of general principles of law.

4. For the opposing party in armed conflicts not of an international character a minimum protection has been included in Article 3 common to the four Geneva Conventions of 1949.

5. International law does not forbid the civilian population to commit acts of resistance, but leaves the Occupying Power free to punish these acts . . .[5]

The conditions enumerated in Article 4A(2) are cumulative, in other words all of them must co-exist for the status of prisoner-of-war to be legitimately claimed and conferred. This emerges quite clearly from the words "provided that . . . such organized resistance movements *fulfill the following conditions.*"[6]

Greenspan points out that resistance movements are to be granted prisoner-of-war status "subject to the proviso that in order to obtain recognition as lawful belligerents all irregulars must fulfill *all* of the following four conditions."[7]

Pictet, in an authoritative commentary on the Third Convention published by the International Red Cross under his general editorship, states: "As we have said already, if resistance movements are to benefit by the Convention, they must respect the four special conditions contained in sub-paragraphs (a) to (d) which are identical to those stated in Article 1 of The Hague Regulations."[8]

A similar position is taken by Lauterpacht's edition of the British *Manual of Military Law.* According to the *Manual,* members of resistance movements are not entitled to prisoner-of-war status if they do not meet the conditions enumerated in Article 4.

The *Manual* states:

> The provisions of Art. 4 do not go so far as may seem at first sight. They do not seriously impede action by the Occupant against resistance movements. For the conditions stated in this article are somewhat stringent inasmuch as they rule out to a large extent the elements of secrecy and surprise which normally accompany resistance movements. Unless these conditions are complied with, members of resistance movements are not entitled to be treated as prisoners-of-war, although they are entitled under the Civilian Convention, Art. 5 and Part III Sec. III, to the rights of protected persons in occupied territories who have committed breaches of the law promulgated by the Occupation Authorities by the use of armed force against the Occupant: such rights comprise humane treatment and a fair trial by a properly

constituted court. The rights to which they are entitled are not limited to the restricted rights conferred by the P.O.W. Convention, Art. 3, since that article does not apply to conflicts between States. If such persons are captured when operating outside occupied territory, and therefore not entitled to prisoner-of-war status under the P.O.W. Convention, Art. 4, then they are illegal combatants, and may be tried as war criminals.[9]

Pictet, and indeed, some other writers, are not quite accurate when they count four conditions only, i.e., those referred to in letters (a)–(d), for in so doing, they omit the conditons mentioned in the preambular part of Article 4A(2).

In a recent study entitled "A Reconsideration of the Law of Armed Conflicts" Professor Denise Bindschedler counts altogether six conditions, for she adds to the above-mentioned four, the requirement of belonging to a Party to the conflict and the requirement of being organized.[10] Professor Bindschedler adds: "Some of these conditions concern the groups themselves, in that case their members enjoy privileged status only if the group to which they belong satisfies these conditions. Other conditions concern the members of the groups; those are the conditions (b) and (c), the other conditions referring to the group."[11] (It will be seen that while this is the situation in general, the pattern of Arab terror activities necessitates certain modifications.)

RELEVANCE OF THE CAUSE OF THE CONFLICT: WARS OF LIBERATION

We shall first consider the question of the relevance of the cause of the conflict or war. The conclusion reached by Mr. Ford to the effect that *jus in bello* must be applied regardless of the cause of the war, and that the question of lawfullness of a war is irrelevant "to the legal status accorded to members of resistance groups," has already been cited. His conclusion is based on numerous authorities, which need not be repeated here.[12]

Dr. Henri Meyrowitz, in his report on "La Guérilla et le Droit de la Guerre" submitted to the Brussels University Conference on Humanitarian Law and Armed Conflicts (1970), discusses this question clearly and succinctly, and concludes that the object and the cause of a particular guerrilla movement must be irrelevant to the objective application of the law of war and cannot justify departures from the law.[13] Indeed, ideology and law must be kept apart if law is to survive. It may be of interest to observe that the Inter-American Commission on Human Rights convened for its twenty-third session, declared in its Resolution of April 16, 1970 entitled "Terrorism for Political or Ideological Purposes," "that the political or ideological aims given as the reasons for those acts do not affect their being classed as serious violations of human rights and basic freedoms, nor can they exempt their perpetrators from responsibility for those violations".

In contemporary literature, the question of motive is closely connected with that of the label given to a particular armed conflict, and particularly to conflicts regarded as "wars of liberation." In particular, it is claimed that the requirements expressed in Article 4A(2) of the Third Convention need not be respected in a war described by the claimants of the prisoner-of-war status as a "war of national liberation." In an interesting study on the Soviet approach to this problem, George Ginsburgs analyzes, and subjects to biting criticism, the Soviet view on the subject:

> Following the German invasion of Russia, the Second World War assumed, in Soviet parlance, the character of a supremely just war. In spite of this designation, however, Moscow did not, in the midst of the fighting, choose to indulge in any wholesale revision or repudiation of the established laws of war and, throughout, insistently demanded that the enemy likewise abide by the letter and spirit of the customary and conventional regulations on modern warfare. Significantly, the only marked departure from the old norms for which the Soviet régime admitted responsibility during the hostilities and which its jurisconsults openly tried to justify concerned rules setting conditons for the conduct of guerrilla warfare. Even so, the pleadings here rested on technical grounds and pursued their objective ostensibly within the frame of reference of established international law.

> As soon as war came to an end, however, the Kremlin's erstwhile caution in handling this sensitive issue suddenly evaporated. Instead, Soviet jurists now rhetorically asked ". . . can we confine a sacred people's war against an aggressor and enslaver, a heroic struggle of millions of people for their country's independence, for its national culture, for its right to exist, can we confine this war within the strict bounds of The Hague rules, which were calculated for wars of a different type and for a totally different international situation?" They forthwith answered their own query in the negative . . .

Things finally reached a point where Soviet publicists denounced outright all attempts to deal with the subject on accepted legal terms and flatly condemned all earlier efforts by their own compatriots to furnish a jural rationale for the changes that the régime had effected in the course of the late war in the stipulations of The Hague accords regarding guerrilla warfare . . .

The net effect of such an outlook would again amount to conferring total immunity on the party said to be waging a just war, irrespective of its actual behavior on the battlefield and behind the front—to giving it *carte blanche* to act as it wishes, while sentencing its opponent to suffer every indignity without recourse. And, it should be stressed, the bulk of these extreme pronouncements were heard well after the signature of the Geneva conventions of 1949, which the Soviets so often cite. There, a partial attempt was made to resolve the legal status of the irregular troops by putting them on equal footing, for certain purposes, with the regular armed forces. Such a venture, in turn, can realistically be expected to *achieve success only if the guerrilla units, too, observe the established laws of war.* The logic of the situation, however, seems to have escaped the Soviets who, instead, altogether absolve one side from any obligation whatever to respect the regulations and concurrently insist that the other side must nevertheless fully conform to the rules.[14]

In the developing countries of the world the argument in favor of special rules which should be applied in regard to "wars of liberation" is largely based on several Resolutions adopted by the General Assembly of the United Nations. These Resolutions declared the "freedom fighters" in South Africa, in Portuguese-administered territories and in Rhodesia "should be treated as prisoners-of-war under international law, particularly the Geneva Convention Relative to the Treatment of Prisoners-of-War."[15]

What do these Resolutions really amount to? The International Committee of the Red Cross (hereafter "ICRC") points out in its "Report on Protection of Victims of Non-International Conflicts" submitted to the twenty-first International Conference of the Red Cross, held at Istanbul in 1969, that in these Resolutions the United Nations expressed the view that armed conflicts or states of tension existing in southern Africa are *international conflicts* involving the application of the laws and customs of war as a whole. This position is based on earlier Resolutions recognizing certain African territories' right to independence.[16]

The ICRC wondered whether it would not be better for the General Assembly to ask that these persons be granted *treatment* as prisoners-of-war rather than prisoner-of-war *status*. It is explained that such a recommendation would be strictly humanitarian with no legal or political connotation and would probably more likely be followed by results beneficial to the persons requiring protection.[17]

The ICRC Report touched on a more fundamental difficulty: the lack of competence of the General Assembly to revise the Geneva Conventions by resolution.

The ICRC thus states:

> In addition, article 4 of the IIIrd 1949 Geneva Convention enumerates and defines exhaustively the persons who, in the event of capture, should be treated as prisoners-of-war. Most of the freedom fighters to which the General Assembly resolutions refer do not fulfill the conditions required by article 4. Is the General Assembly empowered to broaden, merely by a resolution, a definition contained in an article of a Convention which is now binding on more than 120 States?[18]

The question of wars of liberation was also considered by the ICRC in another of its Reports submitted to the Istanbul Conference, namely on "Reaffirmation and Development of the Laws and Customs Applicable in Armed Conflicts." The discussion of the experts consulted by the ICRC on the question of wars of liberation was inconclusive: "While several experts . . . endeavored to find grounds for the political-legal conception of wars of liberation, the majority stressed that the formulation of humanitarian rules applicable to such conflict took first place."[19]

Dr. Kalshoven, in his report on "The Position of Guerrilla Fighters under the Law of War," presented to the International Society for Military Law and the Law of War, criticizes the views of some of the experts consulted by the ICRC who claimed that the conflicts referred to in the above General Assembly Resolutions should be treated as international wars and the groups fighting against colonial governments should be treated as subjects of international law. According to Kalshoven certain objective factors rather than the subjective label should determine which conflicts are to be regarded as international.[20]

Certain conclusions can now be drawn.

The General Assembly recommended treatment of certain conflict-situations as armed conflicts of an international character. It also recommended the application of the Third Convention and the conferment of prisoner-of-war status on "freedom fighters" in such conflict-situations. Whatever the political and moral value of those recommendations may be, they surely cannot modify the Third Convention either on the question of its applicability to the situations in question or on the specific requirements imposed by Article 4A(2) thereof.

THE REQUIREMENT OF BELONGING TO A PARTY TO THE CONFLICT

Doctrine

The requirement of belonging to a Party to the conflict is explained by Meyrowitz as follows:

> This link must exist *between the resistance movements and a party to the conflict*: that means, on the one hand, that the fact that the *members* of the resistance organizations have the nationality of a party to the conflict is not enough, and, on the other hand, that the organizations cannot be considered *themselves* as a party to the conflict. This party is not necessarily the State whose territory is occupied: it can be an allied power of that State, after the government of the latter has signed an armistice or a capitulation or suffered a *debellatio*.
>
> This indispensable link between the organized resistance movements and a party to the conflict does not have to be formal, but it must be *real*. If there does not exist a party to the conflict which recognizes, as to the belligerent State against which the action of the resistance movements is directed, a link with these organizations, these cannot claim the protection of Article 4A(2).[21]

Thus, the fact that members of the group concerned may possess the nationality of a Party to the conflict does not suffice; neither—and this is very important—can the group itself be considered as a Party to the conflict. The Party to the conflict must be a State, and to that Party the group must belong.

Pictet points out that "in our view, the stipulation that organized resistance movements . . . must belong to a Party to the conflict, refutes the contention of certain authors who have commented on the Convention that this provision amounts to a *ius insurrectionis*."[22]

Elsewhere Pictet elaborates that the Party to the conflict is one in the sense of Article 2 of the Third Convention, i.e., a State, "a party to international law." It will be recalled that Article 2 speaks of "High Contracting Parties," or "Powers."[23]

In his lectures delivered at The Hague Academy in 1950, the same author said: "We have seen that what some have feared is the absence of subordination of the resistance movements to a belligerent power, a Party to the conflict."[24]

Having explained the fear of an absence of subordination of movements of resistance to a belligerent power, Pictet concludes that it was decided that such movements must belong to a Party to the conflict. Pictet points out that this fear was to be countered by assimilating resistance groups to militias or volunteer corps.[25]

The type of relationship here envisaged is exemplified by the decree issued by General Eisenhower during the Second World War, with respect to the French Forces of the Interior:

> 1. The French Forces of the Interior constitute a combatant force commanded and directed by General Koenig, and form an integral part of the Allied Expeditionary Force.
> 2. The French Forces of the Interior in the maquis bear arms openly against the enemy and are instructed to conduct their operations against him in accordance with the rules of war. They are provided with a distinctive emblem and are regarded by General Eisenhower as an army under his command.[26]

There is, therefore, a complete chain of command and responsibility assumed by the Allied Command, as well as respect for the provisions of Article 1 of the 1907 Hague Regulations, as proclaimed by the Comité français de la Libération nationale in its ordinance of June 9, 1944:

> The French Forces of the Interior (F.F.I.) are made up of the whole of the fighting units or their services which take part in the struggle against the enemy on Metropolitan territory, the organization of which is recognized by the Government, and which serve under the orders of commanders recognized by it as responsible. These armed forces make up an integral part of the French Army and enjoy all the rights and privileges granted to military personnel by the laws in force. They conform to the general conditions fixed by the Regulations annexed to the Hague Convention of 18 October 1907 concerning the laws and customs of war on land.[27]

It may be concluded that the requirement of belonging to a Party to the conflict is of fundamental importance. Whatever the formal arrangements between a resistance movement and a Party to the conflict might be, it is required that a State should regard the resistance movement as belonging to it and subject to its policy and command. Indeed, that State must be prepared to accept international responsibility for the acts of the resistance group, just as it must bear responsibility for the acts of its regular forces. The resistance group, on the other hand, must regard itself as subordinate to a State, and must accept its overall policy and command, especially as regards respect for the laws and customs of war. The requirement of belonging to a Party to the conflict must have these consequences, or it makes no sense at all.

Do Arab Terrorists Belong to a Party to the Conflict?

The facts of the support, financing, shelter, encouragement, facilities, freedom of movement and diplomatic protection abroad which Arab States render to the terrorist movements are well known. In many cases the rights and duties of the terrorist movements *vis-à-vis* the host Arab States are even prescribed in written agreements. It is not necessary to elaborate on these facts in this paper. We shall only point out that there can be no question that, from the standpoint of international law, the Arab States concerned bear international responsibility *vis-à-vis* Israel, and, indeed, the Government of Israel has always regarded the Arab States as internationally responsible for terrorist attacks emanating from their territories. But the question to be considered is whether the relationship between the terrorist movements and the Arab States is such as to justify viewing such movements as belonging to a Party to the conflict. To do so we must therefore examine the public statements on this question of both the Arab States and the terrorist organizations. It may be observed, in passing, that even the Arab claim that there exists a separate, Palestinian Arab people (without entering here into analysis of such a claim) would amount to a rejection of the traditional criteria of Article 4, for such a people would not qualify as a Party to the conflict in terms of the Geneva Conventions.

The Palestinian National Covenant, adopted by the Palestine Liberation Organization (P.L.O.) in May 1964, in Jerusalem, and amended on June 4, 1968, in the name of "the Palestine Arab people," contained the following provisions concerning the relationship with Arab Governments: "The Liberation Organization cooperates with all Arab Governments each according to its ability, and does not interfere in the internal affairs of any Arab State."[28]

While subsequent experience shows that the idea of non-intervention in the internal affairs of any Arab State has often been disregarded, it may be pointed out that from the start the relationship with Arab States has been described as one of mutual toleration, not subordination.

In March 1969 the P.L.O. submitted a memorandum to the Arab League Council, attended by the Foreign Ministers of the member States, which pointed out, *inter alia,* that

> the P.L.O.'s most sacred duty to our Palestine Arab people was to affirm that our people had the right to liberate their homeland and that their attitude to Arab and foreign States was determined on the basis of the attitude of those States to their cause. Our Palestine Arab people therefore absolutely rejected any form of interference, trusteeship and subservience.[29]

There is no doubt at all that it was Arab States' "interference, trusteeship and subservience" that was being rejected by the P.L.O.

On May 6, 1970, a new program was published in the name of eleven terror organizations, whereby all of them—including for the first time George Habash's Popular Front for the Liberation of Palestine—agreed to join in the P.L.O.'s Unified Command. The program declared: "The Palestine Revolution announces its absolute independence from any Arab regime and its rejection of any attempts at trusteeship, authority and dependence."[30]

Let us now turn from joint statements of the P.L.O. to some individual proclamations made by the leaders of the principal terrorist organizations. These statements show that not only do the Arab terrorist organizations regard themselves as independent of the recognized Governments but that, in certain circumstances, they are willing to actively oppose, even forcibly, such Governments (as in Jordan and the Lebanon).

Yasser Arafat, the leader of Fatah and of the P.L.O., explained to a journalist in April 1970:

> The end of Israel is the object of our struggle which admits neither compromise nor mediation . . .
>
> Revolutionary violence is the only system for liberating the land of our ancestors. The object of this violence is to liquidate Zionism in all its forms—political, economic, military—and to drive it from Palestine. Our revolutionary action must be independent of all control, whether it is exercised by a Party or by a

236

State. This action will last a long time. We know the intentions of certain Arab leaders to resolve the conflict by a peaceful settlement. When this happens we will oppose it.[31]

On April 16, 1970, a number of Arab news agencies reported from Kuwait that a Fatah leader, Hanni El Hassan, declared there on April 13, 1970: "The slogan of the movement which favors non-intervention in the affairs of Arab States is a strategic slogan of Fatah. However, the movement will interfere when any Arab ruler attempts to sign a peace treaty settling the regional crisis, and anyone who signs such a treaty, thereby signs his own death sentence."[32]

He further declared that the movement would not leave southern Lebanon even if it were forced to oppose the Lebanese authorities.

On April 28, 1970, a broadcast of Al Assifa announced that the revolution "rejects the custodianship of Arab regimes."

According to a Reuter report from Beirut dated May 26, 1970, Abu Youssef, Chairman of the Higher Political Affairs Committee in Lebanon, and a Fatah leader, said in a speech in Sidon that "the Palestine Revolution refuses to have its presence in any part of the Arab countries subordinated to the orders of any authority in any country . . . The presence of the Palestine Revolution depends only on the wishes of the masses of the Arab People."[33] A similar position was taken by other terrorist organizations.

George Habash, leader of the Popular Front for the Liberation of Palestine, when asked by the *Time* magazine correspondent in Amman "if the Arab Governments agree to a peaceful settlement short of a return to Palestine, will you oppose them as well as Israel?" replied, "Of course. If any Government tries to stop us, we will have to defend ourselves against that Government, whether or not it is Arab. We will not start the battle against Arab regimes, but if they try to stop us from fighting to regain our homeland, conflict is inevitable."[34]

Interviewed for the West German News Agency, Habash elaborated on the revolutionary plans of his movement. He said:

> The future State of Palestine after the liberation will be run according to Marxist-Leninist principles. There will be a Marxist-Leninist Party, and the People's Front will be the leader of the revolution. The fight for the liberation of Palestine will take another twenty to thirty years, and after victory everything will be different; not only will Palestine be free from Zionism but Lebanon and **Jordan** will be free from reaction and Syria

and Iraq from the petite bourgeoisie. They will have been transformed in a truly socialist sense and united Palestine will be part of a Marxist-Leninist Arabia.[35]

Turning now to the official position taken by the Arab States, we find that while committed to support the Palestinian movements, they refuse to command them, exercise authority over them or accept any responsibility for them. Thus, the Arab League adopted a recommendation that "The Palestinian people have a right to liberate their homeland and decide their own fate; the Arab States should uphold this right of the Palestinians; . . . the Arab States should give all financial and military support to the Palestine Liberation Organization in its present form."[36]

Similar statements were made by various Arab leaders. It will suffice, however, to refer to President Nasser's recent speech at the opening of the Palestine National Council in Cairo, when he restated certain principles of Egyptian policy declared by him in the Egyptian National Council on January 30, 1969:

> The U.A.R. extends to the Palestinian resistance all material and moral help, without any limit, without reservations and without conditions.
>
> The U.A.R. is unequivocally opposed to any attempt to force any trusteeship over resistance organizations. Such trusteeship only brings about interference with the impetus of the resistance and, as a result, interference with its natural development.[37]

In an interview by Charles Holt of *U.S. News & World Report,* Nasser was asked if the fedayeen could be brought under control. He replied, "I say we cannot and do not want to control them if this means preventing them from trying to regain their rights."[38]

From these statements it appears clear that both the organizations concerned and the Arab States deny any link of subordination and command, this being necessary for the fulfillment of the requirement of belonging to a Party to a conflict.

Dr. Kalshoven observed in his report, with reference to the Popular Front for the Liberation of Palestine:

> It is neither an internal conflict nor do Israel's adversaries refuse to admit that they are Parties to the conflict; what they refuse to acknowledge (and even on occasion strongly deny) is that the Popular Front is affiliated to them. This seems to be in the way even of a tacit agreement . . .[39]

The question whether the Popular Front for the Liberation of Palestine belongs to a Party to a conflict arose and was discussed by the (Israeli) Military Court sitting in Ramallah, in the case of the *Military Prosecutor v. Omar Mahmud Kassem and others:*

> If they do not belong to the Government or State for which they fight, then it seems to us that, from the outset, under current International Law they do not possess the right to enjoy the status of prisoners-of-war upon capture.
>
> It is natural that, in international armed conflicts, the Government which previously possessed an occupied area should encourage and take under its wing the irregular forces which continue fighting within the borders of the country, give them protection and material assistance, and that therefore a "command relationship" should exist between such Government and the fighting forces, with the result that a continuing responsibility exists of the Government and the commanders of its army for those who fight in its name and on its behalf . . .
>
> . . . the Convention applies to military forces (in the wide sense of the term) which, as regards responsibility under International Law, belong to a State engaged in armed conflict with another State, but it excludes those forces—even regular armed units—which do not yield to the authority of the State and its origins of government. The Convention does not apply to these at all. They are to be regarded as combatants not protected by the International Law dealing with prisoners-of-war, and the occupying Power may consider them as criminals for all purposes.
>
> The importance of the allegiance of irregular troops to a central Government made it necessary during the Second World War for States and Governments-in-exile to issue declarations as to the relationship between them and popular resistance forces (see, e.g., the Dutch Royal Emergency Decree of September, 1944).
>
> In the present case, the picture is otherwise. No Government with which we are in a state of war accepts responsibility for the acts of the Popular Front for the Liberation of Palestine. The Organization itself, so far as we know, is not prepared to take orders from the Jordan Government . . .[40]

It has already been explained that the Palestinian organizations themselves cannot qualify as a Party to the conflict for the purposes of the Third Convention. Only Powers in the sense of Articles 4 and 2 of the Third Convention can be considered a Party to a conflict. In this connection it is of relevance to point out that the Palestine Liberation Organization made an unsuccessful attempt to accede to the Geneva Conventions of August 12, 1949.

According to a press release published in Geneva, Dr. Mahmoud Hijazy, President of the Palestinian Red Crescent Society, an official body of the P.L.O., on May 6, 1969, addressed a letter to Mr. Willy Spuehler, Chief of the Political Federal Department of Switzerland, which said, in part:

> The Palestine Liberation Organization, which groups all the Palestinian resistance groups, and of which I am the duly mandated representative, has the honour to bring to the attention of Your Excellency that it has decided to adhere to the Geneva Conventions of 12 August 1949 relative to the protection of the victims of war. It has decided, on condition of reciprocity, to fulfill all the duties stemming from these treaties and to apply them in their letter as in their spirit.

> The Palestine Liberation Organization requests the Swiss Federal Council in its quality as the power administering the Geneva Conventions to take note of this adhesion and to inform the other signatory powers.

This application was disregarded by the Swiss Government, as it had to be, in view of the common accession provision of the four Geneva Conventions, according to which only "Powers" are entitled to accede. It may be pointed out that in the same press release, the Palestinian Red Crescent Society announced its wish to be granted observer status in future international conferences of the Red Cross. Dr. Mahmoud Hijazy did in fact arrive at the Istanbul Red Cross Conference, where the Arab delegations present endeavored to obtain observer status for his organization. The Bureau of the Conference allowed Dr. Hijazy to attend the Conference as an observer, *but in a personal capacity only,* thus frustrating the main purpose of the application, i.e., the recognition of the Palestinian Red Crescent Society.

THE PRINCIPLE OF OPENNESS

Doctrine
The requirements contained in letters (b) and (c) of Article 4A(2)—i.e. the duty of having a fixed distinctive sign recognizable at a distance, and

of carrying arms openly—are a reflection of the fundamental principle of openness of guerrilla warfare. (The nonfulfillment of any one of these requirements by an individual member of a resistance movement suffices to deny him prisoner-of-war status.)

The British *Manual of Military Law* points out that irregular combatants may "be refused the rights of the armed forces if it is found that their sole arm is a pistol, hand grenade, or dagger concealed about the person . . . or if it is found that they have hidden their arms on the approach of the enemy."[41]

Pictet observes that a fixed distinctive sign is "an essential factor of loyalty [*"loyauté"* in the French text] in the struggle and must be worn constantly, in all circumstances."[42]

And as regards the duty to carry arms openly, he adds: "The enemy must be able to recognize partisans as combatants in the same way as members of regular armed forces, whatever their weapons. Thus, a civilian could not enter a military post on a false pretext and then open fire, having taken unfair advantage of his adversaries."[43]

Pictet, in his Hague *Recueil* study speaks of the denial of status to *"individus qui mènent des attaques clandestines."*[44] Professor Denise Bindschedler explains the principle of openness as essential for the maintenance of the distinction between the combatants and the civilian population. Under no circumstances may a guerrilla camouflage himself as a civilian.[45]

The principle of openness came under some criticism in the discussions which took place in the Advisory Group of Experts consulted by the ICRC as too difficult for guerrillas to satisfy in modern warfare.[46] The experts did not, however, propose to modify the traditional rules. They referred, in this connection, to the restatement of such rules by the World Veterans Federation in 1967.[47]

It ought to be emphasized once more that the principle of openness should not be regarded as merely an expression of formal requirements. It is necessary, for humanitarian reasons, to maintain the distinction between combatants and noncombatants and thus protect the civilian, non-combatant population. Thus, Professor Bindschedler, referring to the conditions expressed in letters (b) and (c), explains that "these two conditions are intimately connected; they mean that the guerrilla must mark himself off from the civilian population, and they are consequently the expression of the immunity of that population whose fate becomes uncertain when every civilian may be suspected to be a camouflaged guerrilla."[48]

THEODOR MERON

Professor Draper, in a statement delivered during the Istanbul Conference on September 11, 1969, made a plea on humanitarian grounds against any tampering with the requirements of openness established by the Third Geneva Convention:

> Those who framed the Law of War and who came before us in the long line of the development of that branch of Law knew well the essential value of distinguishing those who fight wars as regular combatants "openly and overtly," to use the old medieval expression, i.e., in "Public and Open Wars." They also knew, as they showed quite clearly, in the Hague Conventions of 1907, time and again, that once you allow the irregular combatant—the peasant by day, the soldier by night, the man without a uniform but with a bomb in his pocket, the civilian in the street who throws a bomb through a café window and runs—once you allow such people to be brought within the proper ambit of *jus in bello,* then you open "Pandora's box," and you make unmitigated misery for every civilian, who loses what precious legal protection he has under the Law of War. . . . Once the guerrilla fighter, the man with the bomb who is a civilian in all outward appearances but can blow you to smithereens as you pass him by, once you bring such a person within the framework of the protection given to regular armed combatants under Article 4 of the Geneva Prisoner-of-War Convention, you make life for every single civilian hang upon a thread. . . .
>
> No civilian can then be distinguished from a secret fighter. The uniformed combatant confronted with a civilian in time of armed conflict, even in time of an internal armed conflict, will not know who is his adversary and who is not . . .[49]

And in a report on the Legal Classification of Belligerent Individuals submitted to the Brussels Conference, Professor Draper observed:

> In open international armed conflicts the identifiability of opponents is essential if warfare is not to be more indiscriminate than it is already. The danger to every innocent civilian if the concealed fighter is to be accorded combatant and POW status does not need to be spelt out. The civilian suffers enough in modern armed conflicts. The civilian fighter will make the lot of his innocent civilian brother a daily walk with death.[50]

Those who plead, in the name of effectiveness of guerrilla operation, for the dispensing with requirements of openness for guerrilla fighters seem to overlook the essential need to maintain the distinction between combatant and non-combatant population, on which the whole humanitarian structure of the law of war rests.

Do Arab Terrorists Fight According to the Principle of Openness? As opposed to the requirement of belonging to a Party to a conflict, the non-satisfaction of which disqualifies the movement as a whole, the requirement of openness applies to the individual members of the resistance groups.

The fact is that often members of Arab terrorist organizations, while fighting on or near cease-fire lines, wear a kind of uniform and carry arms openly. However, if they succeed in penetrating deeper into Israeli-held areas, they usually discard their uniforms and, both for fear of being caught and to increase the element of surprise in their operations, wear civilian clothes when on operations. They reveal their arms only at the very last moment of their terrorist missions. Such members of the organizations as have been recruited locally rather than infiltrated from outside act in a clandestine way, in civilian clothes, and bring out their arms at the very last moment necessary for the success of their operations. Numerous operations of both infiltrators and locally recruited terrorists involve grenade-throwing, mostly at civilians, both Jewish and Arab, and laying of anti-personnel mines, button mines, and various devices intended to injure civilians and particularly children.

The Court in the *Kassem* case accepted the following description of the practice of the Popular Front for the Liberation of Palestine: "The Members of the Organization sometimes wear military uniform and openly carry arms outside inhabited areas and sometimes they do not wear uniform in the course of action and do not carry arms openly for fear of being caught."[51]

Obviously, those members of the organizations who act in a clandestine way, in violation of the requirements to operate openly, forfeit their right to be treated as prisoners-of-war, a right which would depend, in the first place, on the fulfillment by the organization itself as a whole of certain requirements. In this connection, it appears that the failure to observe the requirement of openness is part of the *modus vivendi* of the Arab terror organizations and is in accordance with its orders and its tactics. In other words, the individual terrorist, in concealing his arms and identification, normally does not do so on his own initiative, in isolated cases only, but does so according to an organizational pattern.

Such disregard of the requirements of Article 4, as a matter of *policy,* affects the qualifications of the organization as a whole. This situation is, of course, quite different from that in which an individual member forfeits his privileged status because he himself fails to meet the criteria established under Article 4, in spite of the fact that the organization as such observes those criteria as a matter of policy and practice. The fact that a major part of the activities of the Arab terrorist organizations is carried out in deliberate violation of the conditions enumerated in letters (b) and (c) cannot be disregarded.

THE DUTY TO CONDUCT OPERATIONS IN ACCORDANCE WITH THE LAWS AND CUSTOMS OF WAR

Doctrine

It has already been explained that the obligation to conduct operations in accordance with the laws and customs of war pertains to the group as a whole.

Professor Bindschedler explains:

> According to subparagraph (d), Art. 13 of Geneva Convention I, militias and volunteer corps must fulfill the condition "of conducting their operations in accordance with the laws and customs of war." Naturally this is an obligation which is incumbent on all belligerents, but for resistance organizations or guerrilla groups it has a constitutive effect. Indeed, it is only if the given movement or group in its entirety complies as a general rule with the laws and customs of war that its members may claim that these laws are applicable to themselves. It is in this connection that one can appreciate the great importance of the condition—already mentioned—of being organized, according to which the group must be commanded by a responsible person because it is precisely the way in which the commander will interpret his obligations which will be decisive.
>
> The breaches of laws and customs of war which may occasionally be committed, as in every army, will in this case involve only the personal responsibility of the individual guerrilla who has committed them or, perhaps, that of the chief who has ordered them.[52]

This point is of tremendous importance. If it can be shown that although some members of the group conduct their operations according to the laws and customs of war, other members of the group are allowed to carry out operations in violation of the laws and customs of war, e.g., by launching indiscriminate or even deliberate attacks on civilians, then the group as a whole does not qualify for privileged status under Article 4A(2). The question must always be whether the group as a whole follows the laws and customs of war as a matter of policy. If the answer is negative, a major constitutive requirement of the group is not met, and the group does not qualify under Article 4. Pictet observes, in his commentary, that the requirement to conduct operations in accordance with the laws and customs of war is "of course an essential provision which embraces those just listed above."[53]

This requirement is based of course on the assumption, still doubtless true despite the strains imposed by modern warfare, that a distinction must be maintained between legitimate and illegitimate objectives. And if accidents of war inevitably occur, a policy based on deliberate or indiscriminate attacks on civilians can in no circumstances be tolerated.[54]

Professor Bindschedler, in commenting on the problem of guerrilla attacks on civilian population, and on indiscriminate (blind) attacks, had this to say:

> International law cannot—without completely undermining itself—confer privileged status on acts which so clearly run counter to it, whatever may be the motives inspiring those who commit such acts. The principle that the end justifies the means would signify here as elsewhere—if it would be accepted as justification—the end of any limitative regulation. Considered within the framework of a conflict to which, in principle, the laws of war apply, direct armed attacks against the civilian population or attacks striking blindly at civilians and military alike can only constitute—if they are committed by members of the armed forces—war crimes, and if they are committed by civilians—common law crimes. In so far as terrorism *is the usual method of fighting* of groups of guerrillas, this can only deprive the members of the group of the status of privileged combatants. Any other conception would render derisory all efforts which have been undertaken to humanize the conflicts and to protect human rights generally . . .
>
> We may add that terroristic acts against civilian material objectives are no less prohibited.[55]

It is therefore essential to determine whether terrorism is the "usual," habitual way of fighting of a particular group.

Dr. Henri Meyrowitz, in his report referred to above, says that "the prohibition of terrorist bombings is considered by the majority of authors as an imperative principle of the law of war ... it implies an absolute prohibition of terrorism, but resulting from this is, also, that what is forbidden under the term terrorism is attacks directed, with a terrorist objective, against elements of the *civilian enemy population*. This prohibition, which has a general character, *applies also unquestionably to guerrilla warfare.*[56]

The experts consulted by the ICRC before the Istanbul Conference considered the question whether the requirement of conduct of operations in accordance with the laws and customs of war should in any way be mitigated. The Report points out that "most of the experts did not advocate any basic modification in the interpretation of Article 4 in favor of guerrillas, with the exception of two participants who asked that combatants fighting against an aggression or against colonialism should be favored."[57] The Report further says that the practice of terrorism gave rise to discussion, as an expert argued that to condemn terrorism would be equivalent to depriving guerrillas of their only means of combat, and would thus be unrealistic.[58]

But the view of that expert was unacceptable to the majority who felt that "terrorism, in the sense of indiscriminate attacks against the civilian population, should be condemned and that it outlawed guerrilla forces."[59]

Elsewhere in the report, the ICRC said that while it did not advocate the application of humanitarian principles on the basis of reciprocity, it recognized that "in practice it would be difficult to ask Governments to apply these rules to persons who entirely disregarded them."[60]

Professor Jacques Freymond, Vice-President of the ICRC, posed this fundamental question: "Is it possible to get a government, or the population, to regard a terrorist who has thrown a grenade into the middle of a peaceful crowd, and has been seized and detained, as a prisoner-of-war, entitled to the protection of the Geneva Convention?"[61]

In this connection it may be observed that even members of regular armed forces of a State may be tried for war crimes committed prior to their capture, if they conduct their operations in violation of the laws and customs of war. That this is the case is supported by the recent case of *Mohamed Ali and another,* in which the accused, while dressed as civilians, planted a bomb in a Singapore office building, killing several civilians. They were caught while still in civilian clothes and charged with murder under the domestic criminal law. The accused claimed that they were members of Indonesian armed forces and that they should be treated as prisoners-of-war. The Federal Court of Malaysia held that the accused were not prisoners-of-war within the meaning of the Convention, as they committed "not only an act of sabotage but one totally unconnected with the necessities of war." The Federal Court went on to say that

> It seems to us clear beyond doubt that under International Law a member of the armed forces of a party to the conflict who, out of uniform and in civilian clothing, sets off explosives in the territory of the other party to the conflict in a non-military building in which civilians are doing work unconnected with any war effort forfeits his right on capture to be treated as a prisoner-of-war.[62]

The conviction was upheld on appeal to the Privy Council, which ruled that as the saboteurs "forfeited their rights under the Convention by engaging in sabotage in civilian clothes, it is not necessary to consider whether they also forfeited them by breach of the laws and customs of war by their attacks on a non-military building in which there were civilians."[63]

Do the Arab Terrorist Organizations Conduct Their Operations in Accordance with the Laws and Customs of War?

It has already been explained that the requirement of conducting operations in accordance with the laws and customs of war applies to the conduct of the group as a whole, and that it has constitutive effect. If a group as a whole conducts its operations in violation of the laws and customs of war, then none of its members can qualify for prisoner-of-war status although he might not personally have been involved in such violations.

Before examining the record of Arab terrorist organizations, let us briefly review their declared objectives: the "politicide" of Israel and the establishment in its place of a "democratic Palestine." Arabs are regarded as Palestinian citizens, as well as such "Jews who were living permanently in Palestine until the beginning of the Zionist invasion." (According to a resolution of the Palestinian Congress, the year 1917 is regarded as the beginning of the Zionist invasion.)[64]

According to the Palestinian National Covenant, "the liberation of Palestine . . . is a national duty . . . to purge the Zionist presence from Palestine."[65] The goal is not merely to eliminate "the consequences of the aggression committed in 1967," but to "liberate" Tel Aviv as well.[66] These objectives, replete with their genocidal undercurrents, if analyzed in terms of contemporary international law and the law of the Charter, would be viewed as flagrantly incompatible with law, and as internationally criminal.

The examples which follow will bear mainly on the more technical aspects of the violations of laws and customs of war by terrorist organizations at present, rather than with their aims and objectives for the future. An attempt will be made to show that terrorist actions and declarations (which clearly amount to admissions), aim at the deliberate liquidation of Israel's civilian population, or, at best, are aimed blindly and indiscriminatedly at civilians and combatants alike, and are therefore just as illegal.

The acts described below are utterly repugnant to the principles of international law and, according to the authorities and the jurisprudence, are crimes for which their perpetrators must pay a penalty. The immunity of non-combatants from direct attack is one of the basic rules of war, and this immunity is consistently violated by those carrying out such attacks.

As reported by Bernard Jordan in the London *Daily Mail* of January 14, 1969, the orders given to terrorists by their leaders are to "kill Jews. No, we don't care whether the dead are civilians or soldiers. Just as long as they are Jews."[67]

A few examples of terrorist activity:

A child wounded by a detonation pencil on June 8, 1968.

Two button-mine explosives in the form of attractive, colorful buttons placed near a school on June 27, 1968.

A time bomb in a cinema on October 8, 1967, and on May 13, 1968.

Bombs at a bus station in Tel Aviv on September 4, 1968.

A truck blown up in Gaza market place wounding sixteen persons, including fourteen Arabs, on September 9, 1968.

An infernal machine blown up at the Jerusalem market on November 22, 1968, killing eleven persons, including a child, and wounding scores of others.

A bomb at a Jerusalem supermarket on February 21, 1969, killing two university students and injuring many persons, including a U.N. observer.

A bomb in a crowded cafeteria at the Hebrew University on March 6, 1969, injuring twenty-nine persons.

Bombs exploded in the Afula vegetable market on October 6, 1969, killing several civilians and wounding many more.

A series of explosions in civilian dwellings in Haifa in October 1969, causing death and injury to civilian inhabitants.

A series of terrorist attacks aimed at terrorizing the Arab population of the Israel-held areas, causing many dead and hundreds of wounded.

A series of attacks on civilian air transport:

On November 27, 1969, hand grenade attack on El Al offices in Athens. One Greek child was killed, thirteen persons of various nationalities were wounded.

On December 26, 1968, an attack on an El Al passenger airliner at Athens airport. One Israeli passenger killed and some wounded.

On Feb. 18, 1969, an El Al passenger airliner was attacked at Zurich airport. The co-pilot of the plane was killed, others were wounded.

On September 8, 1969, hand grenades were hurled into El Al offices in Brussels.

On Februray 10, 1970, passengers and crew of an El Al passenger airliner were attacked at Munich airport. One passenger was killed, several wounded.

On February 21, 1970, an explosion took place in an Austrian Airlines plane en route from Frankfurt to Vienna.

On the same day a Swissair passenger airliner exploded in the air en route from Zurich to Lod, killing all forty-seven passengers and crew of various nationalities.
Bombing attacks were also carried out against Israel Embassies abroad.[68]

At various times deliberate shelling of Israel civilian towns and villages took place, killing and wounding many, with an especially heavy toll among children. Many such attacks occurred in

May and June 1970, for instance against Kiryat Shmonah, Beit Shean, Tiberias and villages in the Beit Shean and Jordan valleys.

On May 22, 1970, a terrorist attack was carried out against a school bus, killing and wounding many children. The bus carried children and teachers from Avivim village to a regional school.

Reference must also be made to terrorist organizations' taking of hostages in order to force the release of criminals condemned to imprisonment in accordance with due process of law, or awaiting trial. The taking of hostages is—as is well known—prohibited by international law. (e.g., Article 34 of the Geneva Convention relative to the Protection of Civilian Persons in Time of War.)

The above list, ugly as it is, is only partial and non-exhaustive. It gives examples of the actions of the Arab terrorist organizations. Such acts speak, of course, for themselves. But as the Appendix to this paper shows, the Arab terrorist organizations boastfully accept responsibility for their deeds, and their aims and intentions become quite clear.

Although the principal terrorist organization, Fatah, sometimes claims—for propaganda purposes—that it does not engage in activities against civilian objectives, the record shows that like all the other organizations, Fatah engages as a matter of policy in terrorist attacks against civilians. Except as regards operations in the territory of neutral countries, there is no important difference in the methods and objectives of various terrorist organizations concerning conduct of operations in violation of the laws and customs of war.

Moreover, it may be pointed out that the organizations have a common organization and a coordinated joint command.

TERRORISM IN THIRD COUNTRIES

In view of the condemnable chain of attacks by Arab terrorists against civilian Israeli objectives, as well as against innocent persons, in neutral countries not involved in the Middle East conflict, the need arises to comment on the claim of the individuals in such countries to treatment as prisoners-of-war, and not as common criminals triable under the local criminal law. The fact is that even if Arab terrorists were accorded privileges by a belligerent country involved under Article 4A(2), a neutral country whose neutrality they violated would not be under any similar obligation. Indeed, Article 4A(2) speaks only of such prisoners-of-war "who have fallen into the power of the enemy."

It is universally recognized that the belligerents have certain duties *vis-à-vis* neutrals. While Arab terrorists cannot be regarded as belligerents, let us examine briefly the duties belligerents do have with regard to neutral States.

Oppenheim points out that "this duty *excludes,* in the first place, any violation of neutral territory for military or naval purposes of the war, and any interference with the legitimate intercourse of neutrals with the enemy. . . ."[69] Violations of the duty of belligerents to respect neutral territory call for appropriate reparation.

Neutral countries, on the other hand, have certain duties *vis-à-vis* belligerent countries. They are "under a duty to prevent their territory from becoming a theatre of war as the result of passage of foreign troops or aircraft or of prolonged stay of belligerent men-of-war in their territorial waters . . . they are bound to control the activities of their nationals insofar as these may tend to transform neutral territory into a basis of war operations or preparations."[70]

When terrorists carry out attacks against Israel nationals in neutral countries, they do not conform to any of the requirements enumerated in Article 4A(2). It has been pointed out that in no case could they claim the privileges conferred by that Article from a neutral country. They must instead be treated as common criminals under the law of the country concerned.

Professor Draper puts it succinctly:

> We are also confronted today with the phenomenon of isolated acts of violence in different State territories directed against the nationals or property of a specified State, by an organization of concealed fighters with specific political objective directed against that particular State. *Such acts are treated as crimes under the municipal law of the State in which they are committed.* The perpetrators have no international law protection except such as may derive from the existing regime of Human Rights, e.g., under the European Convention on Human Rights of 1950. The feasibility of obtaining for such persons any international law combatant status is remote.[71]

Similarly Dr. Meyrowitz points out:

> The protection accorded by Article 4A(2) to irregular combatants is independent of the place where they carry out their acts of war: occupied territory, enemy territory, the territory of another belligerent, or the high seas. But this protection is only due

from a *belligerent* State party to the Convention. *If the action takes place in a non-belligerent country, this State* (party or not to the Geneva Convention) *is free to prosecute the agents in conformity with its internal penal law.*[72]

Of course, the international community is entitled, not only on legal grounds but also on grounds of morality, public safety and order, to insist that the scope of conflicts be limited geographically, and that neutral territories not be turned into lawless jungles by foreign terrorists.

Some of the considerations against privileged status for terrorists acting in foreign countries find clear expression in the judgment rendered on December 22, 1969, by the *Geschworenengericht* of Canton Zurich against *Abu-El Heiga Mohamed, Yousef Ibrahim Tawfik* and *Dahbor Amena,* who were accused of manslaughter and other infractions of Swiss criminal law as a result of their attack on February 18, 1969, on an El Al passenger aircraft taxiing for takeoff at Kloten airport. In rejecting any claim of privileged status, the Court said:

> Before judicial determination of the actions of which defendants 1, 2 and 3 are accused, it is necessary to proceed to the argument put forth by the defense that it is an error to judge their deed from the standpoint of civil law. According to this theory, the attack at Kloten is an emanation of the war between the members of the Popular Front and the "Zionist usurpers," so that they have a legitimate right to defend themselves with all possible means; that the fighters of the Popular Front are entitled to the status of combatants; that every deed should be viewed as a military action; and that according to the principles of the Hague Convention, they would therefore stand outside of civil law. Thus, attacks on military installations and military matériel would also be legitimate actions. They assert that in wartime, weapons, ammunition and soldiers are transported by "El Al" planes; that they now also serve to bring in war matériel and to transport volunteers; that they are constituent parts of Israel's armaments, thus military objectives, which they are even more justified in destroying, since the Israelis are supposedly constantly guilty of violations of international law.

> It is unfathomable why someone who penetrates into a neutral country having normal diplomatic relations with his State, and who here carries out an attack against the aircraft of another country, should be placed under the law of war. The fact that the

aircraft of the "El Al" Company and its crew are seen as military objectives, because they have been used for military purposes and according to the defendants—the truth or error of their assertion does not have to be decided—still transport war matériel, changes nothing. But the argument of the defense misses its mark because of other considerations as well. The Geneva Conventions of the year 1949, and especially that dealing with the treatment of prisoners-of-war of August 12, 1949 *(Swiss Treaty Series* 1951, p. 228), would be applicable to the defendants and others only if they were members of a resistance movement, and as such carry a fixed sign recognizable at a distance, carry arms openly and conduct their operations in accordance with the laws and customs of war (Art. 4). None of these conditions applies to the defendants. To this must be added that the Geneva Convention merely requires that sentences be passed by a regularly constituted court affording all the judicial guarantees which are recognized as indispensable by civilized peoples (Art. 3, par. 1). That the Court passing sentence does not offer these guarantees is not urged by the defense itself.[73]

The accused were sentenced to twelve years' imprisonment with forced labor. Elsewhere as well, cases involving Arab terrorist attacks against Israel objectives have been dealt with under domestic criminal law and no privileged status has been granted. The Athens Court of Appeals, in a decision rendered on March 26, 1970, in the case of *Mohamed Mahmoud Mohamed* and *Soleiman Maher,* condemned two Arab terrorists to seventeen and fourteen years respectively for a number of offenses arising out of an attack at Athens airport on an El Al airliner on December 26, 1968, an attack which caused the death of one passenger, injuries to others and damage to the aircraft. It is noteworthy that the defense pleaded prisoner-of-war status but that this plea was not accepted by the Court.[74]

An Arab terrorist was also prosecuted and condemned for throwing a grenade at the Israel Embassy in The Hague, but, as he was a minor, the sentence was a light one.[75]

On June 29, 1970, an Arab terrorist was prosecuted and condemned *in absentia* to five years' imprisonment by a Belgian court for aiding the perpetrators of a grenade throwing at the El Al office in Brussels on September 8, 1969.[76]

It is natural that foreign, neutral countries on whose territories terrorist attacks have been carried out express resentment and protest.[77] Following the attack at Kloten airport on February 18, 1969, the Government of Switzerland made protests to the Governments of Jordan, Syria and Lebanon, which by their policy of support of terrorist movements made the attack possible.[78]

On March 18, 1969, Swiss Foreign Minister Spühler, in an important speech in Parliament (*Nationalrat*), set out the reasons why Jordan, Syria and Lebanon carried international responsibility for the attack at Kloten:

> A State is not responsible for the unlawful conduct of individuals in relation to foreign States, but is bound to take preventive and repressive measures against such illicit actions. One cannot speak of acts of war as long as it is not established that the terrorists acted on direct instruction of a State. The penal authorities must clarify in how far one may speak of a war-like action and to what extent our neutrality and sovereignty have been abused. It is established, however, that these States tolerate the liberation organizations, if not facilitate and support them. They must assume the responsibility for that. For that reason the protests to Syria, Lebanon and Jordan ensued on February 28. It is established that the organizations at least partly operate from Lebanon. One of the attackers admitted being an instructor in the Syrian army. Two of the terrorists arrived here from Syria. The headquarters of the National Front for the Liberation of Palestine is located in Jordan. Switzerland awaits measures from these States for the prevention of further designs contrary to international law.[79]

Following the Swissair plane explosion, the Government of Switzerland announced on February 23, 1970, that it "has charged its Embassies in the interested countries to bring these measures to the attention of the governments to which they are accredited. It expects that they will formally disapprove terrorist acts committed abroad and that they will do all within their power to prevent similar acts."[80]

Other States, victims of terrorist attacks, such as Ethiopia, have also expressed their anger at the lawless acts carried out against their national airlines abroad.

ISTANBUL CONFERENCE

An attempt to obtain recognition as prisoners-of-war for Arab terrorists was made during the twenty-first International Conference of the Red Cross, held in Istanbul in September 1969, where the above-mentioned General Assembly Resolutions on the situation in Southern Africa were relied upon as authorities by Arab delegations. The irrelevance of these Resolutions to the Israel-Arab dispute in general and to the status of the Arab terrorists in particular, became obvious to all when the Algerian Red Crescent delegation submitted to the Commission for International Humanitarian Law the following draft resolution on Protection of Victims of Non-International Conflicts:

> The XXIst International Conference of the Red Cross,
> Considering Resolution No. XXXI, in which the XXth International Conference of the Red Cross (Vienna, 1965) urged the ICRC to continue its work with the aim of strengthening the humanitarian assistance of the Red Cross to victims of non-international conflicts and recommended that Governments of States parties to the Geneva Conventions and National Societies support these efforts in their respective countries,
> whereas since the adoption of the 1949 Geneva Conventions internal conflicts have taken on ever increasing proportions and have already caused millions of victims,
> considering further the different resolutions adopted by the UN—in particular No. 2396 of December 2, 1968 on Apartheid and No. 2395 of December 29, 1968 on Angola—declaring that members of resistance movements fighting for their freedom should be treated as prisoners-of-war in accordance with international law and specifically in accordance with the Geneva Convention relative to the Treatment of Prisoners-of-War of August 12, 1949,
> noting the de facto existence of the Palestine Liberation Front,
> declares that the Palestinian combatants such as the combatants of the FRELIMO, MLPA and PAIGC should be treated as prisoners-of-war in accordance with international law and specifically in accordance with the Geneva Convention Relative to the Treatment of Prisoners-of-War of August 12, 1949,
> urges the ICRC to redouble its efforts and take vigorous action to ensure the application of this resolution.[81]

The very same day, September 10, 1969, a far-reaching amendment was submitted by the Danish Red Cross Delegation.[82] A further sub-amendment was submitted on September 11, by the Swedish Red Cross.[83] These amendments reflected the spontaneous and broad opposition which immediately arose to the Algerian initiative. Both amendments dealt with the treatment of members of resistance movements in non-international conflicts, rather than with the question of status of Arab terrorists in the Israel-Arab (inter-state) dispute. Many delegations were particularly concerned about the following difficulties:

1. The Algerian draft attempted to present a particular inter-State dispute as a non-international armed conflict and to provide for a certain treatment of a specific group, all this in violation of the statutes of the International Red Cross which provide in Article II, paragraph 5, that the Conference "may not deal with political matters nor serve as a forum for political debates."[84] The Algerian draft violated a long tradition of the International Red Cross to consider matters of general principle only, rather than particular disputes between States.

2. The Israel-Arab dispute had never before been presented as a conflict of non-international character. On the contrary, it has always been regarded by the States concerned themselves (for instance, by their signature of the General Armistice Agreements) and by the United Nations organs as a typical inter-State conflict. (The practice of the United Nations clearly shows that the dispute is regarded as an exclusively international one. This emerges from a long series of U.N. Resolutions addressed to the States concerned. For example, the cease-fire resolutions of June 1967 were addressed to "the Governments concerned.")[85] Moreover, the draft resolution was itself entirely self-contradictory. For if a conflict was non-international, then only the obligations of Article 3—common to the several Conventions—were applicable.

The Algerian delegation was not concerned by the contradiction inherent in the fact that on the one hand it insisted as Arab States do, that Israel was an "aggressor," and on the other hand that it regarded the conflict as non-international. Indeed, any attempt to treat the conflict prevailing between Israel and the Arab States as non-international is too ludicrous to warrant analysis. In fact, all the classical criteria of an international conflict are present in the case of the Israel-Arab conflict.[86] Neither was the Algerian delegation worried by the contradiction between the demand to have the Israel-Arab dispute treated as international for the purposes of the (Fourth) Geneva Convention Relative to the Protection of Civilian Persons in Time of War, and non-international for the purposes of the Third Convention.

3. In any event, the Convention itself establishes in Article 4A(2) the precise requirements which resistance groups and their members must satisfy in order to claim prisoner-of-war status. A representative of the ICRC on the Commission explained that the ICRC International Conference was not a diplomatic conference convened to consider revisions of the Conventions, and until such revision the status of resistance movements (in international conflicts) was regulated by Article 4A(2).

When it became clear to the Algerian delegation that its draft had no chance whatsoever of being adopted, it decided to join with the Danish and Swedish Red Cross delegations in sponsoring a joint draft (No. 8172), which was accepted by the Conference (50 votes for, 31 against and 19 abstentions). The Resolution read as follows:

Status of Combatants in Non-International Armed Conflicts

The XXIst International Conference of the Red Cross,
   considering Resolution No. XXXI, in which the XXth International Conference of the Red Cross urged the ICRC to continue its work with the aim of strengthening the humanitarian assistance of the Red Cross to victims of non-international armed conflicts and recommended that Governments of States parties to the Geneva Conventions and National Societies support these efforts in their respective countries,
   whereas, since the adoption of the Geneva Conventions of 1949, non-international armed conflicts have become increasingly extensive and have already caused millions of victims,
   considers that combatants and members of resistance movements who participate in non-international armed conflicts *and who conform to the provisions of Article 4* of the Third Geneva Convention of 12 August 1949 should, when captured, be protected against any inhumanity and brutality and receive *treatment similar* to that which that Convention lays down for prisoners-of-war,
   requests the ICRC to make a thorough study of the legal status of such persons and take the action in this matter that is necessary.[87]

Professor Paul Geouffre de la Pradelle, in a report submitted to the Brussels Conference on Humanitarian Law and Armed Conflict remarks about the Resolution as adopted: "Thus the 'freedom fighters,' compared with members of organized resistance groups, persons protected by the 1949 Conventions, must, by their example, observe the rules of conduct laid down since 1899 for militias by the Hague Regulations, in order to receive treatment—and not the status of prisoners-of-war."[88]

It is obvious that the Resolution as adopted is entirely different from the original Algerian draft and not at all helpful to Arab claims for status for Arab terrorists. Not only have all references to a specific dispute and group been deleted, but the Resolution as adopted concerns non-international disputes only. Moreover, the Resolution requires that certain persons participating in non-international armed conflicts should receive treatment *similar* to that which the Convention lays down for prisoners-of-war, *if such combatants conform* to Article 4 of the Third Geneva Convention. This would presumably refer primarily to conditions contained in letters (a) to (d) only, for it is not clear how such combatants could belong to a Party to a conflict.

It may be concluded that the Arab attempt at Istanbul to obtain prisoner-of-war status for Arab terrorists amounted to a clear failure.

CONCLUSIONS

In the preceding pages the record of the Arab terror organizations has been examined in light of Article 4 of the Third Convention and of the contemporary doctrine respecting the rights and duties of resistance movements. Account has been taken of recent developments, including the Red Cross Istanbul Conference, and trials of Arab terrorists in both Israel-held territories and in neutral countries, where attempts have failed to gain privileged status for Arab terrorists. While the ideological aims of the Arab terrorist organizations have been briefly mentioned as objectionable on both moral and legal grounds, the examination itself has been restricted to more technical grounds.

It has been established that whatever the motives of the Arab terrorist organizations might be, they cannot justify departures from the law of war and are not relevant to claims of privileged combatancy.

It has been shown that the Arab terrorist organizations do not satisfy two criteria which are of a constitutive nature for the organizations as a whole, for they do not belong to a Party to the conflict and they do not carry out their operations in accordance with the laws and customs of war. Moreover, many individual terrorists forfeit their claim by violating the principle of "openness," not having a fixed distinctive sign recognizable at a distance, and not carrying arms openly, as required by the

Third Convention. But, the claim of the organizations for privileged status is adversely affected by their disregard of the principle of openness.

Although the Arab terrorists' claims for privileged combatancy has been denied, and they have been treated as common criminals, the Israel prosecuting authorities have refrained from demanding the death penalty even when the terrorists have been convicted of murder and when the death penalty would have been wholly justifiable under the applicable criminal law. Whenever the accused has claimed the protection of Article 4 of the Third Convention, such claims have been thoroughly examined by the Israel Courts, and then denied for juridical reasons. Only terms of imprisonment have been imposed, and regular visits of ICRC are allowed, without supervision, in the places of detention.

APPENDIX:

STATEMENTS OF ARAB TERRORIST ORGANIZATIONS
CONCERNING ATTACKS ON ISRAEL CIVILIAN OBJECTIVES

One of the slogans, which is regularly broadcast to Fatah members is: "From Q to the insurgents: Exterminate, exterminate, exterminate!"

[Voice of Fatah, Cairo, February 18, 1970]

"Special group 277 has been ordered to carry out an operation of deterrence to serve as a warning to the enemy ... This morning our fighters managed to place several high explosive charges in the Afula vegetable market ... As a result of the explosions, several cars were destroyed and it caused many casualties, dead and wounded."

[Voice of Fatah, Cairo, October 6, 1969]

"Two Arab terrorist organizations claimed responsibility for the explosions which took place in civilian dwellings in Haifa in October 1969:

The spokesman of Al-Assifah announced that his organization is responsible for the explosions."

[Radio P.L.O., Cairo, October 22, 1969]

"Statement No. 1202 of the Command of the Palestinian Armed Struggle on the action of Fatah forces ... in Acre:

a. In accordance with orders, group No. 2225 moved to carry out the action ... with the object of detonating explosives somewhere in Haifa.

b. For this purpose our fighters used a vehicle loaded with explosives, driven by two fighters.

c. At the outskirts of Acre, on the way to its target, the force met an enemy patrol and after a short battle, managed to make its way to the target.

d. The enemy sent large forces in pursuit of our force, who found themselves at the entrance to the New City of Acre, in the Jewish quarter.

e. Our fighters had no alternative and decided to blow up the vehicle right there, near the Jewish quarter, while they were inside it."

[Radio P.L.O. Cairo, November 24, 1969]

"During the night of March 20, a special group of Assifah placed explosives in several vital installations of the Avivim village in Upper Galilee, as well as in the public shelter in the heart of the village. During the morning of March 21, the charges went off, destroying essential installations and wounding a number of enemy people."

[Middle East News Agency, Cairo, March 21, 1970]

"On March 9, another group of the Liberation Forces set off explosives in the building housing the post office and labor exchange, on the Jebaliya main street. The building was completely destroyed."

[Middle East News Agency, Cairo, March 21, 1970]

"On March 19, Group 55 of Assifah launched a heavy rocket attack on the town of Nahariya. In a parallel operation, our forces attacked the northern industrial district. Our sources reported that heavy losses in men and property were inflicted on the enemy."

[Voice of Fatah, Cairo, March 21, 1970]

"During the night of March 22, at 19.30 hours, Assifah fighters of Group 1119 attacked al Assi village, using heavy rockets. The attack was directed against the village's vital installations. Our sources reported that the enemy suffered heavy losses in men and installations . . ."

[Voice of Fatah, Cairo, March 22, 1970]

"Our fighters of Group 56 placed delayed action explosives in a two-story building housing a club and night-club. The building is at the junction of Mea She'arim-Musrara Quarter and Aqabat al-Manzal in Jerusalem. The explosives went off during the night of March 22 at a quarter to eight. As a result, a large part of the south side was destroyed. Some of the enemy soldiers were also hit. Our fighters returned to their base unharmed . . ."

[Voice of Fatah, Cairo, March 22, 1970]

"Our fighters of the special group 'S' placed incendiary bombs and explosives in the building of the Zionist youth club in Holon, southeast of Tel Aviv. The explosives went off on March 22 at 11.30 hours. As a result, a large part of the building was destroyed and fire broke out in the whole building which consists of many stores. The fire spread to neighboring buildings and hit some enemy people. Our soldiers returned to their base unharmed."

[Voice of Fatah, Cairo, March 22, 1970]

"The Popular Democratic Front has stated that on March 24 its members launched a large-scale attack on three Israeli villages: Shetula, Zarit and Tarbina."

[Middle East News Agency, Damascus, March 26, 1970]

"A spokesman of the Armed Struggle Command reported that on March 25 'popular liberation forces' destroyed a tractor of the enemy doing construction work in the Al-Hatib area, killing the driver."

[Middle East News Agency, Cairo, March 26, 1970]

"Abstract of Palestine Armed Struggle Command communiqué:
On March 8, Group 13, the 'Clouds of Hell Group,' attacked Beit Shean with heavy rockets, starting fires and inflicting damage and casualties; at the same time Assifah silenced the enemy's artillery fire."

[Voice of Fatah, March 9, 1970, quoted from BBC Monitoring Service]

"Operations placing explosives in enemy restaurants in Arab Jerusalem are part of the revolution's activities . . . The revolution will continue to deal blows to enemy military and tourist meeting places. This will paralyze the enemy's political, economic, military and propaganda resources as part of the overthrow of the synthetic Zionist entity . . . The revolution will go on hitting all enemy entertainment places."

[Voice of Fatah, Cairo, May 11, 1970, quoted from BBC Monitoring Service]

The Popular Front for the Liberation of Palestine admitted responsibility for the Zurich and Athens attacks on international air transport. The Popular Front for the Liberation of Palestine, General Command, admitted responsibility for the Swissair plane explosion.

[Baghdad Radio, February 2, 1970, BBC Monitoring Service]

The Popular Front for the Liberation of Palestine, General Command, admitted responsibility for the attack on the Avivim school bus, which took place on May 22, 1970. The short range attack was described as involving a bus of 'Zionist experts.' It is of interest to observe that a Fatah spokesman in Beirut expressed reservations about the operations.

[Middle East News Agency, May 22, 1970, 22.50 hours]

On the following day, however, a Fatah spokesman in Amman announced that his organization did not condemn, nor did it criticize, the attack.

[As reported by Agence France Presse, May 24, 1970]

NOTES

[1] *El Ahram* (Cairo), April 17, 1970. The article was written in connection with the question of the representation of the Palestine Liberation Organization in the Dar-es-Salaam Conference of Foreign Ministers of Non-aligned States.

[2] *The Geneva Conventions of 12 August 1949.* Jean S. Pictet, ed. (Geneva, International Committee of the Red Cross), 1960, Vol. III, p. 4.

[3] Annex to the Convention Concerning the Laws and Customs of War on Land, 2nd Peace Conference, The Hague, October 18, 1907. *Conventions and Declarations between the Powers* (The Hague), 1915, No. IX.

[4] See, in general: J. S. Pictet, "La Croix Rouge et Les Conventions de Genève," 76 *Recueil des Cours* 1 (1950), Vol. I, pp. 71–81; Zorgbibe, "L'application des Conventions de Genève et le sort des combattants arabes," *Le Monde Diplomatique,* June 5, 1969; "Legitimate Resistance or Murder in International Law," 85 *The Law Quarterly Review* 1 (January 1969); Goodhart, "Terror and International Law," 11 *New Outlook* 34 (November–December 1968); Trainin, "Questions of Guerrilla Warfare in the Law of War," 40 *Am. J. Int. L.* 534 (1946); Draper, *The Red Cross Conventions of 1949* 13–17 (1958); Nurick and Barrett, "Legality of Guerrilla Forces under the Laws of War," 40 *Am. J. Int. L.* 563 (1940); Stone, *Legal Controls of International Conflict* 562–70 (1954); Baxter, "So-called 'Unprivileged Belligerency': Spies, Guerrillas, and Saboteurs" 28 *Br. Yrbk. Int. L.* 323 (1951); "The Privy Council on the Qualifications of Belligerents," 63 *Am. J. Int. L.* 290 (1969); Oppenheim, 2 *International Law* 256–58 (7th ed., Lauterpacht, 1952); Greenspan, *The Modern Law of Land Warfare* 58–62 (1959); von Glahn, *The Occupation of Enemy Territory* 54–55 (1957); "Report of the Secretary General on Respect for Human Rights in Armed Conflicts," U.N.G.A. 24th session, Doc. A/7720 (November 20, 1969). Special attention is drawn to the recent and comprehensive study by Dr. W. J. Ford published in October, November, December 1967 and January 1968, which contains a review of the principal military manuals, a study of the practice of war, jurisprudence

and opinions of authors of many countries. W. J. Ford, "Resistance Movements and International Law," 82 *International Review of the Red Cross.*

⁵ Ford, *op. cit.,* p. 14.

⁶ Italics added.

⁷ Italics added. Greenspan, op. cit., p. 58.

⁸ Pictet (ed.), *op. cit.,* p. 59.

⁹ Lauterpacht (ed.) *Manual of Military Law: Part III, The Law of War on Land* (1958), pp. 46–47.

¹⁰ D. Bindschedler, "A Reconsideration of the Law of Armed Conflicts," paper submitted to the Conference on the Law of Armed Conflicts: Contemporary Problems (Carnegie Endowment for International Peace, 1969), pp. 55, 59, 60, 65.

¹¹ *Id.,* p. 58.

¹² see fn. 4 above.

¹³ "One of the essential conditions for the existence of the law of war is its *indifference.* No matter what may be, concretely, the object, the purpose, the "cause" of a guerrilla war, the law of war can never agree to see in it a motive of justification. However great the desire to extend the protection of the law of war to the various categories of persons participating directly or indirectly in guerrilla warfare, if the general, intrinsic requirements of the law of war trace a limitation in this regard, such a limitation cannot be overcome for the benefit of guerrilla warfare on the pretext that the *cause* of the latter justifies digressions. Inversely, a belligerent collectivity, no matter what it may be, cannot label guerrilla or counter-guerrilla warfare with which it is dealing as illegal, on the pretext that the cause of the guerrilla or counter-guerrilla war is unjust.

This remark, important because of the very marked ideological character which guerrilla wars often present, is valid with regard to persons as with regard to methods of guerrilla warfare. "Henri Meyrowitz, "La Guérilla et la Droit de la Guerre," paper submitted to Brussels University Conference on Humanitarian Law and Armed Conflicts, Doc. R/5, 1970, p. 4.

¹⁴ George Ginsburgs, " 'Wars of National Liberation' and the Modern Law of Nations—The Soviet Thesis," in *The Soviet Impact on International Law* (Baade, ed., 1965) pp. 90–92. Italics added. It may be pointed out that the USSR did not make any reservation to Article 4 of the Third Convention.

¹⁵ Para. 8(c) of G. A. Resolution 2396 (XXIII) on the Policies of Apartheid of the Government of South Africa. G. A. Resolution 2395 (XXIII) on the Question of Territories under Portuguese Administration called on the Government of Portugal to ensure the application of the Third Convention "in view of the armed conflict prevailing in the Territories and the inhuman treatment of prisoners" (para. 12); see also the similarly worded paragraph 13 of Resolution 2383 (XXIII) on the Question of Southern Rhodesia, and paragraph 5 of Resolution 2446 (XXIII) on Measures to Achieve the Rapid and Total Elimination of All Forms of Racial Discrimination in General and of Policy of Apartheid in Particular, which confirmed "the decision taken by the International Conference of Human Rights [Teheran Conference] to recognize the right of freedom fighters in southern Africa and in colonial Territories to be treated, when captured, as prisoners-of-war under the Geneva Conventions of 1949."

¹⁶ "Protection of Victims of Non-International Conflicts," Report submitted by the International Committee of the Red Cross at the 21st International Conference of the Red Cross, Istanbul, 1969, p. 9.

[17] *Id.*

[18] *Id.*

[19] "Reaffirmation and Development of the Laws and Customs Applicable in Armed Conflicts," ICRC Report, 1969, p. 102.

[20] "Indeed, it seems somewhat arbitrary to place the 'wars of liberation' which are covered by the General Assembly's decolonization resolutions in a separate category and to characterize these as international conflicts irrespective of their size, the presence or absence of effective outside support and similar factors, while other conflicts involving issues of self-determination would not be so characterized. In my view, there is little merit in attempts to attribute a particular status to certain armed conflicts merely on account of their cause . . .

"In other words, the qualification of armed conflicts as 'international' or 'non-international' remains to my mind a matter of assessment of available data in each separate case and of basing a conclusion on such relatively vague grounds as scope and duration of the conflict, presence of foreign military intervention, etcetera. Recognition of the insurgents as a belligerent party by the lawful Government will of course be of decisive importance; but such a step is as rare as it is important." F. Kalshoven, "The Position of Guerrilla fighters under the Law of War," Report submitted to the International Society for Military Law and the Law of War, Leiden, 1969, p. 6.

[21] Meyrowitz, *op. cit.,* p. 7.

[22] Pictet (ed.), *op. cit.,* p. 57.

[23] *Id.,* Pictet explains: "The latter category, which includes organized resistance movements, is entitled to benefit by the Convention provided, of course, the general implementing conditions (Article 2) are fulfilled. Resistance movements must be fighting on behalf of a 'Party to the conflict' in the sense of Article 2, otherwise the provisions of Article 3 relating to non-international conflicts are applicable, since such militias and volunteer corps are not entitled to style themselves a 'Party to the conflict' . . . It is essential that there should be a de facto relationship between the resistance organization *and the party to international law* which is in a state of war, but the existence of this relationship is sufficient. It may find expression merely by tacit agreement, if the operations are such as to indicate clearly for which side the resistance organization is fighting. But affiliation with a Party to the conflict may also follow an official declaration, for instance by a Government in exile, confirmed by official recognition by the High Command of the forces which are at war with the Occupying Power. These different cases are based on the experience of the Second World War, and the authors of the Convention wished to make specific provision to cover them." (italics added).

[24] Pictet, *Recueil, op. cit.,* p. 77. Italics added.

[25] *Id.,* p. 78.

[26] Ford, *op. cit.,* p. 20.

[27] *Id.,* p. 19.

[28] Article 26.

[29] From text of broadcast of the "Voice of Palestine" in Arabic, March 13, 1969, 13:30 G.M.T.

[30] Middle East News Agency (hereafter "MENA") Damascus, May 6, 1970.

[31] *Le Monde* (Paris), April 7, 1970, reported by Agence France Presse.

[32] MENA, April 14, 1970; *Al-Siassa, Kuwait.*

[33] Reuter, Beirut, May 26, 1970.

[34] *Time,* June 13, 1969.

[35] DPA, in German, January 18, 1970, quoted from BBC Monitoring Service.

[36] Radio Cairo, March 16, 1969.

[37] Radio Cairo, February 1, 1969 at 17:40 hours.

[38] Radio Cairo, May 13, 1970, quoted from BBC Monitoring Service.

[39] Kalshoven, *op. cit.,* p. 19.

[40] *Military Prosecutor v. Omar Mahmud Kassem and others,* File No. 4/69, *Law and Courts in the Israel Held Areas,* published by the Institute for Legislative Research and Comparative Law of the Hebrew University of Jerusalem (1970), pp. 25–27.

[41] Lauterpacht (ed.), *Manual,* p. 34.

[42] Pictet (ed.), *op. cit.,* p. 59.

[43] *Id.,* p. 61.

[44] Pictet, *Recueil, op. cit.,* pp. 76–77.

[45] "The distinction between the irregular combatant and the civilian population must be recognized as fundamental and allows to comprehend better the meaning of these rules. Thus, the requirement to have a sign does not by any means signify that the guerrilla may not camouflage himself as any regular soldier may, but he may not camouflage himself as a civilian; he may try to become invisible in the landscape, but not in the crowd. This sign must be recognizable at the same distance at which a uniform would be recognizable. It is not necessarily an armband; it may be a military headgear or part of a uniform. In the same way carry arms 'openly' does not mean to carry them 'more' openly than does a regular soldier, but not to hide them at the approach of the enemy so as to be taken for a disarmed civilian.

"The guerrilla who camouflages himself as a civilian for a military action not only loses his privileged status, but may at the same time also violate the laws and customs of war. This will be the case always when such actions constitute a treachery. Thus, the guerrilla will commit a treachery who disguised as an innocent peasant after having overtaken a group of soldiers turns round and fires on them. It will be seen that there exists a close connection between the condition of the compliance with the laws and customs of armed conflicts and the two conditions with which we are dealing here." Bindschedler, *op. cit.,* pp. 64–65.

[46] "Reaffirmation and Development of the Laws and Customs Applicable in Armed Conflicts," *op. cit.,* pp. 116–117.

[47] See text, *Id.*: Annex XIX, particularly paras. 5(b) and 5(c).

[48] Bindschedler, *op. cit.,* p. 63.

[49] Draper, Intervention on September 11, 1969, Twenty-First International Red Cross Conference, Istanbul, Humanitarian Law Commission.

[50] G.I.A.D. Draper, "The Legal Classification of Belligerent Individuals," paper submitted to Brussels University Conference on Humanitarian Law and Armed Conflicts, Doc. R/3, 1970, p. 23.

[51] *Kassem,* p. 23 (see fn. 40 above).

[52] Bindschedler, *op. cit.,* pp. 60–61.

[53] Pictet (ed.), *op. cit.,* p. 61.

[54] In a recent Resolution, the General Assembly of the United Nations reaffirmed the distinction between legitimate and illegitimate objectives. In Resolution 2444 (XXIII) on Respect for Human Rights in Armed Conflicts it stated:

"a) That the right of the parties to a conflict to adopt means of injuring the enemy is not unlimited;

"b) That it is prohibited to launch attacks against the civilian population as such;
"c) That distinction must be made at all times between persons taking part in the hostilities and members of the civilian population to the effect that the latter be spared as much as possible."

G. A. Resolution 2444 (XXIII), unanimously adopted at the 1748th plenary meeting, Dec. 19, 1968.

[55] Bindschedler, *op. cit.,* p. 61. Italics added.

[56] Meyrowitz, *op. cit.,* p. 24.

[57] "Reaffirmation and Development of the Laws and Customs Applicable in Armed Conflicts," *op. cit.,* p. 117.

[58] *Id.,* p. 120.

[59] *Id.,* pp. 120–121.

[60] *Id.,* p. 103.

[61] *International Review of the Red Cross,* May, 1969, p. 228.

[62] [1968] 3 ALL. E.R. 493 (P.C.). Compare, Article 85 of the Third Convention.

[63] *Id.,* p. 497. See also Baxter, "The Privy Council on the Qualification of Belligerents," 63 *Am. J. Int. L* 290 (1969).

[64] The Palestinian National Covenant was adopted by the Palestine National Council's fourth Session, convened at Cairo from July 10 to 17, 1968. The comparison of Article 5 with Article 6 of the Covenant speaks for itself:

> Art. 5. The Palestinians are the Arab citizens who were living permanently in Palestine until 1947, whether they were expelled from there or remained. Whoever is born to a Palestinian Arab father after this date, within Palestine or outside it, is a Palestinian.

> Art. 6. Jews who were living permanently in Palestine until the beginning of the Zionist invasion will be considered Palestinians.

[65] *Id.,* Article 15.

[66] Thus, George Habash, leader of the Popular Front for the Liberation of Palestine, was reported in *Ad-Dustour* of Amman of October 15, 1969, to have said that "the Palestinian people is not prepared to wait, either twenty years or one year, for the Arab armies to conquer and liberate Tel Aviv. The Palestinian forces will make their way to Tel Aviv . . ." See, in general, Harkabi, "The Position of the Palestinians in the Israel-Arab Conflict and their National Covenant" (1968), which is a revised text of a lecture given at Tel Aviv University on May 18, 1969, and which appeared in *Ma'ariv* (Israel) on November 21, 1969. It will appear in the New York *Journal of International Law and Politics.* See also the Symposium on the Democratic Palestinian State held in Beirut on March 20, 1970, under the auspices of the *El Anwar* newspaper, and attended by the representatives of six terrorist organizations.

[67] Article published January 14, 1969 in the London *Daily Mail.*

[68] The Permanent Council of the Organization of American States adopted a Resolution on May 15, 1970 (CP/Resolution 5 (7/70)) entitled "Action Condemning Acts of Terrorism and the Kidnapping of Persons," which considers crimes committed against representatives of foreign States as crimes under common law.

[69] Oppenheim, *op. cit.,* p. 676.

[70] *Id.,* p. 656.

[71] Draper, *op. cit.,* p. 18. Italics added.

[72] Meyrowitz, *op. cit,* p. 9. Italics added.

Legal Aspects of Terrorists' Claims

[73] *Geschworenengericht des Kantons Zürich: Urteil,* Geschw. 6 No. 27/1969, December 22, 1969, pp. 21–22 of the judgment (in German).

[74] Decision No. 383/1969, Athens Court of Appeals, March 26, 1970. The reasons for the decision have not yet been announced.

[75] He received three months' detention, *Ma'ariv,* November 12, 1969.

[76] *Ma'ariv* (Israel), June 30, 1970.

[77] Thus, following the grenade-throwing incident at El Al offices in Athens on November 27, 1969, the Deputy Premier of Greece declared: "The new criminal action by a foreign citizen against the offices of an airline company in Athens, resulting in injuries to fifteen innocent victims, does not constitute an act of war, but is a cowardly act of callous criminals. The Greek people have a long and glorious military history, but all of their military struggles for national rights or cultural values are distinguished by the element of valour, and especially by respect for all that is good in any society not at war. The carrying out of such despicable murderous activities in neutral territories, under guise of supposed military action, proves an absolute lack of spirit of self-sacrifice for a just struggle, as well as cowardice." Bulletin, Athens News Agency, December 1, 1969.

[78] Soon after the attack, on February 28, 1969, the following communiqué was issued by the Swiss Département Politique Fédéral:

> Although the criminal investigation has not yet been completed, it is already certain that the authors of the attack acted for the Popular Front for the Liberation of Palestine. At the microphone of a Lebanese station, these organizations assumed responsibility for the aggression against the El Al airplane. According to their own declarations, the terrorists were trained in Jordan and some of them left from Syria to carry out the attack at Zurich. The Head of the Political Department has protested to the diplomatic representatives of the countries in question, condemning the attack and asking that measures be taken in order to prevent new violations of Swiss territory.

[79] Translated from remarks in German.

[80] Press announcement following extraordinary session of the Federal Council on February 23, 1970.

[81] Draft Resolution of the Algerian Red Crescent, submitted to the Commission for International Humanitarian Law under Item 5: Protection of victims on non-international conflicts and marked P. 8150/IW/10.9.1969 (unpublished).

[82] See preceding note: Amendment of Danish Red Cross, marked P. 8162/IW/10.9.69.

[83] See preceding note: Amendment of Swedish Red Cross, marked P. 8168/EMD/11.9.69.

[84] See also Article III, paras. 1 and 5.

[85] S/RES/233 of June 7, 1967, S/RES/234, of June 7, 1967. Other ceasefire resolutions were addressed to the Governments of Israel and Syria. S/RES/235 of June 9, 1967, also see S/RES/236 of June 12, 1967. The Security Council Resolution 242 of November 22, 1967, addresses itself to "the States concerned" (para. 3) and enumerates the rights "of every State in the area" (para. 1 (ii)).

[86] On the distinction between international and non-international conflicts, see Jean Siotis, *Le Droit de la Guerre et les Conflits Armés d'un Caractère Non-International* (1958), pp. 21, 23, 24, 28, 46, 50, 228.

[87] Resolution XVIII of the International Conference of the Red Cross, Istanbul, 1969, *Resolutions,* p. 14. Italics added.

[88] Paul de Geouffre de la Pradelle, "La Notion de Personne Protégée dans les Conventions Humanitaires," paper submitted to the Brussels University Conference on Humanitarian Law and Armed Conflicts, Doc R/6, 1970, p. 7.

RATIONAL SYMMETRY
IN CHOICE OF LAW

Yuval Levy* and Barbara Marks**

INTRODUCTION

During this past decade, decision-makers have attempted to resolve problems of choice of law in terms of the factors linking the interested states, and the policies underlying their laws, with the controversies at bar. Although these attempts mark a departure from incongruous *rationales* which resulted from analysis based on rules and exceptions, much confusion still obfuscates choice of law.[1] The continuing ambivalence in responses of decision-makers to choice-of-law questions derives not only from failure to clarify long-term national and international interests,[2] but also from a misconception of the general process of decision.[3]

Responses of decision-makers are frequently no more than extrapolations from inherited formulae and catch-phrases which fail to relate decisions to the mores and concepts of justice prevailing in the various social and economic structures of the world community. Societal values and policy considerations, as well as other significant variables affecting long-range objectives of states interested in choice-of-law questions are ignored or remain unarticulated in opinions.[4]

The first essential step toward rational clarification of considerations relevant to choice of law is to understand the process of authoritative decision by which interests of states are honored and protected.[5] The second step is to clarify and appraise certain basic policy-goals[6] which influence choice-of-law questions; and finally, the third step is to outline the methodology employed in promoting such controlling policies.

The numerous factors and considerations which constantly interplay in the dynamic flow of choice-of-law decisions may be related to

* Lecturer of Law, Tel Aviv University
** Member of New York Bar

these broad policy goals. However, such goals should not be deemed mathematical constants purporting to supply ready-made answers.[7] This article will advocate the abandonment of the hitherto futile search for an elusive magic formula: rather it will show that rational symmetry in choice of law can be achieved without resort to black-letter rules.

STEP I—THE AUTHORITY FUNCTIONS

Claims which states make against each other, whether directly, or indirectly through private litigants, may arise from many different types of interactions. Yet, with respect to all such claims, each state is presented with the same basic issue: whether a given claim is one over which it shall maintain effective control or is one properly within the authority of another state or states. Indeed, the most abstract principle of international law is a corollary of this basic issue: the granting of jurisdiction to the most substantially affected state.[8]

Authority to resolve a given claim often stems from major power bases of a state: people, territory and institutions. With respect to events occurring within its bounds, a state quite naturally seeks to protect its resources and the integrity and efficiency of its mores and institutions. Regarding events occurring beyond its borders, a state may act to protect her territorial base and community processes against external attack, to control its nationals and property abroad (*e.g.*, persons, corporations, ships and aircraft), to protect access to common world resources (*e.g.*, the oceans, the moon and outer-space) or to protect so-called international values such as repression of piracy and conformity to the rules of war.

Opposing claims by other states to control such interests create the controversies and resulting flow of decisions which are sometimes described as "private international law" or "conflict of laws."[9] The allocation of authority among claimant states in this flow of decisions is carried out by various decision-makers. The most important decision-makers, resolving the majority of controversies, are state officials who function within the formal judiciary of a state. However, decisions are affected by all branches of government—the legislative and executive, as well as the judicial—through countless interactions in foreign offices, special conferences, national courts and municipal legislatures.

Although such formal national institutions greatly influence decisions, a measure of authority is also exercised by other participants. For example, functions of evaluation, appraisal and criticism are performed by universities, civic groups and political pressure groups which do not participate in the formal decisional process. In addition, decisions may be influenced by international bodies, such as international courts and arbitration tribunals, as well as by various international organizations which appraise and recommend methods of resolving conflict of laws.

The broad term "decision-makers" is therefore used to describe the various officials and other bodies which interact to influence decision. It is also appropriately used to describe national judges functioning within their spheres of authority in the various states; for although they directly resolve the majority of controversies, they are indirectly influenced by the other official and unofficial decision-makers. Interdependence between decision-makers is a significant factor in the process of decision. For example, a judge sitting in one state may be called upon to apply policy declared by the legislature, judiciary, or even the executive of another state.

With respect to claims involving more than one state, the local judge is elevated from his modest role as prescriber of local policies to the role of an international, authoritative decision-maker who prescribes policies compatible with the objectives of the community of states.[10] In accordance with such policies, a national decision-maker may decide to refrain from exercise of authority over a particular controversy in favor of another state's official and to apply policies prescribed by other officials, judges, legislatures or executives, or to enforce such foreign policies as have already been applied by a foreign decision-maker to the specific case at bar.

The process of decision in conflict of laws, *i.e.*, the process whereby decision-makers exercise authority over a given controversy, or defer to the authority of another state and its decision-makers, may be summarized as the exercise of three authority functions, which together comprise jurisdiction: the power to apply policy; the power to prescribe policy; and the power to enforce policy.[11] Focusing upon the three authority functions in examining conflict-of-law decisions, one can observe the sharing of jurisdiction among states, which is the hallmark of the process of decision in conflict of laws.[12]

At times, the forum applies, prescribes and enforces policy, and thus maintains control of all three authority functions. However, often, in a conflict situation, several states, in effect, share jurisdiction (control). For example, if a *tort* in State A occurs between plaintiff from State B and defendant from State C, plaintiff may bring the action in State A, the court of State A may choose to apply the law of State B; and if plaintiff prevails and is awarded damages, he may seek to enforce the judgment in State C. Thus, control of the controversy, *i.e.*, application, prescription, and enforcement of policy, may be shared among three states.

The first authority function, the power to apply policy, is always exercised by the forum, unless it dismisses a case for lack of such power. In other words, the first authority function is similar to the traditional concept of "jurisdiction over parties." A tribunal must first determine whether it has the power to adjudicate a controversy between two or more parties, and in doing so considers traditional bases of *in personam* jurisdiction such as domicile, nationality, presence in the state, and the conducting of business, or the traditional basis of *in rem* jurisdiction: property in the state.

With respect to *in personam* actions, the expansion of the power to apply policy to non-domiciliaries is justified by resort to such terms as consent, submission, temporary allegiance and *locus* of the cause of action. On the other hand, a set of complementary opposing prescriptions purport to reject the power to apply policy *in personam* to non-domiciliaries. Examples are the use of ambiguous labels like *forum non conveniens*, sovereign immunity and public policy.

The variables on which states rely to justify the exercise, or the non-exercise, of the power to apply policy to a particular controversy, whether civil or criminal, are myriad, and a detailed discussion is beyond the scope of this article.[13] The important point to note is the flexibility of the prescriptions conferring and denying such jurisdiction, comprising sets of "rules" and "exceptions."

Once a tribunal is seized with the power to apply policy, it normally must proceed to the task of determining where to allocate the second authority function, the power to prescribe policy. This power may be exercised by the forum, or by another state. If the forum chooses to apply its own law, the forum prescribes its own policy. However, if the forum determines that the law of another state controls a certain issue, it is that state which, in effect, prescribes policy. Thus, the power to prescribe policy may be exercised by several states, each state controlling a different issue in a particular controversy.[14]

The prescribing function has been performed throughout the years in a flow of decisions exhibiting certain uniformities in response, which have resulted in a body of inherited "principles of international law." To a lesser degree, prescription of policies has been through bilateral or multilateral agreement among states.[15]

The power to prescribe policy, also referred to as "choice of law," rests on the principle of allocation of this function to the state most substantially affected by the controversy. To achieve realization of this principle, it is necessary for decision-makers to appreciate the major objectives which are common to all states.

One of the primary objectives, as mentioned above, and as discussed in Step II below, is protection of major power bases: territory, people and institutions. The process whereby decision-makers sitting in forum states defer to claims by other states, designed to protect and enhance their respective power bases, affords a mutual advantage to all states in maintenance of productive transnational processes. However, a concern for protection of power bases is not the only objective which influences interactions among states. Other major objectives, discussed in greater detail in Step II, include meeting expectations of parties, as well as achieving elusive concepts of justice.

The third authority function is the power to enforce policy. This power may also be exercised by the forum of another state. In conflict of laws, this function is described as enforcement or recognition of foreign judgments and decrees. The exercise of this authority in favor of a foreign state has been expressed in various terms, among them "comity" and the recognition of the "obligation" created by a foreign judgment.[16] Whatever the label, the following statement well-summarizes the vital role of the third authority function:[17]

> Perhaps the ultimate justification for some degree of recognition is that if in a highly complex system and interrelated world each community exhausted every possibility of insisting on its parochial interests, injustice would result and the normal patterns of life would be disrupted.

The underlying objective in recognizing foreign judgments is derived from the realization of the long-term common interests of all states, interacting in a common world arena, which grows ever smaller and, consequently, underscores the necessity of states to exercise mutual tolerance and restraints. Decision-makers are aware of the fact that stubborn considerations of forum interests only, and unreasoned refusal to enforce foreign judgments, encourage counter-measures by foreign states, supported by such reprisal phrases as "contrary to public policy" or "lack of reciprocity."[18]

Of course, even the most objective decision-maker may not always recognize and enforce a foreign judgment. Such non-recognition of a foreign judgment is generally based, not on retaliation, but on "non-competency" of a foreign tribunal to adjudicate a controversy (apply policy), or impropriety of the choice of law (prescription of policy) made by the foreign forum.[19] Anglo-American judicial systems traditionally show greater concern for putting an end to litigation, and, accordingly, determine most questions of recognition on the basis of whether the foreign tribunal had adjudicatory jurisdiction over the parties. On the other hand, civil law systems historically place less emphasis on *res adjudicata*. Thus, a tribunal in a civil law state often considers whether it would have prescribed the same law as the foreign tribunal.[20]

However, the difference in emphasis should not be exaggerated. In practice, when presented with a question of whether to give efficacy to a foreign judgment, decision-makers of both legal systems may often concern themselves with exercise of the first, as well as the second authority function by the foreign decision-maker. For example, in the United States, generally the fifty states are required to give "full faith and credit" to the judgments of sister states under Article IV of the Constitution. On the other hand, the non-recognition of a foreign judgment, or refusal to give "full faith and credit" to a sister state judgment may be justified on grounds that such foreign or sister state judgment constituted a denial of procedural or substantive "due process" under the Fifth and/or Fourteenth Amendments to the Constitution.[21] (These constitutional grounds, of course, support non-recognition on the basis of malexercise of the first authority function (application of policy—adjudicatory function) and/or the second authority function (prescription of policy—choice of law).

Because of the unique opportunity the federal structure of the United States provides for conflicts and problems to arise in the ordinary course of decision-making, American precedents are fairly numerous.[22] For this reason, the main text of this article, which specifically discusses the second authority function, choice of law, considers many American decisions.

With respect to choice of law, *i.e.*, the power to prescribe policy, all states interested in a particular issue have at least a potential claim to control its resolution.[23] This is because, until the governing law is determined, the function of the decision-maker is to weigh the policies of competing states and to determine the effects each will have on the forum, the parties, the interested states, and the international community.[24] When the choice of law with respect to the specific issue is made, then, of course, one state predominates and becomes the policy prescriber.

STEP II—BASIC POLICY GOALS

A. The Rule—Exception Dichotomy

It is necessary as a second step to clarify and appraise certain broad policy goals to which tribunals relate the power to prescribe policy. The basic policy goals outlined below should not be treated as rules, but as broad considerations governing the choice-of-law process. In fact, it is submitted that these goals have always controlled behind the scenes of the "rules," "exceptions," and other confusing explanations[25] which have acted as the reasons for decisions.[26] Thus, overt recognition of the policy goals will finally draw the curtain over such portrayals and set the stage for a decisional process based on the real considerations which control choice of law. There was much dissatisfaction[27] with the traditional rules, such as mechanically using "the law of the place of the tort"[28] to determine questions of liability and damage, or "the law of the place of performance" or "place of making" to determine the validity of a contract. Thus a confusing dichotomy of "rules" and "exceptions" evolved. The need to evaluate contents and results, and yet ostensibly follow doctrinal principles loaded the decisions with escape devices.[29]

For example, in the field of torts (from whence are selected many of the illustrative cases cited in this article) courts found ways of freeing themselves from the straitjacket of the *lex loci* rule by means of several types of "exceptions" or counter-rules. One technique, where the forum was not the place of the tort, was to label the *lex loci* rule as "procedural" and conclude, as a fabricated excuse for applying the forum law,[30] that the forum was not bound to apply the rule. Another technique, somewhat more simple in style, was merely to denounce the *lex loci* law as contrary to the "public policy" of the forum.[31] Yet another technique was the use of *renvoi*.[32]

The ambiguity and vagueness of terms used to describe the allocation of prescriptive authority by means of the *lex loci* rule and its exceptions has been the subject of much criticism in the United States, and for the most part, this methodology has already been rejected by American courts.[33] Nevertheless, it should not be forgotten that the determination of the *locus* whose policy would be preferred for controlling the effects of a tort resulted from a series of intellectual functions performed by decision-makers who, in fact, weighed and balanced various factors and policies which found no expression in the label *lex loci delicti*. Equally unexplained in past decisions were the policies and factors which these decision-makers considered in application of the counter-rules of "procedure" and "public policy." Thus, the *lex loci* rule, as well as its exceptions, often masked the weighing and balancing of relevant policies. Not only in torts, but also in other fields of law, the decision-makers of the era of the "rule—exception" dichotomy frequently reached reasonable decisions based on wrong reasoning by articulating what purported to be the governing rules and exceptions. Because these labels did not adequately explain decisions, a series of decisions in any one field often appeared non-uniform and unpredictable.

Decisions cannot be explained by labelling one set of prescriptions "the rules"[34] and the complementary set as "the exceptions."[35] Even if both the "rules" and the "exceptions" were accepted as valid directives for resolution of choice-of-law problems, it would still be impossible to encompass within them all the permutations and combinations of events which give rise to issue.[36] Indeed, Currie, one of the most vehement critics of the traditional rules, observed:[37]

> The rules so evolved have not worked and cannot be made to work . . . (I)n attempting to use the rules, *we encounter difficulties which* do not stem from the fact that the particular rules are bad, nor from the fact that a particular theoretical explanation is unsound but rather *from the fact that we have such rules at all.* (emphasis added.)

Likewise, most attempts to formulate new guidelines, such as the prescription of the law of the "center of gravity,"[38] or the "law of the forum, unless there is good reason to apply the law of another state,"[39] "the better law,"[40] or the "law of the place with the most significant relationship,"[41] as well as the use of "grouping of contacts"[42] or "principles of preference,"[43] merely furnish labels for new sets of rules. These proposed guidelines do not provide adequate assistance in solving choice-of-law problems since, like all rules, they fail to meet and reconcile all possible fact situations which may arise in the decisional process. Indeed, Cavers, the advocate of the "principles of preference" noted that this is the shortcoming of his theory, since many "exceptions" to his "principles" would necessarily be required in the course of decision.[44]

On the other hand, it is submitted that a multifactoral analysis of choice-of-law questions in terms of broad, basic policy goals, which control decisions, may afford patterns for rationally predicting results of future decisions. Decisions will appear "uniform" when underlying considerations are identical or similar; however, when new considera-

tions affect a given type of controversy, or when community policies
dictate that traditional considerations be weighted differently, then
a "new" result may emerge. Nevertheless, the broad policy goals remain
as the bases of resolving the controversies. Resolution of choice-of-law
problems, using the tools of multifactoral analysis to relate various
factors to the broad policy goals, thereby obviates the cumbersome need
to rationalize decisions in terms of "rules" and "exceptions."

B. Basic Policy Goals[45]

It is felt that these policy goals, as outlined below, were the underlying
decision-controllers, even in the days when decision-makers insisted
on articulating their conclusions by the artificial *rationales* of "rules"
and "exceptions." It will be shown that in striking a balance between
exclusive and inclusive claims for exercise of control[46] of a controversy
made by the states concerned, virtually every choice-of-law decision
is affected by the basic policy goals.

It is submitted that the basic policies are:

1. *Concern for exclusive forum interests by seeking to protect three
major power bases: territory, people and institutions.*[47]

2. *Concern for inclusive interests of non-forum states, whereby the
forum state shares authority with other states which claim authority for
protection of their respective power bases.*

3. *Concern for the expectations of parties, both litigants and states,
which encompasses considerations of stability and uniformity of decisions.*

4. *Concern for ideals of justice.*

*1. Concern for exclusive forum interests by seeking to protect three
major power bases: territory, peoples and institutions.*

States quite naturally seek to protect their bases of power, namely,
territory, people and institutions. The following discussion submits
that the so-called "territoriality," "nationality," and "protective"
principles of jurisdiction merely serve as traditional ways of justifying
decisions predicated on the concrete policy of protecting state power
bases.

The exclusive interest of the forum in protecting its territorial mass
is often expressed by reference to the label "territoriality." This label,
of course, is used to support protective interests not only with respect
to events which may clearly be grounded on the territorial mass of the
forum, including its adjacent waters and airspace, but also to events

in areas totally without the immediate bounds of the forum. In the latter situation, the protective label of "territoriality" finds expression in confusing terms such as "impact territoriality," "subjective and objective territoriality," and "extraterritoriality." Whatever the description, the fact that territoriality is a well-recognized major power base is succinctly expressed in the following statement by Cavers:[48]

> Our states and nations are territorially organized; the legal order that each has created impinges on actions and affairs, which, in a very high proportion of all instances, are wholly domestic to the state where they take place. To withdraw like actions and affairs from the reach of domestic law because the persons participating in them are not domestic to the state causes a wrench away from customary attitudes toward law that may lead the disadvantaged party to regard the distinctions as involving a personal discrimination against him rather than as a step toward comity between states.

Protection of the "people" power base entails the objectives of preserving their identifications and loyalties, controlling their movements, and preserving and enhancing their wealth and well-being. As implied in the above statement by Cavers, this second major power base is closely connected with the territorial power base. In addition to protecting its domestic inhabitants, the forum naturally seeks to protect "strangers" within its immediate bounds, as well as individuals without its bounds who may nevertheless incorporeally fall within the penumbra of the forum's interests. As with territoriality, decision-makers have developed curious technical labels, such as "active nationality," or "passive personality" to support claims of interest in protecting people in situations other than the simple case of domestic inhabitants.

Institutions, the source of the third major power base, are also subject to protective efforts. The forum strives to protect its institutions in order to preserve its substantial interests against external injury. For example, states are extremely interested in protecting their fiscal institutions in order to ensure their interests in collection of revenues. The fundamental goal of preserving institutional processes, of course, has often been blessed by decision-makers with a technical descriptive term, namely, the "protective principle."

Thus, it may be seen that while the all-important policy of protecting power bases may be described in simple terms of protecting territory, people and institutions, the decision-makers of the past have chosen to enunciate this broad policy goal in terms of ambiguous references covering a vast spectrum. The above-mentioned terms like "impact territoriality," "passive personality," and "protective principle" are by no means exhaustive. Many more have been utilized by decision-makers as conventional justifications to support decisions which, in fact, encompass the very distinct policy goal of protecting power bases.

Hence came the theories based on "connecting factors" which in some cases lost their identity as such and became inflexible points of reference embodied in so-called choice-of-law rules and counter-rules, as noted in the above discussion of the rule—exception dichotomy. It is interesting to observe that now that the catch phrases such as *lex loci delicti* are out of vogue as "rules," they have been retained and used as "connecting factors,"[49] or "significant contacts,"[50] by some writers and decision-makers. It was noted above that these "new" techniques also fail because they neglect to distinguish such variables from the overriding policy goals; and thus, the erroneous belief that solutions to choice-of-law problems may be found in mere technique is perpetuated.[51]

An illustration of how the relabelling of the old variables as "connecting factors" instead of "rules" merely continues to disguise the real basis of a decision (which is in fact related to the overriding policy goal of protecting power bases), may be seen by reference to the recent English decision, *Miller* v. *Whitworth Street Estates.*[52] The main issue presented was whether a Scottish arbitrator could be ordered to prepare findings of fact and conclusions of law for review by an appellate court. Such an order is common to English procedure; whereas, under Scottish procedure, the opinion of an arbitrator is final with respect to both fact and law. The parties contracted to build premises in Scotland and made their agreement on a well-known English standard construction contract. The operation was supervised by an English architect. The agreement provided for submission to arbitration of any dispute but failed to specify the governing law of either the contract or arbitration.

The Court of Appeal added up the "connecting factors" in favor of English law as "the proper law of the contract," and concluded that English law would also govern the arbitration poceeding. This decision was made on the basis the "controlling" factor was that the agreement had been made on the English standard form.

On the other hand, when the House of Lords heard the case on appeal, it treated the controversy as presenting two separate issues, namely, what was "the proper law of the contract," and what was the proper law of the arbitration. Manipulating connecting factors, the Lords found—by majority of three to two—in favor of English law with respect to the first issue. (The majority saw the fact that the contract had been made on the English form as the controlling factor; whereas, the minority regarded "the place of performance"—Scotland—as the dominant factor.) With respect to the second issue, the Lords were unanimously in favor of application of Scottish law to the arbitration proceedings and reinstated the order of the Master of the English High Court, which the Court of Appeal had reversed; but their reasons varied; this aspect of the House of Lords decision is considered below under discussion of the policy goal of reciprocity.

When a decision-maker merely makes reference to "connecting factors" and fails to articulate the overriding policy goals relevant to the weighing of variables against the background of such goals, he creates a shaky precedent. This is because the precedent leaves the impression that one or another of the factors was arbitrarily chosen as overriding, which, of course, makes the outcome of a subsequent controversy presenting similar facts seem "unpredictable."

With respect to the law governing the contract, the Miller decision, on closer examination, seems to reflect an unexpressed concern for protecting an institutional power base of the forum state in order to preserve stability in business relations, at the expense of Scottish territorial and personal interests. It would seem reasonable to relate the prescription of the law governing the agreement to an overriding concern for protecting an English business institution which had been established on the basis of an English standard building contract. Had the *rationale* of this issue been expressed in such terms, instead of by means of an apparently arbitrary choice among connecting factors, the choice of English law would appear less haphazard.

2. Concern for inclusive interests of non-forum states, whereby the forum state shares authority with other states which claim authority for protection of their respective power bases.

Protection of power bases of the forum is a consideration which is too exclusive. It eliminates the basic conept of choice of law—namely, the sharing of the authority to prescribe policy on a reciprocal basis.[53] If the forum state were always to exercise exclusive concern for its own interests, there would be a complete collapse of the system of private international law, in which the forum state often shares control of a controversy with other interested states and considers whether it should exercise self-restraint with respect to its own interests in favor of prescription of the law of another interested state.[54]

The first policy goal of protecting state base values is therefore complemented by the second policy goal of "reciprocity,"[55] the sharing of authority to prescribe policy[56] among all states interested in a controversy showing concern for the base values of each. Long range protection of common power bases of the world community braced by a common interest in maintaining international order depends on reciprocal self-restraint on a mutually satisfactory basis.[57]

As noted above, in the Miller[58] case, the House of Lords decided that Scottish law should govern the arbitration proceedings, even though "the proper law of the contract" was English. Thus, the Lords indeed recognized, though not expressly, Scottish, as well as English interests in the protection of their power bases and the importance of the sharing of authority to prescribe policy among states interested in a controversy, which is the cornerstone of the policy goal of reciprocity. As his reason, Lord Reid relied on the conduct of the parties after appointment of the Scottish arbitrator.[59] Lord Hudson preferred the "rule" that,[60]

> Whatever relates to the remedy is to be governed by the *lex fori*, the law of the country to whose courts application is made for performance. I see no reason why this principle should not be applied to arbitration proceedings.

Lord Guest emphasized that "the territorial nature of arbitration is important."[61] Viscount Dilhorne observed that it was not unreasonable for the law of a country other than the seat of arbitration to govern a contract even though the proceedings themselves must be governed by the country of arbitration, as "most closely connected with the proceedings."[62] Finally, Lord Wilberforce, relying on the "rule" that the *lex fori* determines procedure observed:[63]

> It is a matter of experience that numerous arbitrations are conducted by English arbitrators in England on matters governed by contracts whose proper law is or may be that of another country, and I should surely be surprised if it had ever been held that such arbitrations are not governed by the English Arbitration Act in procedural matters . . . The principle must surely be the same as that which applies to court proceedings brought in one country concerning a contract governed by the law of another . . .

From the above-cited reasons of the various Lords, it should be obvious that whatever the label for choosing Scottish law as governing the arbitration proceedings ("conduct of the parties," "territoriality," "the law of the *lex fori*," etc.) all of the reasons given reflected a concern for protecting the governmental institution of Scottish arbitration procedures on the facts of the case. If this restraint on the part of the English court in deferring to Scottish procedure had been so expressed, the diversified reasons of the Lords could have been brought together "under one roof" to afford a sounder precedent.

Two recent American decisions, *McCulloch* v. *Sociedad Nacional*[64] and *Incres S.S. Co.* v. *International Maritime Workers*[65] also serve to illustrate the role which the policy goal of reciprocity plays in the decisional process of balancing forum interests in protecting its power bases with the interests of other affected states. The issue in each case was whether the U.S. National Labor Relations Board should permit American unions to hold elections for representation of alien seamen on ships of foreign registry. The Court noted that Congress had not exercised its potential power to grant such authority to the N.L.R.B. and further observed that for Congress to do so would contravene a well-established policy of international law, recognizing the authority of the country of the flag of a vessel to control its internal affairs.[66] The Court held in both cases that the law of the country of registry of the ship on which the foreign seamen worked should control their internal activities on the respective vessels. This decision is a clear instance of a decision-maker exercising reciprocity by honoring the claim of the non-forum state for authority over its people, even though arguably, the forum state, in this instance the United States, might have a legitimate interest in controlling and supervising the conduct of all seamen, on all vessels in ports within her territorial domain.

In showing concern for power bases of interested states in addition to those of the forum state, decisions thereby subordinate, coordinate, and integrate policies related to considerations which affect the national or international community.[67] The art of choice-of-law decisions lies in striking an appropriate balance between the legitimate exclusive claim of states (the attainment of the first basic policy goal) and inclusive claim (the attainment of the second basic policy goal)[68] for authority to control given events by weighing myriad variables in relation to the overriding policy goals.

In a typical controversy involving choice of law, different issues presented may be the concern of two or more states. This may be illustrated by a wrongful death claim arising from an automobile collision affecting parties from different states. One issue might be which state's law should govern the legal relationship of the parties in determining the qualification for recovery of damages, and another might be which state's law should determine questions of negligent conduct of parties.

The sharing of authority to prescribe policy among the interested states serves to protect domestic values of the forum state as well as to preserve the legitimate interests of other affected states in striving to ensure inter-community relations.

Thus, in determining a balance of exclusive and inclusive interests of affected states, a decision-maker may well decide that the optimum method of preserving domestic, as well as inter-communal interests, would be to apply different state laws to the various issues. In the above example, he may determine that to protect the territorial interests of the state where the accident occurred in maintaining order on its highways, the law of that state should control questions of negligence; whereas, to protect the personal interests of the state which houses dependent survivors of the deceased, the law of that state should control questions of qualifying status for wrongful death compensation.[69]

A decision such as this shows that each claimant state may be granted a degree of authority to prescribe policy to the extent that a given issue most significantly affects its interests. A similar sharing of authority to prescribe policy is discernible in virtually all choice-of-law cases.[70] Indeed, the old escape device of mapping artificial boundaries between "substance" and "procedure" to chart areas of tolerance and intolerance in prescribing the law of a state other than the forum, or the forum law instead of the state law prescribed by a given "rule," derived from the often unarticulated policy goal of sharing of authority to prescribe policy among states substantially affected by a controversy.[71] This sharing of authority to ensure reciprocal protection of interests among states interacting in a national or international community may be regarded not only as a major policy goal, but also as the veritable cornerstone of the choice-of-law process.[72]

3. *Concern for the expectations of parties, both litigants and states, which encompasses considerations of stability and uniformity of decisions.*

By reference to several cases above, it was seen that the policy goal of reciprocity, the goal complementary to that of protecting the exclusive interests of the forum and its power bases, acts as a stabilizing factor in the relations of states and contributes to the maintenance of national and international order. Frictions are minimized and decisions generally meet with expectations of the individual litigants, as well as states affected by a choice-of-law controversy.[73] Thus, the interaction of the first and second policy goals in the decisional process is closely connected with the third major objective, the policy goal of meeting expectations of parties to controversies, both individuals and affected states.

This basic policy goal embodies two objectives, namely "stability" and "uniformity." "Stability" encompasses the idea that parties[74] who structure a relationship in a given manner may expect certain results among themselves; whereas, "uniformity" encompasses the idea that in respect to a given type of controversy, decision-makers will reach the same result regardless of forum.[75] This point may be illustrated by again reverting to the *Whitworth*[76] decision discussed above. One recalls that the individual parties made a building contract according to a standard form. Such forms, of course, are designed to stabilize the operation and outcome of certain types of agreements. Thus, parties who enter into a standard contract rely on and anticipate "stability" in their relationships; whereas "uniformity" reflects their expectations that a litigated controversy arising under a contract will be resolved in the same manner, regardless of forum.

The third basic policy goal embodying expectations of parties plays an important role in relationships of a contractual or semi-contractual nature because such relationships involve pre-planning by the parties. On the other hand, this goal plays a less significant part in legal relationships which arise from torts, since torts are unplanned events.[77]

Domestic relations is an area of the law where the objectives of stability and uniformity are extremely vital. It is generally considered undesirable for the marital status of parties to change from state to state; and consequently, there is a greater tendency on the part of a forum state, not the state of domicile, marriage, or divorce of the parties to an action related to marital status, to prescribe the law of one of these other states, in order to preserve the status of individuals. This point is illustrated by the readiness of English courts to recognize a foreign divorce decree if the bases of adjudicatory jurisdiction (power to apply policy) were substantially identical with those bases recognized by the United Kingdom.[78] Likewise, with respect to marriage, English courts have refused to permit non-residents to use England as a marriage haven when their states of nationality, domicile or permanent residence bar their marriage.[79]

Commercial transactions are, of course, also greatly influenced by the objectives of meeting expectations of parties.[80] Businessmen cannot tolerate application of capricious and coincidental prescriptions and strive to arrange their relationships in a stable manner.[81] The expansion of business and industry crossing state lines demands that the consequences of trade relations will not vary and oscillate from forum to forum. A striking example of recognition of the importance of the third policy goal to commercial transactions lies in the fact that both the Anglo-

American and Napoleonic Code legal systems uphold the right of parties to an agreement to choose the governing law.[82] In addition, case law is studded with instances where decision-makers tried to prescribe that law which would uphold agreements.[83]

In some areas of law, objectives of stability and uniformity are reflected in patterns of decision showing preference for certain classes of persons. Claims involving benefits, wills and community property rights tend to resolution in favor of widows, widowers and children;[84] decisions arising from insurance claims show a bias in favor of recovery for the insured; thus, although decision-makers may seem sometimes haphazardly to justify a decision in favor of prescription of the law of "place of making" of the insurance contract, and sometimes in favor of the law of "place of delivery" or "place of performance," on closer examination, it may be observed that any given series of insurance decisions consistently favors the insured.[85]

These examples again emphasize how the reference merely to connecting factors tends to distort the rationality of decisions. Thus, "inconsistent" selection of different connecting factors to serve a community policy such as favoring the cause of insured parties, make decisions appear "uniform." Analysis of choice-of-law questions in terms of policy goals would often reach the same result and the decisions would appear "uniform" because of the fact that the objectives remained constant. Articulation of a preference for insureds, wives, widows, children, or the sanctity of agreements in terms of meeting expectations of parties and promoting stability in relationships between individuals and states would far better explain such decisions.

Reverting to the illustration from insurance law, one can see that considerations of stability and uniformity control whether the "connecting factor" chosen is the place of making or the place of performance of the insurance contract. In articulating the objective of uniformity, it is therefore important to distinguish this concept as embodied within the policy goal of meeting expectations of parties, from the misplaced idea that uniformity contemplates application of a rule or a single connecting factor to resolve decisions. The desired uniformity will be achieved in recurring patterns of decision, all resulting from a pertinent weighing of various factors against the background of generally acceptable policy goals. The fallacy of seeking uniformity of decisions in terms of rules and exceptions, or selection of "most significant contacts" or "connecting factors" will be further discussed below by reference to recent American tort decisions involving interstate automobile accidents.[86]

4. *Concern for ideals of justice.*

The following words of Harper well describe the nature of the amorphous basic policy goal of concern for ideals of justice:[87]

> Justice is always administered in particular situations which involve particular litigants. Adjudication is concrete rather than abstract. It is the business of courts therefore to administer the law in such a way as to reach fair and just results between particular litigants except in situations where some paramount policy may require an undesirable disposition of the immediate controversy . . . Subject to other policy considerations a court may with complete propriety exploit the flexibility of the legal situation to produce a result in conformity with the merits of the case.

Although it is difficult to define the concept of justice, it seems generally understood that a desire to reach decisions fair to the parties is the cornerstone of this policy goal.[88] This desire, of course, often collided with the "legal results" dictated by the so-called choice-of-law "rules."

However, decision-makers avoided the "legal results" by testing the "rules" in terms of practical resolutions of controversies and by modifying the "rules" to suit normal human activities and expectations. In an article which has become a choice-of-law classic, Cavers described this technique as the "result selective" process.[89] In effect, what a court frequently did was to weigh the result dictated by application of a choice-of-law "rule" against the desired "just" result; and if the two did not balance, the court would chip away at the rule by means of "exceptions," "escape devices," or "connecting factors."

In contrast to this method of reaching a "fair" result in any given case, the method suggested in this article, whereby decision-makers would articulate the basic policy goals, removes the "blindfold" which courts were forced to put on in order to ignore the so-called "rules."[90] On re-examination of the policy goals, it may be seen that articulation of these guidelines in choice-of-law cases would provide decisions with solid foundations to support the multifactoral set of variables, such as "significant contacts," and local policies, which influence the process of decision, but which *per se* cannot adequately explain decisions. A final reference to the *Miller* decision[91] illustrates this important point. Assuming that it was a "fair" and "just" decision, one naturally asks why. The answer lies in this rhetorical question: Was it fair because it seemed to meet reasonable expectations of the individual parties and at the same time preserve the integrity of both English and Scottish institutions?—or—Was it fair because the contract in controversy was made on an English standard form and because the arbitration was carried out in Scotland? It should be clear from this question, that the factors mentioned in the second half merely influenced the decision, but could not adequately justify the prescription of English law instead of Scottish law.

C. Conclusion

The above discussion of the basic policy goals submits that choice-of-law decisions are in fact influenced by heretofore substantially unarticulated efforts to strike a balance between exclusive and inclusive claims of states and parties interested in choice-of-law controversies. These efforts are guided by policy goals of protecting base values of substantially affected claimants, along inclusive lines of shared authority, with a view to meeting the expectations of all participants and doing justice to the immediate parties involved. It is submitted that the international community shares these basic goals as the product of centuries of past decisions; and thus, the basic policy goals may serve as foundations of past, present and future decisions. In the final section of this article, further case illustrations will attempt to show that by setting up a multifactoral framework of inquiry for choice-of-law questions, it is possible to reconcile the spectrum of decisions by reference to the basic policy goals.

STEP III—THE METHODOLOGY EMPLOYED IN PROMOTING THE POLICY GOALS: A MULTIFACTORAL FRAMEWORK OF INQUIRY

The process of decision has been described above in terms of weighing and balancing of myriad factors and variables, which influence decisions against the background of certain overriding basic policy goals. In clarification of these goals, their integration and subordination in various contexts were illustrated in order to show that no ultimate, paramount policy goal can be singled out and deemed prevailing in all decisions.

A number of relevant factors were considered in outlining the process of rationalizing decisions in terms of the policy goals. These included *locus* of the interaction, nationality or domicile of the litigants, impact on internal processes, local community mores, policies of claimant states, characterization of a cause of action, as well as other factors. Of course, the complete set of factors and variables which may influence decisions is infinite. Considering both the differences in claims presented to decision-makers and the differences in local policies and prescriptions which decision-makers deem relevant to the respective types of controversies, it should be clear that no unique factor may reasonably be described as "determinant" in the prescription of policy (choice of law) to control the outcome of a given decision.

When presented with a specific controversy, a decision-maker must face a peculiar constellation of various factors in the given context of that controversy. Thus, at the outset, he is confronted with the complex task of appraising the relevance of numerous elements. To pretend that such a task may be satisfied by resolution of the controversy in terms of one of those factors is indeed an artifice. Rather, a decision may adequately be explained only in terms of recognizing and discussing the various elements comprising its facts in terms of a weighing and balancing process encompassing consideration of the basic policy goals. Indeed, it has been emphatically stated that "a policy-oriented approach is not a single factor, but a multifactoral approach."[92]

A panoramic view of the great range of factors which may influence decisions is supplied by the following outline which roughly groups the factors into three major categories:[93]

1. *The Nature of the Controversy.*
Among relevant factors requiring consideration in this category are:
a. The manner in which the controversy arises, *e.g.*, whether by omission, agreement or wilful conduct.
b. The manner in which the controversy is characterized (tort, contract, etc.) by the forum and claimant states claiming the power to prescribe policy.
c. The effect on the states and individual litigants of different characterizations of a controversy (if they exist), by the forum and claimant states competing to prescribe policy.[94]

2. *The Relationship of the Controversy to Individual Litigants, the Forum, and States Competing for the Authority to Prescribe Policy.*
Among relevant factors requiring consideration in this category are:
a. The effects of the controversy upon each of the litigants and interested states.
b. The relationship of each individual litigant with the interested states in terms of such variables as identity, nationality, domicile, residence, presence at the time constituting the controversy arose, etc.
c. The resources sought to be controlled or protected and the

relationship of interested states and individual litigants in terms of location, identity and ownership.

d. The actual interests of the litigants sought to be protected and the extent and scope of the authority claimed by interested states and required for such protection.

3. *Local Policies of the Forum State and Other Claimant States Competing for the Authority to Prescribe Policy.*

Among relevant factors requiring consideration in this category are:

a. Objectives of the competing prescriptions as revealed by case law, comment and legislative history.

b. Effects of the competing prescriptions on the interested states and individual litigants.

c. Effects of objectives upon promotion of basic policy goals.

These categories are intended only as guidelines to assist in selection of elements of controversies which influence decisions. It is re-emphasized that merely to discuss the influencing elements is not sufficient, and that relevance of such elements to achievement of the basic policy goals should be articulated in the opinions of decision-makers. As noted above, it is submitted that only discussion of the influencing elements in relation to the basic policy goals provides a methodology which may create reconcilable patterns of choice-of-law decisions. This is because uniformity of decisions is a legitimate goal only insofar as it is openly related to the promotion of community policies; on the other hand, uniformity is an unrealistic goal if its achievement is sought in terms of rules and exceptions or the haphazard selection of connecting factors. It is necessary that conflicting policies be articulated in decisions, in order to make possible reconciliation of the outcome of controversies which differ even though their facts are identical or similar.[95] Of course, since community policies change with time, uniformity of a pattern of decisions is limited to the time span of a given policy. It should be pointed out that as changes in community policies evolve, so should patterns of decisions.[96] This makes choice of law a dynamic process.

The various rules of preference purporting to describe responses and also the seemingly opposed exceptions, attain a surprising measure of consistency and purposefulness when considered against the background of the above described multifactoral framework and conceived as consequences of the interplay of numerous variables and community policies sought to be effectuated. The fallacy of searching for a uniform method of reconciling choice-of-law decisions in terms of "connecting factors" may be compared with the credibility of reconciling such decisions in terms of a policy-oriented approach (employing a multi-factoral framework of inquiry which relates the decision-influencing elements to the policy goals) by examining two recent series of American interstate automobile cases from New York and Wisconsin. The *rationales* of the New York decisions, although marking a brave departure from analysis by means of black-letter rules and exceptions, are tangled in an irreconcilable web of "connecting factors." On the other hand, the cases in the Wisconsin series, which have been articulated in terms of certain "choice-influencing considerations," are more reconcilable and more closely reflect an approach to choice of law as advocated by this article.

The New York series, from *Babcock v. Jackson*[97] to *Tooker v. Lopez*[98] has already received much attention from scholars.[99] Each case in the series considered the question of whether to apply the New York common law rule of negligence holding a defendant host-driver liable to a guest injured in his automobile, or whether to apply the law of another state concerned with the controversy, which exempted a host-driver from such liability under a guest statute. This issue, as it has arisen in these cases, so far has presented itself against a backdrop of four factual patterns. In Pattern I, a host and guest from New York made a short trip to a state with a guest statute, where the accident occurred.[100] In Pattern II, the facts were similar, except that the guest and host temporarily resided in and met in a guest-statute state.[101] In Pattern III, the guest and host came from a guest-statute state and were involved in an automobile accident during a short trip to New York state.[102] In Pattern IV, a guest from a guest-statute state and a host from New York suffered an automobile accident in the guest-statute state.[103]

In respect to Patterns I, II, and III, with the exception of one Pattern II case,[104] the New York courts applied New York law and not the law of the guest-state; thus, the host-driver was held liable to the injured guest. The federal court, in which the Pattern IV case was brought, applied the foreign state guest statute, instead of the New York common law negligence rule.[105] Since each of these cases has been the subject of much comment, this article will not discuss them in great detail. It is most important to note that despite reference to competing state policies in the opinions handed down in these cases (*e.g.*, a policy favoring tort liability as opposed to a policy designed to protect insurers from collusive hosts and guests, or a policy to protect hosts from ungrateful guests), the commentators attempted to search for a magic connecting factor which would reconcile all of the decisions in the series. Although this series marked a significant step away from the use of "rules" and "exceptions," the seemingly haphazard selection of a dominant "connecting factor" or a "most significant contact" in each of the opinions led the commentators into the trap of searching for a golden thread in terms of a specific factor. The possible "key factor" most frequently discussed was the place where the guest-host relationship had been formed.[106]

It was this factor which caused the debate over whether the first Pattern II decision, *Dym* v. *Gordon*,[107] could be reconciled with *Babcock* v. *Jackson*,[108] a Pattern I decision. In the latter, the guest and host had gotten together in New York and made a short motor trip to Ontario, Canada, where the accident occurred. As noted above, New York law was applied and the host was held liable; however, if the law of the place of the tort rule had been applied, the host would not have been liable, thanks to the guest statute. On the other hand, in the former decision, *Dym* v. *Gordon*,[109] the host and guest, although both New York residents, had never met in New York. They met while they were students in Colorado, and their accident occurred on a drive to a golf course in that state. The majority opinion of the New York Court of Appeals, in an ambiguous fashion, seemed to place great emphasis on the fact that the Colorado guest statute was properly applicable because the parties had met and made their drive in Colorado.

The New York Court of Appeals recently overruled this case in *Tooker* v. *Lopez*.[110] In this case, two New York residents, who had become acquainted as students in Michigan, met with an accident on a drive to Detroit, Michigan. Michigan, like Colorado, has a guest statute; but this time the New York common law liability rule was applied, and the host was held liable to the guest. Judge Fuld, who wrote the landmark majority opinion of *Babcock* v. *Jackson*,[111] and dissenting opinion in *Dym* v. *Gordon*,[112] delivered a concurring opinion in this case, in which he advocated that the time had come for new choice-of-law rules, as well as for new choice-of-law methods.[113] Such a demand for choice-of-law rules, by the very judge who made history in rejecting the old rules and exceptions, clearly shows the misplaced efforts of a methodology solely dependent on connecting factors. (To many observers, the place of the "seat of the relationship" was an inadequate explanation for the non-applicability of New York law in *Dym* v. *Gordon*.[114])

One should consider whether *Dym* v. *Gordon*[115] would have been more reconcilable with *Babcock* v. *Jackson*[116] if these opinions had been articulated in terms of the basic policy goals outlined in this article. It is submitted that perhaps a reasonable opinion supporting the application of Colorado law in *Dym* v. *Gordon* could have been written by means of weighing Colorado's territorial interests against New York's strong interest in protecting its power base of people. Such an opinion, which would have treated the so-called connecting factors merely as decision-influencing elements supporting the potential application of Colorado or New York law, and which would have expressed the ultimate choice of Colorado law in terms of legitimate interest in protection of its power bases (*i.e.*, in terms of the first policy goal), would have made a clearer precedent. This type of analysis in the written opinion would have avoided the subsequent debate on whether the "seat of the relationship" test had been the determining factor in applying the guest statute on the facts of *Dym* v. *Gordon*,[117] or the New York common-law negligence rule on the facts of *Babcock* v. *Jackson*.[118] This would also have obviated discussion on whether such test would form an adequate "rule" for determining all future decisions involving interstate automobile torts. It is re-emphasized that the search for any single key factor would be irrelevant, because a choice-of-law process oriented in terms of basic policy goals precludes the need for choice-of-law rules.

That such a choice-of-law methodology is indeed workable may be seen by examining the Wisconsin series of decisions referred to above. The Supreme Court of Wisconsin has recently handed down several opinions involving issues presented by interstate automobile torts by noting various connecting factors and treating them as decision-influencing elements, but making choices of law in terms of the following five "choice-influencing considerations:"[119]

1. Predictability of results.
2. Maintenance of interstate and international order.
3. Simplification of the judicial task.
4. Advancement of the forum's governmental interests.
5. Application of the better rule of law.

The leader in this series was *Heath* v. *Zellmer*,[120] an action which presented the claims of Wisconsin and Indiana guests injured in an accident in Wisconsin. The car was owned by an Indianan and driven by a host of Ohio residency. Wisconsin law imposes common law liability on host drivers, whereas Indiana has a guest statute.

The Wisconsin Supreme Court first examined Wisconsin and Indiana contacts, such as residences of the parties and the place of the accident,[121] and then compared the policies behind the law of Wisconsin and the law of Indiana.[122] It concluded that there was merit to the application of either law and summarized its observations as follows:[123]

In this case, the choice of law is outcome-determinative of the case. In the event Indiana law is used, the guests who traveled with Miss Meyer from Indiana will not be compensated by their negligent host and the deterrent factor that Wisconsin law attributes to damages for negligent conduct will not be imposed upon the driver. Moreover, the Wisconsin driver of the second car, will not be entitled to contribution from the other negligent tortfeasor, since no common liability would then exist. If Indiana law is applied, those policies favored in the Wisconsin law will suffer. In the event Wisconsin law is applied, the kindly host and his Indiana insurer, the objects of the bounty of the Indiana guest-law, will suffer or at least be answerable in damages.

From the above discussion, it is seen that the Wisconsin Supreme Court in *Heath* v. *Zellmer*[124] properly treated connecting factors merely as decision-influencing elements, pointing to the competing state laws and policies. This approach indeed parallels the consideration of decision-influencing elements as roughly grouped into the three categories outlined above: the nature of the controversy; the relationship of the controversy to the individual litigants, the forum and states competing for the power to prescribe policy; finally, the court's consideration of local policies of the forum state and other claimant states competing to prescribe policy is clearly reflected in the above quotation.

The court ultimately chose application of Wisconsin law by discussing the choice between Wisconsin and Indiana law in terms of choice-influencing elements. It noted that consideration no. 1., predictability of results, was not a vital consideration in torts, since they are unplanned events.[125] This attitude parallels thoughts expressed in this article regarding the significance of the role of uniformity and stability in achieving the basic policy goal of meeting expectations of parties.

Discussing consideration no. 2, the maintenance of interstate and international order, the court emphasized that "no state should impose its law in a situation when its parochial rules would unduly and without substantial reason so impinge upon another state as to interfere with the free flow of commerce or the exercise of another state's legitimate policies in such a manner that would invite retaliation from another jurisdiction."[126] This statement, of course, reflects a philosophy similar to the considerations of the importance of the role of "reciprocity" as a hallmark of the choice-of-law process in the above discussion of the second basic policy goal.

With respect to choice-influencing consideration no. 3, simplification of the judicial task, the court noted that no difficulty would be presented to it in applying the law of either of the two states competing to prescribe policy, namely, Wisconsin and Indiana.[127] Although this choice-influencing consideration played an insignificant role in *Heath* v. *Zellmer*,[128] it is submitted that it should be completely discarded as a relevant consideration. With respect to laws of a state of the United States, there is no need to prove "foreign law" because each state is required to recognize the law of sister states under the "full faith and credit" clause of the U.S. Constitution.[129] It is, therefore, hard to understand why the court in *Heath* v. *Zellmer*[130] discussed the issue of the relative ease or difficulty in applying Indiana law, if necessary. The U.S. Constitution has been interpreted as requiring that in applying the law of any given state to a controversy, the court must choose the law of a state which may reasonably be applied on the facts of the case. Thus, there is no constitutional requirement that an American state court sitting as the forum in a choice-of-law controversy must apply the law of a sister state. However, this notwithstanding, the above-noted interpretation of the "full faith and credit" clause implied that such sister-state law must be considered regardless of possible difficulties involved.

It is deemed that consideration of simplification of the judicial task as determinative in applying the law of a foreign state is dangerous. Although parties generally prove such foreign law, a court's outright rejection of it on grounds of difficulty could conceivably interfere with the achievement of the policy goals of reciprocity and justice, which basically allow for mutual deference to legitimate claims of substantially affected states. The simplicity consideration suggests a blatant bias toward forum law and should be discouraged, if not completely discarded.[131] One American judge has indeed stressed, "Only in those cases in which foreign law is either very complex or very obscure will simplification of the judicial task be a weighty consideration."[132]

In reviewing choice-influencing consideration no. 4., advancement of the forum's governmental interests, the court noted:[133]

> The question in private litigation, such as in an automobile-accident case, is whether the proposed nonforum rule comports with the standards of fairness and justice that are embodied in the policies of the forum law. If it appears that the application of forum law will advance the governmental interest of the forum state, this fact becomes a major, though not in itself a determining, factor in the ultimate choice of law.

Thus, this so-called choice-influencing consideration, like the previous one, also reflects a serious forum bias. It is re-emphasized that the duty of decision-makers in the choice-of-law process is to weigh and balance, in as objective a manner as possible, the interests of all states concerned with a controversy, as well as the interests of the forum state, with the goal of achieving an inclusive allocation of authority to prescribe policy. It is therefore advocated that "advancement of the forum's governmental interests" should be considered equally with interests of other concerned states. Forum interests and supporting local policies should not be mistakenly considered to be a basic policy goal; rather, the forum's governmental interests are properly treated as a decision-influencing element[134] within the third category outlined above.

In its discussion of choice-influencing consideration no. 5, application of the "better rule of law,"[135] the Supreme Court of Wisconsin in *Heath* v. *Zellmer*,[136] made a survey of the general attitude toward guest statutes throughout the U.S.A. and compared it with the attitude toward the common-law negligence rule. It concluded that such statutes were generally deemed outmoded by commentators and decision-makers,[137] and expressed the following reasons for favoring the common-law rule:[138]

1. Providing compensation for persons injured by negligent conduct.

2. Ensuring the equal protection of the laws required by the U.S. Constitution to residents and non-residents injured in a common-law negligence state.

3. Enabling injured persons to pay their medical bills.

4. Discouraging and penalizing negligent driving.

5. Effecting sharing of the burden of loss among joint tortfeasors (for example, if a non-resident from a guest-statute state, as well as a resident of a common-law negligence state were responsible for an auto accident in the common-law negligence state, the burden of compensating the accident victims would be spread equally between them, regardless of competing state laws with respect to the liability of each of them).

In summarizing its reasons for applying the Wisconsin law, the court noted:[139]

> And in this case the Wisconsin driver, if Indiana law were used, would also be liable for all injuries sustained by the guests in the Meyer car, with no opportunity to seek contribution from their negligent host, Eileen Meyer, even though it might be her negligence that was the principal cause of the accident. This would

defeat Wisconsin's policy of spreading losses and assessing damage against all tortfeasors in proportion to their causal negligence. To employ Indiana law in this instance would remove the deterrent effect of our law of negligence, while the choice of Wisconsin law would further this state's interest in regulating conduct on Wisconsin highways and penalizing that conduct when it is negligent. It would promote safe driving on Wisconsin highways.

The above quotation clearly shows that the court could equally well have expressed itself in terms of protecting its power bases, *i.e.*, its highways—territory; people on its highways—people; its welfare programs and attitudes toward negligent conduct—institutions. The opinion could have been articulated in favor of such protection of Wisconsin power bases—first policy goal; after weighing and balancing elements supporting the alternative of exercising reciprocity by applying Indiana law—second policy goal; discussing expectations of the parties—third policy goal; and examining fairness of the application of Wisconsin law to the parties—fourth policy goal. It is submitted that a decision which weighed and balanced the influencing elements and discussed the ultimate choice of law in relation to achievement of the basic policy goals would more clearly disclose the "real reasons" for applying Wisconsin law. Such expression would certainly be more objective and would avoid any intimation of a forum-prejudiced approach to choice of law. Unfortunately, forum prejudice is the natural consequence of decisions rationalized in terms of the third, fourth, and fifth choice-influencing considerations discussed in *Heath* v. *Zellmer*.[140] This is especially true of the "better law" consideration, which indicates a misplaced subjectivity in the choice-of-law process.

The application of the better rule of law may be one decision-influencing element within the general policy goals of meeting expectations of parties and doing justice to them. However, it should not be regarded as a primary objective or an isolated determinative factor; rather, it is an element to be considered within the third category of factors outlined above. Thus, the concept of "a better rule of law" can be acceptable if it is applied to a scrutiny of the contents of the relevant prescriptions and the weighing of the effects of its application on the expectations of parties and the doing of justice to them on the merits of the case.

That the concept of choice of the "better law" invites dangerous and misleading subjectivity into the choice-of-law process is well illustrated by subsequent cases in the Wisconsin series. For example, in the case which followed *Heath* v. *Zellmer*,[141] namely, *Zelinger* v. *State Sand and Gravel Co.*,[142] the discussion of choice of Wisconsin law in terms of the "better law" definitely obscured the actual weighing of decision-influencing elements in terms of the first and second policy goals, protection of power bases and reciprocity, which the court seems actually to have engaged in without so stating.

In *Zelinger*,[143] the wife and daughter of an Illinois plaintiff were injured in a collision in Wisconsin with a truck owned by a Wisconsin defendant. The wife was the host-driver of the car, and the minor-daughter was the guest. In the husband's action for the injuries suffered by his spouse and child, the defendant sought contribution by way of a counter-claim against the wife, and a third-party complaint against her insurer. Illinois has a statute which bars spouse from suing spouse for a tort committed during coverture, as well as a statute limiting suits between parent and child to actions claiming compensation for injury as a result of wilful and wanton conduct. Thus, interspousal and parental immunities under Illinois law, if applied in this case, would have barred the defendant from recovering contribution from the wife, a joint tortfeasor. Wisconsin law posed no such bars to contribution. Wisconsin follows the rule of allowing contribution among joint tortfeasors within the limits of a comparative negligence doctrine which apportions liability according to relative fault of the tortfeasors.

Comparing the policies of the Illinois law and Wisconsin law in *Zelinger*, the court observed:[144]

> The interspousal and parental immunities rest on the proposition that family peace is promoted thereby and perhaps as a by-product collusive suits are held to a minimum. The host-guest policy is basically the good Samaritan argument that one should not be liable for negligence in the performance of a good deed. On the other hand, Wisconsin's interest in the nonexistence of such rules is to promote the spreading of the risk and fasten liability in torts on a moral basis of fault. Such moral considerations leave little room for a justification of immunity for collateral reasons.

In examining the above conclusions quoted from *Zelinger*, it should be obvious that instead of speaking in subjective terms of the "better law," the court could have more accurately framed its opinion by a discussion of the actual contents of the competing laws, the policies underlying them, the ends sought, and the effects of preferring one over the other, upon the parties, against the background of the first and second policy

YUVAL LEVY AND BARBARA MARKS

goals. However, instead of so doing, the court merely described Wisconsin law as "better:"[145]

> ... the considerations of advancing this state's interest and what it considers to be the better law dicate that these defendants are entitled to the benefits of the Wisconsin law of contribution and the subsidiary rules on which it rests ... Interspousal-immunity and the host-guest limitations are subsidiary issues upon which contribution stands or falls since in this state contribution must be based upon joint or common liability. For the purpose of determining whether a Wisconsin resident involved in a Wisconsin accident can recover contribution from an Illinois wife when her husband sues in Wisconsin, we think the Illinois interest of the preservation of family integrity seems hardly to be in jeopardy and also the interest served by the host-guest statute and parental-immunity is scarcely impinged upon.

The above quotations from *Zelinger* show that as in *Heath* v. *Zellmer*,[146] the Wisconsin Supreme Court again applied its local policy in favor of promoting contribution and compensation in tort claims, which in fact reflects a preference for protecting its own power bases, *i.e.*, its people (residents) and institutions (methods of compensation), as well as its territory (highways). Such preference was made at the expense of the Illinois policy of protecting its internal social processes— stability in family relationships. The court deemed Wisconsin to be the more substantially affected state, since Wisconsin's interest in promoting safety on its highways would be more severely jeopardized[147] than Illinois' interest in family stability. Discussion of the choice of Wisconsin law in reference to the basic policy goals clearly provides a more objective explanation for the choice than does the mere selection of what the court "considers to be the better law."[148]

The danger of relying on the so-called "better law" in choice of law was made very clear by the decision which the Supreme Court of Wisconsin handed down two months after *Zelinger*.[149] In *Conklin* v. *Horner*,[150] plaintiff-guests brought an action against host-defendant for injuries suffered when his car went off the road and hit a tree in Wisconsin. All parties were residents of Illinois.

Before evaluating the conclusion actually reached by the court in this case, one should make reference to the first two policy goals and consider whether they indicate that Illinois law should have determined the question of liability.[151] It would indeed seem reasonable for the court to have exercised reciprocity and applied Illinois law, rather than to have weighted various influencing elements in favor of protection of Wisconsin power bases. After all, despite such interest of Wisconsin, the interaction in that state was with a tree. On the other hand, the entire interaction *vis-a-vis* the parties was among Illinois residents. Nevertheless, the court applied Wisconsin law.

The majority opinion well illustrated the shortcomings of the forum-prejudiced approach encouraged by the concept of the "better law," although the court stated that its choice of Wisconsin law as "better" was not forum-prejudiced:[152]

> We emphasize that we prefer the Wisconsin rule of ordinary negligence not because it is Wisconsin's law, but because we consider it to be the better law. In three cases within a year, *Heath*, *Zelinger*, and this case, we have preferred Wisconsin law, but it should be noted that the merits of the competing rules of law were carefully considered, and the choice was made not as a matter of parochial preference but in the honest belief that, given the opportunity to apply either a forum or non-forum law, the better law in each case proved to be that of the forum.

One questions the sincerity of the above statement, since the opinion expressed a blatant forum prejudice, and curiously referred to the old "place of the tort" rule to support its forum bias:[153]

> Wisconsin is not only the state where the tortious conduct and injury occured—facts that in themselves would compel the use of Wisconsin law under the Bealian rule of the 1st Restatement—but it is the forum as well. Thus this court is specially charged as an instrument of the Wisconsin government to further the interests of Wisconsin, if to do so furthers the underlying policies of our law.
>
> ***
>
> . . . (T)he place of injury and the forum coincide. Accordingly, the whole gamut of the responsibilities of a concerned forum court come into play.

On the other hand, the dissenting view in support of application of Illinois law written by Chief Justice Hallows, the author of the opinion in *Heath* v. *Zellmer*,[154] poignantly expressed the objective format which the majority should have followed, as well as the danger of the forum prejudice invoked by the "homing instinct" of the "better law" concept:[155]

299

. . . But in *Heath* and in *Zelinger*, we made it clear that none of the choice-influencing considerations standing alone is to be considered controlling.

***

The application of the choice-influencing factors should be consistent in every case with respect to the same issue although the relative importance of each factor will vary with the kind of tort or isssue involved in relation to the factual contacts. If we are going to be consistent only in applying the law of the forum, then we are merely giving lip service to the new "significant contacts" rule. The result reached by the majority and its reasoning of the overpowering local concerns and better law logically and easily support the rule of the mechanical application of the law of the forum in every case, but this rule was rejected years ago in *Bain* v. *Northern Pacific R. Co.* (1904), 120 Wis. 412, 98 N.W. 241.

The *rationales* of these three Wisconsin cases, *Heath* v. *Zellmer*,[156] *Zelinger*,[157] and *Conklin* v. *Horner*,[158] in terms of the "choice-influencing considerations" stand as significant precedents for a policy-oriented approach to choice of law in terms of multifactoral analysis of elements which influence decision. This point should not be overlooked, despite the above criticism concerning the drawbacks of "considerations" 3, 4 and 5, in encouraging a forum-biased approach. It has been seen that "considerations" 1 and 2 indeed show recognition of two of the basic policy goals— expectations of parties and reciprocity. It is submitted that future precedents in terms of the basic policy goals along the lines of analysis embarked upon in *Heath* v. *Zellmer*[159] naturally follow as the next step on the trail blazed by these Wisconsin decisions. This could be done by simply discarding "consideration" 3 and treating "considerations" 4 and 5 merely as decision-influencing elements to be placed in the third category outlined in this article, and introducing discussion of the basic policy goals of protection of power bases and justice.

It is interesting to note that none of the five so-called "choice-influencing considerations" specifically considers the concept of fairness and justice to the litigants.[160] Overt discussion of this policy goal may have avoided the application of Wisconsin law in *Conklin* v. *Horner*.[161] It could certainly be argued that "fair and just results between particular litigants" (to requote the words of Harper)[162] demanded application of Illinois law rather than Wisconsin law in that case.

In contrast to the series of Wisconsin interstate automobile tort cases discussed above, several maritime cases of an earlier vintage of choice-of-law precedents showed a more keen concern for the policy goal of justice. Of course, these cases did not specifically express the basic policy goals outlined in this article so nearly as did the "choice-influencing considerations" in the Wisconsin cases noted above. Nevertheless, these maritime cases could well be regarded as having sown the seeds of a policy-oriented approach to choice of law.[163]

The first example is the landmark U.S. Supreme Court decision in *Lauritzen* v. *Larsen*[164] per opinion of Justice Jackson. The issue presented was which law to apply to a libel brought by a Danish seaman, a temporary resident of New York who had signed ship's articles providing that Danish law should govern rights of crew members. He suffered injury in Cuban territorial waters on a ship of Danish ownership and registry. Danish law provided for twelve weeks of maintenance and cure at shipowner's cost, regardless of fault; whereas, the U.S. Jones Act,[165] gave the seaman a cause of action in negligence and placed no limits on recovery. Negligence had been proved.

Although Jackson did not express his opinion as a policy-oriented analysis within a multifactoral framework, the following statement generally embodies this approach:[166]

> International or maritime law in such matters as this does not seek uniformity and does not purport to restrict any nation from making and altering its laws to govern its own shipping and territory. However, it aims at stability and order through usages which considerations of comity, reciprocity, and long range interest have developed to define the domain which each nation will claim as its own. Maritime law, like our municipal law, has attempted to avoid or resolve conflicts between competing laws by ascertaining and valuing points of contact between the transaction and the states or governments whose competing laws are involved. The criteria, in general, appear to be arrived at from weighing of the significance of one or more connecting factors between the shipping transaction regulated and the national interest served by the assertion of authority.

These words of the U.S. Supreme Court, as early as 1952, surely reveal that even prior to the recent Wisconsin decisions discussed above, the advantages of a multifactoral approach were recognized.

The court made a thorough examination of the many elements linking the parties and interested states with the controversy,[167] as well as the contents of the competing prescriptions of Danish and U.S. law and their effects upon the litigants:[168]

> The two systems are in sharpest conflict as to treatment of claims for disability, partial or complete, which are permanent, or which outlast the liability for maintenance or cure, to which this class belongs. Such injuries Danish law relieves under a state-operated plan similar to our own workmen's compensation systems. Claims for such disability are not made against the owner but against the state's Directorate of Insurance Against Consequences of Accidents. They may be presented directly or through any Danish Consulate. They are allowed by administrative action, not by litigation, and depend not upon fault or negligence but only on the fact of injury and the extent of disability. Our own law, apart from indemnity caused by the ship's unseaworthiness, makes no such compensation for such disability in the absence of fault or negligence. But when such fault or negligence is established by litigation, it allows recovery for such elements as pain and suffering not compensated under Danish law and lets the damages be fixed by jury. In this case, since negligence was found, United States law permits a larger recovery than Danish law. If the same injury were sustained but negligence was absent or not provable, the Danish law would appear to provide compensation where our law would not.

This decision closely parallels the considerations for examination of elements influencing decision as outlined in this article. In deciding which law to apply, the Court found in favor of Danish law from the cumulative weight of three elements, which were all Danish—the flag of the ship, the nationality of the injured seaman, and the registry of the ship. However, the Court did not treat such factors as the grounds for choosing Danish law. Instead, it measured these factors against expressed concern for expectations of the parties and justice to the litigants. Further, it made its final decision in favor of Danish law only after comparing possible grounds for application of American law, since the place of the "locus contractus" was New York. The court concluded that even though non-application of the Jones Act to the facts of this case might discourage some foreign seamen from signing articles in New York (because they could not be certain of claiming the same high standard of care afforded by the U.S. to her seamen), this was of less importance than the arguments in favor of applying Danish law.

Lauritzen v. *Larsen*[169] was not the only early example of a decision relating influencing elements to community policies. One should also compare the cases of *Nakken* v. *Fearnley and Eger*,[170] and *Uravic* v. *F. Jarka Co.*[171] The first case concerned a Norwegian seaman who signed articles in New York for service on a ship of Norwegian ownership and registry. The articles expressly provided for application of Norwegian law. The seaman sustained injuries on the vessel while it was docked in New York. If application of the law of the place of injury were a valid mechanical rule, U.S. law would have been applied; however, the court recognized that the American *locus* factor was of relative insignificance and ruled in favor of Norwegian law because of Norway's interests in protecting her seamen. This reflected an appreciation of the important role of reciprocity, which defers to the interest of states other than the forum in protecting their power bases.

On the other hand, the *locus* factor in the *Uravic*[172] was of great significance. Its facts were similar to *Nakken*,[173] in that an accident occurred on a ship of foreign registry (a private German vessel) docked in New York. An American stevedore brought an action to recover for injuries suffered aboard the vessel through negligence of a fellow-servant. In justifying application of the U.S. Jones Act, Justice Holmes observed:[174]

> The conduct regulated is of universal concern. The rights of a citizen within the territorial limits of the country are more extensively determined by the scope of actions for torts than even by the law of crimes. There is strong reason for giving the same protection to the person of those who work in our harbors when they are working upon a German ship that they would receive when working on an American ship in the next dock. . . It would be extraordinary to apply German law to Americans momentarily on board a private German ship in New York.

Thus, Justice Holmes seems to have considered the importance of justice to the individual litigant and the interest of the U.S. in protecting her people (seamen).

Any attempt to reconcile the *Uravic*[175] decision with the *Nakken*[176] decision in terms of "connecting factors" is futile. The *locus* factors (U.S. port, flag, and registry) were identical. Only the nationality of the injured party in each case differed. However, relating these influencing elements to the basic policy goals provides grounds for reconciling these cases. To honor the interest of Norway in protecting her people power base (seamen) in *Nakken*[177] seems reasonable, just as to apply U.S. law to the American stevedore from New York in *Uravic*[178] seemed fair. *Nakken* shows recognition of the second basic policy goal of reciprocity; whereas, *Uravic* reflects strong interests of the U.S. in protecting her power bases.

The following cases preceding the Wisconsin decisions also seem to have appreciated the fact that only awareness of the basic policy goals may provide rational symmetry to decisions. In *Southern Steamship Co. Ltd.* v. *Dillon*,[179] the "connecting factors" *per se* overwhelmingly pointed to application of English law, yet the application of American law was clearly mandatory for achievement of justice (fourth basic policy goal.) In brief, the facts were that a British seaman brought an action to recover half-wages under the U.S. Seamen's Act,[180] legislation which proscribes payment of advance wages to seamen. This act makes such payment a misdemeanor and permits a seaman to recover any such payment of half-wages.

The Court deemed the act applicable to foreign, as well as American vessels, so long as no U.S. treaty indicated otherwise. In supporting this contention, the Court emphasized that the purpose of the act was to protect all seamen from "bad men," out to take advantage of them. In its opinion, the Court made reference to an earlier decision, *The Eudora*, which had declared that this was the purpose of the act:[181]

> If the necessities of the public justify the enforcement of a sailor's contract by exceptional means, justice requires that the rights of the sailor be in like manner protected. The story of the wrongs done to sailors in the larger ports, not merely of this nation but of the world, is an oft-told tale, and many have been the efforts to protect them against such wrongs. One of the most common means of doing these wrongs is the advancement of wages. Bad men lure them into haunts of vice, advance a little money to continue their dissipation, and having thus acquired a partial control and by liquor dulled their faculties, place them on board the vessel just ready to sail and most ready to return the advances. When once on shipboard and the ship at sea the sailor is powerless and no relief is availing. It was in order to stop this evil, and to protect the sailor, and not to restrict him of his liberty that this statute was passed. And while in some cases it may operate harshly, no one can doubt that the best interests of seamen as a class are preserved by such legislation.

***

We are of the opinion that it is within the power of Congress to protect all sailors shipping in our ports on vessels engaged in foreign or interstate commerce, whether they belong to citizens of this country or of a foreign nation, and that our courts are bound to enforce these provisions in respect to foreign equally with domestic vessels.

Although the above quotation well expresses the social purposes of the Seamen's Act, a shortcoming of the *Southern Steamship*[182] was its failure to mention the strong economic interest of the U.S. which was at stake. While the opinion indicated strong support for the U.S. interest in protecting its people power base, the omission of discussion of the desire of the U.S. to protect the institution of her shipping interests makes difficult the reconciliation of the later *McCulloch*[183] and *Incres*[184] decisions discussed above, in which the Court refused to apply the National Labor Relations Act to foreign seamen.

The brief of the U.S. Government in *The Eudora*[185] had stressed protection of the economic position of American shipping interests as a justifiable ground of extraterritorial application of the Seamen's Act:[186]

Moreover, as ninety per cent of all commerce in our ports is conducted in foreign vessels, it must be obvious that their exemption from these shipping laws will go far to embarrass domestic vessels in obtaining their quota of seamen. To the average sailor it is a consideration while in port to have his wages in part prepaid, and if in a larger port like New York ninety per cent of the vessels are permitted to prepay such seamen as ship upon them, and the other ten per cent, being American vessels, cannot thus prepay, it will be exceedingly difficult for American vessels to obtain crews.

The task of decision-makers, in addition to examining the relevant variables within the broad framework outlined above, is to evaluate and weigh such considerations in terms of competing policies and the policy goals. Choice of law within this framework is not without recognition of the fact that this analysis is made by a national decision-maker. Consequently, the so-to-speak "human condition" of the law may occasionally justify a decision which considers local political or economic considerations.

Such less objective grounds should be articulated. Unfortunately, the Court, in *Southern Steamship*[187] did not mention the above-quoted point discussed in the government's brief for *The Eudora*.[188] It is submitted that concern for protection of U.S. shipping interests and their position in the American economy should have been expressed. This would have made *The Eudora* and *Southern Steamship* more distinguishable from *McCulloch*[189] and *Incres*,[190] where non-extraterritorial application of the National Labor Relations Act apparently was less of a threat to American shipping interests.

As a matter of fact, overt reference to political considerations, even though not entirely objective considerations, is the only plausible way in which to make politically-oriented decisions valid precedents *vis-a-vis* other decisions on similar facts, which, under different circumstances, are not dependent on transient political attitudes. For example, generally a state will not accord extraterritorial effect to war decrees issued by another state. Yet, in *Lorentzen* v. *Lydden and Co.*,[191] an English case which arose during World War II, such a decree was given extraterritorial effect. The issue was whether to recognize war decrees issued by the Norwegian government requisitioning all ships flying the Norwegian flag. Although previous case law indicated that a government could not expect such an order to be binding with respect to property located outside its territory, wartime conditions presented unusual circumstances, and English political interests dictated the necessity of assisting Norway, her ally, whose provisional government was then in England. Thus, the Court honored the decree and allowed ownership of a vessel, which was then in England, to pass to a curator appointed by the Norwegian government. However, this decision seemed irreconcilable with previous precedents, because the court did not articulate the above-noted political considerations.

Across the Atlantic, twelve years later, a case with similar facts arose and an American court refused to given extraterritorial effect to such a decree. In *Latvian State Cargo and Steamship Line* v. *United States*,[192] Latvia claimed title to a vessel, owned by a Latvian company, which had been requisitioned by the U.S. Government in 1942, and had not been in Latvia or its territorial waters since that time. The U.S. Court of Claims, noting that the property "taken" was a ship outside Latvian territory on the effective date of the decree, held against the claim. The Court further articulated its holding on the ground that the U.S. would not recognize such decrees, since it had refused to recognize Soviet annexation of Latvia. Thus, *Latvian State Cargo*, by expressing political considerations behind the decision, is a more valuable precedent than *Lorentzen*, in which the English court did not express such interests.

The above-discussed decisions from maritime law and recent American interstate automobile tort law, all of which were supported by opinions progressing beyond the application of choice-of-law rules and exceptions, have been examined in light of the basic policy goals in order to demonstrate that only overt articulation of these policy goals by decision-makers may create reconcilable patterns of decisions. This is because the many elements which influence decisions, as well as local community policies are too myriad in variety to be used as the criteria which make it possible to reconcile one choice-of-law decision with another in a system of precedents. Of course, it should be pointed out that the broad policy goals outlined in this article are functions of "reasonableness"— reasonable protection of power bases, reasonable shareability of authority, and reasonable expectations of parties. Fairness and justice are also to be regarded as basic components of "reasonableness." The concept of reasonableness in the common law, like the policy goal of justice, is a reflection of contemporary social values, and it is the criterion of reasonableness which accurately describes the various resolutions of controversies resulting from the constant weighing and balancing of decision-influencing elements and policies within a framework of multifactoral analysis.

CONCLUSION

The approach to choice of law suggested in this article calls for a methodology independent of "rules" and "exceptions" or "dominant connecting factors." However, fears that such a system will open the door for decision-makers to hand down capricious decisions are unfounded. A high degree of uniformity in response by decision-makers, due to constantly recurring patterns of decision and uniform social and legal trends has been attained in the past and is likely to continue in the future. The role of overt articulation of the basic policy goals in choice-of-law decisions is to afford rational symmetry to these patterns. The proponents of mechanical choice-of-law jurisprudence or new rules in order to attain uniformity in decision, who would resort to technical doctrinal formulae, must admit the practical hopelessness of their quest.[193] The lesson of the past demonstrated that resort to rules bred numerous escape devices and exceptions, resulting in a multitude of complementary opposite prescriptions. By the evolution of these sets of opposed prescriptions, mechanical choice-of-law jurisprudence defeated its own ends and showed the futility of its approach.

On the other hand, the policy-oriented approach, is "not a chaotic, anti-rational method," to use the words of Harper; and, "the alternative to a hard and fast system of doctrinal formulae is not anarchy. The difference is not between a system and no system, but between two systems; between a system which purports to have, but lacks complete logical symmetry and one which affords latitude for the interplay and clash of conflicting policy factors."[194]

The task of evaluating the various decision-influencing elements is somewhat simplified by common trends in legal thinking, resulting from the growing similarity in objectives and principles underlying various competing prescriptions of individual states in the world arena. This trend facilitates mutual tolerance and restraint without unduly offending any decision-maker's concept of justice or expectations of parties. The prescription of policies springing from common grounds and having substantially similar objectives, accords with the general interests and expectations of most claimants and diminishes possible frustration due to preference for one claim over another.

Common trends in legal thinking and general homogeneity in community policies, which may afford some formal uniformity in the evaluation of decision-influencing elements and local policies, are attained within the broad multifactoral framework of inquiry of a policy-oriented approach to choice of law. However, this uniformity is meaningful only when integrated with the basic policy goals. The flexible approach advocated in the foregoing discussion is best suited for such coordination and integration of decision-influencing elements and presents a new perspective to that branch of law commonly referred to as choice of law. The analysis of choice-of-law questions articulating the basic policy goals is the means of providing rational symmetry to past, present and future decisions.

NOTES

[1] For an excellent scholarly survey of the several approaches to choice of law advocated by contemporary American Judges and scholars, see Juenger, *Choice of law in Interstate Torts*, 118 U. Penna. L. Rev. 202 (1969).

[2] Private international law should not be ascribed exclusively to recognized territorial authorities. See generally Yntema, *The Objectives of Private International Law*, 35 CAN. BAR REV. 721, 722 (1957); Zeballos, *La nationalité au Point de Vue de la Legislation Comparée et du Droit Privé Humain* (Paris 1914); Stevenson, *The Relationship of Private International Law to Public International Law*, 52 Colum. L. Rev. 561 (1952).

In *International Law, Power and Policy: A Contemporary Conception*, Hague Receuil 165, 217–18 (1953), McDougal observed:

(D)ecision makers upon problems of private international law act within the context of a world power process and, hence . . . their decisions are affected by all the variables that affect other decisions within this context.

[3] See R. Crampton and D. Currie, *Conflicts of Laws* 257 (1968).

[4] An excellent example of such non-articulation and a rationale based on grounds of the vague notion of "public policy" is Wyatt v. Fulrath, 16 N.Y.2d 169, 264 N.Y.S.2d

Rational Symmetry in Choice of Law

253, 311 N.E.2d 637 (1965). A deceased husband and wife, domiciliaries of Spain, had placed funds in joint New York bank accounts which gave the wife rights of survivorship. On the other hand, Spanish law forbade a spouse to deprive the other spouse of community property rights by *inter vivos* gifts creating rights of survivorship. The husband predeceased the wife, which under Spanish law would have automatically vested in his estate one-half of the funds in the bank accounts, which meant that two-thirds of this half would pass to his heirs at law. One account and the wife's will provided for application of New York law. The court applied New York law. The Columbia Law Review gave the following critique, Recent Development, 66 Colum. L. Rev. 790, 793–94 (1966):

> Rather than relying on the "public policy" of one of the concerned jurisdictions, it seems clear that the court should have undertaken a more extensive inquiry into such factors as the purpose underlying the potentially applicable local law rules, the dominance of one state's interest in regulating the particular legal relations, the expectations of the parties, and desirability of certain and easily applied principles, and the reduction of complications caused by the existence of complex interstate and international systems.

[5] The desire to promote common long-range interests was long ago recognized by Story, *Commentaries on the Conflict of Laws*, art. 35, p. 33 (8th ed. 1883):

> The true foundation on which the administration of international law must rest is, that the rules which are to govern are those which arise from mutual interest and utility, from a sense of inconveniences which would result from a contrary doctrine, and from a sort of moral necessity to do justice, in order that justice may be done to us in return.

[6] A policy-oriented approach to law regards law as a means to securing social, public and private interests. Projecting this view to conflict of laws, Heilman, *Judicial Method and Economic Objectives in Conflict of Laws*, 43 Yale L. J. 1082, 1108 (1934) wrote:

> The chief functions which the rules of conflict of laws ought to be made to serve are . . . to provide to the greatest extent possible, through the imposition of legal consequences of the kind generally thought desirable throughout the larger commonwealth. The domestic rules of particular states should be excluded from application to the extent that their employment might impede or defeat this accomplishment.

Clarification of policy goals is indispensable to the concept of law which does not insist upon technical rules, but regards law as a "flow of decisions in which community prescriptions are formulated, invoked, and in fact applied in the promotion of community policies" (McDougal, *International Law, Power and Policy: A Contemporary Conception*, Hague Recueil 165, 181, see also p. 183 (1953)).

[7] The difficulty of describing decisions in any field of law in terms of a mathematical formula has presented difficulties in the success of computerized research. See Dennis, *Shall We Put the Law into the Computer?*, Law and Computer Technology, vol. 1, no. 1, p. 25 (Jan. 1968); Von Briesen, *Status of Legal Use of Computers*, Law and Computer Technology, vol. 1, no. 4, p. 9 (Apr. 1968); compare *Use of Computers to Predict Appellate Judge Decisions*, Law and Computer Technology, vol. 1., no. 5, p. 11 (May 1968).

[8] The term "international law" is used here to describe the flow of decisions governing interactions between states which are sometimes labeled "public international law," as well as those decisions commonly called "private international law." See note 9, *infra*.

[9] See Nussbaum, *Principles of Private International Law* 3 (1943): "Private International law, or Conflict of Laws, may be broadly defined as that part of private law which deals with foreign relations." This definition is vague and "offers, therefore, a shelter to an immense variety of existing and contradictory opinions." See also Beckett, *What is Private International Law?* B.Y.B. Int. L. 73 (1926).

Wolff, *Private International Law* 10 (1950) wrote: "The usual titles of our subject are 'Private International Law' or 'Rules on Conflict of Laws.' Both are open to objection—the first seems to suggest that there are two kinds of international law, Public and Private . . . and the second is no more satisfactory because it is the task of this branch of the law to avoid conflicts." See also Stevenson, *The Relationship of Private International Law to Public International Law*, 52 Colum. L. Rev. 561–88 (1952) and McDougal, *International Law, Power and Policy: A Contemporary Conception*, Hague Recueil 165 (1953).

For a comprehensive discussion of the merits and demerits of a variety of labels proposed to describe the flow of decisions allocating authority, see Komar, *International Private Law: Its Name and Nature,* Int. L. Assoc. 312, 313–21 (31st Rep., Buenos Aires 1920).

[10] See McDougal, Burke and Vlasic, *The Maintenance of Public Order at Sea and the Nationality of Ships,* 54 Am. J. Int. L. 23, 50 (1960). Other variables such as culture. personality and group affiliations may also influence individual decision-makers and affect their decisions. Differing evaluations may derive from differing cultural backgrounds and traditions. Political and social environment influence decisions, as do different perspectives of underlying goals and policies expressed in various concepts of public policy, moral rights, security, democracy, totalitarianism, due process, fraud, justice, crime and the like. Any study of decision-makers cannot ignore these variables.

[11] For expansion of the ideas expressed in this section of the article, see McDougal, Laswell, Vlasic, *Law and Public Order in Space* 646 ff. (1963); see also Von Mehren. *Conflict of Laws in a Federal System*, 16 Int. and Comp. L.Q. 681, 687 (1969).

[12] It should be noted that many writers fail to make the distinction between the term "conflict of laws" which embraces all three authority functions, and the term "choice of law" which embraces only the second function. When many scholars refer to a "conflict of law" they, in fact, mean only "choice of law," *i.e.*, the second authority function, prescription of policy.

[13] For an excellent survey, see Von Mehren and Trautman, *The Law of Multistate Problems, Survey of Accepted Bases for Jurisdiction to Adjudicate 652–747*, and *Departure from Normally Accepted Jurisdictional Bases 747 f. (1965).*

[14] For example, note the following observation of U.S. District Judge Pettine in Tiernan v. Westext Transport, Inc. 295 F. Supp. 1256, 1262 (R.I. 1969):

> In Woodward v. Stewart, R.I., 243 A.2d 917 (July 9, 1968) a Rhode Island citizen and resident riding in the vehicle of another Rhode Island citizen and resident was killed in Seekonk, Massachusetts in an accident with a vehicle owned by still another Rhode Island citizen and resident and operated with the consent of the latter, by yet a fourth Rhode Island citizen and resident. The parties in the Stewart vehicle had begun their trip in Barrington, Rhode Island, to which they were returning after a dinner engagement in Newport, Rhode Island, when the accident occurred. On appeal from the trial court's dismissal of the decedent guest's administrator's case against the host-driver, *the Rhode Island Supreme Court, reversing all previous law to the contrary, held that in those circumstances the wrongful death law of Rhode Island should be the governing substantive law with respect to the*

> *legal relationship between the parties in the Stewart vehicle, the liability arising from*
> *that relationship, and the damages recoverable for such liability. The court further*
> *noted that Massachusetts law should govern with respect to the wrongful conduct*
> *of the parties.* (Emphasis added.)

[15] Until the process of decision-making shall have as its only objectives the perspectives and goals of the world community, and shall be free from environmental predispositions and political considerations of individual states, conflict of laws shall remain a necessary field of law in controversies which cross state lines. Nevertheless, despite seemingly insurmountable difficulties, there have been attempts to draft multistate agreements. For a list of conventions, see Cheshire, *Private International Law* 12–16 (6th ed. 1961).

Conventions and treaties, of course, have not been limited to resolving allocation of the second authority function (the power to prescribe policy), but also have been made with respect to adjudicatory jurisdiction (the power to apply policy), and recognition of foreign judgments (the power to enforce policy). An example of a convention for allocation of the power to apply policy is the Warsaw Convention of 1929 (for discussion and summary see Honig, *The Legal Status of Aircraft* 115 (1956) and Verplaetse, *Sources of Private International Law*, 7 Int. and Comp. L.Q. 405–416 (1958).

Conventions with respect to the second authority function are especially difficult to formulate because of the utopian character of universality in choice of law (see Niboyet, *Territoriality and Universal Recognition of Rules of Conflict of Laws,* 65 Harv. L. Rev. 582, 584 (1952). For a recent successful choice-of-law statute, see Uniform Commercial Code, Sec. 1–105(1), which has been adopted by a majority of U.S. states and requires application of the Code to any transaction bearing a reasonable relation to the forum state unless the parties otherwise agree. See also, The Universal Copyright Convention (Sept. 1952) Article I and Article II, Secs. 1 and 2.

With respect to conventions concerning enforcement of foreign judgments, see Anton, *The Recognition of Divorce and Legal Separations* 18 Int. and Comp. L.Q. 620 (1969) discussing the Draft Convention on the Recognition of Divorces and Legal Separations signed at the Hague, Oct. 26, 1968. See Toepper, *Comments on Sec. 20 of the Rome Convention,* 19 J. of A.L. and Comm. 420–30 (1954).

In the United States, recognition of sister-state judgments is guaranteed by the "full faith and credit" clause of the Federal Constitution, see Von Mehren and Trautman, *The Law of Multistate Problems* 840 f. (1965).

[16] American courts have frequently used the term "comity" to express the recognition of a foreign judgment. This term has been defined as "the recognition which one nation allows within its territory to the legislative, executive and judicial acts of another nation, having due regard both to international duty and convenience, and to the rights of its own citizens or of other persons who are under the protection of its laws," Hilton v. Guyot, 159 U.S. 113, 163–64 (1895). English courts speak of the "legal obligation" of foreign judgments, see Cheshire, *Private International Law* 629–30 (6th ed. 1961). The obligation theory is based on the idea that foreign judgment, rendered by a court of competent jurisdiction, creates a contractual or quasi-contractual obligation. The theory brings a fictitious contract into play. See Wolff, *Private International Law* (1950).

[17] Von Mehren and Trautman, *The Law of Multistate Problems* 834 (1965).

[18] Von Mehren and Trautman, *ibid* at 835 have outlined this recognition as follows:

> A desire to avoid the duplication of effort and consequent waste involved in recon-
> sidering a matter that has already been litigated; a policy against making the
> availability of local enforcement the decisive element, as a practical matter, in

plaintiff's decisions respecting the initiation of litigation, as well as a desire to protect defendants from exploitation by unsuccessful plaintiffs of further choice among forums; an interest in fostering the elements of stability and unity essential to an international order in which many aspects of life are not confined within the limits of any single jurisdiction; a concern to protect the successful litigant from harrassing or evasive tactics on the part of his previously unsuccessful opponent; and a belief, in certain classes of cases, that the rendering of jurisdiction is a more appropriate forum than would be the recognizing jurisdiction either because the former was a more convenient forum or because as the predominantly concerned jurisdiction or for some other reason its views as to the merits should prevail.

[19] A critical examination of the "rules" or "factors" which have influenced enforcement or non-enforcement of foreign judgments will not be made in this article. Such decisions are described under various labels. Most decision-makers would decline recognition of a foreign judgment if the foreign court had no "competent jurisdiction," see, *e.g.*, Wolff, *Private International Law* 258–69 (1950). Generally, the prerequisite to enforcement of a foreign judgment is that it must meet certain standards of morality and justice; hence, a judgment obtained by fraud, whether on the part of one of the parties or the court, would not be recognized, see, *e.g.*, Wolff, *id.*, at 267–70. A court may refuse to enforce a foreign decision as being contrary to natural justice or failing to give a party due notice and thus denying the opportunity of presenting his case, Wolff, *id.*, at 266.

[20] For an enlightening comparison of recognition of foreign judgments in different legal systems, see Von Mehren and Trautman, *The Law of Multistate Problems* 836–37 f. (1965).

[21] See Stumberg, *Principles of Conflict of Laws* 108–110 (1937); Reese, *The Status in this Country of Judgments Rendered Abroad*, 50 Colum.L. Rev. 783 (1950); see also Dowling and Gunther, *Constitutional Law* 544 f. (1965).

[22] Von Mehren, *Conflict of Laws in a Federal System, Some Perspectives*, 18 Int. and Comp. L.Q. 681, 685 (1969):

> Whatever may have once been the fact, today both family and economic life within the United States frequently transcends the legal unit defined by the territorial boundaries of a given state. As a moment's reflection reveals, the combination of varied and quite intense multistate activities with the legal arrangements already described creates a veritable conflict-of-laws paradise—at least for the scholar and the lawyer, if not always for the individual citizen with legal difficulties. In a real sense, the United States is a conflict-of-laws laboratory, a uniquely favorable setting in which to observe—and to reflect upon—the problems of private international law.

[23] *Ibid*:

> The first proposition of general significance that can be validated on the basis of the experience of the American Federal system is that *no private international law structure serving communities with substantial social and economic relations inter se can ultimately function effectively in terms of approaches based solely on the policy of one jurisdiction*, whether that jurisdiction be—to name a few of the many possibilities that have been embraced in the past—the forum, the place of contracting, or the place where the tort occurred. (Emphasis added.)

[24] See Tiernan v. Westext Transport Inc. 295 F.Supp. 1256, 1262 (R.I. 1969).

[25] It should be noted that this article does not consider what some writers label, with

varying definitions, a "false conflict;" rather it is submitted that there is "no such animal." For example, the observation that the laws of two interested states are identical does not create a "false conflict;" instead, it points to the conclusion that no matter which law is applied the outcome will be the same. The fallacy inherent in the term "false conflict" is that it creates the impression that choice of law is irrelevant in such a situation. Thus writers who discuss "false conflicts" tend to forget that to conclude that the laws of two states do not materially vary, it is necessary first to examine the respective laws and their underlying policies. For an excellent discussion of the various ways different theoreticians define false conflicts, see Juenger, *Choice of Law in Interstate Torts,* 118 U. Penna. L.R. 202, 211–12 (1969); see also Leflar, *American Conflicts Law* 237–41 (1968); Cavers, *The Choice of Law Process* 30, 75, 82, 89, 128, 137, 167 (1965); Ehrenzweig, *Private International Law* 175 f., 216 n. 1 (1967); Heath v. Zellmer, 35 Wis. 2d 578, 589–90, 592–95; Zelinger v. State Sand and Gravel Co., 156 N.W.2d 466, 470 (1968).

[26] Professor Myres S. McDougal intimated that certain broad policies indeed govern the choice-of-law process and wrote as follows upon the dawn of the space age, McDougal, Laswell, Vlasic, *Law and Public Order in Space* 662 (1963):

> The overriding objective sought in the pre-space earth arena by the general community in its allocation among the different particular communities of competences to prescribe and apply policies with respect to particular events has been, as in other areas of international law, that of clarifying and implementing the common interests of all the different particular communities. The historic aspiration of the established process of authoritative decision, embracing large parts of both public and private international law, has been, regarding the planet as a whole as one huge shareable resource or domain exploitable for the benefit of all mankind, to encourage and facilitate the movement of resources and peoples across particular territorial boundaries best designed to promote the greatest production of net values (the largest possible "pie" in goods and services) and to secure the most equitable distribution of these values by persuasive, nonviolent processes among all peoples.

[27] Both Lorenzen and Cook were pioneers in outlining a modern approach to conflict of laws urging departure from the traditional rules. See particularly, Lorenzen, *Territoriality, Public Policy and Conflict of Laws,* 33 Yale L.J. 736, 745 (1924) and Cook, *The Logical and Legal Bases of the Conflict of Laws,* 33 Yale L.J. 456, 487; *The Logical and Legal Bases of Conflict of Laws* (1942). The work of these two men hastened the evolution of conflict of laws "from a mechanical oversimplified machine to a body of legal principles incorporating some of the most profound of our notions of social policy," Harper, *Policy Bases of the Conflict of Laws, Reflections on Rereading Professor Lorenzen's Essays,* 56 Yale L.J. 1155, 1156–57 (1947).

[28] See Note, *Post Transaction or Occurrence Events in Conflict of Laws,* 69 Colum. L. Rev. 843, 847 (1969).

[29] The most notorious escape device was bowing to "public policy" as an excuse for not applying the "applicable law." Harper, *Policy Bases of the Conflict of Laws, Reflections on Rereading Professor Lorenzen's Essays,* 56 Yale L.J. 1155, 1175 (1947) remarked:

> The "public policy" formula is a striking instance of how courts have thrown off the judicial inhibitions of the jurisdictional or territorial approach to the conflict of laws . . . This escape from what would be regarded as an improper or undesirable result has, perhaps, become palatable because it is treated as an "exception" to the usual treatment.

See also, Currie, *Notes on Methods and Objectives in the Conflict of Laws*, (1959) Duke L.J. 171, 175.

Other escape devices included novel and ingenious "characterization." (See generally, Hoff, *Intensity Principle in the Conflict of Laws*, 39 Vir. L. Rev. 437, 442–45 (1933) and particularly Levy v. Daniel's U-Drive Auto Renting Co., 108 Conn. 333 (1922) *cf.* Young v. Masci, 289 U.S. 253 (1933); the concept of "fraud on the law," (See Cheatham, Griswold, Goodrich and Reese, *Cases and Materials on Conflict of Laws* 519 (4th ed. 1957)); manipulation of "connecting factors," (Compare Mutual Life Ins. Co. v. Dodge, 246 U.S. 357 (1918); see also Currie *op. cit.* at 175); "alternative references," (see Morse, *Characterization, Shadow or Substance?* 49 Colum. L. Rev. 1027, 1057 (1949)); and expansions or contractions of the dichotomy between "substance" and "procedure" (See generally Leflar, *American Conflicts Law* 287–90 (1968)).

[30] See e.g., Grant v. McAuliffe, 41 Cal. 2d 859, 264 P. 2d 444 (1953).

[31] See *e.g.*, Kilberg v. Northeast Airlines, 9 N.Y.2d 34, 172 N.E.2d 526, 21 N.Y.S. 2d 133 (1961).

[32] See *e.g., University of Chicago v. Dater, 277 Mich. 658, 270 N.W. 175 (1936).

[33] Von Mehren, *Conflict of Laws in a Federal System, Some Perspectives*, 18 Int. and Comp. L.Q. 681, 687 (1969) wrote:

> American thinking tends to assume that jurisdictional and recognition problems are less complicated and, perhaps more important, that they are susceptible of solutions that can give quite firm and authoritative guidance for future decisions. These assumptions go far towards explaining why the Supreme Court of the United States has been willing to regulate state practice under constitutional provisions in the jurisdictional and recognition fields but not in choice of law.
>
> Today there is in the United States general agreement that choice of law is intrinsically a highly complex area, one in which it is often impossible to do more than formulate directive rules and principles, indicating the elements in the situation that a court should consider in seeking to resolve a choice-of-law question.

[34] Yntema, *The Hornbook Method and the Conflict of Laws*, 37 Yale L.J. 468. 480 (1928) observed:

> The important problem in the conflict of laws is not the formulation of the rule but the ascertainment of the cases to which, and the extent of which, it applies. And this, even if we are seeking solely uniformity in the administration of justice, will lead us again to the circumstances of the concrete case, and to the careful study of foreign practices. The reason why the general principle cannot control is because it does not inform.

[35] Ehrenzweig, *Conflict of Laws*, Part 1, p. 16 (1959) noted:

> Above all, courts have resorted to the exception of "public policy" in order to reach the proper result where a rigid formula would have sacrificed common sense to "logic" . . . (W)hat at first appears as an exception based on public policy or other general considerations, at some points must become a new conflicts rule demanding formulation without regard to dogmatic conceptions such as vested rights, legislative jurisdiction, or local sovereignty.

Judge Traynor also expressed the same sentiment in *Law and Social Change in a Democratic Society* (1956) U. Ill. L. For. 230, 234:

> (T)he compelling logic of the proposition that . . . local law is supreme has made it necessary to search for acceptable doctrines to govern the making of exceptions to the local law, and serve as the basis of a new and realistic system of conflict of laws.

[36] Lorenzen forcefully attacked traditional formalists in *Territoriality, Public Policy and the Conflict of Laws*, 33 Yale L.J. 736, 744 (1924) as follows:

> (T)o those who believe that there ought to be as far as possible one body of rules governing the problems of the conflict of laws in all countries, or to those who believe that the domestic rules should be the expression of fundamental principles, nothing can be gained by hiding the truth and making it appear that certain rules govern in the nature of things. Such rules have not been discovered by the theoretical writers of the greatest eminence, nor has a consistent set of rules been worked out as yet by either British or American courts . . . Sound progress in this field of law, as in all other departments of knowledge, can be made only if the actual facts be faced, which shows that the adoption of the one rule or the other depends entirely upon considerations of policy which each sovereign state must determine for itself.

[37] Currie, *Notes on Methods and Objectives in the Conflict of Laws* (1959) Duke L.J. 171, 174.

[38] Restatement (second) Conflict of Laws, Secs. 379, 379-a, and 379-b (Tent. Draft No. 9, 1964). See Harper and Taintor, *Cases and Other Materials on Judicial Technique in Conflict of Laws* 173–208 (1957); Sohn, *New Bases for Solution of Conflict of Laws Problems*, 55 Harv. L.Rev. 978 (1942); Morris, *The Proper Law of a Tort*, 64 Harv. L.Rev. 881 (1951); Childres, *Toward the Proper Law of a Tort*, 40 Tex. L.Rev. 336 (1962).

[39] Preference for the law of the forum has its strongest supporter in Ehrenzweig. See Ehrenzweig, *A Treatise on the Conflict of Laws* (1962) and *Foreign Guest Statutes and Forum Accidents: Against the Desperanto of State Interests*, 68 Colum. L.Rev. 49 (1968); *Private International Law* (1967).

Von Mehren has criticized the forum-oriented approach as follows, *Conflict of Laws in a Federal System, Some Perspectives*, 18 Int. and Comp. L.Q. 681, 686 (July, 1969):

> Probably because it permits certain short-cuts and simplifications, the single-jurisdiction fallacy still persists—it is perhaps seen, for example, in the writings of Professors Currie and Ehrenzweig. However, the dominant theme in contemporary American thinking in choice of law is clearly a recognition that more than one community may have relevant rules and policies and that these should, in a sound conflicts system, be mutually accommodated to the greatest extent practicable.

See Currie, *Notes on Methods and Objectives in the Conflict of Laws* (1959) Duke L.J. 171. Currie has suggested that when a court is asked to apply the law of another state, it should first consider the policies of each state and should apply the law of the forum, where it appears that no state has a greater interest than another, or where it appears that conflicts of interest will result in a different disposition, depending on where the action is brought, *Comments on Babcock v. Jackson, A Recent Development in Conflict of Laws*, 63 Colum. L. Rev. 1212, 1233 (1963).

[40] See *e.g.*, Leflar, *Choice Influencing Considerations in Conflict of Laws,* 41 N.Y. U.L.Rev. 267 (1966).

[41] The "most significant relationship" test, as set forth in the Restatement (Conflict of Laws) 29 (Proposed Official Draft II, 1968) provides as follows:

> The rights and liabilities of the parties with respect to an issue in tort are determined by the local law of the state, which, as to that issue, has the most significant relationship with the occurrence and the parties.

For comment, see Shapira, Amos. *A Transatlantic Inspiration: The Proper Law of the Tort Doctrine,* 33 Mod.L.Rev. 27 (Jan. 1970).

[42] See cases cited in Tiernan v. Westext Transport, Inc., 295 F.Supp. 1256, n. 5 at p. 1262–63 (1969).

[43] Cavers' most complete statement of his theory may be found in *The Choice of Law Process* (1965). Ehrenzweig predicted that this work "will for some time to come, be regarded as the most important contribution of our era in this field," *A Counter-Revolution in Conflicts Law? From Beale to Cavers,* 76 Harv. L. Rev. 377 (1967). For reviews of this work, see Cheatham, *Book Rev.* 19 Vandervilt L.Rev. 558 (1966); Greenspan, *Book Rev.* 27 U.Pitt.L.Rev. 924 (1966); Kroner, *Book Rev.*, 41 N.Y.U.L.Rev. 851 (1966); Leflar, *Conflict of Laws,* 1966 Ann.Sur. Am. L. 1 and *Book Rev,* N.Y.L. Forum 178 (1966); and Reese, *Book Rev.*, 55 Fordham L.Rev. (1966).

[44] Cavers, *Choice of Law Process* (1965):

> Another possibility, indeed, a probability, is that, in the course of decision, the principles which I have stated in very broad terms—again, more for purpose of exposition than from conviction—would be subjected to fission as distinctions were drawn on grounds that I have not attempted to identify and consider.

For some previous attempts to define controlling policies relevant to conflict of laws, see the following: Goodrich, *Public Policy in the Law of Conflicts,* 36 W. Va.L.Q. 156 (1930); Heilman, *Judicial Method and Economic Objectives in Conflict of Laws,* 20 Can. Bar. Rev. 479 (1942); Harper, *Policy Bases of the Conflict of Laws,* 56 Yale L.J. 1155 (1947); Kronstein, *Crises of "Conflict of Laws"* 37 Geo.L.J. 483 (1949); Morse, *Characterization, Shadow or Substance?* 49 Colum. L.Rev. 1027 (1949); Salonga, *Conflict of Laws: A Critical Survey of Doctrines and Practices and the Case for a Policy-Oriented Approach,* 25 Phila. L.J. 501 (1950); Briggs, *"Legislative Jurisdiction Principle" In a Policy-Centered Conflict of Laws,* 4 Int. and Comp. L.Q. 329 (1955); Dainow, *Policy Problems in Conflict Cases,* 35 Tex. L. Rev. 759 (1957); Kramer, *Interests and Policy Clashes in Conflict of Laws,* 13 Rutgers L. Rev. 523 (1959); Currie, *Notes on Methods and Objectives in the Conflict of Laws* (1959) Duke L.J. 171.

[45] Cheatham and Reese outlined nine "policy factors" in *Choice of the Applicable Law,* 52 Colum. L. Rev. 959 (1952), and Yntema outlined seventeen policy considerations which he further separated under two main headings—"security" and "comparative justice," *The Objectives of Private International Law,* 35 Can. Bar Rev. 721, 734–35 (1957). For further discussion of the policy principles of these three scholars, see Leflar, *American Conflicts Law* 241–43 (1968).

[46] "Exclusive control" means that all three authority functions are exercised by officials of one state to the exclusion of all other states; whereas, "inclusive control" means that the exercise of the three authority functions is distributed among two or more states. This sharing also comprises sharing of a single authority function, such as the power to prescribe policy among two or more states, in the course of the decisional process, whereby the decision-maker weighs the factors and variables which connect each state with a given controversy and balances such considerations in terms of the broad policy goals.

[47] See McDougal, *International Law, Power and Policy: A Contemporary Conception,* Hague Recueil 165, 198–205 (1953).

[48] Cavers, *The Choice of Law Process* 35 (1965). Cavers has also displayed a preference for territoriality in his seven "principles of preference," *id.*, at 136. (Note: The close of the quotation cited in the text are the words of Judge Wyzanski in Gordon v. Parker, 83 F.Supp. 40, 43 (D.Mass. 1949).)

Cavers has intimated that the traditional conflict of laws rule which favored application of the law of the place of the tort emphasized a territorial concern; whereas, the recent trend of examining policies and other relevant factors to determine choice of law in tort cases, rather than mechanically to apply a rule, reveals a greater concern for people, *i.e.*, it has become distasteful to apply the law of a certain state to persons who have no other relationship to the state save for an accident within its borders, *id.*, at 176.

[49] See note 38, *supra*. The term "connecting factor" is used in decisions and by scholars in two ways. Some use the term as including community policies, as well as personal and territorial factors. This seems to be the way Judge Fuld used the term in the following quotation, Babcock v. Jackson (1963) 2 Lloyd's Rep. 286, 289 (N. Y. Ct. App.):

> The "center of gravity" or "grouping of contacts" doctrine adapted by this court in conflicts cases involving contracts impresses us as likewise affording the appropriate method for accomodating the competing interests in tort cases with multi-state contacts. Justice, fairness and "the best practical result" . . . may best be achieved by giving controlling effect to the law of the jurisdiction, which, with the occurrence or the parties has the greatest concern with the specific issue raised in the litigation . . . The relative importance of the relationships or contacts of the respective jurisdictions is to be evaluated in the light of the issues, the character of the tort and the relative purpose of the tort rules involved.

The *Restatement (Second) Conflict of Laws* (Tent. Draft No. 9 1964) also includes policies underlying the laws of interested states, see secs. 379, 379-a and comments of Reese, *Conflict of Laws and the Restatement Second*, 28 Law and Contemp. Prob. 679, 681 (1963).

On the other hand, some decision-makers use the term "connecting factors" in a manner whereby the old rules are treated as "factors" to be added up for each side in such fashion that the side with the most "connecting factors" wins. Thus, the "connecting factors," instead of having significance relative to state interests involved, have attained significance only in terms of metaphysical theory, lending to decisions a very capricious air. Thus, the "connecting factor" becomes a manipulative escape device. Compare Mutual Life Ins. Co. v. Liebing 259 U.S. 209 (1909) with New York Life Ins. Co. v. Dodge 246 U.S. 357 (1918).

[50] See, *e.g.*, Turner v. Pfluger, 487 F.2d 648 (7th Cir. 1969).

[51] Katzenbach summarized this view as follows, *Conflict on an Unruly House: Reciprocal Claims and Tolerances in Interstate and International Law*, 65 Yale L.J. 1087, 1127 (1956):

> The problem is not—and indeed, never has been—one of finding the greatest number of contacts, or the "center of gravity" of the transaction, or the "proper law" by crude addition of contacts, but one of the measuring the policies of the several states against the facts of the particular controversy, the rules against their origin and purpose. These formulae are useful only in that they are flexible. Whether a foreign rule can in fairness or does in policy, touch a particular transaction is dependent upon the evaluation of the policy, the parties, the events and the contact.

[52] (1970) 2 W.L.R. 728 (H.L.(E.)), reversing, (1969) 1 W.L.R. 377 (C.A.).

[53] Sharing of authority has two meanings:

> (1) Sharing of total authority, *i.e.*, sharing of the three authority functions among two or more claimants.
> (2) Sharing of one authority function. The concept of sharing of the authority of the power to prescribe policy in the decisional process is basic to the operation of private international law.

[54] See Falk, *International Jurisdiction: Horizontal and Vertical Conceptions of Legal Order*, 32 Temple L.Q. 295 (1959).

[55] This policy-goal has sometimes been described as "comity," a notion of voluntary concession to other states, namely acts of courtesy dictated by *comitas gentium*. (This article avoids this term as descriptive of the second basic policy goal because of confusion with the term "comity" as frequently used to describe mutual recognition by states to foreign-state judgments, *i.e.*, the recognition of the power of another state to exercise the third authority function; see note 16, *supra*.) One of the greatest proponents of the theory of comity as the basis for prescribing foreign law was Story, who was greatly influenced by Dutch legal scholarship (especially by the writings of Ulric Huber and Johannes Voet). See Story, *Commentaries on the Conflict of Laws, Foreign and Domestic* (8th ed. 1883); Wheaton, a contemporary of Story, observed, *Elements of International Law* 112 (ed. 1866):

> (T)he application of foreign laws is founded upon reciprocal wants, [so that a state's] subjects] may find in foreign countries a reciprocal protection for their interests.

A British contemporary of Story and Wheaton who was an outstanding advocate of the comity doctrine was Lord Phillimore, see 4 Phillimore, *Commentaries upon International Law, Private International Law or Comity* 8 (3rd ed. 1874).

Many juristic writings and judgments have been based on the principle of comity. See especially Barry, *Comity*, 12 Va. L.Rev. 253, 364 (1926). (This writer regarded the doctrine of comity as based upon the principle of reciprocity and identified comity as the root of the second and third authority functions, choice of law and enforcement of judgments); see also Kuhn, *Comparative Commentaries on Private International Law* 28–33 (1947); Nussbaum, *Principles of Private International Law* 17 *and authorities cited* (1943); Wolff, *Private International Law* 14–15 (1950); Graveson, *The Conflict of Laws* 9 (1955); Ehrenzweig, *Conflict of Laws* 5 (1959); Lenhoff, *Reciprocity: The Legal Aspects of a Perenial Idea*, 49 N.Y.U. L.Rev. 619 (1955); Katzenbach, *Conflicts on an Unruly Horse: Reciprocal Claims and Tolerances in Interstate and International Law* 65 Yale L.J. 1087, 1102–04 (1956). Hilton v. Guyot, 159 U.S. 113 (1895); Disconto Gesellschaft v. Umbreit, 203 U.S. 570 (1908); Opinion of Judge Cardozo clarifying concept of comity, Loucks v. Standard Oil Co. of N.Y., 224 N.Y. 99 (1918); Simpson v. Fogo (1863) 1 Homm. and M. 195, 247; Lorentzen v. Lydden and Co. Ltd., 58 T.L.R. 178 (1942); United Africa Co. Ltd. v. Owners of M.V. Tolten (The Toltin) (1946) 2 All E.R. 372 (C.A.); Szalathay-Stacho v. Fink (1947) 1 K.G. 1; *Re* a Debtor (1948) 2 All E.R. 533, 539 (C.A.), *aff'd sub. nom.* Theophile v. Solicitor General (1950) 1 All E.R. 405 (H.L.).

[56] See note 14, *supra*.

[57] *Ibid.*

[58] (1970) 2 W.L.R. 728 (H.L.(E.)).

[59] *Ibid.*, at 734.

[60] *Ibid.*, at 735.

[61] *Ibid.*, at 738.

[62] *Ibid.*, at 741.

[63] *Ibid.*, at 744.

[64] 372 U.S. 10, (1963) A.M.C. 283. An American company was the beneficial owner of vessels which sailed regularly between the U.S. and Latin America for purposes of transporting goods produced by the said company. Each vessel was owned by a foreign subsidiary of the American company, was crewed by foreign seamen recruited in Honduras who were members of a Honduran union, and flew the flag of a Latin American country. However, the American parent company managed the business of all shipping, such as designation of ports of call, cargoes and sailing dates.

⁶⁵ 372 U.S. 24, (1963) A.M.C. 293. A Liberian corporation, wholly-owned by Italian nationals, operated cruise ships which flew the Liberian flag and were manned by foreign crews. A New York corporation acted as agent for the cruise business.

⁶⁶ Compare Ehrenzweig, *Private International Law* 209 f. (1967).

⁶⁷ See Falk, note 54, *supra*.

⁶⁸ See note 46, *supra*.

⁶⁹ See note 14, *supra*.

⁷⁰ See Falk, note 54, *supra*.

⁷¹ See McDougal, *International Law, Power and Policy: A Contemporary Conception*, Hague Recueil 137 (1953).

⁷² Yntema suggested that the three objectives of private international law are (1) the minimization of conflicts; (2) cooperation among states; and (3) the respect for the interests of states, *The Objectives of Private International Law*, 35 Can. Bar Rev. 721, 734 (1957).

⁷³ As mentioned in note 16, *supra*, the theory of "comity" urges the importance of stabilizing sovereign relations with respect to the third authority function, embodying the recognition and enforcement of foreign judgments. A further discussion of this subject is beyond the scope of this article, which focuses on the second authority function, namely prescription of policy (choice of law).

⁷⁴ Unless otherwise indicated, the term "parties" includes affected states and individuals involved in a controversy not actually before a tribunal, as well as actual litigants named in a controversy.

⁷⁵ Harper, *Policy Bases of the Conflict of Laws, Reflections on Rereading Professor Lorenzen's Essays*, 56 Yale L.J., 1155, 1159 (1947).

Harper and Taintor observed, *Cases and Other Materials on Judicial Technique in Conflict of Laws* 58 (1937):

> (T)he problem is presented whether uniformity in result can ever be wholly attained. If it be assumed or demonstrated that complete uniformity is impossible, the problem still remains to what extent should this policy be subordinated to other policies, and to what extent, therefore, the tribunal which is adjudicating a particular controversy will defer to the legal ideas of other communities.

⁷⁶ See note 52, *supra*.

⁷⁷ Heath v. Zellmer, 35 Wis.2d 578, 596 (1967).
Travers v. Holley (1953) 2 All E.R. 794, 800 (C.A.). Husband unsuccessfully contested a divorce his wife had obtained in New South Wales by arguing that neither he nor his wife had obtained a domicile of choice there. See also Auten v. Auten, 308 N.Y. 155, 124 N.E.2d 99 (1954) and Comment in Cheatham Griswold, Reese, Rosenberg, *Conflicts of Laws, Cases and Materials,* 5th ed. (1964) at 534; Leflar, *Conflict of Laws* (1963) Ann. Sur. Am.L. 57, 70. In Auten, a husband and wife, who were married in England, executed a separation agreement in New York which included a clause stipulating that neither party would commence an action relating to the agreement, separation, marriage or divorce. When her ex-husband defaulted in payments under the agreement, the wife commenced an action for separation in England on advice of counsel. Still unable to collect any alimony from her elusive ex-husband, she thereafter went to New York to bring an action on the agreement, and the husband's defense was that under New York law this repudiated the agreement on the basis of the clause mentioned above. The lower court (Appellate Division) had held summary judgment for the ex-husband. The Court of Appeals, per opinion of Judge Fuld, expressed doubt that such was the law of New York, but reversed on the ground that English law should apply, because that was where the seat

of the marital relationship had been. The wife had come to New York to make the agreement as a result of the husband's remarriage in the U.S. to an American woman.

[79] Regina v. Brentwood Superintendent of Marriages, *Ex parte* Areas (1968) 3 H.L.R. 531 (Q.B.). Denied order of *mandamus* compelling defendant to issue marriage license on application by a Spanish spinster who wished to marry a divorced Italian national. Both she and her prospective husband were domiciliaries of Switzerland. The Swiss courts barred their marriage, notwithstanding the fact that the man's former wife had remarried.

[80] See generally Heilman, *Judicial Method and Economic Objectives in Conflict of Laws*, 43 Yale L.J. 1082, 1168–69 (1934).

[81] Yntema, The Objectives of Private International Law, 35 Can. Bar Rev. 721, 735 (1957) stated:

> For the purposes of conflicts law, the objective of security seeks to maximize uniformity in defining the legal and socio-economic consequences of transactions and events by the selection and application of the corresponding law . . . From a jurisdictional point of view . . . the principle implies reciprocity and respect for the interests of the states concerned, in particular it requires deference to the effective law, namely, that of the state which is in a position to control. Without such cooperation in regard to the policies the respective states enforce, there will be anarchy in the choice of law instead of the certainty that business and commerce demand.

[82] See Ehrenzweig, *Private International Law* 76 (1967).

[83] Hoff contended that this policy, sometimes called "the doctrine of efficacy," was adopted from the Roman law maxim of *favor negotii*, Intensity Principle in the Conflict of Laws, 39 Vir. L. Rev. 437, 453 (1953).

[84] See authorities cited in Harper, *Policy Bases of the Conflict of Laws, Reflections on Rereading Professor Lorenzen's Essays*, 56 Yale L.J. 1155, 1168–70 (1956); See also, Royal Private International Law Committee, 4th Rep. (Formal Validity of Wills) 3–9 (July 1958); Morris, 22 Modern L. Rev. 65 (1959); Bland, 8 Int. & Comp. L.Q. 213 (1959); Cohn, 22 Modern L. Rev. 413 (1959); *Formal Validity of Wills*: Committee's Rep., 266 L.T. 218 (1958). Lorenzen suggested the principle of "alternative reference" with respect to will formalitites, *Validity of Wills, Deeds and Contracts as Regards Form in the Conflict of Laws,* 20 Yale L.J. 427 (1911). See Morse, *Characterization, Shadow or Substance?* 49 Colum. L. Rev. 1027, 1057, n. 119, 1059–1060. See also, with respect to trusts, Shannon v. Irving Trust Co. 275 N.Y. 95, 9 N.E. 792 (1937) and Land, *Trusts in the Conflict of Laws* 61, 71 (1940).

[85] See Zogg. v. Penn Mutual Life Ins. Co., 276 F.2d 861 (2d Cir. 1960), plaintiff's decedent, a New York resident, purchased a life insurance policy in Massachusetts while stationed there as a naval officer, and committed suicide before the expiration of two years from the purchase date, which barred recovery of the proceeds under Massachusetts law. The New York Court of Appeals applied New York law, which did not bar recovery. See also Jones v. Metropolitan Life Ins. Co. 158 Misc. 466, 286 N.Y. Supp. 4 (Sup. Ct. 1936). See also Fleet Messenger Service, Inc. v. Life Ins. Co. of No. America, 315 F. 2d 593 (2d Cir. 1963); Lowe's No. Wilkesboro Hardware, Inc. v. Fidelity Mut. Life Ins. Co., 319 F. 2d 469 (4th Cir. 1963); White v. Motor Vehicle Accident Indem. Corp., 39 Misc. 2d 678, 241 N.Y.S. 2d 566 (Sup. Ct. 1963). See Urhammer v. Olson, 39 Wis. 2d 447 (1967), a "grouping of contacts" decision which presented a conflict between Wisconsin insurance law, which prohibited family exclusion clauses, and Minnesota law, which absolved Minnesota insurers from liability to members of insureds' families. The

facts were that as a result of an automobile accident in Wisconsin between a car driven by a Wisconsin resident and one driven by a Minnesota resident with his wife as passenger, the said wife sued the said Wisconsin resident and his insurer. The latter sought contribution from the insurer of the plaintiff's husband. The court found in favor of Minnesota law on the following grounds:

(1) The husband's insurance contract was made and delivered in Minnesota.

(2) The purpose of Minnesota law was to protect insurers from liability to insured parties who are likely to be partial in cases of injury where there are close family ties.

(3) It was not against the public policy of Wisconsin to recognize and enforce an inter-spousal immunity clause in a sister-state insurance contract.

(4) Minnesota courts enforced such contracts.

The court made the following statement distinguishing contract and tort aspects of stability and meeting expectations of parties, *id.*, at 451.

> There are no significant contacts with Wisconsin. While the appellants correctly state that the place of the accident and the residence of one defendant and his insurance carrier are in Wisconsin, these factors, though relevant to the tort aspects of this case, have nothing to do with the contract question. Certainly one would not argue that the policy limits in this contract would change when state lines are crossed.

cf. Clough v. Liberty Mutual Ins. Co., 282 F. Supp. 553 (E.D.Wis. 1968).

[86] See p. 292 ff. *supra*.

[87] *Policy Bases of the Conflict of Laws, Reflections on Rereading Lorenzen's Essays*, 56 Yale L.J. 1155, 1174 (1947).

[88] See International Shoe Co. v. Washington, 326 U.S. 310 (1945), which equated justice with "fair play." Charles Rembar has expressed the role of justice in enlightening decision-makers regarding bases of decisions and litigants as to the reasons they are successful or unsuccessful, as follows, *Xenophelia in Congress: Ad Interim Copyright and the Manufacturing Clause*, 69 Colum. L, Rev. 770, 774 (1969):

> The function of judicial opinion, of course, is enlightenment, for the benefit of other courts, the bar and eventually the public, and—last but not least but not totally unimportant—the parties. Justice requires the ruler to tell a man ruled against, who thinks he is right, why he is wrong. More broadly, a system of precedents need reasons as well as results; otherwise the data from which we are to derive principles (or, if you will, base our predictions) are rich in ambiguity and poor in interconnection, too particularized and too scattered to support a legal structure.

[89] Cavers, *A Critique of the Choice-of-Law Problem*, 47 Harv. L. Rev. 173 (1933).

[90] *Ibid.*

[91] See note 52, *supra*.

[92] McDougal and Feliciano, *The Initiation of Coercion: A Multitemporal Analysis*, 52 Am. J. Int. L. 241, 258 (1958). This article was influenced by the analysis presented therein. That in choice of law, it has been recognized that the courts should be governed by a "defined but flexible methodology" rather than rules and exceptions was well expressed by U.S. District Judge Pettine in Tiernan v. Westext Transport Inc., 295 F.Supp. 1256, 1262 (R.I. 1969):

> As this court perceives that methodology, it requires a four-step analysis: (1) what factual contacts are there with the states whose laws are alleged to conflict; (2) what is the nature of the conflict between the laws of those states whose contacts are mini-

mally sufficient constitutionally to allow application of their laws; (3) what are the interests to be considered in choosing the applicable law; (4) weighing those interests, what law should be applied.

[93] These categories comprise a revision of the multifactoral framework outlined in Levy, Yuval, *Delimitation of State Competence in International Law: A Special Reference to Jurisdiction over Events Aboard Aircraft* 184–87 (1960) (A Doctoral Thesis on file at the Yale Law School Library, Yale University).

[94] See generally, Leflar, *American Conflicts Law* 139–43, 206–16 (1968).

[95] See comments of Cavers in Cheatham, Griswold, Goodrich and Reese, *Cases and Materials on Conflict of Laws* 539 (4th ed. 1957). Legitimate considerations which may cause difference in prosecution and outcome of a decision or decisions on similar facts, depending on the forum where an action is brought, are noted in the following statement of Von Mehren, commenting on choice of law in the United States, *Conflict of Laws in a Federal System, Some Perspectives*, 18 Int. and Comp. L.Q. 681, 682 (July 1969):

> There will be differences that can be important between the procedures followed in the several possible courts. For example, the federal courts provide more comprehensive pre-trial procedures—including wide opportunitites for discovery—than do many state court systems. The general quality of the judges can vary; different types of persons may be likely to serve on the jury because of different practices in making up jury lists. Considerations respecting convenience and expense in litigating will play a role; there may be significant advantages from this point of view in prosecuting the matter in a court near the place where the accident occurred.

[96] See Note, *Post Transaction or Occurrence Events in Conflict of Laws*, 69 Colum. L. Rev. 843 (1969).

[97] 12 N.Y. 2d 473, 191 N.E. 2d 279, 240 N.Y.S. 2d 743 (1963). Compare Clark v. Clark, 107 N.H. 351, 222 A. 2d 205 (1966). See Leflar, *Conflict of Laws* (1963) Ann. Sur. Am. L. 12–13; see also Kopp v. Rechtzigel 141 N.W. 516 (1966); Wilcox v. Wilcox, 26 Wis. 2d 617, 133 N.W. 2d 408 (1965).

[98] A copy of Tooker v. Lopez, No. 356 (N.Y., May 1969) was not available in Israel; for summary, see 69 Colum. L. Rev., note 83 at 864 (May 1969).

[99] Among commentaries, see Cavers *et al, Comments on Babcock v. Jackson, Recent Development in Conflict of Laws*, 63 Colum. L. Rev. 1222 (1963); *The Proper Law of the Tort Again*, 79 L.Q.R. 484 (1963); Dicey and Morris, *The Conflict of Laws* 916–18 (8th ed. 1967); see notes to dissenting opinion of Chief Justice Hallows, Conklin v. Horner, 38 Wis. 2d 468, 157 N.W. 2d 579, 588 f. (1968). Compare Boys v. Chaplin, 2 All E.R. 1085 (H.L. Aug. 1969) citing Babcock, wherein the English law of measure of damages was applied to the case of two English officers involved in a motor accident while stationed in Malta. The analysis in tort cases by means of "connecting factors." in place of application of the *lex loci delicti* rule or one of the various English exceptions. Consideration of this decision is not expanded here in view of the fact that several American courts have already progressed beyond analysis by "connecting factors" to a policy-oriented approach, as discussed in this article. See Shapira, Amos, *A Transatlantic Inspiration: "The Proper Law of the Tort" Doctrine*, 33 Mod. L. Rev. 27 (Jan. 1970) and Graveson, *Towards a Modern Applicable Law in Torts*, 85 L.Q.R. 505, 508 (1969). Compare Krieger v. Amigues (1963) 2 Gazette du Palais 355, Goldman, note 91 J. Droit Int. 103 (1964) where French law was applied to a French defendant who negligently killed a French plaintiff's son in an auto

collision in Germany, thus marking departure from the application of the "law of the place of the tort" rule traditionally employed by French courts. See Dym v. Gordon, 16 N.Y. 2d 120, 209 N.E. 2d 463 (1965); Macey v. Rozbicki, 18 N.Y. 2d 289, 221 N.E. 2d 380, 274 N.Y.S. 2d 591 (1966). See Kell v. Henderson, 26 A.D. 2d 595, 270 N.Y.S. 2d 552 (3d Dept. 1966), Rosenberg and Trautman, *Two Views on Kell v. Henderson, An Opinion for the New York Court of Appeals*, 67 Colum. L. Rev. 459 (1967); Ehrenzweig, *Foreign Guest Statutes and Forum Accidents: Against the Desperanto of State Interests*, 68 Colum. L. Rev. 49 (1968).

[100] Babcock v. Jackson, *supra*, note 97.

[101] Dym v. Gordon and Macey v. Rosbicki, *supra* note 99 and Tooker v. Lopez, *supra*, note 98; compare Turner v. Pfluger, 407 F. 2d 648 (7th Cir. 1969).

[102] Kell v. Henderson, *supra*, note 99.

[103] Cushman v. Evans, 249 F.Supp. 273 (S.D.N.Y. 1966); compare Turner v. Pfluger, 407 F. 2d 648 (7th Cir. 1969).

[104] Dym v. Gordon, *supra*, note 99.

[105] See note 103, *supra*.

[106] See Cavers, *The Choice of Law Process* 295 (1965). See also, reference to appellant's brief in Heath v. Zellmer, 35 Wis. 2d 578, 588 (1966).

[107] Note 99, *supra*.

[108] Note 97, *supra*. For detailed discussion, see Cavers, *supra*, note 96 at 296–99, 302 (1965).

[109] Note 99, *supra*.

[110] No. 356 (N.Y. May 1969).

[111] Note 97, *supra*.

[112] Note 99, *supra*.

[113] See 69 Colum. L. Rev., note 83 at 684 (1969).

[114] Note 99, *supra*.

[115] *Ibid.*

[116] Note 97, *supra*.

[117] Note 99, *supra*.

[118] Note 97, *supra*.

[119] Leflar, *American Conflicts Law* 233–65 (1968); 1966 Ann. Sur. Am L. 1, 12–13; *Choice Influencing Considerations in Conflicts Law*, 41 N.Y.U. L. Rev. 267 (1968).

[120] 35 Wis. 2d 578, 151 N.W. 2d 664 (1967).

[121] *Ibid.*, at 590. The court did not consider Ohio law.

[122] *Ibid.*, at 590–92.

[123] *Ibid.*, at 592. The court considered the competing policies in great detail, *id.*, 592–95.

[124] Note 120, *supra*.

[125] 35 Wis. 2d at 596:—

> Predictability is one of the choice influencing considerations that deserves special emphasis in consensual arrangements. In those cases, since a legal relationship is entered into by pre-arrangement, it is imperative that the parties know that their rights will be the same, irrespective of the forum, and that their agreement will have the same consequences, irrespective of where the contract is performed or where a dispute in regard to it is resolved. Predictability is an essential in the law of wills, descent and distribution, trusts, contracts, land titles, and conveyancing. It has little or no relevancy to an automobile accident or other tort that was never intended or planned.

[126] 35 Wis. 2d at 596–97.

[127] *Ibid.*, at 597–98.

[128] Note 120, *supra.*

[129] See Cheatham, Griswold, Reese and Rosenberg, *Conflict of Laws* 629–37 (5th ed. 1964). See especially, Von Mehren and Trautman, *The Law of Multistate Problems*, 250–53, 255–59, 342–45, 1242–45, 1297–1302, 1343–54 (1965).

[130] Note 120, *supra.*

[131] Here it is worth noting an old device that was formerly used to avoid the "difficult" task of prescribing foreign law—namely, the "equality of laws" doctrine. See *e.g.* Tidewater Oil Co. v. Waller, 302 F. 2d 638 (10th Cir. 1962). An American employee was injured in the course of employment by an American employer in Turkey. Following the *lex loci delicti* "rule," the U.S. Court of Appeal "applied" Turkish law by assuming that Turkey was a civilized country and would therefore permit recovery on the same grounds as Oklahoma.

[132] U.S. District Court Judge Pettine, Tiernan v. Westext Transport, Inc., 295 F. Supp. 1256, 1264 (1969).

[133] 35 Wis. 2d at 598.

[134] Currie was the principal advocate of the forum-oriented governmental interests approach, see Currie, *Notes on Methods and Objectives in the Conflict of Laws* 1959 Duke L.J. 171. Currie subsequently changed his mind in favor of a weighing and balancing of interests of all states concerned with a choice-of-law question; see Currie, *Selected Essays on the Conflict of Laws* (1963) and *The Disinterested Third State*, 28 *Law & Contemp. Prob.* 754 (1963); see also Juenger, *Choice of Law in Interstate Torts*, 1969 U. Penna. L.Rev. 202, 205–207 (1969).

[135] For further discussion, see Juenger, note 134, *supra* at 230–35.

[136] 35 Wis. 2d at 600.

[137] *Ibid.*, at 602–04.

[138] *Ibid.*

[139] *Ibid.* at 604.

[140] Note 120, *supra.*

[141] *Ibid.*

[142] 38 Wis. 2d 98, 156 N.W. 2d 466 (Feb. 1968). Compare Satchwell v. Vollrath, 293 F.Supp. 533 (E.D. Wis. 1968), an interstate wrongful death action where the U.S. District Court stated a presumption in favor of forum law. Compare also, Angel v. Ray, 285 F. Supp. 64 (E.D. Wis. 1968), where Wisconsin law was applied in a case involving a collision between an Illinois resident with a Wisconsin resident in Tennessee.

[143] 38 Wis. 2d 98, 156 N.W. 2d 466 (Feb. 1968).

[144] 156 N.W. 2d at 472. The format of the Zelinger opinion, unlike that of Heath, did not utilize a three-step method of noting connecting factors, comparing policies, and then reaching conclusions in terms of the "choice-influencing considerations." Instead, the court wrote a brief history of the various choice-of-law theories it had followed before adopting "choice-influencing considerations" analysis.

[145] 156 N.W. 2d at 473.

[146] Note 120, *supra.*

[147] Note 145, *supra.*

[148] *Ibid.*

[149] Note 143, *supra.*

[150] 38 Wis. 2d 468, 157 N.W. 2d 579 (1968).

[151] The defendant had argued in favor of application of Illinois law on the basis that

it was the "reverse situation" (157 N.W. 2d at 582) of Wilcox v. Wilcox (26 Wis. 2d 617, 133 N.W. 2d 408 (1965)), the Wisconsin counterpart of New York's Babcock v. Jackson (Note 97, *supra*.) Both cases involved plaintiff-guests from common law liability states who made short trips with a host-driver from the same state to a bordering guest-statute state. However, in the New York counterpart of Conklin v. Horner, *i.e.* Kell v. Henderson (Note 99, *supra*) the New York Appellate Division applied New York law, in a very superficial opinion without analysis. For an interesting scholarly critique, see Trautman, note 99, *supra*. The accident in Kell had involved two Ontario (guest-statute Canadian province) residents (host and guest) who met with an accident on a short trip to New York. Trautman advocated application of New York law after determining that Ontario law had carved many exceptions to its guest statutes. Query, whether he was not, in effect, applying Ontario law.

[152]   157 N.W. 2d at 587.

[153]   *Ibid.* at 585. This is similar to Trautman's theoretical opinion for Kell v. Henderson (see article cited at note 99, *supra*).

[154]   Note 120, *supra*.

[155]   157 N.W. 2d at 587.

[156]   Note 120, *supra*.

[157]   Note 143, *supra*.

[158]   Note 150, *supra*.

[159]   Note 120, *supra*.

[160]   Reese listed justice as an important policy factor in *Restatement (Second) of Conflict of Laws* Sec. 6(2)(d)(Proposed Official Draft, part 1, May 2, 1967).

[161]   Note 150, *supra*.

[162]   Note 87, *supra*.

[163]   The following cases were originally discussed in Levy, Yuval; *Delimitation of State Competence in International Law: A Special Reference to Jurisdiction over events aboard Aircraft*, Ch. III, *A Multi-Factoral Framework of Inquiry*, p. 182 f. (1960) (Doctoral Thesis on file in the Yale Law School Library, Yale University.)

[164]   345 U.S. 571 (1952).

[165]   46 U.S.C. 688.

[166]   345 U.S. at 582. But compare the view of Ehrenzweig, *Private International Law* 209–10 (1967).

[167]   345 U.S. at 575–76. The Court independently considered Cuban law, which was not urged as applicable by either party. It noted that Cuba did not apply the "locality" test to torts aboard ships of Cuban registry and it concluded that the accident did not substantially affect Cuban interests. Compare The Assunzione (1954) 1 All E.R. 278, Cheshire, *Private International Law* 212–14 (1957); Note, 3 Int. and Comp. L.Q. Rev. 356–59 (1954) and 17 Mod. L. Rev. 255–59 (1954).

[168]   345 U.S. at 575–76.

[169]   Note 164, *supra*.

[170]   137 F. Supp. 288 (1955).

[171]   282 U.S. 234, 51 S.Ct. 111, 75 L.Ed. 312 (1931).

[172]   *Ibid.*

[173]   Note 170, *supra*.

[174]   51 S. Ct. at 112.

[175]   Note 171, *supra*.

[176]   Note 170, *supra*.

[177]   *Ibid.*

[178] Note 171, *supra*.

[179] 252 U.S. 348, 40 S.Ct. 350 (1920).

[180] 38 Stat. 1164 (1915).

[181] Patterson v. The Eudora, 190 U.S. 164, 175, 179, 23 S.Ct. 827, 47 L.Ed. 1002 (1902). Compare McQuade v. Compañía De Vapores San Antonio, S.A. *et al*, 131 F. Supp. 365 (1955), Honduran law was applied in an action by a Greek seaman, who had signed articles in New York for service on a ship of Honduran registry owned by a Panamanian company, to recover wages and other benefits on grounds of allegedly wrongful discharge in Persia. Here it was deemed that American interests in seamen's wages were not substantial.

[182] Note 179, *supra*.

[183] Note 64, *supra*.

[184] Note 65, *supra*.

[185] Note 81, *supra*.

[186] 190 U.S. at 179.

[187] Note 179, *supra*.

[188] Note 181, *supra*.

[189] Note 64, *supra*.

[190] Note 65, *supra*.

[191] (1942) 2 K.B. 202.

[192] 126 St. Cl. 802 (1953).

[193] See *e.g.* Juenger, *Choice of Law in Interstate Torts*, 118 U. Penna. L. Rev. 202, 221 (1969) where Juenger suggests the possibility of a return to the *lex loci delicti* rule, but at the same time mentions that "certain refinements" might be made where the rule is too simplistic.

[194] Harper, *Policy Bases of the Conflict of Laws, Reflections on Rereading Professor Lorenzen's Essays*, 56 Yale L. J. 1155, 1157–58 (1947).

LAWS AND CRIME

CRIMINOLOGY AND THE
PENAL SYSTEM

Franco Ferracuti* Giuseppe Di Gennaro**

The social concept of crime and the reaction to crime has undergone a greater evolution in modern times than has the penal law.

Rather than a manifestation of damage to the individual person, his rights, and property, criminality in present day society is considered a social problem requiring appropriate means for its repression and prevention. This view applies also to other endemic evils which trouble the harmonious evolution of the community.

This sociological view of crime must not, however, obscure the system of moral values on which the penal law is based, and which is the model for individual responsibility.

The recognition (and the reaffirmation) of the human values which sustain the penal imperative is a fundamental requirement for the survival of civilization, since with the advancement of technological progress, the amount and the variety of illicit behavior has been growing. Modern social achievements, which have resulted in an expansion of man's possibilities, seem indeed to be accompanied by erosion of respect for moral norms, and by a greater discrepancy between the normative system and the values system.

New or relatively new concepts, such as those of social deviation, appear frequently in current writings and research, contributing to increased anxiety in those who open-mindedly seek guidance and support from the social and behavioral sciences and from legal principles which no longer seem tenable.

Criminology, once it overcame the many misunderstandings connected

* Professor of Criminology, University of Rome
** Director, Research Unit, Italian Ministry of Justice

with restricted "schools" with which it struggled in its infancy, has now attained scientific maturity, pragmatically oriented towards the solution of the problems which both society and the jurist set for it.

The present trend of the discipline is of absolute adherence to factual reality; barren doctrinal disputes, which characterized the first phases of its development, no longer suit it. In this changed perspective analysis of the division between clinical criminology, criminological medicine, and criminal sociology is a preoccupation of marginal relevance or none at all.

What actually matters is the progressive utilization of the achievements of criminology at all levels of the penal system. Such a system should today be conceived as a single entity, from the legislative process, through its judicial application, the implementation of the penalty, on up to and including the post-detention phase. Sectional fragmentation between police action, verdict and penal implementation have been overcome through a perspective which sees the system as a global one, with continuous "osmosis" between its various parts.

It is in the light of such a concept that the task of criminology in the penal system should be indicated. Numerous authors in our country, as well as abroad, have dealt with the problem, and recently their writings have enormously increased in number.

In our country, as elsewhere, the penal system is tottering on its original, narrow, retributive foundations, which no longer appeal even to the popular conscience; it is inclining toward "reeducation and treatment," and in this domain the frontiers between juridical-penal acts, social work, administrative welfare and medico-social prevention are vanishing. The current framework is one of "social defense," in which various disciplines and their exponents combine in an unprecedented example of social architecture.

The Penal System

The penal system consists of three components: the legal basis, the instrumental apparatus, and the disposition.

These are actually the components of every social system, and thus do not represent a characteristic peculiar to the penal system.

The identity (and the specification of the latter) derives from the nature of the norms which govern it, and from its particular purpose.

The purpose of the penal system is a complex one, so that it may assume different dimensions and emphasis both in interpretation and in fulfillment.

From the point of view of the interest of the social group, it is regarded as aimed at controlling criminal manifestations and reducing them as much as possible.

The forces which work toward this end are two: the first belongs exclusively to the field of general prevention: the deterrent force of the threat inherent in penal law and of the social pressure of judiciary, penitentiary and police operations.

The second is made up of activities converging on single individuals, such as accusation, arrest, trial, and punishment.

As far as the victim is concerned, the penal system appears to aim directly at morally redressing the wrong suffered, and indirectly, at facilitating civil reparation.

As far as the author of the unlawful act is concerned, the same system appears to aim at retributive, and also, in a way less clearly perceptible, at therapeutic action.

It is evident that we refer to penal regulations, understood in their widest meaning: that is, laws and rules governing police, courts, preventive and penal institutions, and including also the personnel and material organization of the various sectors indicated, and the activities carried on within them.

Criminology

Criminology, from a theoretical point of view, has been allotted a field of study and action which goes beyond the limits of the penal system; indeed, it has expanded to a consideration of the causes of crime both immediate and remote, both individual and social, and to the proposal of the proper steps for prevention and remedy. Thus there is no biological or social reality which is disregarded by criminology. This legitimizes the criminologist's interest in personality theory, in medical pathology, in social organization in all its demographic as well as economic and political components.

It is certainly not our task, and it is at any rate superfluous here, to search for a new definition of criminology, or to make a choice among the numerous definitions that have been supplied by the literature on the subject. Still we have made a rapid "content-analysis" of the several definitions at our disposal. One of the first problems to be solved is that of overcoming differences—largely fictitious and frequently only terminological—between differently named disciplines which overlap and intersect without a clear delimitation.

Criminal sociology, criminal anthropology, clinical anthropology, criminological medicine are terms which, in our country, have defined particular aspects, often as an expression of extra-disciplinary efforts or of theoretical conflicts which have fragmented the common ground of criminology.

We conceive criminology as an integrated science where biological and social contributions converge in the study of behavior which according to the substantive legal norm is unlawful. We do not, however, exclude the possibility that criminology may assume the character of a "meta-discipline" of penal law. The scientific analysis of what behavior a democratic society wishes to penalize from among a large selection of deviations—against a background of unceasingly changing social values—is certainly pertinent. Criminological medicine represents the wedding of legal medicine and forensic psychiatry. A fruitful collaboration between jurists, biologists, and students of social problems will doubtless develop on this interdisciplinary bridge.

Criminology is, in fact, that science which logically coordinates and arranges all knowledge on the particular aspect of human and social reality which is known as crime, and on the individuals who are actually engaged in it.

It is from such a concept that the relationship between criminology and the penal system inevitably derives.

Recent extensive inquiries on the criminal phenomena in other countries, e.g. American studies such as "The Challenge of Crime in a Free Society," on violence, obscenity, and pornography; as well as a most recent Canadian one on penitentiary problems, and current studies on the same themes in England, in France, at the Council of Europe and at the U.N., have united jurists and criminologists in research efforts in the course of which the boundaries between the individual specializations of the researchers have largely disappeared.

It is useful to recall, in this connection, an explicit declaration of Bettiol, in 1955: "The belief that there may exist an opposition between penal law (a normative science connected with the imposition of values) and criminology (an experimental science connected with facts) is an error from which we have recently freed ourselves."

Relationship Between Criminology and the Penal System

In regard to the operation of the penal system, criminology has in fact become an applied science. As such, it does not renounce its methods, but, at least on the operational plan, it is bound to coordinate its aims with those of the system, as is necessary if an integrated contribution is to be made.

The assumption which supports the alliance between the penal system and criminology is that of admitted utility, so that the former may get help from the latter in order to function better.

The contributions that criminology can offer are manifold. They fall into general categories for which the following classification is proposed:

a: Analysis of the operation of the system in order to check the adequacy with which each part, in the best and most economical way, attains its specific ends, and contributes to the attainment of those of the whole system.

b: Suggestions for the adoption of means and scientific procedures to increase the efficiency of the normative system.

Penal law exists in order to compel respect for certain properties and interests, where it is feared that some members of society might violate these interests without the restraints of penal law.

As is known, other laws, both civil and administrative, have the same function and structure. They nevertheless differ from penal law in the different character of the penalties. In the case of civil law, this amounts to compelling restitution or proper compensation; in the case of administrative law, it entails also pecuniary and disciplinary punishment of various kinds, as well as the restriction of individual liberties.

To define, in principle, the differential character of penal law, in comparison with other laws, is an extremely arduous task. It is enough to think of the cases, drawn from the legislation of other countries, including our neighbors, in which penal sanction consists exclusively of indemnification, or in which the civil sanctions take the form of deprivation of liberty.

The task of definition becomes possible only within the framework of a given regulation, based on conventional concepts.

As far as Italy is concerned, it is agreed that a law has a penal character when its violation is followed by sanctions that are qualitatively heavier than those provided by other laws.

This qualitative gradation in penalties is, within certain limits, merely a convention. In reality, especially if we take into consideration individual situations, a civil or administrative penalty may turn out to be heavier and more damaging than a penal one (e.g., loss of employment).

The authority to choose the kind of sanction (a penal, civil, or administrative one) and its category (death, life imprisonment, detention, arrest, fine, or damages) is the legislator's, and in choosing these he is engaging in the establishment of legislative policy.

Making legislative policy involves a broad vision of the ends which society has decided (in our country, freely) to take as its own, and of the means to attain them.

It is a difficult task, and its realization requires the contributions of the most diverse components, first and foremost among them the general political orientation of the government.

Legislative policy must harmonize innumerable and contradictory interests of individuals and groups with the renunciation, by some of the individuals, of those "minimum portions" of liberty, which, according to Beccaria, everyone gives up in order to build the penal system. The task is not only to supervise an existing reality, but also to stimulate its development in a pre-planned evolution.

Where the legislator believes that any one interest is more substantial than others, and therefore its non-realization would be more dangerous and harmful, he takes care of it in the way he deems most efficient; that is, by resorting to penal sanctions.

Criminology does not aspire to guide the legislator in the choice of great social ends. It accepts the political restrictions of the system, and puts its resources at the system's disposal.

It may even happen, and it has indeed happened, that a politically "unjust" system asks and receives from criminology scientific help to increase the efficiency of its control. The scientific value of this science precludes an evaluation in moral terms: its instrumental value absolves it from an ethical judgment which should be applied to the political system.

Criminology, in any case, may usefully assist and facilitate the politician's choice, transforming intuitive data into objective knowledge, correcting wrong prognoses, offering manifold choices for the attainment of definite ends. Nor should we ignore the fact that criminology may, through clarification, indirectly influence even final decisive operations intended to orient the general policy of the regime.

The legislator, especially in democratic nations, is interested in interpreting the scale of moral values current in society, in order to fit the variety of sanctions to it.

This operation is generally performed on an intuitive basis with preconceptions and prejudices.

The modern criminological approach, on the contrary, is in a position to analyze and measure the values and supply a basis for objective and real evaluation. It may also warn the legislator against the foreseeable negative consequences of penal legislation which ignores or is even in conflict with social feelings.

The police, the courts, the penal institutions, and those which deal with the ex-convict's re-entry into society are, as already mentioned, integral parts of a unique social defense system. They are elements in a single function.

Yet this truth is not entirely perceived by the various participants, and still less by the public.

Thus it happens that the ideal picture of penal regulation, in practice, disintegrates into segments, often not aligned, and even not converging toward the same end.

The police, in closest contact with the immediate reality of the offense, may be tempted to assume a competitive attitude. Such temptation may distort the self-perception of the agent and the institution, to the detriment of their operations.

In Italy, the position of the judicial police, which is administratively dependent on the Executive, and functionally directed by the judge, could bring about the emergence of two conflicting souls in the same body.

Functional subordination to the judge may be more tolerable when it is thought that the judge, concerned with safeguarding liberties, opposes the operational interference of the police.

People who have investigated this field well know that under the rhetoric of devotion to the unitary functioning of the penal system there is often a feeling of frustration, perhaps stronger in other countries.

It may happen, in fact, that the police feel that the fight against crime is their own exclusive goal, and perceive the judicial authority as a filtering superstructure which disperses and weakens the achievements of the police.

On the other hand, the public lives daily in the presence of police activities, while feeling the courts to be remote and detached. The police, then, are regarded as having an autonomous function, so that conflict and collaboration with the penal system are seen in terms of either struggle against or assistance to the police.

The courts, as they are in closer contact with the laws and procedures than with social and penitentiary reality, actually run the risk of taking action while being isolated in their formal structure from the larger system of which they are a part.

The activity of the courts may be regarded by the judges, as well as by the other judicial agents, as a non-coordinated series of procedures, each of them starting and ending with the individual case. This could generate conflicts between the ascertained fact and the typical normative example, in an atmosphere of social irresponsibility. In that case the judge would feel himself bound only to the right definition of the typical normative example, without adequate consideration of the extent to which judicial activity makes a more or less effective contribution to the aims of the entire system. What happens to the individual offender and his family, and the social consequences of the particular judgment would be considerations not necessarily present in his consciousness.

The public, for its part, sees the courts as a complex, distant, and incomprehensible mechanism whose operation appears bound to ritual formulas totally lacking reason and whose judgments are meted out at random.

For the penitentiary institutions the verdict generally appears to be an order which is given by a third party and which is "suffered" not only by the "client" but also by the implementors to whom the "client" has been committed. Custody combined with reeducation becomes an autonomous act, an end in itself, disconnected from the framework of its social perspective.

What has been observed subtracts nothing from the merits of the different sectors. We wished only to stress how the penal system has the tendency to break up into operational segments, each of them losing contact with the others, and finally creating its own philosophy and purpose.

Criminology, through modern methods of "operational research" and of "systems analysis," may contribute to reassembling the parts into one whole.

In fact these methods make it possible to evaluate the effectiveness of each sector's means of attaining the institution's single end. They also make it possible to evaluate the relevance of the apparatus to the general ends of the law through the examination of the existing situation, thereby opening the way to useful rationalization. With these ends in sight, the procedures and the activities can be evaluated according to their efficiency, so that better alternatives may also be provided.

Criminology, apart from introducing structural changes in the system, may also supply knowledge on the means and procedures for increasing its efficiency, and so contribute to the activities of all the sectors.

The contributions of criminology may follow three concurrent paths:

The first consists of the preparation and training of personnel at the various levels, so that each category acquires the scientific understanding necessary for a more complete knowledge of the substance of the problems it is called upon to solve.

The second consists of the incorporation of the criminologist in the machinery of the administration of criminal justice.

Still more important is the third path, that of scientific research directed towards concrete topics of specific interest for the penal system.

Future Perspectives

At this point we must indicate, if only briefly, the future lines we believe the development of an operational relation between the penal and criminological systems is to follow. We shall do so with reference to current experience in other countries.

Before dealing with specific areas of activity, a further point must be made. The topics we are presenting by no means exhaust all possible areas of the operational convergence of criminology and the penal system. They are only examples dictated partly by our personal experience, partly by our present interest of study and research. We have not established any priorities, nor have we tried to order the material according to urgency and importance.

The sectors chosen by us all belong to the larger field of the relations between the penal system, criminological research, and social planning; this is in fact the frame of reference which seems to us to be most fruitful.

In most countries, and obviously in ours too, social planning has been developing along with material and economic planning. The "social planning" of the Anglo-Saxon authors indicates a network of activities, generally at the governmental level, which aims to raise and coordinate the interventions and the social effects of the developmental initiatives of a nation. The influence of the penal system in social planning, by hastening or delaying initiatives, by limiting or enlarging the boundaries of human action, is undeniable. Equally undeniable is the influence of every other social reality on the penal system. When the society changes in an orderly way and towards clear and well defined goals, (if the social planner has something to say in the evolutionary process) normative variation may become a fundamental component of the evolution. The dialectic between an evolving society and the norm which guides it involves a series of problems in which criminological research may lend valuable assistance.

For criminological activities relevant to social planning to be really operational, they should have some characteristics in common: an awareness of urgency in the first stage of the planning process; a broad social significance in the process of national development; direct relation with the control and prevention of antisocial behavior. They should also have available qualified personnel to study these and use them effectively.

The process of modernization, development, and change that society is undergoing in our country; the large population displacements, the demographic variations producing a considerable increase in percentage of the young generation in the population; all these constitute the social phenomena on the basis of which the penal system must perform its complementary functions and within which the planner works. The progress of change leaves behind islands of backwardness, in which certain groups may organize themselves subculturally, in a deviant or even in an antisocial way in regard to which proper norms should be adopted.

It should be clear, in any case, that we do not affirm (and the point has academic value only) that the modernization and development of society inevitably have a "criminogenic" effect. A causal relationship of this kind has not been proved; but, even if it should be proved, there would be no change in the terms of interaction between criminology and the penal system in a society in evolution—either planned or spontaneous. Social change, in a free society, is irrepressible. The course of progress which involves all of us is autonomous; it may only, in the best of hypotheses, be very delicately guided, with well-regulated interventions, and without sharp strains on normative reins.

Among the methods used by the social planner, especially during the research stage before the moment of decision (in which he does not take part, leaving this to the politician to whom the responsibility has been delegated), are those of "systems engineering" and "experimental social innovation." Although they appear to be of considerable complexity, they are based on relatively simple principles. Their moment of perception and the "test" of the proposals for action which constitute the basis belong to that large area of governmental activity with the initials R & D (research and development) to which the literature, chiefly the American, has accustomed us. These techniques entail the application to social problems of the same technology, depersonalized but extremely efficient, which dominates modern life, removing the exclusive responsibility of operational choice from intuition, from genius, and from artistic improvisation, and allowing effects of alternate decisions to be tested. For congruous and specific purposes, the latter achieves the best results at the cheapest cost in economic and social terms. These operations are already among us, and the increasingly numerous perforated forms which dominate our collective life are the external symptoms of it. Very recent are the attempts to use computers to facilitate the question of penal jurisdiction. The most recent application in Italy is the mechanographic analysis of judicial decisions. All this is "research and development" which, in the penal system, can no longer disregard criminological information.

It is not simple to establish the probable sectors of future activity, where data of criminological pertinence and the normative as well as the practical operation of the penal system will be based on the harmonizing efforts of the social planner.

The former will probably have as its object the gathering of the necessary data for the "decision" process, including, obviously, criminal statistics. The choice among the possible alternatives is based, whenever it is made rationally, on the construction of reasonably certain projections on the basis of the available data. The extent and validity of data are correlated mathematically to the validity of the projections and, therefore, of the choices.

Crime will never become a "certain variable" like that which actuaries are used to handling in their "econometrical" models. But there is ample room for improvement in the criminal statistics field; this may be achieved both in the direction of reduction of the "dark number" or in the more exact typological classification of the infinite variety of criminal behavior according to parameters not only juridical, but behavioral as well. Criminal statistics may still improve considerably both on the national level and on the level of international comparison.

Another sector today included in the gamut of interests of the researchers in several subjects concerns the "analysis of variations on the concept of deviance." The discrepancies between the scale of values applying in the moral sphere and that of legality (limited to the normative function of law), which increase with the accelerated rhythm of social change, often constitute a very sharp rift between the penal system and social reality.

The question may be presented in terms of conflict-conciliation between the value of legal certainty and the value of justice in the concrete case. In this enormously interesting sector too, social and criminological information may help the legislator and the agent of the law to correct imbalance and to prevent incongruities.

A problem of great timeliness, which in some countries has assumed dramatic aspects, is that of police activity, at which we briefly hinted earlier. The traditional lines of police activity are now being sifted through a broadened reconsideration of human rights; almost everywhere an image of "service to community" counters the traditional authoritarian image of the police. This broadens the scope of the "forces of order," immersing them more and more in the social fabric of the nation. The analysis of the image that the public has of the police is a meeting ground for criminological research and penal function.

Today penal sanctions are subjected to continuous revision in regard to cost and efficacy. Recent features, like "probation" and "parole" emerge from the inclination to reduce "detentive" measures to the indispensable minimum.

The effect of sanctions, their individualization, the analysis of the cultures and subcultures in which they occur are topics which have been extensively investigated by "research and development" activities.

The training and selection of personnel, which is bound to affect the various elements of the penal system, and which must characterize its work in the area (among which reeducational goals have been of special importance), will be based upon a fund of information. The modern achievements of criminology will surely no longer be considered informational luxury, but will be a prerequisite for judicial or administrative action. This, of course, will require the acceptance of a penal theory courageous enough to give up the narrow retributive view.

The differential characteristics of criminals will be examined in the light of alternative etiological theories of deviant and antisocial behavior which will allow refutation of "typologies" and "nosographies," inspired by a "pathologism" which the facts deny and which present day psychiatry and clinical psychology reject. In such an operation, for example, criminological medicine will be obliged to join with criminal sociology in an effort to define that human reality (which is quite individual and inimitable though it follows general laws of behavior) which causes transgressions of the law.

The treatment of the criminal, although it remains an art, entrusted to the quite personal and often hard-to-define qualities of the penitentiary operators, will face a critical evaluation of its success or failure, which will constitute the basis of choice for possible alternative or cumulative modes of treatments.

Many of the factors which are part of the "etiological" process of variables inherent in sectors previously mentioned cannot be dealt with experimentally and sometimes they cannot be quantitatively defined. This permits an affirmation that our concept of the relationship between criminology and the penal system is far from that "quantomania" whose risks are well known to the biologist and against which Sorokin warned the student of social facts. Number, in any case, has never replaced informed understanding of phenomena and of the goals of an action.

Nevertheless, scientific progress now imposes group actions and decisions in the field of general plans, and leaves little room for intuition.

It is in this concept, when man extends his actions by means of the controlled use of new technologies, that law and criminology will finally be able to join forces to achieve orderly progress in our society.

THE DIRECTION AND EVOLUTION OF THE JURY SYSTEM

JEAN GRAVEN*

Justice H.H. Cohn, to whom this present collection of essays is dedicated, had shown us in his papers prepared for the conference of the International Association of Penal Law—whose Israeli section he founded and presided over—that the penal legislation in Israel is neo-classical and is inspired by *common law* and the British system; but that, nevertheless, that legislation is "progressive" and has been able to adapt itself to modern demands and to the present problems of "criminal policy," as well as to the aims of "social reclassing." He also showed us to what extent Israeli law and procedure are concerned with the proper exercise and the protection of the rights of the accused in the course of the penal process.

These tendencies are on the one hand demonstrated by the type of extenuating circumstances which the Supreme Court most frequently encourages the courts to take into account (e.g.: age, psychological and social background, recidivism and the dangerous state of the offender, his attitude toward the court, his relationship to his victim, etc.). At the same time, the application of numerous penal laws "individualizing" sanctions shows that the present aim is not to avenge or expiate the delinquent act, but first and foremost "to cause a change in the behavior of the offender."

Following the codification of the rules of penal procedure in the Criminal Procedure Act (5725–1965), published in the official journal on July 15, 1965, and put into practice on January 5, 1966, Justice Cohn was kind enough to make us aware of the great changes which had occurred in the judicial system[1].

This Israeli legal system is at the judicial frontier between two systems of criminal law and procedure, and therefore is particularly instructive and worthy of study by both penalist and magistrate.

* Honorary President, International Association of Penal Law

Starting from the protective and traditional principles of *British law*, it has given up reinforcing it by means of the *British* type of jurisdiction, namely the jury, in favor of our familiar courts of the judicial system, with its two-level jurisdiction.

On the occasion of recent cases tried in Switzerland by juries, which whipped up renewed interest in the problem, and in face of the debates on the continental jury system which have been raised and are likely to be raised again in Belgium, it seemed to us interesting and relevant to take up the whole problem.

I. Introduction: Statement of the Problem

1

So much has been written and said on the problem of the jury that the debate appears to have been exhausted long since, and one might wonder whether it is worthwhile returning to it again. This continuing controversy recalls the moralist's formula according to which one ordinarily convinces oneself and not one's interlocutor. Indeed, there are questions so bound up with existing judicial systems, with conventions and rules obtaining in each country, and also with the unshakable innermost convictions of each person, that it would seem wise to leave them out of the controversy. This is the case particularly with the need for and usefulness of the death penalty, for example, and the indispensability or the desirability of having recourse to the jury as an instrument of penal justice. It is less the advantages or defects of the system and its analysis than the innermost conviction or prejudice, which affect each individual. The person most unaware of this is the one who is sincerely convinced that he is right, for all sorts of reasons which he no longer articulates because they are so self-evident to him. Thus "trial by jury" is judged the way juries themselves judge a judicial problem, by simple intuition or innermost conviction, by a "Coupable" or "Non coupable," or *guilty* or *not guilty*.

Two recent trials in Switzerland had a psychological aspect which awakened thought, and caused certain people to consider basic problems. One of the trials, the echo of which hardly crossed our borders, was held at the Court of Assizes at Tavel, one of the judicial districts of the canton of Fribourg. The result was, that on December 15, 1969, the newspapers squarely put the question that had already frequently been debated: "Should the Court of Assizes with jury be abolished?". The case involved a poacher who killed the gamekeeper who had caught him *in flagrante delicto*. The jury had to define the crime within the subtle variations of the system regulating homicides, introduced after 1942 in the Swiss Penal Code of December 21, 1937. They rejected the provisions dealing with murder or assassination and applied the article dealing with murder "through passion" which is punishable less harshly[2].

The second trial had international reverberations; its consequences were more far-reaching and it is still in everybody's memory. This was the case which the Canton of Zurich's Court of Assizes heard at Winterthur on April 9, 1970, against the perpetrators of the attack on the El-Al plane at Kloten airport. The judgment was appealed before the Supreme Federal Tribunal by the three condemned Palestinian attackers, and likewise by a representative of the Public Prosecutor in regard to the acquittal of the security man on the Israeli plane, who had killed one of the Palestinian gunmen (who were about to be arrested) on the ground. On one hand, it was the provisions concerning assassination (art. 112) that were applied to the accused Palestinians, rather than those on murder, or attempted murder with legal extenuating circumstances: on the other hand, the accused Israeli, Mordechai Rahamim, was acquitted through benefit of doubt, it having been impossible to establish definitely whether or not he was in a state of legitimate defense. It must be clear, however, that such delicate problems of law would have had a better chance of being resolved more subtly in a debate between higher justices. The latter would be more familiar with the application of the Penal Code and federal jurisprudence in such matters, and psychologically better equipped to withstand the reaction of the public or of citizens aroused to passion by the unprecedented seriousness of the case. Since the verdict and judgment was given by the Fribourg Court of Assizes in December, 1969, the problem of reconsidering the Assizes system itself has been taken up again. Among other arguments, the gist of the question is as follows: The scope of the Court of Assizes introduced at Fribourg by the March 4, 1848, Constitution to judge all crimes[3], has gradually been so reduced, because of its rigidity and its contested verdicts, that it deals only with "crimes against the state" and "murder and assassination." It has no other jurisdiction. "This means that it meets very infrequently (once or twice a year) and that, because of its very rarity, a Court of Assizes decision gives rise to extensive discussions and criticisms. Thus after the accused is tried, the sentence and the institution which pronounced it are nearly always tried as well. The verdict of the Fribourg court," concludes the opinion we have quoted, "does not close the conflict but rather reopens it: In order to safeguard the laws of justice, should the Courts of Assizes with jury, as they function at present, be abolished?" It is this question which the present article aims to answer.

2.

If one wishes to consider the problem of the jury, its usefulness and its scope, its reform or its abolition[4], it is indispensable to consider its origins, its function and its aim, what it has become and what meaning it still has today.

Switzerland, where, in the wake of political developments between 1830 and 1850, the jury was adopted in eight out of the 22 cantons, has already reconsidered the question three times. As far back as 1863, when the jury still enjoyed wide popularity, there was consideration of improving it by changing the special interrogation, which was deemed responsible for astonishing acquittals and incomprehensible verdicts[5]. In 1881, the jury system was examined and found more or less useless; however, the Swiss Society of Jurists decided to refrain from a clear-cut decision. Since opinions were still divided, its abolition did not seem "a necessity."[6] In 1938, before the general convention of the Swiss Society of Jurists in Geneva, the entire problem of the jury and alderman courts was reconsidered.

The profound transformation from the jury system to one of mixed juror-assessor or alderman courts was then closely analyzed.[7] There was consideration of whether the transformation itself was really opportune, and whether it would not be better to abandon entirely an institution foreign to our customs and unsuited to our needs, whose function was being criticized, reduced and ignored, and which the vast majority of cantons had in any case rejected and were managing very well without. However, the principle of cantonal "sovereignty" in matters of judicial organization and penal procedure has remained so much alive that the majority of the convention defeated the proposal put forth by the President, Federal Judge Bolla, who suggested that the Swiss Society of Jurists should "give the cantonal legislators guidelines, at least on the question of abolishing juries, if not on the choice between ordinary and alderman courts."

It was thus possible to evade the question, leaving to each canton a free choice. But it was not possible to suppress the problem itself, which judicial practice, the evolution of customs and institutions and unfavorable experiences repeatedly brought up, and which finally forced a decision.

Whoever follows Professor Clerc's interesting "Chronicles of Penal Procedure" in the *Revue Pénale Suisse*[8] will see very clearly that for

346

the cantons who have the jury system its modification or abolition is the crucial issue in the administration of criminal justice.

This movement to change the jury system is rather old and universal. Let us recall that the International Penitentiary Congress held in Budapest in 1905 had on its program the question of whether there was room for making corrections in the jury system[9]. On its part, the International Congress of Penal Law convened in Palermo in 1933, and put on its agenda the question: In criminal cases, should the jury or the alderman system be accepted?

As Switzerland, Germany, Austria, and Italy discussed the question extensively, France, the creator of the continental type of "classic" jury, had to consider the issue as well, in view of disappointing and often demoralizing results. In 1899, the General Society of Prisons engaged in a wide-ranging debate, which was not followed up, but was reopened in 1928–29. It finally ended—after the partial modification of March 5, 1932—with a completely different solution, which, in 1941, transformed the Court of Assizes, separating the judges and jurors and their respective tasks, in a jurisdiction formed of a single mixed body. In it, jurors, who formerly judged guilt alone, thenceforth decided jointly with professional magistrates on the facts, on guilt, and on the sentence. This joint system has also prevailed in Germany and Italy, and is becoming more and more common in Swiss jury cantons.

Since the discussion was likewise reopened in various other countries including Belgium[10], it behooves us to see *why* the need for these profound changes was imperative, what they really mean, what was their aim and outcome, and whether they solved the problem of criminal jurisdiction in the best—the most rational—way.

II. The Origin and Objectives of the Jury

1.

What then is the jury, and for what purpose was it initiated? The first point that arises, and without which the implications of the problem cannot be understood, is that the jury was supposed to be *an instrument of fact-finding and conviction and not of sentencing*.

It was born in England in the 13th century in the form of a "jury of accusation," when the judge—who was itinerant and lacked information on local custom—had two methods of fact-finding: by ordeal (the judgment of God), and by the hearsay of neighbors. In the latter mode of evidence the judge established guilt through the squires of the country who were in the best position to know the defendant and the circumstances of the act of which he was accused.

On the continent, where the institutions of the late Roman Empire were influential, recourse was had to proof *per inquisitionem*, i.e. by questioning, which culminated in secret sessions and the use of coercive methods, especially judicial torture and harsh detentions, for the purpose of obtaining a confession, the "queen of proofs." This was a "judicial certainty" which appeased the conscience of the judges and allowed the application of the rough penalties of the period, i.e. almost always a sentence of death or the most severe and mutilating corporal punishments.

In feudal England, on the contrary, where the influence of Roman law was not widespread, and where traditional institutions were maintained, the procedure of private accusation (*per accusationem*) was retained. In this system, an accused person who had not confessed was brought before a jury. Its role was limited to the enunciation of the words "guilty" or "not guilty" to proclaim the guilt or innocence of the accused, and unanimously, at that. It did not need to be concerned with the sentence, which was pronounced by the magistrate. It is still true today that the accused who confesses or "pleads guilty" need not appear before a jury (whose task is thus useless), and is simply and briefly sentenced by the magistrate who metes out the customary punishment.

The judge was gradually led to transfer to the jurors—whose role was by no means limited to penal cases—the entire range of fact-finding. This had far-reaching consequences: the opinion of the jurors acquired special weight, and the judge always conformed to it in the end. In the final analysis, however, the judge maintains absolute control of the entire procedure, he sums up the affair at the end as he sees it, explains the effect of the relevant law, and can thus try to guide the jury. The latter may question the witnesses, but only on the facts, and only through the intermediary of the judge, if he believes the questions to be pertinent. The jury decides on the weight of the proof and has the power to acquit an accused regardless of the value of the proof. Only in this sense is the judge bound.[11]

For this reason, however, the juries, which were considered the "guardians of popular feeling", gradually earned a reputation as "guarantors of the independence and impartiality of the sentence" as well; the institution was viewed as a barrier to the arbitrariness or omnipotence of judges appointed by those in power. The English jury did not appear only as a local judicial institution, but as a *political and democratic* institution safeguarding individual rights.

It is for this reason above all and as an antidote to secret inquisitorial methods which make use of torture, forbid any defense during the investigation, and give unlimited powers to the judges, that the French became enamoured of the institutions native to England. In the wake of laudatory statements by Montesquieu, Voltaire, Mirabeau and so many others, the jury was enthusiastically introduced in 1790 by the Constituent Assembly. Its essential character was clearly proclaimed: "Without juries, there is no freedom in a country"; the jury was supposed to "reconcile humanity with justice, liberty with the law."

Along with the new revolutionary institutions, administration and legislation, the jury procedure was brought to—or forced upon—the adjacent countries on the Rhine, in the present territory of Belgium, Holland, Luxembourg, and Switzerland as well, by the French invasion. At Berne, while proclaiming the "Rhodian Republic" on the 26th of Ventose, in the year IV, General Brune declared that the legislature would "place the institution of juries in its criminal procedure." The ephemeral "Helvetian Republic" included it in its program and discussed it at the sessions of its Legislative Commission. Nevertheless, neither the legislation of 1799, nor the Helvetian Constitution of 1802, nor the Federal Pact of 1815, sanctioned the jury.[12]

In a democratic country such as ours, where all magistrates are elected by the people or by representatives of the people, and are all closely involved with the population, it should have been realized that the foreign institution of the jury made no sense, *provided that the old inquisitorial procedure was reformed* by adding humaneness, rights to defense, and sufficient guarantees for the accused.

2.

Precisely from this point of view, *the jury experiment was so decisively disastrous* that at the time that the relevant French legislation—the 1808 Code of Criminal Investigation—was enacted, the jury seemed condemned, with no appeal. In the preliminary inquiry opened at the appellate courts and criminal tribunals, the vast majority preferred the immediate abolition of the jury, and the Supreme Court of Appeal put the question in the following terms: "It is doubtful whether the institution of the jury which is so beautiful in theory has not been more harmful than useful in its effects . . . Perhaps today we should examine in the light of experience what was no more than speculation for the Constituent Assembly . . ."

After fiery discussions and long hesitation, Napoleon, who had "found

France lacking criminal law," decided to retain the jury in order to "yield to the revolutionary tradition".[13]

Geneva, which in imitation of France had introduced juries for all types of trials, with the Constitution of February 5, 1794 (the year III of Equality), and had used juries in the French manner throughout the period of its attachment to France as the "Department of Léman," had no hesitation in abolishing them as soon as it regained its independence in 1813, as the Netherlands and Luxembourg were to do in 1814 and 1815.

Thus the problem seemed clearly *solved in regard to the intrinsic value of the jury* as an instrument of penal justice.[14]

3.

A not unimportant point which explains the wide variety of Swiss judicial systems more than a century later is that the jury was later accepted, *only through political pressure* as an achievement of the "liberal" revolutionary movement.

Geneva, after vain attempts in 1827, 1828, 1830, and 1839, re-established it through a law in January, 1844. The cantons of Vaud and Berne did likewise in their constitutions of 1845 and 1846. Valais (which never put it into effect), Fribourg, and Neuchâtel did so in 1846.

Swept by the current, like all the cantons bordering France, the moment the "radical party" gained a majority in the Federal Government and replaced the old conservative parties, the Confederation, in the Constitution of 1848, also instituted the jury for the Federal Assize Court, and then in 1851 established it for military offenses. German-speaking Switzerland partially followed these examples in the constitutional revisions of the period; Thurgau in 1849; Zurich in 1851, though unenthusiastically, and following the English model; Aargau and Solothurn in 1852 and 1856. Ticino did this in 1855, but was to become quickly disenchanted with the jury and reject it after the first experiments. Solothurn did not put it into effect till 1862, and from the outset, jury judgments raised controversies, produced sharp parliamentary questions, and were lampooned even in the schools. Proposals for abolition of the jury were made at Thurgau in 1869, Berne in 1879, and at the Swiss Society of Jurists in 1881. In Ticino, where it was "completely discredited after unfortunate verdicts," the jury was abolished in 1883: "Condemned almost universally on all sides . . . it died without a struggle, without even the honor of a funeral oration."

In instituting the jury for federal offenses in the Constitution of 1848, the dominant idea had been that the jury was "in essence bound to democracy," and contrary to "judicial absolutism." The Federal Council recognized, however, that the people were not familiar with the institution. If the jury was to fulfill the hopes placed in it and become popular, it was necessary to simplify its function as much as possible. In 1893 the new federal judicial organization set up a Federal Penal Court of five magistrates, in order to divest the Assize Courts of everything that could be withdrawn from them. Furthermore, in certain elections of federal juries, it was noted that the electors did not bother to do their duty, and in Vaud, for instance, citizens on the electoral board found it expedient to appoint themselves . . . .[15]

As to the military jury,[16] experience was likewise negative, and the situation rapidly became so "untenable" that after the military reorganization of 1874, a conference of experts was in agreement in condemning the artificial and harmful system of dividing "fact" and "law" in the same judgment. They rejected the jury "which had proved to be slow and costly, unhealthy because of its uncertainty, constituting a source of trouble in military life, and which moreover was a foreign import condemned even in France which had given it to us," since the experiments with military juries had failed. The jury system was then replaced by mixed permanent tribunals composed of judges with military jurisdiction and civilian jurists.

III. The Choice of Systems

1.

In 1881, Professor Hornung of Geneva had already advised the Swiss Society of Jurists that the *tribunal échevinal or Schöffengericht* as had been conceived in German doctrine was the "felicitous means of retaining the jury without its dangers." This entailed the combination of magistrates and popular assessors (inspired by the ancient *échevins* of German common law) to decide on both guilt and punishment. In 1883 at Berne, Professor Carl Stooss, the future author of the Swiss penal code, demanded the replacement of the Assize Court by a mixed criminal tribunal of this sort. In 1884 in the canton of Aargau, *échevinage*, and, in the course of the debate, the return to ordinary courts, was likewise officially proposed. In November, 1894, as we have indicated, the canton of Ticino at the time of its constitutional revision, finally accepted the replacement of the jury by *échevinage*. Their law on judicial organization and the code of penal procedure established "district Assize courts" to try misdemeanors, and "cantonal Assize courts" to try felonies. The second solution was the attempt, not to *replace* the jury by this system of *tribunaux mixtes*, but to *modify* it internally by endeavoring to find a balanced system that would make it possible to retain the Assize Court with the double function of fact-finding and sentencing, with judges and jurors chosen by lot for each session. This was done fairly successfully in the canton of Geneva in 1889. Contemporary witnesses were convinced that if the people had been consulted at the moment, they would without doubt have agreed to the abolition of the jury and its replacement by *échevinage*. It was, however, impossible to achieve this (the absence of a few deputies favoring the fundamental structural reform was enough to block it), and the law of October 1, 1890, accepted the "compromise" which is known as "the Geneva system." It consists of having the presiding judge attend the secret deliberations of the jury in an advisory capacity, enabling him to respond to their requests for information or clarification. Once the jurors have decided about the guilt, the judge sits together with them to determine sentence.

It is between these two paths that contemporary choices have been made. Since the jury in its pure state has become discredited, *the choice tends more and more toward a mixed assessorat system.* Germany sanctioned it in 1924, the canton of Berne in 1928, Italy in 1931, Austria in 1934, France, after the 1932 reform involving the jury in the determination of the sentence, instituted a radical reform in its November 25, 1941 law which was based on the system of *assessorat*.[17] In Switzerland, convinced by the Berne example, the cantons of Neuchâtel (1938), Vaud (1940), Geneva (1957 bill), Aargau (November 11, 1958 law), Solothurn (March 5, 1961 law), Thurgau (1962 bill), Zurich (new 1967 law) have put into effect the same amendment.[18] The institution of the "single body" of magistrates and *assesseurs-jurés* was also the path indicated by the International Congress of Penal Law at Palermo in 1933.[19]

In the canton of Zurich, the new 1947 law brought about a fundamental change. The original system based on the English example was radically changed. The law on judicial organization sanctions the *Geschworenengericht* composed of the president and two other judges of the cantonal Tribunal (*Obergericht*), and of nine jurors; together they constitute a judicial body. The 1947 law fixes the precise procedure whereby preliminary questions are judged by the Court (the magistrates), but the whole *Tribunal* decides on the proof of guilt. The president conducts the debate and the vote, he explains points of law, and presents the questions to be resolved. In the discussion, the "juror judges" have the right to express themselves before the judges. Voting is not by secret ballot but openly, with the jurors first giving their opinions in random order. The president votes last. A majority of at least eight votes is necessary for a verdict of guilty. For all other points a simple majority is sufficient. In case of a tie or when the required majority is not obtained, it is the opinion most favorable to the accused which prevails. This certainly seems the best solution, assuming that the retention of a half-professional, half-lay type of judiciary is desired.

For the sake of appearance, the traditional terms "Court of Assizes" and "jurors" are preserved. But this is no more than a front. The Court of Assizes system which separates fact from law, the lay members from the professionals, the role of the jury from the role of the judge, the verdict from the sentence, *in fact no longer exists.* To conclude, we may point out that if one compares the jury's origin and aim with its evolution and present status, it must inevitably be concluded that it is anachronistic. Historically and logically, it has lost its meaning and justification.

Another conclusion is that in the cases of the jury's collaborating with judges in determining the sentence, or of the jury and judges sitting together in a mixed assessorship tribunal, *jurors have become judges* and fill their role. They need no longer be concerned exclusively with facts, and their proof, giving their opinion of the accused's guilt by a simple "yes" or "no" answer.

Now, these jurors who have no legal training have been assigned the role of judge, which is becoming more and more difficult as the penal code becomes more complicated and modernized. At the same time they continue to be regarded as jurors originally were, *i.e.* "the first citizen to appear," chosen by chance, "the man in the street," whose very incompetence seemed to be his essential quality. In fact he could be challenged with no reason given—and was challenged—the moment he seemed to be somewhat cultured and could be suspected of "intellectualism."

It was certainly a fundamental error to imagine, when the modern continental jury was instituted as an imitation of the English jury, that it would be possible to *separate fact from law*: to require people to establish the guilt of an accused person and disengage themselves completely from the practical results of their verdict, *i.e.* from the sentence passed on the accused who has been declared guilty. Indeed, that famous article 342 of the Code of Criminal Procedure states that: "The jurors should concern themselves with facts only . . . The object of their mission is not to seek out or punish offenses; they are only called upon to decide whether or not the accused is guilty of the crime imputed to him."

But it was unrealistic from the outset to imagine that a rational "division of labor" could be instituted between the two elements of fact-finding and sentencing. As far back as 1790, Tronchet had found the rule "silly and chimeric."

IV. The Real Problem at Present

1.

The moment that jurors, échevins or assessors received the right and function both of declaring guilt and of determining the penalty as well, the problem was knowing if they were qualified and were capable of doing their duties. Personally, on the basis of a long comparative study of the problem, and a penal judicial practice of more than 25 years, I believe that this is not the case. The common sense, good will, and good faith which were adequate for the purpose of replying "in honor and conscience", "Guilty" or "Not guilty," no longer suffice.

People who are certainly generally honest, sincerely desirous of doing the right thing, but absolutely unprepared for and inept at their new task, have been assigned a role which was not, and could not be theirs. In the course of an 1845 discussion on juries in the canton of Vaud, a representative of the minority opinion could say: "It does not matter whether the jury is more or less enlightened. The questions submitted to it are simple, and the sense of an unschooled man can be as useful in solving them as the knowledge of a scholar." That may have been so. But at present to judge and to have to apply "learned" penal law (with the complexity and variety of recent codes), is no longer a matter of pronouncing "yes" or "no" on the basis of simple intuition.[20] As early as 1928 Glaser stated in his contribution to the "*Etudes Criminologiques*" on the suicide of the jury, that when changed political conditions reduced the importance of the jury as a liberal achievement, it finally began to be appreciated from the point of view of judicial utility, "and its slow decline dates from there": because from this point of view, the balance sheet everywhere was a disaster.

Here a lesson taught from experience must be frankly admitted: *échevinage* or assessorship is infinitely better than the jury. It has corrected the worst faults and the most shocking errors. And it functions well and without any marked friction between the professionals and the laymen, between the magistrates and the juror-assessors. In the 1938 report and during the discussion of the jury or *échevinage* problem at the Swiss Society of Jurists, it was recalled that after some experience with the new mixed tribunals in Ticino in 1896 and 1897, the president of the Court of Assizes declared that he was "more than satisfied with the collaboration of the juror-assessors," and that *échevinage* in criminal cases "earned only praise." On his part, a former president of the Assizes could confirm that the system "had proved itself very well" and that "in any case, it satisfied the opinion and conscience of the country." The canton of Berne as well, after the introduction of the new system of mixed Courts of Assizes in 1928, officially proclaimed itself "very satisfied" with the new criminal jurisdiction, which was simpler, more convenient, and provided justice that was more regular and more certain. There too a cantonal judge who had presided over the Court of Assizes for years both before and after the reform evaluated the system as "very superior" to the former one, and indicated that the juror-assessors had a lively sense of justice, a consciousness of their responsibility and the courage of their convictions. According to him the collaboration with the judges operated naturally and without incident, and in the ten years to which the comments applied, neither their decisions nor the new system had ever been publicly criticized.

Let us take note of this, and also of the fact that, in view of these favorable experiences, and the opposite experience with juries, the former example has been generally followed in our country. The new mixed and unified Court of Assizes of the Berne type is on the way to becoming "the Swiss judicial system" in criminal jurisdiction in those cantons which in the initial political fervor of 1844 to 1848 and later had allowed themselves to be seduced by the political idea of the jury as a "democratic institution." Neuchâtel, Vaud, Solothurn, Thurgau, and finally Zurich—the most loyal to its origins and special form—are proof of this.

We cannot, however, ignore another very significant point either. This is that the function of the Court of Assizes, whatever form it may take, has been continually restricted everywhere. This has resulted from the more or less extensive *correctionalization*—legalized or otherwise—of numerous criminal cases. For a large number of crimes, the prerogative of the Court of Assizes has been legally transferred to correctional tribunals. This is the case at Geneva for all crimes punishable by imprisonment for less than five years. The necessity of indicating the grounds for the sentence so as to permit a review of the correct application of federal penal law by the Supreme Court of Appeal also operates to increase this tendency, since juries are not required to explain or motivate their sentences. Thus the recent Commission for the revision of the Code of Penal Procedure was of the opinion that it was sensible to abolish the jury, even of the assessor type. The Government, never-theless, "did not hesitate to retain the institution so as not to provoke discussions among the electorate when constitutional modifications were on the agenda. The debate might have taken a passionate turn, for fear of seeing a guarantee abolished, especially in political cases." In the canton of Thurgau the revision bill of 1962 chose neither the jury form nor that of the assessors, but provided for the constitution of a Criminal Tribunal made up of three cantonal judges and four other members. The Government also anticipated objections and recalled Professor Clerc's view: "First of all, he justly notes that nowadays people are less excited than formerly about political questions; the present generation prefers technical solutions. Secondly and primarily, what's the use of discussing the jury question *ad infinitum*, when we know that in Thurgau today the Court of Assizes is convoked at most three times a year to try three accused persons?"

It is superfluous to belabor the well known phenomenon of the *correctionalization* of criminal cases, whether done in practice or sanctioned legally. It is a phenomenon which the widely quoted French "dismissal" procedures have brought to the fore, as has the "legal disqualification" of infanticide, bigamy, and usury. Belgium as well, has been making recourse to the Assizes rarer. Making the correctional tribunal legally competent to try all infractions punishable by from three to five years in prison, and allowing the Council Chamber to "correctionalize" crimes punishable by 10 to 15 years of forced labor by the exceptional recognition of extenuating circumstances will have reduced the cases henceforth submitted to the jury as much as possible. In fact, according to the report of the 1958–1959 debate on jury reform in Belgium, 98% of criminal cases were referred to correctional tribunals.

The decisive question which really remains to be solved is whether in our era, in the present state of our laws, our ideas, our customs, and our needs, it is still fitting to "submit the most serious crimes to the sovereign examination of public opinion," or whether they should be judged rationally and technically in the best, surest and most regular manner possible by the appropriate jurisdiction. For our jurists and penalists, this is, in the final analysis, the entire problem.

The fact is that specialized doctrine, all the well-informed criminalists, and the scientific movements of modern penal law, criminology, and social-defense protagonists have long been demanding penal judges who are trained for their essential and delicate task. I may be allowed to recall the fact that the cause of the "necessary specialization" of the penal magistrate was already debated and recognized as desirable at the Third International Congress of Penal Law at Palermo in 1933, at the Eleventh International Penal and Penitentiary Congress in Berlin in 1935, at the First International Congress of Criminology at Rome in 1938. It was warmly defended again at the Second International Congress of Social Defense at Liège in 1949, and in 1950 at both the First International Course of Criminology at Paris and the United Nations Colloquium at Brussels.

If the battle is won in theory, it is far from being so in the minds of the public, the magistrates themselves, and the legislators! The latter must "open up to new horizons," and finally understand, that the role of the penal judge is not what it was. It is no longer a matter of simply applying the most severe "legal tariff" possible to all, without distinction, in order to make the offender expiate his fault, and give him "evil for evil," in order to frighten him and prevent his recidivism (what a vain hope!), while at the same time also intimidating all the potential offenders by means of the resultant "general prevention."

If one takes the trouble to think about it, it is precisely because of this old and necessarily severe attitude of vindictive and punitive law that the magistrates who shared these ideas and were supposed to apply them acquired a reputation for inhumanity and inexorable severity. For these reasons, the feeling arose that they must be countered by the "humaneness" of jurors, who came from "the people" and are the incarnation of the popular conscience.

However, I am convinced that to achieve real justice, nothing better has been invented than a good judge, and I also agree with the opinion of Federal Judge Cavin, that the man appearing before a court has to be more on guard against the popular judge than the career judge. The absolute power to judge and condemn, given to any person with no knowledge of law and with no need to account for his reasons, involves great risks.

The fact that some well-established jurymen or *assesseurs-échevins* happen to deliver a good judgment, and some judges happen to deliver a mediocre or even bad judgment, is not a reason to give preference and predominance to the former. All things considered, the "layman," whatever his name and whatever he does, will always hamper the administration of justice. Modern penal and judicial systems can no longer rely on the itinerant judge—accompanied by twelve men of experience and integrity (*prud'hommes*), representing in some eyes the twelve Apostles inspired by the Holy Spirit descending upon them at Pentecost—who administered punitive justice throughout the country.

To sum up, I believe, as Binding said, that now that "the sin of the old judges has been expiated" and the modern judges—humane, enlightened, and competent—has retrieved the indispensable confidence which his important task deserves, the time has come for the jurors, the gentlemen of experience and integrity, who are the ordinary judges in punitive customary law, to disappear as naturally as they appeared. And so the normal end will come to the evolution of an institution which has come down through history but has no more place in a world of electronic computers and the scientific conquest of outer-space. It belongs to the era of the "judicial duel," "trial by ordeal," and the feudal "judgment of God." In these times of the "end of myths," one should finally find and establish a real instrument of modern justice in a judiciary organization which is well thought-out, modernized and scientifically adapted to its lofty and arduous task.

NOTES

[1] See H. Cohn: LES CIRCONSTANCES AGGRAVANTES AUTRES QUE LA RECIDIVE ET LES DELITS SIMULTANES (CONCOURS) DANS LE DROIT ISRAELIEN, *Revue Internationale de droit pénal*, Paris 1965, No. 3–4, pp. 587–595; LES DROITS DE L'ACCUSE DANS LA PROCEDURE PENALE EN ISRAEL, in the same journal, 1966, No. 1–2, pp. 173–198; LES DELITS CONTRE LA FAMILLE ET LA MORALITE SEXUELLE EN DROIT ISRAELIEN, in the same journal, 1964, No. 3–4, pp. 813–833. Mention must also be made of Justice Cohn's valuable contribution (as a member of the U.N. Human Rights Commission) to the great studies of the International Association of Penal Law for the U.N., such as THE PROJECTED INTERNATIONAL CONVENTION ON THE INDEFENSIBILITY OF WAR CRIMES AND CRIMES AGAINST HUMANITY, *same journal*, 1966, No. 3–4, pp. 451–459.

[2] In order not to repeat the entire doctrine and commentaries, see Graven: LE SYSTEME DE LA REPRESSION DE L'HOMICIDE EN DROIT SUISSE (study for the British Royal Commission on capital punishment), in *Revue de droit pénal et de criminologie*, Brussels, Jan. 1951, No. 4, pp. 353 *ff.*; LA REPRESSION DE L'HOMICIDE EN DROIT SUISSE, *Revue de science criminelle et de droit pénal comparé*, Paris, 1966, No. 2, pp. 234 *ff.*, with references and bibliography, pp. 295–297; MEURTRE, ASSASSINAT, OU MEURTRE PAR PASSION? *Revue pénal suisse*, Berne, 1946, vol. 61 (collection in honor of Professor Hafter), pp. 347 *ff.*; THE PROBLEMS OF THE APPLICATION OF LEGAL DECISIONS TO MURDER THROUGH PASSION (focussing on the development of jurisprudence and the study of practical cases), same journal, 1960, vol. 76, pp. 164 *ff.* It is striking to note that in a case very similar to the Fribourg one of the murder of a gamekeeper by a poacher, the Swiss Federal Court (in a decision against the public prosecutor of the canton of Berne on Feb. 11, 1944, Official record of 1944 Federal Court decissions, vol. 70, sec. IV, pp. 5 *ff.*) confirmed the judgment of the Berne cantonal court condemning the murderer for "assassination"

(according to Art. 112 of our Penal Code), and admitted that "the offender has killed in circumstances or with premeditation indicating that he is particularly perverted or dangerous," the only case requiring life imprisonment.

[3] In the jury system of the canton of Fribourg introduced by the liberal constitution of 1948, the present forms are those provided for by the Code of Cantonal Procedure of 1927 revised in 1944, and by the cantonal law of 1949 on judicial organization. It is, moreover, no longer the classical form of the "jury à la française," which has been replaced in each of the three "judicial districts" of the canton by an Assize Court composed of a presiding judge and three members.

[4] This presentation is the synthesis of an introductory report entitled: EVOLUTION, DECLINE, AND TRANSFORMATION OF THE JURY, which we presented for the third Jean Dabin juridical day, held at the Law Faculty of the Catholic University of Louvain on May 19–20, 1967, on the theme of *The Jury Confronts Modern Penal Law*. It takes into account also those discussions and their conclusions. See volume IV of the *Bibliothèque de la Faculté de Droit de Louvain* (Brussels, 1967), pp. 79–122, with an extensive Swiss bibliography, pp. 123–131.

[5] On the problems and evolution of the jury in Switzerland as a whole, see especially Rothenberger: GESCHICHTE UND KRITIK DES SCHWURGERICHTSVER-FAHRENS IN DER SCHWEIZ, *Dissertation*, Berne, 1903 (Considerable data and general view); Cavin: FROM JURY TO ALDERMANRY, *Dissertation*, Lausanne, 1951.

[6] Ruttimann: WAS SIND DIE GESETZLICHEN BESTIMMUNGEN IN DEN-JENIGEN KANTONEN, WELCHE GESCHWORENENGERICHTE HABEN, IN BETREFF DER AN DIE GESCHWORENEN ZU RICHTENDEN FRAGEN? Report to the Swiss Society of Jurists, *Acts of the Society*, 1863, p. 42.

[7] Favey: DE LA VALEUR DE L'INSTITUTION DU JURY EN SUISSE. Report of the Swiss Society of Jurists, 1881. *Actes (Verhandlungen)*, p. 19; Hornung: LE JURY ET LE TRIBUNAL ECHEVINAL. Memorandum to the Swiss Society of Jurists, 1881. *Acts of the Society*, 1881, p. 99; Schneider: WERT DER INSTITUTION DES SCHWÜRGERICHTS IN STRAFSACHEN NACH DEN ERFAHRUNGEN IN DEN SCHWEIZ. KANTONEN. Reports to the Swiss Society of Jurists, *Acts of the Society*, 1881, p. 96; Gaven: LE JURY ET LES TRIBUNAUX D'ECHEVINS EN SUISSE. *Rapport à la Société Suisse des Juristes, Acts of the Society*, 1938, pp. 1–213; and discussion at the 73rd annual convention, minutes, *ibidem*, pp. 817–837. Pfenninger: SCHWUR—UND SCHÖFFENGERICHTE IN DER SCHWEIZ. Report to the Swiss Society of Jurists in 1938, *Acts of the Society*, 1938, pp. 700–747, and discussion pp. 838–856; GEDANKEN ZUM SCHWÜRGERICHTS PROBLEM, Collection in honor of Carl Stooss, Rev. pén. suisse, 1929, 43, p. 295; GESCHWORENE ODER SCHÖFFEN. *Neue Zürcher Zeitung*, July 5, 1941, No. 1308; BUNDESGERICHT GEGEN SCHWUR-GERICHT (re the Schürch affair), *Rev. suisse de jurisprud.*, 1952, 48, p. 349; VOM SCHWURGERICHT ZUM GESCHWORENENGERICHT IM KANTON ZURICH, Neue Zürcher Zeitung, April 14, 1966, No. 1623.

[8] Clerc: CHRONIQUE DE PROCEDURE PENALE, REFORMES EN COURS, *Rev. pén. suisse*, 1966, p. 200, and numerous subsequent notes.

[9] Borel: LES RESULTATS DE L'INSTITUTION DU JURY, ONT-ILS ETE TELS QU'IL Y AURAIT LIEU D'Y APPORTER DES REFORMES? Swiss report to the International Penitentiary Congress of Budapest in 1905, 1st section, question IV, *Acts of the Congress*, 1906, II, p. 345.

[10] See, in the Dabin Collection: Professor P. Bondue, attorney-general at the Brussels Appellate Court, president of the School of Criminology, *Introductory Report*, pp. 13–22;

R. Charles, attorney-general at the Supreme Court of Appeal, *General Report*, on the situation and prevailing opinion in Belgium (pp. 23–50); P.E. Trousse, counselor to the Supreme Court of Appeal, *Belgian Report*, pp. 51–77, especially the following sections: VI: LE MAINTIEN DU JURY, EST-IL COMPATIBLE AVEC L'ORIENTATION DU DROIT PENAL? p. 62; VII: LE JURY, PEUT-IL ETRE REFORME? p. 70; VIII: L'ADMINIS-TRATION DE LA JUSTICE CRIMINELLE PAR DES MAGISTRATS DE CARRIERE p. 74. Also, in the discussions, the presentations of Professor P. Cornil, former secretary-general of the Ministry of Justice and honorary president of the International Association of Penal Law; Professor R. Legros, counselor at the Supreme Court of Appeal, and MM. P. DeCant, deputy attorney-general at the Brussels Appellate Court; Professor A. Fettweis; Judge S.C. Versele, representative of the Belgian League for the Defense of the Rights of Man; Judges J.Y. Dautricourt and L. DeClercq, pp. 183–200. Mr. Legros' presentation was the strongest defense of the jury system.

[11] See the presentation of Judge C.D. Arvoold on LES FONCTIONS DU JUGE ET DU JURY DANS LE SYSTEME ANGLAIS DU DROIT PENAL, Dabin Collection, 1967, *History*, pp. 217–220. The author stresses that "the English system of judgment by judge and jury is a system which was developed in the course of centuries, which has been sanctioned by time, and which has been found compatible with the character and mentality of the English people." He wishes to "advance no argument as to its merits, nor state any preconceptions regarding its value in the search for truth." It is not at all a matter of a "system developed by philosophers or sociologists or practitioners of the law in seeking the best system for bringing out the truth, either guilt or innocence of a suspect," nor is it "a plan conceived in order to achieve a result," but rather a regime "born of social necessity and of the development of the conscience of the community." It is "something that has been found suitable to operate in England, and whose development has been allowed." It was "not a system utilized in the administration of justice," but "a system used by the Norman kings to obtain information they wanted from a person. They forced an oath on this person, and under the influence of the religious character of the oath, they demanded that he inform the king's officers of the facts they wanted to know, of which that person, who was a resident of the district, had special knowledge." This practice was later extended to the community, "requiring it to point out and bring to judgment those of its members suspected of having committed certain crimes." Juries did not at first have to judge or decide on the guilt or innocence of a person; the jury was the body which accused him or could exonerate him of a crime. When Pope Innocent III in 1215 abolished the "judgment of God" and the "ordeals", "judges made use of the jury system in the vacuum that had been created; the accused was asked to put himself at the disposal of his countrymen, and he was judged by a jury of neighbors who were themselves familiar with the case." But, once again, and the author stresses this, "this was not a system that had been carefully worked out to assign certain powers or duties to a judge and certain others to a jury; it was an improvisation by the judges and it worked." *Cf.* Bach: LE DEVELOPPEMENT DU JURY EN ANGLETERRE. *Dissertation*, Geneva, 1915. On the choice between the original system and the French system at Zurich, see von Orelli: DIE JURY IN FRANKREICH UND ENGLAND, Zurich, 1852.

[12] Luthi: REGENERATIONS BEWEGUNG UND EIDGEN-STRAFRECHTS-PFLEGE, *Rev. pén. suisse*, 1932, p. 61; DIE GESETZGEBUNG DER HELVETISCHEN REPUBLIK ÜBER DIE STRAFRECHTSPFLEGE, Berne, 1938.

[13] We shall again find Sabatier's study in the discussions, the reports and debates of the International Colloquium of Louvain in 1967 (J. Dabin Day).

[14] On the jury at its beginnings in Switzerland and on its subsequent direction, see especially De Vegobre: SUR LE JURY DANS LES PROCES CRIMINELS, Geneva, 1827; Wessel: SUR LE JURY CRIMINEL, *Dissertation*, Geneva, 1849; Masse: GUIDE ANNOTE POUR LES DEBATS CRIMINELS ET CORRECTIONNELS AVEC LE CONCOURS DU JURY, Geneva, 1850; OBSERVATIONS SUR LA POSITION DES QUESTIONS AU JURY EN MATIERE CRIMINELLE, Geneva, 1856; Mitesco: DU JURY, *Dissertation*, Geneva, 1874; Karcher: LE JURY CONSIDERE DANS L'AD-MINISTRATION DE LA JUSTICE PENALE, *Dissertation*, Geneva, 1878; Laloir: ETUDE SUR LE JURY CORRECTIONNEL DANS LES CANTONS DE LA SUISSE ROMANDE, *Bulletin de la Société de Législation comparée*, Paris, 1888, vol. 17, p. 547; Gautier: L'AFFAIRE BLANC, *Rev. pén. suisse*, 1891, p. 45; LE PROCES LUCCHENI (the assassination of Empress Elizabeth of Austria); Same journal, 1898, p. 333; Lorenzelli: IL GIURI. ORIGIN, ORGANIZATION, OPERATION, *Dissertation, Fribourg*, 1911.

[15] Gretener: ZUM ENTWURF EINES GESETZES ÜBER DIE ORGANISATION DER BUNDESGERECHTSPFLEGE (with the creation of the Federal Penal Court to the detriment of the Federal Assize Courts). *Rev. pén. suissé*, 1888, p. 234. On the impor-tant trials at the federal Assize Courts and their difficulties, see especially Kraft: A PROPOS DU PROCES CONRADI-POLOUNINE (Federal Assize Court, assassination of a U.S.S.R. delegate at Lausanne), *Rev. pén. suisse*, 1924; Pfenninger: NACH DEM URTEIL VON LAUSANNE (Conradi-Prozess), BUNDESGERICHT ODER SCHWURGE-RICHT?, *Zürcher Post* of Nov. 19, 1923, No. 272; Rott: SUR L'AFFAIRE SCHILL, *Rev. pén. suisse*, 1888, p. 314; DER NEUENBURGISCHE ANARCHISTENPROZESS. Same journal, 1890, p. 51; Stampfli (Attorney-general of the Confederation, writing re the jurisdiction of the Federal Assize Courts): ZUM FALL JUSTH (case of outrage before the League of Nations), *Rev. suisse de jurisprud.*, 1927, p. 257; ZUM FALL BASSANESI (pilot who crashed in the Gothard mountains on the way to drop anti-fascist leaflets over Milan), *Ibid*, 1931, p. 1; ZUM FALL NICOLE (Communist-influenced riot at Geneva), *Ibid*, 1933, p. 420. On the extremely reduced competence of the Federal Assize Courts, see especially von Salis: DIE KOMPETENZEN DES BUNDES IN STRAFSACHEN, *Dissertation*, Berne, 1927; Rais: LA JURIDICTION FEDERALE EN MATIERE PENALE D'APRES LES PROJECTS DE CODE PENAL ET DE CODE DE PROCE-DURE PENALE, Report to the Swiss Society of Jurists, *Acts of the Society*, 1931.

[16] Schneider: ZUR GESCHICHTE DES MILITARISCHEN RECHTSPFLEGE MIT BESONDERER RÜCKSICHT AUF DIE SCHWEIZ TRUPPEN, *Zürcher Zeitschr., f. Gerichtspraxis u. Rechtswissenschaft*, 1847. vol. 25; Dubs: DAS NEUE SCHWEIZ MILITÄRSTRAFRECHT, im *Gerichtssaal*, 1852, IV, 2, p. 219; Kocher: DIE MILITÄRGERICHTSORGANISATION DER SCHWEIZ, Zurich, 1894; Pictet: LA JUSTICE MILITAIRE EN SUISSE, *Revue internationale de criminologie et police technique*, Geneva, 1951, No. 2, p. 86.

[17] Professor Vouin's exhaustive presentation of LE DESTIN DE LA COUR D'ASSISES FRANÇAISE at the Dabin Day gives a detailed overview of the evolution, as well as useful specific points, Collection cited, 1967, pp. 132–40, partial bibliography, pp. 146–147. We ourselves have provided a detailed French bibliography for the preceding period, in our *Report to the Swiss Society of Jurists*, 1938, *Acts*, pp. 211–213.

[18] For the present composition of cantonal Courts of Assizes, see the Berne law of 1928 on judicial organization, arts. 20–35; the 1945 Neuchâtel code of penal procedure, art. 33; the new 1967 Vaud code of penal procedure, Criminal Tribunal, art. 12. (The term Court of Assizes (Cour d'assises) is no longer known; the Criminal Tribunal is com-posed of three professional judges and six jurors; during deliberations, the jurors give

their opinions first, in a sequence fixed by lot, in order to avoid both the preponderant role of the one previously called the "leader", and the risk of having the jurors too over-whelmed by the magistrates, art. 386). The Geneva bill is still under discussion. The 1958 Aargau law of penal procedure mentions a "Schwurgericht" composed of two judges of the cantonal Tribunal and five jurors, who cannot be on the police force of the cantons or the districts, employees of the penal investigation department or of the prosecutor-general, nor "lawyers for minors", nor juvenile judges (par. 8). The judgment is discussed and passed in common between the jurors and "the other judges" and this is the rule also for decisions taken in the course of the trial. The judgment must be pronounced in its entirety (*in vollständiger Ausfertigung* and thus in writing, par. 179). The 1961 Solothurn law on judicial organization retains the *Schwurgericht* composed of three judges (*Schwurgerichtskammer*) and six jurors, thenceforth combined (par. 31), and who likewise judge "*als enheitliches Gericht über Schuld und Strafe*" (par. 42) thus merging the mixed court and assessorship systems.

[19] J. Steinhaver, a Fribourg correspondent, in the *Tribune de Genève* of Dec. 15, 1969: The new 1961 Solothurn law of judicial organization provides that "jurors shall be elected in the various electoral districts of the canton in the same numbers as the *Kantonsrate* (cantonal deputies).

[20] See, for example, our paper on this subject: EXISTE-T-IL UN CHROMOSOME DU CRIME (*Comment juger le porteur d'une anomalie génétique XYY?*) in *Revue inter-national de criminologie et de police technique*, Geneva, 1968, No. 4, pp. 277 *ff*. and 1969; No. 1, pp. 21 *ff*., and on the particular point of judicial expertise and the evaluation of responsibility (re the expertise of Art. 13 CP competing with that of the new article 43, No. 1, subpara. 4), pp. 21–22.

DIVERSION

Gerhard O. W. Mueller*

I THE DEVELOPMENT OF DIVERSION

1. *Introduction*:

The term Diversion is defined in Webster's Third New International Dictionary Unabridged (1a) as

> *"the act or an instance of diverting from one cause or use to another."*

Black's venerable law dictionary knows the use of the term only in explanation of the unauthorized changing of the course of a water stream.

But during the last two or three years the term has appeared with increasing frequency, mostly in unpublished (usually xeroxed) research reports and documents, presaging its appearance in the archives of official legal and criminological terminology, in expectation of one of the most significant phenomena in the history of criminal justice administration.[1]

2. *Procedure as a Flow of Events*

Most of those engaged in various tasks or aspects of criminal procedure view the totality of procedure as a series or sequence of chores to be performed. Those who view procedure from the outside see it as a more or less disjointed system, in which given functionaries perform expected services, for an anticipated purpose. On more sophisticated examination, criminal procedure turns out to be a machinery, a production mechanism, with a certain input and a certain output, managed by mechanics or functionaries, seemingly without the supervision of a master engineer. This machinery is capable of being observed and stated in terms of the steps of production, from raw material (reported crimes) to finished products (disposition of offenders). Such observations and statements

* Professor of Law, Director, Criminal Law Education and Research Center, New York University

form the traditional content of the text books of our craft. Each step is treated with the same attention and respect.

It is the hallmark of primitive and static society that it views all given aspects of societal living as unavoidable, birth and death, diligence and reward, acquisition and taxes, crime and punishment, sickness and health. Status is lost with the discovery that what was hirtherto regarded as unalterable may indeed be changed. Sickness may be avoided or healed, birth and death may be subjected to some control, crime and punishment may be discovered as parts of a social game capable of being manipulated. Soon it appears that the ancient seemingly fatalistic flow of events from crime to punishment, without totally predictable stages, is neither unique nor unavoidable. Other measures of social control are invented or detected. It appears that the flow of events from crime to punishment has many competitors; rivers in the same valley of social control. The stream of criminal procedure flows side by side with the streams of civil procedure, of administration, indeed, of religion, of ostracism and stigma, of witchcraft, and of other powers—even chemical. Society discovers that if one stream is clogged, shallow or otherwise unpassable, another stream can be used to make progress toward the goal. With this discovery, the view of criminal procedure as a series of unavoidable events has disappeared.

Let us concentrate on the stream which we have called criminal procedure. We have said of it that its stages had once been regarded as predictably and unavoidably following each other, from crime and arrest to conviction and the gallows—a view, incidentally, which lasted from primitive times, well past the end of the Middle Ages, with very few and minor exceptions, whose number and significance has increased toward modern times. (Thus, for example, the gallows could be avoided by pleading "the benefit of clergy.")

But the inevitability of the sequences seems less overwhelming when the power and discretion of the functionaries is taken into consideration. Perhaps it is true that the functionaries of a very primitive system view themselves fatalistically merely as executors of fate, while the functionaries of more advanced society appreciate that fate is not at all that demanding. In any event, it is my contention that primitive and modern criminal procedure can be contrasted basically in these terms:

Primitive criminal procedure is regarded as the sole and inevitable sequence of events leading from apprehension of a culprit, to disposition, allowing only for an uninterrupted and unalterable flow from one source to one end. Sophisticated and/or modern criminal procedure, on the other hand, recognizes that (1) it is not the sole sequence of events which may befall a "culprit;" that (2) both the source and the end, input and output, are capable of being manipulated; and that (3) its sequences are not at all inevitable, allowing, rather, for frequent diversions from the mainstream.

The least controversial discovery or statement is the third one, pertaining to the multiplicity of sources and of ends. Modern law allows wide choices at the input and output points. At the input point, the manipulators of the system have discovered the power to select the stream on which the voyage should be commenced: civil liability, criminal liability, administrative disposition, juvenile proceedings, community care, or completely ignoring the event. At the end of the stream, the manipulators have a wide choice of dispositions—as contrasted with the once inevitable gallows—including a diversity of punishments, correctional measures, social and therapeutic interventions, or complete avoidance of any consequence.

In this essay, we shall concentrate on the second statement, which pertains to the flow manipulation, or the discovery of the power—and the actual exercise of that power—to alter the downstream voyage, to change the course and fate of a float travelling downstream. In fact, the discovery is really only recent in American law, dating from Goldstein's article, *Police Discretion Not to Invoke the Criminal Process*[2] and similar works about the discretion of all law enforcement organs,[3] and other functionaries in the system who similarly have the power to alter the course of events.

What is even younger is the movement to regularize all such diversions from that criminal process which at one time was regarded as fatalistically predictable. It is that which I mean by diversion.

3. *The Precedents of Diversion*

Official diversions from the criminal process have not been totally unknown in our process for a century; they simply had not been regarded as such. A few significant early diversions from the American criminal process deserve special mention:

(1) The establishment of juvenile jurisdictions in the late nineteenth and early twentieth century by which a significant proportion of offenders was withdrawn from the criminal process and dealt with by an alternative, less onerous method.

(2) The advent of forensic psychiatry with the passing of legislation concerning the "criminally insane" as well as other deviant offenders (e.g., psychopaths), allowing for diversion from the criminal process of wrongdoers for whom the criminal process was regarded as unsuitable.

(3) The invention of the suspended sentence, of probation and parole, allowing for the diversion from the otherwise ordinary course—which led to imprisonment—of all those who, at that juncture, were regarded as within the reach of help short of imprisonment.

Each one of these by now fairly well established procedural diversions drains a substantial portion of the procedural flotsam off the mainstream, diverting it to other channels. The amount of the diversion itself may be manipulated. By way of example, a simple increase in the age of offenders subject to juvenile court jurisdiction drains a substantial proportion of defendants from the mainstream of criminal trial jurisdiction, diverting it to juvenile court jurisdiction.

It is my contention that the number of diversions, and their intensity, have increased significantly in recent years—at least for American criminal procedure—and that these new types of diversions are being regularized through an experimental process. I should like to give some recent examples, one each for several of the more significant stages of American criminal procedure.

II: THE ACTUALITIES OF DIVERSION

1. *The Arrest Stage.*

A considerable portion of police manpower is devoted to removing intoxicated persons from the public thoroughfares, where they are an aesthetic nuisance, and a danger to themselves (and rarely to others). Traditionally, the police deliver these usually chronic alcoholics to a detention cell for overnight holding, from which they are brought for a court hearing and trial the next day. Traditionally the trial judge will sentence these hopeless human beings to a short jail term. Thereafter, they will promptly appear drunk in public again, and then the cycle starts once more.

Recently, there has come into existence a new type of social service agency, of which the Manhattan Bowery Project is an example. An agreement was reached among all authorities concerned—the police, the prosecutor, the criminal court and the health authorities—according to which the police will no longer patrol the traditional haunts of the chronic alcoholics for purposes of starting the old carousal. Rather, the "Project" will cruise the area, with a social worker and a rehabilitated alcoholic, gather the derelicts—with their permission if they are capable of giving it—take them to the shelter with its hospital and social work facilities, clean them up, dry them out, and care for them *without* adjudication or use of police—and court time and energy—i.e., without punitive intervention. If nothing else, this new method of intervention—of diversion from the criminal process—is more humanitarian and much cheaper. Indications are that the new mode of intervention has slowed down the pick-up cycle for chronic alcoholics by several weeks, indicating that the social intervention method—while not completely curative—has at least a temporary beneficial effect on the alcoholic which is longer in duration than that of the traditional adjudicative intervention.

2. *The Custody Stage.*

Skolnick has established that, at the police arrest stage, diversions in significant numbers take place, determined by criteria which have nothing to do with any of the criteria posited in criminal codes.[4] Some criminologists harbor the suspicion that it is preferable by far not to be held in custody following arrest than it is to be locked up at this stage. I need remind only of three major inconveniences which arrest and detention upon identification for wrongdoing entails: (a) detention makes it more difficult to prepare one's defense, (b) it brings about identification with other wrongdoers, with the possible acceptance of their negative values, and (c) it is costly for the state. Consequently, while in many jurisdictions, law enforcement officers always had the power—at least in the case of the vast proportion of offenses—to refrain from arresting a suspect after identification, this power too was rarely used, until in Manhattan, the Vera Institute of Justice—a private organization which cooperates with the authorities for the improvement of criminal justice—instituted the Manhattan Summons Project.

> Under this program, persons charged with certain misdemeanors and violations are released directly from the stationhouse and ordered to appear in court for arraignment at a later time. The program, supported by a generous grant from the Ford Foundation, was initiated by the New York City Police Department and the Vera Institute of Justice in order to test the hypothesis that persons charged with minor offenses who possess verifiable roots in the community can be relied upon to appear in court voluntarily and need not be held in custody until arraignment. The primary purpose of an arrest—to bring the suspected offender before the court—can thus be accomplished in a way that frees police manpower for preventive patrol, preserves the rights of individuals, and reduces expenses to the taxpayer.[5]

3. *The Pre-Trial Detention Stage.*

According to the traditional American rule, a person charged with crime has to remain in custody pending his trial, unless he can post a bail bond deemed sufficient by the court to guarantee his appearance at court if set free pending trial. As early as 1927, Beeley demonstrated the inadequacy—nay, the complete absurdity—of this system which rewards the rich and punishes the poor with no discernible beneficial impact upon the criminal justice system, and no regard for criteria which really matter, namely dangerousness.[6]

Thanks to the personal efforts of a few scholars, reformers and philanthropists, massive research and demonstration programs were started all over the United States, culminating in the National Conference on Bail and Criminal Justice,[7] with the result that, today, in many jurisdictions, notably in New York, tested criteria are employed to determine risk factors for court appearances. The result is, once again, a significant diversion from the theretofore inevitable flow of the criminal process, into more humanitarian, less costly, and certainly no less effective channels.

At the Criminal Law Education and Research Center of New York University, efforts are currently underway to devise a new pre-trial supervisory system for federal defendants who cannot be freely discharged pending trial. What may emerge is a new form of pre-trial control for persons theretofore invariably detained pending trial—perhaps in the form of a pre-trial halfway house, from which pre-trial detainees could be furloughed for hours or days.

There is no limit to human imagination at this or any other stage of the criminal process. No heretofore inevitable next step is regarded as sacrosanctly mandatory. The search for alternatives—for diversions—is on.

4. *The Accusation Stage.*

That prosecutors have a certain amount of discretion has long been recognized in those European countries who regarded their systems as government by the "opportunity principle," as distinguished from those countries in which a "legality principle" demanded a prosecution in all cases where the evidence warranted it. We have been slow to recognize the difference in the United States, but once we did, we left no doubt about the fact that our prosecutors possess and in fact exercise a vast amount of discretion whether to prosecute, and for which greater or lesser crime or degree thereof to prosecute in any given case. If it were not the case that close to ninety percent of all criminal defendants in American courts plead guilty, the system plainly would be incapable of handling the flow of offenders. Thus, necessity seems to be

the principal reason for today's diverting of perhaps ninety percent of all criminal defendants from the once seemingly unavoidable
next step, trial. But it is, perhaps, not the only reason—especially in
a society which can afford more courtrooms and more judges, if it
really needed them. There is, perhaps, the feeling that the definitions
of offenses are so all-encompassing as to include far more persons within
the sweep of their definition than merit inclusion; that the punishments
provided for all these offenses are far more exacting than deserved for
the conduct in question, and that the prognosticated benefits of the
imposition of sanctions are all but fictitious. Under those circumstances,
it seems quite plausible to do what seems more humanitarian than,
and at least as efficacious as, that which the law seems to postulate as
inevitable. Modern literature, both American[8] and Canadian,[9] abounds
with accounts of the prosecutor's discretion not to invoke the criminal
process, and of judicially stimulated avoidance of criminal trials.

Two years ago an offspring of the Vera Institute of Justice, the Manhattan Court Employment Project, made its appearance. This project

> is an experimental attempt to intervene in the usual court process
> just after a defendant's arrest, to offer him counselling and job
> opportunities and, if he cooperates and appears to show promise
> of permanent change, to recommend that the prosecutor (District
> Attorney) and the judge dismiss the charges against him without
> ever deciding whether he is guilty. Thus, the MCEP attempts to
> convert a participant's arrest from a losing to a winning experi-
> ence. The system stands to benefit from this conversion as much
> as the defendant. Successful participants leave the project
> working and earning an honest living, the community gains
> a taxpayer, and the resources of the over-burdened criminal
> justice system are freed to attend to serious cases.[10]

In its two years of operation, this project has already benefited
hundreds of defendants for whom a prison career had theretofore
seemed inevitable, until this diversion system was invented.

A word seems necessary about the occasionally voiced danger which
inheres in any system that assumes control over the life and conduct
of a human being who has not yet been adjudicated. The danger does
exist, and care must be taken to advise all participants of their right to
trial whenever they propose to contest their criminal liability, so that
this diversion project is applicable only to those who would normally
propose to plead guilty or expect to be convicted on the basis of all
available evidence.

5. *The Adjudication Stage.*

It was already noted that American law has now reached the stage at which it regards criminal trials as a fiscal evil to be avoided. The question is, what is to take the trial's place whenever a criminal defendant can be profitably diverted from the regular flow of the criminal process.

For many years, the therapists of the New York Chapter of the Association for Psychiatric Treatment of Offenders (APTO), had an arrangements with certain trial judges. They would stay further proceedings if a defendant—who was unquestionably bound to be convicted—would consent to accept psychotherapeutic care by one of the APTO therapists. If that therapist could report to the court within the period specified (e.g., six months) that the defendant was on the road to successful adjustment, the defendant would never be found guilty; he would not have the stigma of a "record."

Diligent observers of our system have long been troubled by the show of majesty with which our trial judiciary imposes its pronouncements, including the raised bench, the black robes, the national colors, the subservient attendants and what not. The majesty seems shaky—particulary when God is invoked for the evidence, and all "the People" are called upon for the verdict—in view of the fact, and it is fact— that the sanctions imposed by the tribunal are the merest guesswork, and the ends to be achieved—justice and criminal prosecution—are less predictable than the pronouncements of astrologers. It was perhaps with such thoughts in mind that the American Arbitration Association recently took steps to develop a system of arbitration in some situations involving community disputes and controversy in which the existing system proscribes the use of the traditional mediating of criminal justice. Another recognition of the need to divert from the criminal process! A successful pilot project has already been carried out in Philadelphia.[11]

6. *The Sentence Stage.*

Earlier I had taken note of the invention of alternatives to imprisonment (which itself had already become an alternative to capital punishment), in the by now traditional forms of probation—in lieu of all imprisonment, and parole—in lieu of the last remaining portion of imprisonment. But recent years have seen further experimentation at this stage of the criminal process, with the invention of two significant diversion methods: work release and halfway houses, both less onerous restraints than straight imprisonment, more humanitarian, and, according to the evidence at hand, not merely *as* effective in preventing recidivism, but perhaps more so. It is noteworthy that the United Nations Secretariat Report on the "Standard Minimum Rules for the Treatment of Prisoners in the Light of Recent Development in Corrections," of 1970, has paid special tribute to these innovative methods of diversion from the criminal process.[12]

III: THE IMPACT OF DIVERSION

1. *The Flow of Criminal Defendants*

National statistics are only a very rough, gross estimate as to the true extent of the diversion process. For individual states or cities the figures are somewhat more accurate. But for New York, estimates of diversion based on different types of statistics, collected for different purposes, also vary widely. A LIFE Magazine report stated: "the appalling arithmetic is that in New York if you commit a felony, the chances of being arrested, indicted, found guilty of the original charge and then going to prison, are a great deal less than one in 200."[13] However, if one begins with the detection of crime as a starting point for the system, the actual diversion rate for the City would appear to be much smaller. A recent Rand Institute study shows the diversion rate to be as follows: of 330,243 persons arrested or summoned for crime in 1967, 181,063 pleaded guilty, 14,310 were convicted and 13,173 sent for disposition to a higher court (i.e. almost 2/3). But only one in ten of those determined to be guilty in one way or another, ultimately went to prison.[14]

2. *Some Basic Questions About Procedural Diversions.*

The enormous extent and frequency of diversions in American criminal procedure raises some fundamental questions about the philosophy of such a system. There can be very little doubt that historically—and for both old and new forms of diversion—the impetus for diversion derived from the overburdening of the system, coupled with the unwillingness or incapacity of the administrators and guardians of the system to expand it in such a way as to accommodate smoothly the new burdens. But there is also little doubt that this impetus has given rise to the invention of procedural ideas and methods—namely diversions, which constitute not only relief but often improvement. The diversions were instituted after all, with the blessings of the administrators and guardians of the system, who thereby indicated their dissatisfaction with old methods, with the overextension of the reach of substantive and procedural criminal law, and with the effects of the old system.

The efficacy of the old American criminal procedure was frightfully small. Dissatisfaction with the system is great: in terms of input (who was subjected to the system and should not really have been), output (who comes out of the system in a deteriorated condition) and the flow in between (the millions frustrated by delay and inefficacy). The diversions, on the other hand, have proven to be "curative" in many respects: more humanitarian than other regular approaches, not less efficacious in terms of control of the crime rate and the correction of offenders, and furthermore, less expensive. Diversions, then, while seemingly temporary emergency measures in the face of a bulging, bursting criminal procedural apparatus in the United States, may well point the way toward a new procedural system which regularizes these "emergency" measures.

3. *Decriminalization: Diversion in the Substantive Criminal Law*

It is possible to view diversion as simply the procedural aspect of a significant overall development aimed at decriminalization of social norms and remedies. It is perhaps true that, in the past, society has been overly eager to relegate every difficult social and/or economic problem to the cultural refuse dump, the criminal law, in hopes that somehow the problem would then solve itself. Such expectations have proven unjustified.[15] Deep dissatisfaction with the overburdened criminal justice system has set in, and an effort to decriminalize conduct norms has set in. By way of example, Illinois has begun decriminalizing its victimless sex offenses.[16] New York has removed abortion from legal to medical control,[17] and has diverted much of its traffic control from criminal to administrative jurisdiction.[18] There is a serious debate on whether traditional criminal law sanctions are useful for economic regulation.[19]

An astute observer of these developments, Nicholas Kittrie, has called it "The Divestment of Criminal Law," and, not without some misgivings, anticipates the criminal law's replacement by the therapeutic state.[20]

"Criminal Law in the United States has been undergoing a process of divestment resulting in the relinquishment of its jurisdictions over many of its prior subjects and areas," says Kittrie.[21] The debate on the *pros and cons*[22] of what is here viewed as a necessary reduction of the criminal law's reach, is now in full progress. The interesting thing is that, regardless of the philosopher's debates, the tide seems to have turned from overcriminalization[23] to decriminalization.

Overcriminalization was the scare reaction which the rapid social change flowing from industrialization brought about. Scare has given way to reflection and contemplation. Of course, the rapid social change which is taking place in the United States, and perhaps in all highly industrialized societies, has posed challenges to traditional modes of repressive penal policy. As yet, we—industrialized society—have not even developed an adequate theoretical framework for the study of the interaction of penal law and policy, on the one hand, and social change on the other.[24] We are, thus, compelled to observe and record more or less episodically, lacking the skill to intervene with predictable effect.

A new philosophy, an outlook on life, makes itself heard and felt with its clamor for greater tolerance of opposing views and unorthodox mores. In the same vein, where scholars work toward recodification of criminal laws, they are also cutting down on the vast sweep of prohibitions which has marked all penal law. In particular, where criminal justice will be computerized, the aim and necessary consequence will be a reduction of inflated and multiple criminal liabilities to small and essential cores.

It may be too early to assess the entire movement. At this point, decriminalization of substantive law and social order, and its procedural counterpart, diversion, seem nothing more or less than a healthy, natural reaction to an opposing tendency which until recently had so overburdened the criminal law and its processes as to drive it virtually to the breaking point.

NOTES

[1] The term may have originated in the report of the President's Commission on Crime in the United States, *The Challenge of Crime in a Free Society*, 133 (1967): "Procedures are needed to *divert* from the criminal process mentally disordered and deficient persons." (Emphasis supplied.) To my knowledge, only one title has used the term diversion so far: Brakel and South, *Diversion from the Criminal Process in the Rural Community*, 7 Am. Crim. L. Q. 122 (1969).

Upon completion of the manuscript, an article by Eleanor Harlow was received, *Diversion from the Criminal Justice System*, 2 Crim. & Del. Lit. 136 (1970). This is a review of several diversion projects currently being conducted in the U.S.A.

[2] Goldstein, J., *Police Discretion not to Invoke the Criminal Process:* Low Visibility Decisions in the Administration of Justice, 69 Yale L.J. 543 (1960).

[3] Kadish, *Legal Norms and Discretion in the Police and Sentencing Processes,* 75 Harv. L. Rev. 902 (1962): La Fave, *The Police and Nonenforcement of the Law,* 1962 Wis. L. Rev. 104; La Fave, *Arrest: The Decision to Take a Suspect into Custody* (1965); Newman, D., *Conviction: The Determination of Guilt or Innocence without Trial* (1966); Goldstein, H.,

Administrative Problems in Controlling the Exercise of Police Authority, 58 J. Crim. L., C. & P. S. 160 (1967); id., *Police Discretion: The Ideal versus the Real,* 23 Pub. Admin. Rev. 140 (1963); Kaplan, *The Prosecutorial Discretion—A Comment,* 60 Nw. U. L. Rev. 174 (1965); see also, Davis, *Discretionary Justice* (1969). Schwartz, L.B., *Federal Criminal Jurisdiction and Prosecutor's Discretion,* 13 Law & Contemp. Problems 64 (1948).

[4] Skolnick, *Justice Without Trial* (1966).

[5] *The Manhattan Summons Project,* published by the Criminal Justice Coordinating Council of New York City and Vera Institute of Justice 1 (n.d., 1970?).

[6] Beeley, The *Bail System in Chicago* (1927).

[7] See Freed and Wold, *Bail in the United States: 1964* (1964); Proceedings, National Conference on Bail and Criminal Justice (1965); Proceedings, Bail and Summons: 1965 (1965).

[8] See *op. cit.* above, n. 3.

[9] Grosman, *The Prosecutor: An Inquiry into the Exercise of Discretion* (1969).

[10] The Manhattan Court Employment Project of the Vera Institute of Justice 7 (1970).

[11] Communication of February 11, 1970, from the American Arbitration Association to the author.

[12] The Standard Minimum Rules for the Treatment of Prisoners in the Light of Recent Developments in the Correctional Field—Working paper prepared by the Secretariat, United Nations, 1970. A/Conf. 43/3.

[13] *Logjam in Our Courts,* LIFE 69 No. 6, 18, 20 (August 7, 1970).

[14] Oelsner, *Criminal Courts: Statistical Profile,* N.Y.Times, (March 28, 1970).

[15] See Packer, *The Limits of the Criminal Sanction* (1968); Morris and Hawkins, *The Honest Politician's Guide to Crime Control* (1969); Kadish, *Crisis of Overcriminalization,* 7 Am. Crim. L. Q. 17 (1968); Mueller, *Human Rights and the Treatment of Offenders,* 10 Can. J. Corr. 352, 357–358 (1968).

[16] Ill. Rev. Stat. Tit. 38, Crim. Code of 1961, punishing "deviate sexual conduct" only if committed by force or threat thereof, §11–3, or on children, §11–4; §11–5.

[17] N.Y.P.L.»125.05.3

[18] Laws of New York, 1969, ch. 1075, amending §155 of the Vehicle and Traffic Law, effective July 1, 1970.

[19] Kadish, *Some Observations on the Use of Criminal Sanctions in Enforcing Economic Regulations,* 30 U. Chi. L. Rev. 423 (1963). Decriminalization, see: C. M. Friedman, *Use of Criminal Sanctions in the Enforcement of Economic Legislation: A Sociological View,* 17 Stan. L. Rev. 197 (1965).

[20] Kittrie, *The Divestment of Criminal Law and the Coming of the Therapeutic State,* (Suffolk U. L. Rev. 43 (1967); see also Allen, *The Borderland of Criminal Justice* (1964).

[21] *op. cit.* above, n. 20.

[22] Devlin, *The Enforcement of Morals* (1959).

[23] Kadish, *The Crisis of Overcriminalization,* 7 Am. Crim. L.Q. 17 (1968).

[24] See Rose, *The Use of Law to Induce Social Change,* 6 Transact. 3rd World Congr. Soc. 52 (1956); Mueller, *Changing Law in a Changing Society and Social Change and Legal Change in Puerto Rico,* in Hansen (ed.), *Social Change and Public Policy* 118 (1968).

VICTIMOLOGY *

During recent years, the public interest in the penal system has sharply increased, and has been reflected in the daily press, the radio and television. The trend has been toward advocating the humanization of penal law and prison administration, and a movement in this direction has originated with legal sociologists. They have noted that a lot of relatively serious transgressions never become known to the police, or that insufficient evidence for indictment is provided. Among other things, sociologists have become interested in the relationship between criminal records and social status. It has been pointed out that the risk of discovery decreases with higher social status. On the other hand, the lower the social status, the fewer are the acquittals, and the more frequent are prison terms rather than fines. Sociologists believe that social injustice underlies these facts. Society's legal view of theft is still marked by concepts belonging to an era when economic prosperity was restricted, and when possessions of value consisted, as a rule, of cash, food supplies, and tools, the loss of which might spell disaster. In a more general way, the modern trend is based on the assumption that the dividing line between the "criminal" and his "victim" ought to be less pronounced than was the case under previous criminal policies.

It would, however, be wrong to assume that the modern views have achieved any clear victory. It is worthwhile to notice various undercurrents.

As an example, one might quote a reader's letter in the daily *Aktuelt* of January 21st 1967:

> An old lady is attacked while asleep in her bed and brought to hospital in terrible shape. The guilty young man is sentenced to a year of prison and after his release he gets a job and makes good

---

* This term has been gaining ground in modern criminology to denote "the science of the victim."

** Ombudsman for Civil and Military Administration, Denmark

money. Society has done all it could to straighten him out and help him to a fresh start. So far, so good, but the affair also has another aspect, which has apparently been completely forgotten: the innocent victim of the crime.

To her, it meant a long and painful hospital stay, and a lot of expenses. She has had to pay it all out of her modest pension, as she has not seen one penny of the damages awarded her, although two years have passed by now. Upon repeared inquiries, she is told just to be patient. She is approaching the age of 80.

Can society really do nothing to gain justice for her? Aren't we going to extremes, when everything is done for the criminal, while the victim is allowed to pay?

The opinion expressed in this letter undoubtedly enjoys wide support, and in various countries, bills and proposals are being introduced with the aim of providing some sort of help to the victims of criminal acts. But there does not appear to be any deeper theoretical research into the subject.

Although Professor Hans Von Hentig has published a major work with the title *The Criminal and his Victim* (Yale University, 1948) only a small section at the end of the book—which is, incidentally, interesting in several respects—deals directly with the subject reterrea to. The author is concerned mainly with the role of the victim as a provoking agent in relation to the criminal.

One might also mention the more recent work by Dennis Chapman in his book, *Sociology and the Stereotype of the Criminal.*[1] Here, under the heading: The Role of the Victim in Crime, the author rejects the common view of the "victim" of the crime as an innocent participant with a claim to the support of society and an interest on a level with that of the police and the Attorney General, in the prosecution of the criminal. According to the author, this is the victim's role in only a minority of cases. Who, in the final event, plays the role of victim or criminal may often be altogether accidental. Reference is made, in this connection, to the investigation by Kaare Svalastoga, into the relationship between manslaughter and previous contact, in the killer-victim relationship.[2]

Furthermore, in Danish literature, the subject is touched upon by Carl Popp-Madsen in the book *Bod* (amends),[3] particularly as regards cases of damage of a non-economic kind. See also Von Eyber,[4] who contends that it is more important that persons who have suffered receive compensation than that the state gets its fine.

Of particular interest is the development in this field in England. The plea for a reform movement there may be found in an article by the highly esteemed Margery Fry in the Observer of July 7, 1957, entitled *Justice for Victims*. But before this subject was closely considered in England, it had been made the subject of legislation in New Zealand, which must be regarded as the pioneering country.

On October 25, 1963, the Criminal Injuries Compensation Act was enacted in New Zealand. The law deals with cases where bodily harm is done to a person in a manner subject to punishment. The compensation includes expenses as a result of the injuries or death of the victim, loss resulting from inability to work, and compensation for sustained pain. A special commission was established to administer the law: the Crimes Compensation Tribunal.

As to the development in England, the following details should be mentioned:

In February, 1959, a special report on Penal Practice in a Changing Society was presented to Parliament. It stated *i.a.*, "Indeed in the public mind the interests of the offender may not infrequently seem to be placed before those of his victim."

A new working committee appointed in this context presented its report in a new White Paper of June, 1961, entitled Compensation for Victims of Crimes of Violence. This report, in turn, provided the basis for the White Paper of 1964, whose conclusion in regard to this point reads as follows: "The proposals are put forward as a practical method of meeting what is now an acknowledged need simply and quickly, and of ensuring that, in all the consideration which is being given to new and more effective methods of treating offenders, the sufferings of innocent victims of violent crimes do not go unregarded."

Important for the development in England has also been the positive attitude in regard to this issue displayed by the English association, Justice. In its 9th Report dated July, 1966, "Compensation for Victims of Violence", it expresses regret that, in practice, the measures introduced are inadequate, since the claim for compensation has been rejected in cases where the guilty party is a child below the age of 10 or an insane person.

The same report states that applications for compensation and approval of such applications have been increasing greatly in number. In 1965, 757 applicants were granted 295,000 pounds sterling; during the first three months of 1966, the sums paid amounted to respectively 34,000; 45,000; and 50,000 pounds sterling. More information on the steadily accelerating increase in the number and size of compensations may be found in the first four annual reports of the Criminal Compensation Board, 1965–1968.

It should be noted that the development which has taken place in England, was not based upon—nor has it brought about—any actual legal measures, but is merely the result of government decisions, which were announced to Parliament.

In the USA, signs similar to those in England are apparent. In New York State, on October 1, 1966, a regulation was enacted introducing a Crime-Victims Compensation Board with wide powers.[5]

The subject has been dealt with in recent German and French theoretical works, e.g., Fritz R. Paasch has published an article entitled *Problèmes Fondamentaux et Situation de la Victimologie*,[6] which appears to consist of excerpts from a German doctoral thesis. The author deals with works by Edgar Dénez[7] and H. Ellenberger[8]. Paasch mentions the Jerusalem attorney B. Mendelsohn as the "founder of modern victimology." According to him, it was a lecture by the latter in 1947, in Bucharest, which inspired the subsequent research.

Mendelsohn—who, unfortunately, is referred to here through a second source—deals with the very theoretical question whether victimology is a new and independent science or merely a new subdivision of criminology. It does not seem fruitful to pose this question. It should be sufficient to establish the fact that there is so much practical interconnection between the subjects constituting the core in criminological research on the one hand, and the study of the victims' conditions on the other hand, that it would be useful to include these conditions in the province of criminology.

Another and more important field of activity for criminology is the determination of factors which expose the potential victim to a particular risk. Mendelsohn is apparently inclined to apply methods of psychological investigation in order to estimate the potential victims' vulnerability. Here, undeniably, one moves on grounds calling for caution.[9]

The subjects referred to above have not attracted any great attention in Scandinavian literature. However, one might point to deliberations at the Scandinavian meeting of criminologists in Oslo in 1957, where one of the subjects was: What measures should be taken to safeguard the interests of injured persons? Professor Bo Palmgren[10] briefly summarizes the discussion in the relevant section as follows:

The section was unanimous in the conclusion that, to a large extent, consideration of the compensation claims of the injured party must be an integral part of criminal policy. The confidence of the public in the justice of penal law would be strengthened very considerably if the injured parties could expect not to have to suffer economically. Under the existing penal code, there is little consideration for the injured party. In legal procedure, recent developments have tended to weaken the position of the victim. At least in cases where considerable compensation claims are at stake, it would be desirable to make available to the injured party, an appropriate machinery to assist him to make the compensation claim before, during, and after the trial, just as support is provided to the accused by making legal defense available to him.

The same report in the 1957 yearbook, makes it clear that in the Swedish *Riksdag* (Parliament) a proposal was introduced in 1956 to place a certain proportion of the fines in a special fund to provide compensation for injured persons.

The prevailing opinion, however, appears to be that there is no prospect of ensuring, to any considerable extent, economic compensation for the injured party through the system of fines. Only if claims in this respect could be enforced by withholding salaries and wages, could anything of greater practical value be achieved.

It might be pointed out that in Finland persons not paying fines imposed upon them may be placed in working camps. One might also note the stipulations in the Danish penal code according to which payment of compensation becomes an integral part of conditional verdicts.[11]

A question which may not as yet have found its final solution is whether anything could, and should, be done to grant the injured party greater influence than he now has regarding the question of whether a case should be brought before the court or prosecution be discontinued.

As a matter of principle, the injured party enjoys no rights in this respect. He is not a "party" to the case. If he is called upon to testify, he does so as a witness, not as a party. The Attorney-General enjoys a monopoly as prosecutor. There exists a need for safeguards against unjustified waiving of indictment and against refusal of the police to undertake investigation and prosecution following a private complaint. A safeguard of sorts exists in the right to appeal to a higher authority the decision not to prosecute. Thus, the decision of the police may be appealed before the State Attorney and, in turn, to the Attorney-General, the Minister of Justice, and from there further to the *Ombudsman* of the *Folketing* (Danish Parliament). Furthermore, in practice, a set of rules has been developed recognizing the claim of the injured party to be heard and to give his version in the course of the trial.

Let us now discuss briefly the regulations placing the decision to initiate and maintain the criminal prosecution in the hands of the injured party, *i.e.* the so-called private penal cases.

In my description of *Danish Penal Law and Procedure*[12] I have expressed sympathy with the introduction of general rules concerning private accusation, such as exist in Norway and Sweden. This suggestion, however, has not gained any wider measure of support. Nor, I must admit, have my experiences as *Ombudsman* provided material proof of the advisability of allowing extensive rights for private criminal charges.

In the existing Danish penal code, the so-called joint trial—*i.e.*, legal prosecution of civil claims in connection with the criminal case— deserves major attention. Regulations in this respect are to be found in chapter 89 of the Law on Legal Procedure. According to § 991, in police trials and cases, where the accused admitted the charge, damages may be awarded the injured party from the accused for harm or injuries sustained as a result of the crime. But the general rule in these cases is that the injured party must himself file the compensation claim. In other penal cases initiated by the public prosecutor, the latter may— if this can be done without considerable inconvenience—sustain the compensation claim of the injured party at the latter's request.

The court may, however, at any stage of the trial deny the right to maintain this claim. With particular regard to cases of motor vehicles, under § 67 of the Traffic Law, the insurance company involved is entitled to appear in the trial with the status of a party to the case.

Finally, an important element in safeguarding the rights of the injured party is the effort to achieve a proper treatment of court cases in the press. Here, one might refer to the publication issued in 1960, by the Joint Committee of Danish Daily Newspapers, which states, *inter alia*:

> Reporting . . . must be performed with due consideration to avoid causing anyone—including the party injured in the course of the offense—losses or inconvenience, which are not justified by the public's interest in information.
>
> Much care should be taken not to publicise unduly the name of the injured party, particularly in cases concerning moral offenses.

The time is obviously ripe for undertaking a deeper investigation of whether or not to enact in Danish law an arrangement along the lines of that existing in the English legal system to defend the interests of the injured party. The investigation would have to include all aspects of regulations already in existence to secure the rights of the victim. From the outset, there would be no reason to let the regulations apply only to crimes of violence. Neither would there be adequate grounds to grant the injured party only an *ex gratia* sum of compensation rather than an amount which would be based on the actual losses sustained by him. The issue may also be seen as some sort of insurance against loss resulting from criminal acts.

NOTES

1. Dennis Chapman: *Sociology and the Stereotype of the Criminal,* Tavistock Publications. London. 1968. pp. 153–166.
2. The American Journal of Sociology, 1956, p. 37 *ff.*
3. Carl Popp-Madsen: *Bod,* Copenhagen. 1933.
4. Von Elber: *Festskrift til Ussing,* 1951. p. 126 ff.
5. Revue de Science Criminelle et de Droit Pénal Comparé, 1968, p. 166, and, in more detail, Gerhard O.W. Mueller: in the Minnesota Law Review, 1965, p. 213 *ff.*
6. Revue Internationale de Droit Pénal, 1967, p. 121 *ff.*
7. Edgar Denez: *Der Betrogene,* Hamburg. 1961.
8. H. Ellenberger. *Relations Psychologiques Entre le Criminel et sa Victime.*
9. Paul Cornil: Revue de Droit Pénal, 1959, p. 559.
10. *Nordisk Kriminalistisk Arsbok,* 1957. p. 201 ff.
11. §84, Danish Penal Law, regarding compensation for damages.
12. *Danish Penal Law and Procedure,* first edition. 1940. p. 346 ff.

THE CONTRIBUTORS

CASSIN, RENE-SAMUEL (b. Bayonne, France, 1887). Nobel Peace Prize winner, 1968; Member of the Conseil Constitutionnel, Professor Emeritus of the Law Faculties of Lille and Paris, Member and past-President of the Commission on Human Rights of the United Nations, President of the European Court of Human Rights, President (since 1943) of the *Alliance Israélite Universelle*; *Doctor honoris causa* of the Universities of Oxford, Mainz, Hebrew Union College-Jewish Institute of Religion, Brandeis, London, Mayence, and Hebrew University of Jerusalem. Between the two World Wars, was President of the *Union Fédérale des Mutilés et Anciens Combattants*; Active in Free French political activities, and in the beginnings of the U.N. (he was eventually the principal author of the Universal Declaration of Human Rights, 1948). A prolific writer, he has published numerous books, and concentrated much of his writing, both in books and articles, on the problems of human rights. *Decorations*: Among others, Grand-Croix de la Légion d'Honneur, Officier de la Résistance et Compagnon de la Libération, Commandeur de l'Ordre des Palmes Académiques.

COHEN, MAXWELL (b. Winnipeg, Canada, 1910). Professor of Law, McGill Univ., since 1952; Dean, Faculty of Law, 1964–1969; Director, McGill Institute of Air and Space Law, 1962; President, International Law Association (Canadian Branch) 1952–58; Chairman, Constitutional & International Law Committee, Canadian Bar Assn.; Chairman, Minister of Justice Special Committee on Hate Propaganda in Canada, 1965–66; Chairman, Royal Commission on Labor Legislation in Newfoundland and Labrador, 1969–70.

FERRACUTI, FRANCO, (b. 1927). Medical psychologist, Professor of Criminology, University of Rome, School of Law; presently engaged as consultant to the Observation Center of the Italian Ministry of Justice and to the United Nations Social Defense Research Institute. Has beeen a member since 1966 of the Criminological Scientific Council of the Council of Europe. Worked for many years in the United States, at the University of Wisconsin, at New York University, at the University of Pennsylvania, at the United Nations Secretariat, and as Director of a Criminology Program at the University of Puerto Rico. Has contributed many papers and monographs to criminological and psychological journals.

FOIGHEL, ISI (b. 1927). Professor of Law (International Law and Danish Civil Law) at the University of Copenhagen, since 1965. Director of the Institute of International Law and European Community Law, Copenhagen, active in his legal capacity in many international organizations, and has fulfilled numerous tasks in that connection as teacher and adviser; a member of UNESCO since 1966, and of the Executive Board for United Nations High Commissioner for Refugees since 1968. A prolific writer of books and articles. Member of Editorial Board of Common Market Law Review.

DI GENNARO, GUISEPPE. An Appeal Court Judge, presently Director of the Research Unit of the Correctional Administration of the Italian Ministry of Justice; has for many years conducted research and training in the Italian Criminal Justice System. He is Consultant to the United Nations Social Defense Research Institute in Rome; has authored many papers on different aspects of criminal justice.

GOLDBERG, ARTHUR (b. Chicago, Illinois, 1908). At present with the law firm of Paul, Weiss, Goldberg, Rifkin, Wharton and Garrison, in New York City. Became Associate Justice of the Supreme Court of the United States in 1962; served as Permanent Representative of the United States to the United Nations, 1965–1968; was President John F. Kennedy's Secretary of Labor, 1961–1962. Has engaged alternately in practice in private law firms and in public office; also served as legal counsel to many organizations, mainly in union matters. Author of articles in American legal publications and journals of opinion, also the author of several books.

GRAVEN, JEAN (b. Switzerland, 1899). Professor Emeritus of the University of Geneva, where he held the Chair of Penal Law and Civil and Criminal Procedure from 1943, and served subsequently as Dean of the Law Faculty, vice-rector and in 1963–64 as rector. Has also had a long legal career at the Court of Cassation of Geneva. Doctor of Law honoris causa of the Universities of Rennes, Lyon, Liège, and Fribourg-en-Brisgau. Member of the Board of the International Faculty of Comparative Law at Strasbourg. Member of many international legal associations, and holder of many distinctions. Devoted much of his efforts since World War II to the problems of war victims, indemnification, and human rights. Among his legal achievements: the Ethiopian Penal Code of 1957. Has been the scientific director of the International Review of Criminology and Police Science of Geneva. His latest book, in honor of René Cassin, has just been published.

HURWITZ, STEPHAN (b. Copenhagen, 1901). Parliamentary Commissioner (ombudsman) for civil and military state administration, Denmark since 1955. Started as a barrister, 1929–35, went on to a teaching career, became lecturer in 1931, and was eventually appointed Professor of Law, University of Copenhagen, 1935. Doctor honoris causa of the Universities of Stockholm, Oslo, and Helsinki. Among his public functions, served as chief of the refugees' office in Stockholm in 1943–44, and was a member of the War Crimes Commission in London in 1945. Author of numerous legal works.

KOREY, WILLIAM. Director of the U.N. Office of the B'nai B'rith International Council since May, 1960; represents B'nai B'rith and the Coordinating Board of Jewish Organizations at the U.N. Was Assistant Professor of History and Social Sciences at Long Island University and at City College of New York. Has also lectured at Howard University, University of Maryland and Brandeis University. In 1962–63 lectured at Columbia University on Russian History. Has written many books, articles and reviews.

KONVITZ, MILTON. Professor of Law and Professor of Industrial Labor Relations at Cornell University. Has been a Guggenheim, Fund for the Republic, and Ford Foundation Fellow, a member of the Institute for Advanced Study at Princeton, and a fellow at the Center for Advanced Study in Behavioral Sciences at Stanford. Has also been Paley Lecurer, Israel Goldstein Lecturer, and Visiting Professor at the Hebrew University of Jerusalem.

LEVY, YUVAL (b. Tel Aviv, 1932). Lecturer on Criminal Law, Hebrew University, Tel Aviv University; Deputy-Director, Tel Aviv University Institute of Criminology and Criminal Law; Member of Israel Bar. M. Jur., Jerusalem, 1955; Research Assistant, Hebrew University and Tel Aviv High School of Law and Economics, 1954–55. Defense Counsel, Prosecutor, Legal Adviser and Instructor Judge Advocates Corps, 1955–58. Doctor of Laws (J.S.D.) Yale, 1960. Author of many publications.

MARKS, BARBARA JOAN (b. New Haven, U.S.A., 1942). Degree in English Literature from Brown University in 1964, J.D., Columbia University, 1967. A member of the New York Bar, was associated with Greenbaum, Wolff & Ernst in New York City; immigrated to Israel in November, 1968. At Columbia, was on the editorial board of the Columbia Journal of Transnational Law.

MERON, THEODOR (b. 1930). M.J., Hebrew University of Jerusalem, LL. M. Harvard University. Legal Adviser, Israel Ministry for Foreign Affairs since 1967; Arlozoroff Prize in International Law (Jerusalem, 1958). Has represented Israel before various international bodies and before the United Nations in various functions, since 1959. Author of numerous articles on international law, mostly in relation to Israel.

MUELLER, GERHARD, O.W. (b. Germany, 1926). Professor of Law, Director, Criminal Law Educations and Research Center of New York University since 1958. Since 1960, Director of that university's Comparative Criminal Law Project. Studied in Germany, Switzerland and the United States, where he got his Doctor Juris (University of Chicago, 1953).

Professor Mueller has held visiting appointments in various United States and European universities. He was President of the American Society of Criminology in 1967–68, Vice-President of the International Association of Penal Law since 1964, and its permanent representative to the United Nations. In addition, Professor Mueller serves as adviser or consultant to several government agencies. He is most active in fostering intensive international and comparative research on crime, delinquency and criminal justice. His published works include about 200 scientific articles concerned mostly with problems of criminal law and criminology, and ten books.

NEWMAN, RALPH A. Professor of Law, University of California Hastings College of the Law; Professor Emeritus, American University, Washington, D.C.; Member, Board of Directors, and Past President, American Society for legal History; Member, Committee on Research of the Association of American Law Schools. Has taught and lectured extensively in many countries, including France, Germany, Israel, Brazil, Belgium, Luxembourg and England. Author of several books.

OTTOLENGHI, SMADAR (b. Haifa 1937). Lecturer in Commercial Law at Tel Aviv University. Ph. D., 1968. Was an assistant to Judge Haim Cohn.

ROSENNE, SHABTAI (b. London, 1917). LL.B., London; Ph. D., Hebrew University of Jerusalem. Israel's Deputy Permanent Representative to the United Nations since 1967; former Legal Adviser, Israel Ministry for Foreign Affairs, 1948–67; Formerly a colleague of Haim Cohn in the Secretariat, Legal Commission, the Preparation Committee of the State of Israel (Vaadat ha Matsav), January-May, 1948. "Israel Prize" winner, 1960. Certificate of Merit, American Society of International Law, 1968. Has represented Israel abroad on various international legal bodies and in numerous cases. A prolific writer, he has published contributions in many journals in Hebrew, English, and French, on questions of Israeli and international law. Among his books is a two-volume work on the International Court of Justice. Member of the International Law Commission.

SILVING, HELEN (b. Krakow, Poland). Professor of Law at the University of Puerto Rico since 1957. Holder of two doctorates (University of Vienna and Columbia University), was admitted to the New York Bar in 1944, to practice before the Supreme Court of the United States in 1951, and to the first Bar of Korea in 1964. Has had an active legal teaching and research career in various positions: Attorney in the U.S. Department of Justice, Research Associate at Harvard Law School assigned to the Harvard-Israel Cooperative Research for Israel's Legal Development; and adviser to the former Penal Reform Commission of the Legislature of the Commonwealth of Puerto Rico. Has contributed to numerous legal and other periodicals, and written several books.

STONE, JULIUS (b. England, 1907). Challis Professor of International Law and Jurisprudence, University of Sydney, Australia. Studied and received his degrees in England and the United States (Harvard). He taught in several U.S. Universities, and was guest lecturer in Delhi, Jerusalem, and the Hague. In a rich and varied career, he combined specializations in both Jurisprudence and International Law, and is one of the world's best-known authorities in both. His achievements received recognition in the form of awards, such as that of the American Society of International Law in 1956, the World Law Research Award of the Washington Conference on World Peace through Law in 1965. His written works, which include 26 volumes, have been standard sources for legal scholars. His numerous articles (65 major ones) have been published in most Anglo-American legal journals, as well as in European and Indian periodicals.

ZELTNER, ZEEV (b. Kiev, Russia, 1909). Chief Justice of the Tel Aviv District Court since 1965. Lecturer at the Tel Aviv Branch of the Hebrew University, later Assistant Dean of the Law Faculty; Chairman of the Board of Restrictive Trade Practices; Professor at the Law Faculty of Tel Aviv University. As a member of many public committees, participated in the drawing up of their reports, such as the report on secondary education, and that of the committee for the amendment of company law. For many years, editor of *Hapraklit* and of a journal on law and economics. In that capacity, wrote numerous articles, mainly in Hebrew, and is the author of several books.